Dictatorland

PAUL KENYON has travelled all
over Africa in the footsteps of the
dictators. He is a distinguished BBC
correspondent and BAFTA award-
winning journalist and author.

Dictatorland

The Men Who Stole Africa

Paul Kenyon

First published in the UK in 2018 by Head of Zeus Ltd

9 7 5 3 1 2 4 6 8

A catalogue record for this book is available from
the British Library.

ISBN (HB): 9781784972134
ISBN (XTPB): 9781788541909
ISBN (E): 9781784972158

Maps by Jeff Edwards
Typeset by Adrian McLaughlin

Printed and bound in Germany by CPI Books GmbH

Head of Zeus Ltd
First Floor East
5–8 Hardwick Street
London ECIR 4RG

WWW.HEADOFZEUS.COM

To my mother and father, Betty and Neville,
who have always encouraged me to be inquisitive, to question
authority, and to give a voice to those who do not have one

Also in memory of my father-in-law,
Gheorghe, who spent most of his life living
under the tyranny of a dictatorship

Contents

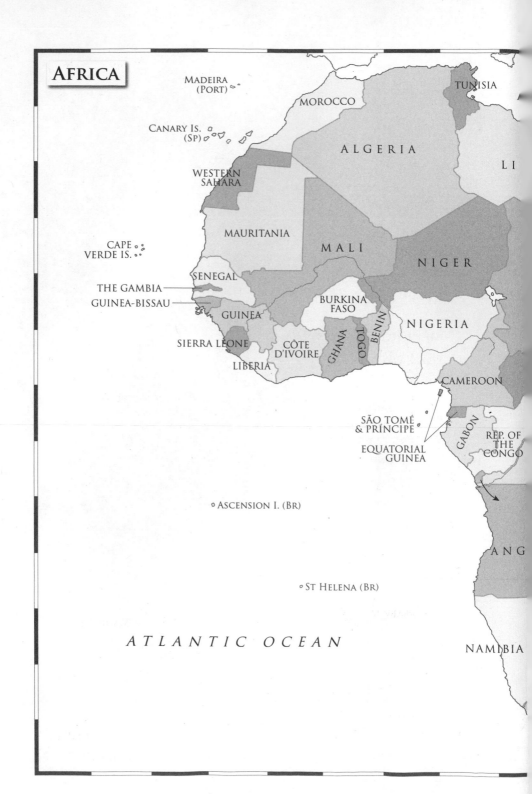

AFRICA

MADEIRA (PORT)

MOROCCO

TUNISIA

CANARY IS. (SP)

ALGERIA

LI

WESTERN SAHARA

MAURITANIA

MALI

NIGER

CAPE VERDE IS.

SENEGAL

THE GAMBIA

GUINEA-BISSAU

BURKINA FASO

GUINEA

NIGERIA

SIERRA LEONE

CÔTE D'IVOIRE

GHANA

TOGO

BENIN

LIBERIA

CAMEROON

SÃO TOMÉ & PRÍNCIPE

EQUATORIAL GUINEA

GABON

REP. OF THE CONGO

ASCENSION I. (BR)

ANG

ST HELENA (BR)

ATLANTIC OCEAN

NAMIBIA

N

DITERRANEAN SEA

EGYPT

RED SEA

ARABIAN SEA

YA

CHAD

SUDAN

ERITREA

DJIBOUTI

ETHIOPIA

CENTRAL
AFRICAN REP.

SOUTH
SUDAN

SOMALIA

INDIAN
OCEAN

UGANDA

KENYA

DEM. REP.
OF THE
CONGO

RWANDA

BURUNDI

TANZANIA

COMOROS

MAYOTTE
(FR)

OLA

MALAWI

MOZAMBIQUE

ZAMBIA

MADAGASCAR

MAURITIUS

ZIMBABWE

RÉUNION
(FR)

BOTSWANA

SWAZILAND

LESOTHO

SOUTH
AFRICA

0   800 MILES

0   1000 KM

Introduction

IT SEEMED A hopeless place to search for human remains, a wilderness of volcanic rock and ancient river sediment on a scorched hillside in East Africa. Everything was lunar grey, not a blade of green, not a glint of water, just the rubble of an ancient planet. Chalachew Seyoum clambered up a slope of slippery scree and found a desolate, windless plateau. It was a January morning in 2013, and he was with a team from Arizona State University, revisiting his Ethiopian homeland for an anthropological dig. Nothing had been found on these remote slopes for more than a decade, but when Seyoum looked down at the bleached stones around his feet, he noticed something out of place.

Jutting from the ground was a small fragment of something smooth and pumice-grey that seemed organic in origin. When he bent down to examine it properly, taking care not to disturb the stones on either side, he saw that it was about eight centimetres in length, a narrow bone-like fragment that was shaped like a beckoning finger. Seyoum lowered his head to the ground, and noticed several protrusions along its length, each about the size of a river pearl, grey, and worn flat on their exposed side. He knew immediately what he had found, although he didn't yet know the age of it.

This was the lower left side of a human mandible with five teeth still attached. Seyoum began shouting for his colleagues.

A man had once sat where Seyoum sat, surveying vast open grasslands where zebras and giant pigs grazed. He may have been up there hunting, when the hillsides were lush green and streams ran along the valley bottoms, before the wild swings in climate and the clashing of the earth's plates plunged the region into a barren wilderness. This was an era before man knew how to fashion spears from the branches of a *Curtisia* tree. Instead they hid in the tall grass, and ambushed their prey with rocks and clubs. If that failed, they would search the caves for remains of a kill by leopards or lions. The meat they scavenged would have been eaten raw. Man still hadn't learned to control fire.

The fragment of mandible represents the burst of evolution that gave rise to humankind 2.8 million years ago, shortly after we had left the forests and stood upright for the first time. Its owner and his tribe were the forefathers of every one of us, chewing raw meat on the gentle, fertile hillsides of East Africa. The rest of the planet was empty of the genus *Homo*. That fragile stick of bone is the closest we have come to the missing link, the point in time when modern humans split from their more ape-like ancestors. It is 400,000 older than any other found in our lineage. Scientists named it LD 350-1. But we should call him Adam.

When Adam's people set off westwards into the scrublands of what is now the Kalahari, and knelt to drink beside a pool of late summer rain, they would have seen sparkling crystals among the sand left in their palms. When they paused at a stream to bathe dust from their rough, chimp-like hair, they would have seen veins of copper-coloured silt, or tiny golden flecks dancing in the currents. The primordial African landscape was full of such wonders: basins of speckled bauxite, pink lakes of trona, canyon walls patterned with livid orange iron ore. Adam might have paused to dip his finger into the glutinous black drips leaking from rock faces near to the coast – oil seepages that were already many millions of years in the making.

Adam expired on that Ethiopian hillside when he was no more than forty years old, birds of prey circling overhead. It would be several millennia later that his ancestors would undertake the great migration, driven from their land by endless drought and volcanic eruptions, to discover new territories beyond Africa's shores. The scattering of mankind to every corner of the earth began relatively recently, just 70,000 years ago. One group crossed what is now the Bab-el-Mandeb straits, the pinch-point between East Africa and the Arabian Peninsula, sculling across the shallow seas on rafts secured by vines. Others headed north, to milder and more fertile climes. When they found their route blocked by the Mediterranean Sea, they were forced across the Sinai into the Middle East, and then spread into the tropics of central Asia. Others edged closer to the ice, and the snowy wilderness of the north, finally pushing over the top of the world from the East Asian Arctic to the Americas. But wherever mankind travelled and prospered, nothing would match the natural riches that they had left behind in Africa.

By the time Adam was born, the continent's wealth was already ancient, mostly created as the earth cooled and a crust formed over its molten rocks about 3.5 billion years ago. Diamonds were forced to the surface when dinosaurs still grazed the grasslands, and when Africa was still attached to the Americas, 150 million years ago. Formed in a furnace of carbon just above the earth's mantle, they were blasted to the surface from spectacular diamondiferous volcanoes that hurled them a mile into the Jurassic sky. In the middle of the nineteenth century our most respected geologists would have scoffed at the idea that diamonds were showered over the landscape by explosions deep inside the earth. They believed the gems came from alluvial deposits, dislodged from the earth by ancient rivers, and swept along in the mud and silt. But then came an event that changed all previous scientific thought, and led to a diamond rush like no other.

A group of prospectors known as the Red Caps were passing through a barren, rock-strewn wasteland in southern Africa, just beyond the border of Britain's Cape Colony, when they stopped for a half-hearted inspection of the land. It was 1871, and a series of high-profile finds along the banks of the Vaal and the Orange rivers had attracted diggers from around the world. Some became rich with a single, spectacular discovery; most returned home exhausted, disease-ridden and penniless. The Red Caps were on their way to join the hopeful throng, and had no intention of starting a 'dry dig' away from the water's edge. They had stopped for a rest when their leader, Fleetwood Rawstone, sent his cook to the summit of a small hillock, known in Afrikaans as a *kopje*, as punishment for being drunk the previous night. While up there, in the searing afternoon heat, the cook kicked the dusty soil and felt something hard beneath his boot. It was a large, translucent stone. He shouted for the others to join him, and within hours they had found many more. The hillock was, in fact, the peak of the first diamondiferous volcano ever found, and was sitting on top of a diamond 'pipe' that stretched almost a quarter of a mile down, its contents studded with gems like raisins in a cake. Tens of thousands of prospectors descended on the *kopje* from Europe and America. Diamond fever gripped the region. The land where the volcano stood was part of a farm owned by two Boer brothers who began renting out plots for excavation. Their name was de Beers.

Among the first to arrive, in October 1871, was an eighteen-year-old British youth dressed in school flannels, his fair hair doused in fine orange dust. He was often to be seen seated on an upturned bucket beside the deepening hole, supervising black labourers while reading the classics. His name was Cecil Rhodes.

By the second month of digging, weekly discoveries had reached a value of £50,000, a staggering £5.5 million in today's money. Three more diamondiferous volcanoes were discovered nearby, all within a radius of two miles of each other. The finds eclipsed anything that had been seen before. Within a year, the de Beers had sold up and moved out. Cecil Rhodes remained, shrewdly trading plots of land, eliminating his competitors one by one, until his company, De Beers Consolidated Mines Ltd, controlled all four diamondiferous volcanoes, and with them, the bulk of diamond production in the world.

The question was, however: who actually governed this previously undesirable, largely uninhabited region? Sovereignty would undoubtedly bring with it economic and political dominance right across the region. Borders were fluid at the time, but the Boer republic of Transvaal had the strongest claim. Britain's Cape Colony lay twenty-five miles to the south. Its claim was so thin as to be non-existent, but its governor had an idea. Why didn't they appoint an arbitrational court to settle the issue? The chairman would be Robert William Keate, an old Etonian who had played cricket for Oxford University and for England. The Transvaal Boers were right to be suspicious. It was a stitch-up. In 1871, Keate awarded the diamond fields to a local chief called Nicholas Waterboer, who had already secretly agreed to hand the territory to Queen Victoria. The British colonial secretary, Lord Kimberley, arrived to celebrate, and instructed his underlings to anglicize the local place names so he could feel more at home. The young men of the Colonial Office knew how to get ahead. The mine, if Lord Kimberley would be so gracious, was to be called Kimberley, and the town was to be named Kimberley too. Even the diamond-bearing volcanic rock was given the colonial stamp. It was named kimberlite, and has been known as such ever since.

The scramble for Africa began in earnest shortly afterwards, culminating in the famous Berlin Conference of 1884–5, when European powers formally divided the continent among themselves. In its aftermath came a series of diamond discoveries: in Congo Free State – owned at the time by Leopold, king of the Belgians – Portuguese Angola, and British-run Sierra Leone. Several diamond mines were dug by Cecil Rhodes's British South Africa Company in his privately run colonies of Matabeleland and Mashonaland, two territories that would later be fused together to form Southern Rhodesia. Spectacular discoveries followed much later in the British protectorate of Bechuanaland, starting in the 1950s, and transforming once again the world diamond markets. Surveys of the region had begun inauspiciously, with geological analysis of dozens of large termite mounds found on the parched, near-lifeless plains of the Kalahari Desert. The insects had burrowed down to find moisture and damp clay with which to construct their homes, but when scientists examined tiny particles of mud in the tall, tapering structures, they found traces of kimberlite. The termites were bringing to the surface evidence of diamonds somewhere beneath.

Teams began excavating and found a diamondiferous pipe, just like the ones in Kimberley. More followed. Eventually, Bechuanaland, one of the most sparsely populated countries in Africa, was found to possess a dozen diamond-filled volcanoes. After independence in 1966, it became known as Botswana, and developed into the second-largest diamond producer in the world.

Gold was delivered to our planet by asteroids when the earth was still young. It first attracted our ancestors' attention about 40,000 years ago, when ancient people took tiny flecks back to their caves to wonder at their deep sun-glow lustre. The first evidence of gold becoming a prized commodity was in Ancient Egypt, when the pharaohs began shaping it into jewellery, and even using it for the caps on the great pyramids of Giza. And then come the Europeans. They arrived on the coast of West Africa 500 years ago, drawn by rumours of entire cities built from gold and set up trading posts, where the precious metal was tricked from the natives in exchange for mirrors, cotton and rum. The whole coast of Guinea was divided according to the resources it could provide to Europeans: Grain Coast, Slave Coast, Gold Coast. Forts were built, first by the Portuguese in 1482 at Elmina in what is now Ghana, and then by the British, Dutch, Danish and Swedish, as European powers battled for dominance and conquered the tribal armies of indigenous chiefs. So much gold poured out of the region that it gave its name to the guinea coin. Again, it was Africa that provided the single game-changing discovery.

In 1886, fifteen years after the diamond discoveries, prospectors in the Boer republic of Transvaal, just up the road from Kimberley, found seams of gold that sliced through the mountains of Witwatersrand like pages of a giant book, forty miles long and two and a half miles wide. Gangs of fortune-hunters hurriedly relocated from the diamond digs; others charged in from Europe and America. Tough and filthy men swarmed the dusty hillsides with pick-axes and buckets, crushing the gold from rocks with primitive stamping machines. Sprawling camps took root, fuelled by cheap alcohol and served by European prostitutes. They grew into a town of huts

and makeshift bars that would become known as Johannesburg.
The gold digs at Witwatersrand were soon recognized as the richest
in the world, and were to become the source of fifty per cent of all
the gold ever mined. Watching from next door in Cape Colony, the
British were hardly going to stand quietly by. Cecil Rhodes was, by
this time, the Cape's prime minister, and owned large gold-mining
interests at the Transvaal dig. He wanted it in reliable and friendly
hands. In 1896, he secretly tried to inspire an uprising among the
British inhabitants of Transvaal against the republic's Boer president,
Paul Kruger. The idea was that, once a revolt had begun, he would
send in armed forces from the British South Africa Company, led by
Sir Leander Starr Jameson, on the pretext of restoring peace. Britain,
he anticipated, would then step in, annex the territory, and help
itself to the gold. The Jameson Raid ended in humiliating failure.
Rhodes's men were arrested, and, under a cloud of international
condemnation, Rhodes himself was forced to resign. But, six years
later, Britain did succeed in annexing the territory and Transvaal's
gold became central to the republic's future as part of South Africa.

Africa's colossal oil reserves were only unlocked relatively recently.
For centuries, nomadic tradesmen crossing the Sahara Desert in
Libya had reported finding curious rainbow sheens on the surface
of oasis water. As far back as the mid-eighteenth century, Portuguese
sailors had observed dribbles of hot tar seeping through the rocks
along the coast of Angola. It was sticky, filthy and unmanageable,
and certainly couldn't be used as fuel. Instead, they collected it in
buckets and used it to plug holes in their ships' hulls. The race to find
oil in Africa only began in earnest after the Second World War, when
Europe recognized the strategic error of relying almost exclusively
on capricious sheiks in the Middle East.

Cocoa may seem a strange inclusion among the precious resources
that have helped shape Africa's recent history, but it shares some of
the attributes of gems and rare metals, in the sense of its restricted
supply coupled with the world's seemingly endless demand. Cocoa
bushes only thrive in very particular conditions, on a narrow belt
of land ten degrees either side of the equator. They need the shade

of a jungle canopy, regular rain, and an absence of hot winds: a rare climatic combination offered by just a few regions of the world. West Africa is among them. Almost every chocolate bar we eat in Europe today originates from the cocoa bushes of Ghana and Côte d'Ivoire, the two biggest producers in the world. Whoever controls cocoa in West Africa possesses considerable power.

It is the era that followed Europe's decolonization that this book chiefly explores, although the tendency towards authoritarian rule can only be properly understood in the context of what went before. The colonial retreat came about as a result of the rise of nationalist movements in the 1950s and '60s, and the realization that attitudes towards imperialism had changed forever. Suddenly indigenous rulers were in control of the precious resources that had previously been in the hands of London, Madrid, Lisbon and Paris. Most were unprepared for governance. The nations they inherited were coarsely mapped European constructs, with borders that took little account of age-old tribal rivalries. Families were left separated by the draftsmen's blunt pencil. Hostile people were thrown together and told to sort out their differences at the ballot box. The newly empowered leaders chose to advance the interests of their own tribes above the rest. Gems and precious metals were used to reward the loyal and silence the foes. Leaders clung to power for fear that their rivals would corner Africa's resources and impose their own way of life. Maintaining dominance of a single clan or family mattered above all else. In the tiny oil-rich state of Equatorial Guinea, the Nguema family began a dynasty that has ruled since the Spanish relinquished control in 1968.

Some European governments lingered after independence to keep a hand in Africa's mineral wealth. Belgium retained its military presence in Congo, not only to hold back the perceived communist threat, but to shamelessly channel profits from diamonds and copper back home to Brussels.

Multinational companies cut deals with authoritarian African rulers, closing their eyes to human rights abuses and securing lucrative mineral rights. BP continued to prosper in Nigeria as successive dictators tortured and massacred tribes in the oil-producing regions for protesting about the devastating damage to their land. De Beers enjoyed diamond contracts throughout much of Mobutu's rule in Congo. Western governments did the same, sustaining some of the continent's most brutal dictators, in Libya, Nigeria and Sudan, in order to get their hands on Africa's oil.

This is the story of how a whole continent has been robbed in broad daylight. And how it is still going on today.

This is the story of the men who stole Africa.

PART ONE

Gold and Diamonds

CHAPTER ONE
Congo

DEMOCRATIC REPUBLIC OF THE CONGO

At the start of things, God travelled the world placing precious minerals in the earth, a little gold here, some diamonds there. When he came to Congo he was tired and lay down and left everything that he had beneath the soil.

PAPA MARCEL, CONGOLESE BOXER

ON A BLOWY evening in August 2016, I met Papa Marcel and a gang of his old boxing buddies outside a quiet street bar in Kinshasa. The last time I had met him was at the Fédération congolaise de boxe, where cockerels pecked around an old punching bag slung over a wooden frame that looked like a gallows. Papa Marcel was the federation's secretary, a former amateur boxer whose sixty-five years had reduced him in volume but not in spirit, and left his giant frame poking through his zoot suit like a sack of elephant bones. On that occasion he had been silenced by a retired army officer who told him never to speak with journalists, but the subject matter had proved just too enticing.

Now he was among friends, lounging on plastic chairs around a carton of cheap red wine, pensioners, several of them, passing an uneventful Saturday on a patch of dust beneath a shady tree. When I told them where I was going, all six folded themselves into the back of the Land Cruiser and began shouting directions.

In the bowels of what used to be called the 20th May Stadium is a cavernous dark space full of broken furniture and scraps of cardboard. 'This is where he stood,' proclaimed Papa Marcel. 'This is where Muhammad Ali prepared himself,' and at the mention of his name they all began jabbing and sparring as if, somewhere in the urine-soaked shadows, a giant brass bell had been struck. The whole room was filled with those noises boxers make, 'Phhtt, phhtt', and they were back there, upper cut, jab to the jaw, 'Ali, bomaye! Ali, bomaye!' The chant in Lingala means 'Ali, kill him!' and it swirled around the stadium as Ali emerged to take on George Foreman for the world heavyweight championship, the fight forever known as the Rumble in the Jungle, the most intoxicating bout in boxing history. 'Over there,' pointed one of them. 'That is where he entered the stadium.' He made a long guttural noise like the gathering roar of a plane, and the whole carnival of dancing Alis jostled towards a square of light, up a short flight of stairs, and out onto the turf, wheeling and jabbing while a group of uninterested youths hoofed a heavy ball around where the boxing ring used to be. The old men pointed high up on the concrete terraces, trying to recall their places on that humid October night in 1974. From up there, right at the top, the ring had looked like a raft on a tempestuous sea. Floodlights struck it from every direction. Knots of officials clambered on board and squinted towards the tunnel, looking for the two fighters. It was 3.45 a.m. and still nothing. The start was tailored for US television schedules, and the crowd was becoming restless.

John Matadi, a restless antelope of a youth who would have fought himself given half the chance, was midway up the terrace, near to Ali's corner. And what a few weeks he had just had. Since Ali's circus had moved into town it was like half of America wanted a ride in his cab. There were men in perma-shades and sheepskin coats, bantering journalists wearing Stetsons and women's heels, TV producers handing out hundred-dollar bills. Some of the guys even said they had seen James Brown, who was headlining the rock concert at the president's private amphitheatre. And now it was Matadi's turn. He was waiting for a fare outside the Intercontinental Hotel and Muhammad Ali himself had walked out onto the pavement! There was a proper maul, all of them trying to catch a glimpse, a hand-shake even, but John Matadi had stood taller than the rest because of his giant Afro hair, and Ali had pointed at him and bellowed, 'You! Who do you want to win?' The cameras were flashing, the hangers-on grinning and gesturing. 'Foreman!' shouted Matadi, all mock defiance. 'ONE HUNDRED PER CENT FOREMAN!' Ali widened his eyes like a demon. Left hook, jab, jab, his head was down and he was sparring with the spindly taxi driver, the crowd cheering them on. Another driver, Pierre Mambele, wanted a bit of it too.

He squeezed between them, hands in the air like a referee. 'Break... keep it moving... keep it clean.' Ali danced around, waiting for Mambele's signal, and the two men were at it again, Matadi parrying and bantering like a pro, 'Foreman, he gonna win,' he kept saying, and Ali's fists were so close he could feel the swish of air across his face. Matadi was an Ali supporter really – they all were. He just wanted to vex the man, provoke him into a performance, and a few days later both taxi drivers were in the 20th May Stadium cheering for their hero.

'And here comes Muhammad Ali out of the dressing room! It is what Muhammad Ali lives for...!'

At his hilltop palace, overlooking Kinshasa, President Mobutu Sese Seko was preparing for a very satisfying night in. The event's promoter, Don King, had been trawling the world for any government or company willing to stump up the $10 million prize money and host the event, and he hadn't been choosy about their credentials. In Mobutu he had found a headline-grabber who was bound to attract a curious TV audience worldwide, a maverick African chief who was rumoured to torture his opponents and who dressed more wildly than James Brown himself. But Mobutu would watch the event he was paying for from the comfort of his own sofa. He didn't want to be upstaged by Muhammad Ali, and anyway there was something nonchalantly powerful about staying away from his own party, not to mention avoiding some lunatic rebel who might be armed with a grievance and a gun. It wasn't worth the risk. He had already milked several photo opportunities. The PR job was done and the international chorus of endorsement had been so loud, so emphatic, that the spoilsport rights groups were mere mosquitos in Kinshasa's humid night air, their whine drowned out by 70,000 cheering fans.

'It changed our view of Mobutu for two years, maybe three,' says Papa Marcel, surveying the scene of his most precious memory. 'It made us proud to be Zairians. The whole world was watching. Now everyone knew about Zaire!'

But the US government and the CIA knew exactly what Mobutu had been up to in Zaire. They had been working with him behind the scenes, funding and encouraging him, from the start.

In March 1960 a young African hurried along a breezy Brussels street bundled up in a heavy overcoat against the end-of-winter chill. He was a slight, earnest man, disorientated by his new environment, and one of just a handful of black Africans in Belgium. He also had every reason to feel conflicted. This was the home of his colonial masters, the Belgians he so passionately wanted to drive from his homeland, but it was also the home of everything he had been taught to respect and admire and, as such, it possessed an unshakeable allure.

The roads leading to the Institute of Social Studies were busy. Elegant Renault saloons cruised by carrying government officials. Men in dark suits fanned out of the Gare Centrale. Barmen tweaked tablecloths inside smoke-filled Flemish cafés. And, to the hurrying young man, everything must have seemed so orderly, so conservative, so colourless.

He was born a world away, Joseph Désiré Mobutu, under a blazing sky in a village of straw shacks and a single Belgian Catholic church. Lisala was situated on the northernmost loop of the Congo, a river whose course had only been charted two generations before by the expedition of Henry Morton Stanley. Women pounded yams and men cast off each morning from the muddy shore to fish from dugout canoes. Mobutu's mother had been the prettiest girl in the village, by his own account, and the subject of much male attention. After giving birth to two children from her first relationship, she was passed on to a local chief and became pregnant with twins. The children died at birth, and Mobutu's mother was convinced she was being persecuted by witch doctors hired by another of the chief's wives. She fled into the jungle and walked for days to the village of a relative, where she met and married a local cook. He was to become Mobutu's father.

The young and rebellious Mobutu had an itinerant schooling, usually at the hands of Catholic monks, whom he impressed with his intelligence, but less so with his discipline. He was famously kicked out of one missionary school for making a 'little expedition' of his own to the capital – Leopoldville back then, now Kinshasa – where he travelled in search of women and alcohol, an adventure for which the monks banished him to the army. But let's pause there, because, in those early years, there is a scene that will help give a sense of the man: Mobutu as a child walking hand in hand with a middle-aged white lady as if he were her own son. She is Belgian, a liberal-minded progressive and the wife of a Belgian judge. Mobutu's father is their cook, and she has seen something in the small African boy, perhaps wit, curiosity, a young mind ready to open, and she tutors him in French and lets him sit at her table, and walks with him through staring crowds; and she fills his mind with everything a young Belgian boy would have as of right.

So, when he is conscripted to the army, Mobutu finds he can speak as well as the Belgian officers. He gallivants through his training, employing his crisp and eloquent French to mock anyone trying to give him orders, failing dismally in disciplinary routines, shining in anything that requires the application of intelligence. And soon, his eye is caught by a profession known, then and now, to accommodate both indiscipline and wit. Mobutu wants to be a journalist, an opinion-writer, an agenda-setter, a person of influence. It would have been laughable just a few years before that an African could harbour such grand ambitions, but Congo was starting to change.

An irresistible force was sweeping the whole continent. What had been viewed as an extreme position at the start of the twentieth century, supported by a handful of cranks and troublemakers, had grown into a popular mainstream movement after the Second World War. Colonialism could be extinguished. It *would* be extinguished. Nationalist movements had won the argument. Now, it was just a matter of time. The Europeans were poised to move out. Ghana had set the pace, winning independence from Britain in 1957, and even de Gaulle was preparing to get rid of his African assets, contemplating the unthinkable by withdrawing from Algeria. But Belgium was standing firm, its leaders suggesting it would take another three decades before Congo was ready for self-governance, some said even longer. In Leopoldville and Stanleyville, however, the fledgling Congolese leaders were already filling stadiums for their rallies and speeches.

There among the crowds in 1958 was Pierre Mambele, the taxi driver who would spar with Muhammad Ali outside his hotel. He was still a child back then, but a precocious one swept along by the emergence of an inspirational young nationalist in his home town of Stanleyville. That man was Patrice Lumumba, a thirty-three-year-old intellectual in a frock coat and irreverent bowtie who captivated audiences with his wild talk of independence, and whose popularity was already alarming the Belgians. 'He was like no one else I had ever met,' says Mambele. 'I used to run to buy him soft drinks when he worked in the post office. He was an *évolué*, and that was rare.' An *évolué* was a creation of the Belgian and French colonial governments. He or she was a native who was judged to have evolved, in the social Darwinist language of colonial administrators, to have risen above primitive tribal traditions, and assimilated European attitudes. So few were awarded the title that they were treated as local celebrities. In Congo, acquiring *évolué* status often involved passing a series of written exams, and even tests of eating habits and manners, to make sure the candidates could behave themselves at the table. It was a sly enterprise on the part of the Europeans. Not only was it a form of sanitized cultural cleansing, encouraging the rejection of a supposedly inferior native heritage, it offered special status to the brightest and most ambitious, the very people who might be tempted to rebel against colonial injustice. The title gained the *évolués* some small privileges, nothing that would raise them to the level of a white man or allow them to enjoy his rights, but enough to make them feel part of the wider club. In Patrice Lumumba's case, it failed to work.

'When he began making speeches,' continued Mambele, 'he was mesmerizing. He denounced the white colonialists, and described in detail how the Belgians had treated the blacks, how they had brutalized them and kept them down. He talked about the millions who had died under the regime of King Leopold, working in rubber

plantations where they starved or were overcome with ex
and disease. He talked about the brutal murders of theose
to deliver the quantities of rubber the Belgians demanded. I
made independence our most cherished hope.'

Lumumba quickly became a national hero. Once, aft
arrested for anti-colonial activity and jailed, groups of y
porters went on the rampage, demanding that the Bel
him. Mambele, by then thirteen years old, was given a pa
dangerous job. Armed with a hacksaw and a packet of m
was despatched to petrol stations to cut through the rubber
set the pumps alight. He ended up in jail himself, but was p
serving fifteen days alongside his hero. It was while Lum
incarcerated that he came across an inspiring new journal
in the newspaper *Actualités Africaine*, the first weekly p
written for Congolese by Congolese. It was that of Joseph

We can picture the nationalist leader, his fashionable
replaced by a prison uniform, propped against a thin ma
crowded and noisy cell. He would have been hungry for any
the demonstrations were continuing outside, that the mo
had helped create was not diminishing. Mobutu's restrai
argued prose would have offered a glimpse of hope amo
and the sticky squalor. Lumumba was eager to meet this
star, and when he was released, he and Mobutu beca
racing between political rallies together, drinking beer la
muggy tropical night, and sharing Sunday lunch with Mob
The pair would ride pillion on a scooter – Lumumba or
shouting directions, Mobutu, in his owlish glasses at th
slaloming through Leopoldville's busy streets, trying to n
treacherous flooded potholes. When they arrived, Lumu
take to the stage while Mobutu watched from the wings.
the first meetings in Congo's history where people had
to the call of a compatriot, instead of to the instruction
men. Mobutu quickly fell under his spell.

The prospect of achieving independence any time soo
was still seen by many as fanciful. Just about every count

was closer to the prize. Many had named a date. Colonial adminis-
trations were staying behind just to tie up loose ends. Newly designed
flags had been delivered to government buildings. Indigenous
political parities had been formed and were preparing for elections.
Belgian Congo seemed like an anachronism. Then, almost overnight,
everything changed. Indpendence was suddenly upon them.

The turnaround began on 4 January 1959. A crowd had gathered
in the sweltering streets arounnd the YMCA building in Leopoldville
for a political rally. The mayor, a Belgian, heard about what was
happening and didn't fancy dealing with a mob of angry nationalists
– not in the holiday season, not just four days after New Year.
He banned the event. The crowd milled around for a while, hot,
frustrated, and looking for purpose. They alighted upon a belligerent
white bus driver who had raised his fist at one of them during an
argument. The driver was swallowed by the crowd and beaten to
the ground. Police poured in, and a single violent episode turned
into a riot. The riot then turned into street battles that engulfed the
entire city.

Three days later forty-seven people were dead. Some say the true
figure was closer to 300. It was a catastrophe. The Belgians had
promised to announce a new colonial policy that very month. Now
it was imperitive that the document made mention of independence:
nothing specific, perhaps, but enough to keep the crowds off the
streets. In the event, the publication was accompanied by a speech
from the king of the Belgians, Baudouin, that was broadcast across
Congo. 'Our decision today,' announced the king, 'is to lead the
people of Congo in prosperity and peace, without harmful procrastination, but also without undue haste, toward independence.'

It was a sensation. Not only was independence now certain, it
would come without procrastination. They had it on the authority of
the king. Of course, it was without undue haste too, but how could
liberation ever be too hasty?

Belgian officials announced there would be a series of round-table
discussions with a delegation from Congo. Independence would be
discussed, although only in the most general of terms. There was no

intention of committing to a date. That was out of the question. This
was more about showing willing.

The meetings were to be held held in Brussels in January 1960
at the very same time the young Joe Mobutu was rushing along the
damp streets for a lecture at the Institute for Social Studies.

It was thanks to the judge's wife that Mobutu was there at all,
having been accepted to study journalism and sociology on account
of his facility with the French language. It was not by design that his
course coincided with the arrival of the Congolese delegates, but he was
delighted to have their company, particularly that of his friend Patrice
Lumumba. There was a snag, however. By the time the Congolese
arrived, Lumumba was in prison again. The promise of independence
had failed to soften his rhetoric. Two months before, he had called
for a campaign of civil disobedience. The Belgians had responded by
sending in the Force Publique – the army – and a riot had erupted
across Stanleyville. By the time the streets were cleared and the fires
put out, seventy of Lumumba's supporters were dead, and 200 injured.
Lumumba himself was jailed for six months, a period that happened to
coincide with the round-table talks in Belgium. The first item of business
for the Congolese delegation in Brussels was to have him released from
prison. The Belgians, anxious to avoid further unrest, soon capitulated.
They released Lumumba, handed him a shirt and tie, and put him on
a plane bound for Brussels. 'In less than twenty-four hours,' Mobutu
would later say, 'the prisoner had become a statesman.'[1]

Lumumba joined the other ninety or so Congolese at the round-
table discussions, which were scheduled to last a month. Sitting near
to him was a delegate whose star was rising almost as fast as his
own, a moon-faced young businessman turned politician named
Moise Tshombe. He was the leader of a popular political party in the
copper-mining province of Katanga, and his objectives differed from
most of those present. Although Tshombe supported an independent
Congo, he wanted it split into self-governing regions: perhaps no
surprise, as Katanga, the region he wanted to lead, was by far the
wealthiest in the country. Tshombe's role would be pivotal in the
events of the next few years.

The round-table talks quickly took an unexpected turn. The Congolese tried their luck by throwing in an implausibly hasty date for independence, 1 June 1960, just four months hence. A deadline was never on the agenda, but now that the Congolese had opened the bidding, an uncomfortable realization dawned on the Belgians: if they countered with a date that was too distant, they would appear attached to an imperialist agenda that was out of step with the rest of the world. The UN was backing self-determination, and so, too, were the US and the USSR. Not only that, any delay might be perceived as procrastination. Riots would almost certainly follow.

But the Belgians couldn't simply surrender their treasured African asset. It had been in their possession for eighty years. They had to be seen to be countering. What about independence in six months' time? The Congolese were astonished. They had been expeting a rebuke for their impertinence, not a bartering match. What about splitting the difference, they shot back, independence in five months' time and be done with it? The Belgians looked at each other helplessly. Why quibble over a day here and there? Five months' time it would be – 30 June 1960. Spontaneous applause broke out around the room. But, in truth, the Belgians never really intended a complete withdrawal at all. This was just decolonization-lite: a simulacrum of self-determination while holding on to the country's most precious resources.

Before Lumumba dashed back to Congo to begin preparations for independence, he made a job offer to his journalist friend. Mobutu should remain in Brussels and negotiate the second phase of the round-table conference, along with a group of equally green Congolese students. At stake was the return to the Congolese people of their gold mines, their diamond fields, and the sprawling copper belt, not to mention the cobalt, uranium and zinc. In short Mobutu and the others would be responsible for taking back their economy from the Belgians, who had no intention of letting it go. The additional problem was that none of the Congolese contingent were qualified in economics or business. The Belgians had deprived their colonial subjects of a higher education. Only seventeen men and women in the entire country had been educated to degree level.

'I, a poor little hungry journalist,' said Mobutu, 'found myself at the same table as the biggest Belgian financial sharks. I felt like the cowboy in the western who is systematically ripped off by city slickers.'[2] With the economy at stake, the Belgians began playing hardball.

Where should all the Belgian-owned businesses have their registered offices? they asked. If Congo was no longer Belgian, the mining companies might want to relocate their financial and administrative operations so they could operate under Belgian governance, rather than take a chance with the new regime.

Many of the companies transferred to Brussels, taking their tax revenue with them.[3] One nil to the Belgians.

Then Mobutu fought hard to ensure customs duties would no longer go to Brussels and Antwerp, only to discover the next morning that the Belgian parliament had already redirected payments of the duty straight into the Belgian treasury, rendering the discussions pointless.[4]

Two-nil. And so it went on.

The worst bungle came with Congo's most lucrative asset, the one which, if managed properly, could ensure that the new nation was one of the wealthiest in Africa: the giant mining consortium Union Minière, which operated in the resource-rich province of Katanga, the powerhouse of all Congo's economy.

Katanga, in the southeast of the country, had a unique administration that was an artifact of the earliest days of colonialism. The province was part run by the Comité Spécial du Katanga (CSK), a powerful and privileged company that had overseen mining operations since 1900, distributing profits between private businesses and the state. In return, it had been given a degree of sovereignty similar to that of Cecil Rhodes's British South Africa Company, and was allowed to run its own police force until 1908. By 1960, the CSK operated as a state within a state, a part-public, part-private hybrid that had more influence over the running of Katanga than the province's governors had over the company. It was CSK that had initiated the creation of mining giant Union Minière, and had become its most important shareholder, as it grew into the largest producer of cobalt in the world and the third-largest producer of copper. The profits of Union Minière the year before independence were no less than 3.5 thousand million Belgian Francs.[5]

Historically, the colonial state had interfered little in the running of the consortium, but now, at the round-table discussions in Brussels, Joe Mobutu and the others had an opportunity to do precisely that. Through the CSK they could begin influencing the complex structure of Belgian trusts, and British and French private capital that lay behind it, allowing the new leaders to bring millions of dollars into the public purse, and ensuring that, in future, Union Minière was run in the interests of the people of Congo.

Instead, in their eagerness to dismantle all colonial structures, Mobutu and his colleagues opted to disband the CSK altogether. In one spectacular miscalculation, they had lost their potential to dominate the country's largest mining operator, with the state now just a minority shareholder in *Union* Minière along with several others.[6]

Perhaps Mobutu's mind was elsewhere. Political independence had been the priority, the economy was secondary. But there was another distraction too. Soviet and US intelligence officers were circling the delegates in Brussels, and Mobutu had already been approached by the CIA.[7]

Picture him now, back in Leopoldville. It is May 1960, and the mood is euphoric. Lines of men are forming outside polling stations. Street drummers are weaving through the crowds, and the young journalist Mobutu has the story of his life. Elections are being held in preparation for independence. The country has only had three months to prepare for this momentous event. There's no one with any experience of government, there are no structures in place, and no history of political dialogue. After years of pushing for self-rule, change is thundering down the track too quickly. Mobutu is supporting Lumumba and his Mouvement National Congolais (MNC). Unlike the dozen or so new parties that have been hurriedly thrown together, the MNC has been at the heart of protests for the past eighteen months, and it isn't based on a single ethnic group. Instead, MNC wants an end to regional separatism, and is calling for tribal communities to put aside their differences and help create a strong, unified Congolese nation. Its main appeal, though, is Lumumba himself, the father of the independence movement. Mobutu, on the other hand, is still barely known outside the small circle of activists who attended the Brussels talks.

As expected, the MNC wins the election handsomely. But Congo is a territory twice the size of Western Europe. The fishing communities of Bas-Congo on the wind-whipped Atlantic coast have little in common with the copper-mining villages on the high plateau of Katanga, which lies 2,500 kilometres to the east. There are ancient antagonisms at play throughout the land, and now they have expressed themselves through the ballot box. A plethora of regional parties have won seats, splitting the country into a jigsaw of tribal interests. The challenge for the new leaders is to select a cabinet that will satisfy an almost ungovernable variety of views. Aside from Lumumba, the two strongest winners are both leaders of regionalist parties: Moise Tshombe, who won control of Katanga, and Joseph Kasavubu, representing the people of Bas-Congo. Kasavubu is a quiet, monkish character whose views have evolved through slow and sombre analysis, and who looks with suspicion upon the flamboyant, politically intuitive Lumumba. Nevertheless, these three men – the holy trinity of Lumumba, Tshombe and Kasavubu – dominate the political landscape of the newly independent nation.

It is 30 June 1960. Fireworks streak across the night sky. Partying crowds gather in the streets, dancing and drinking. After much horse-trading, it is Joseph Kasavubu who has become president of the newly named Republic of the Congo, on the understanding that he will subdue his separatist instincts. Patrice Lumumba, the peoples' favourite, will be Congo's first prime minister. There, sitting beside him, is the boyish, bespectacled figure of Joe Mobutu. The journalist has been transformed into the prime minister's private secretary. It is an astonishing turn of fortune facilitated by Lumumba himself, and now, instead of reporting on the historic events, Mobutu has a place at the top table. Before him lies the beginning of his country's history, the fashioning of a nation that stretches from the yawning mouth of the Congo River, through rainforest and savannah, to the snow-capped peaks of the Blue Mountains to the east. The fledgling nation awaits, exhilarated, expectant, determined that lives will be transformed now they are free from the Belgians.

LEOPOLDVILLE GARRISON, 5 JULY 1960

Number of days since independence: 6

It is early morning. All is quiet. A pair of polished boots stands by the side of a metal-framed bed. A khaki dress cap lies on a chair. Pressed trousers hang in a locker from which drifts the familiar tropical aroma of mildew. A steamship horn sounds from somewhere down on Stanley Pool. We are in the room of Lieutenant-General Émile Janssens, head of the Force Publique. The military command is entirely Belgian, the rank and file entirely Congolese. That's how Janssens likes it. He is up early as usual, brushing his moustache and oiling his hair, but today he's a little anxious. He pulls his door to, and marches crisply to the officers' mess, where he finds his colleagues reading the Belgian papers that have reported on little other than Congo's independence all week. Others are gathered around the breakfast table discussing the implications of an ugly scene that occurred yesterday on the parade ground. A few of the Congolese troops disobeyed orders. It had been simmering for a while, the wearisome complaints about cramped conditions, poor pay, inedible food, and, as usual, segregation in the army, racism as they liked to call it. Now independence had come, and with it their insistence they should be running the show, not the whites. Well, it wasn't going to happen, not in his army.

Janssens calls his men into the mess hall. He needs to nip this in the bud.

'Independence brings changes to politicians and civilians,' he announces to 500 black faces, 'but for you, nothing will be changed.' The white officers sitting at the front nod in agreement. 'None of your new masters can change the structure of the army,' he continues.

'The politicians have lied to you.' And then, to underline his message, Janssens turns around, takes a piece of chalk, and writes in large letters across the blackboard, BEFORE INDEPENDENCE = AFTER INDEPENDENCE.

CAMP HARDY, THYSVILLE GARRISON

Later that same day

Reports of the general's speech have reached another garrison. An incensed group of black soldiers has had enough. They walk into the officers' mess, and take the Belgians hostage at gunpoint. Soon, the whole garrison is rising up against the former colonial officers. They had assumed independence meant an immediate end to Belgian control of the army, but now the general is scoffing at the idea it will happen any time soon. Bedlam quickly spreads to the streets outside the garrison. Gangs race through the European quarter looking for whites to attack. European women are captured and raped. Word spreads to other military bases, and soon General Janssens' speech has helped provoke the whole of Congo's armed forces into mutiny. The troops are hostile not just towards the Belgians, but towards their own leadership for allowing the Europeans to remain in positions of power in the first place.

ELIZABETHVILLE, KATANGA PROVINCE, 9 JULY 1960

Days since independence: 10

Away to the southeast, high on a plateau, is the Katanga provincial capital, Elizabethville. Just a week ago the elegant European quarter, La Ville, was busy with Belgians enjoying imported oysters and crayfish in the smart restaurants, or shopping along the boulevards where blue jacaranda trees blossom. More than 30,000 live here, mostly working for Union Minière or one of its satellite industries, but today they are hiding inside their villas or packing possessions into their Renaults and Volkswagen Beetles ready to flee across the border into Northern Rhodesia, where the white minority government is offering them protection. Congolese soldiers have mutinied here, as they have in the rest of the country, and fighting has spilled into the town centre, with white-owned shops being looted and torched. Later in the day, news emerges that raises the crisis to a new level. Five Europeans have been murdered in the town.

ELIZABETHVILLE, KATANGA PROVINCE, 10 JULY 1960

Days since independence: 11

The art deco airport building outside Elizabethville looks like a Belle Époque villa uprooted from the Cannes seafront. At air traffic control they hear the voice of a Belgian pilot asking for permission to land. Out of a cobalt-blue sky, several military aircraft appear, and land in quick succession on the waiting tarmac. Each is carrying several dozen Belgian paratroopers, and more will follow. Their mission, they say, is to bring order to the province and to protect the Europeans. You might expect the new Congolese leaders to resist them, but Katanga is different from the rest of Congo. The businessman-turned-politician Moise Tshombe, the new president of the province, has long wanted Katanga to be separate from the rest of the country. He welcomes the Belgian troops and holds a series of meetings, to which he invites Belgian administrators and representatives from Union Minière. A plan is hatched and Tshombe will announce it to the world tomorrow morning.

As he composes his speech, more Belgian troops are fanning out across Congo, all under the banner of protecting their own citizens. They seem to have forgotten this is no longer Belgian territory. They are undertaking a military operation on foreign soil. It is, effectively, an invasion.

Over in the capital Leopoldville, Prime Minister Patrice Lumumba watches helplessly. His priority is to bring his army under control and so he sacks the bombastic General Janssens, and replaces him with one of his own cousins. More eye-catching is the appointment of the army's new chief of staff. His image has already been captured by British Pathé News. Gone are the studious glasses and the mischievous smirk of a month ago; now 'a military strongman' has emerged, all prowling sneers and dead eyes. Joe Mobutu, the journalist-turned-politician-turned-colonel of the National Congolese Army, is rising ever higher.

ELIZABETHVILLE, KATANGA PROVINCE, 11 JULY 1960

Days since independence: 12

Moise Tshombe has called the press into his government building. He sits behind a desk, immaculate in beige tie and pressed suit, and waits for the journalists to be seated. The announcement he has prepared, with the help of the Belgians, is astonishing. Katanga will no longer be part of Congo. It is breaking away to form an independent republic. 'This independence is total,' says Tshombe, and explains that Belgium has offered the assistance of its troops. Within a year, personal currency transfers out of Katanga back home to Brussels will reach 100 million Belgian Francs a month.[8] Despite the fact Katanga is a rogue state, supposedly unrecognized by any country in the world, the UK and France will send officials to help, advising Tshombe, and ensuring that their own economic interests are protected.

Over in Leopoldville, Lumumba is fuming at the news. He boards a plane to Elizabethville with the intention of talking some sense into Tshombe. Without Katanga, the rest of Congo will hardly function. Its mining industry provides sixty per cent of state revenue. But when Lumumba's plane begins circling above Elizabethville's airport, air traffic control is no longer in the hands of the Congolese. Instead, a Belgian military officer answers the request to land, and refuses it.

Of course, although Tshombe pretends that it is he who is running the new republic, he knows that, without the Belgian military and the hordes of Belgian political advisors, Lumumba and the new government would simply steam in and take back control. The new country will effectively be run by Belgium, and by the wealthy foreign trusts that control Union Minière.

LEOPOLDVILLE, 12 JULY 1960

Days since independence: 13

Back from his failed trip to Katanga, Patrice Lumumba has almost run out of options. The Belgians have just bitten off a large copper-filled chunk of his country, and he doesn't even have an army to push them back. He and his president, Joseph Kasavubu, decide to approach the UN for emergency assistance. They want the blue helmets on the ground to eject the Belgians and re-establish order. But the UN in 1960 is still a young organization, still feeling its way. Of course it will demand the withdrawal of Belgium troops, and will even send soldiers from neutral countries to help, but it will not be drawn into Congo's internal affairs. In other words, the UN is not going to march into Katanga and seize back the new republic on behalf of the new government. It will protect civilians from violence, if it can, and not much else.

Katanga has broken away with relative ease and established what is effectively a privately run state for the benefit of a small cabal of businessmen and politicians. Now that a precedent has been set, another resource-rich province wants to follow suit.

South Kasai is home to Congo's vast diamond mines, owned by businessmen in Brussels and New York, and is the largest producer of industrial diamonds in the world. Within a month, it, too, will become an independent republic.

But where is the newly elevated Colonel Mobutu in all of this?

He is buzzing high over the forests of Bas-Congo, seated in a military helicopter alongside his closest advisors amid metal boxes full of ammunition and weapons. The newly installed chief of staff is about to begin a most delicate and dangerous operation – travelling the country and bringing mutinous soldiers back to order. Some garrisons are hidden so deep in the forest, the only way to reach them is on foot, and when Mobutu approaches they shoot at him. To the enraged rank and file he's simply an apologist for the Belgians, part of the conspiracy to keep the Congolese subservient. When Mobutu does manage to address troops, he must tread a treacherously fine line. He, too, wants the former colonial administration out, he tells them, but not like this. He needs the troops unified, and obedient to him. 'Keep hold of your weapons,' he tells them. 'Don't hand them over to the UN or the Belgians, but keep them to protect the Congo, only the Congo. Not for pillaging or to serve the ambitions of some little princeling, but for your country.'[9]

Just twelve days after independence, Lumumba, the idealist from Stanleyville, the man who coaxed the timid masses into roaring stadiums, is watching his country disintegrate. Belgian troops are occupying his cities, and Belgian businessmen are looting his precious natural resources. In desperation, he decides on one final throw of the dice. It is a decision that will come to define the rest of his short life. Lumumba, along with Joseph Kasavubu, asks the Soviet Union for help. The Americans, in their Leopoldville embassy, are left blinking in disbelief.

Enter Colonel Joe Mobutu. He has returned from his assignment, battle-weary but elated, having managed to charm his way into several garrisons and calm the marauding soldiers. He could easily have been found dead in a ditch, but instead Mobutu's wit and courage have won the soldiers over, transforming his journey into something like a triumphant papal tour. Mobutu is now the soldiers' favourite. They will do as he asks. With the embryonic republic breaking up, he has the personal support of the army. The political significance of his newly acquired popularity will not have escaped Mobutu. But Lumumba seems unconcerned. After all, Mobutu is his friend and close ally. He assumes he can trust him not to abuse his position.

What he doesn't know is that Mobutu has become close to a man called Larry Devlin, the CIA station chief in Leopoldville.

In the fiercely simple, binary world of Cold War politics, Patrice Lumumba appeared to have confirmed what his detractors had always suspected, that he was a crypto-communist. Never mind that his request for Soviet assistance was made along with President Kasavubu; it was Lumumba who attracted America and Europe's opprobrium. It was he whose seditious activities led to rioting under Belgian rule, he whose belligerent stance against Belgium derailed any hope of ending the crisis. Lumumba, they reasoned, must have been behind the telegram asking Soviet leader Nikita Khrushchev to provide assistance. But Lumumba was no communist. He had no interest in collectivism or a proletarian revolution. His approach to Moscow was simply the last resort of a panic-stricken novice who felt abandoned by the rest of the world. Nevertheless, it was a fatally ill-judged decision.

For the superpowers, Congo represented the most glittering of Africa's jewels. Not only did it possess near-unparalleled mineral wealth, it shared borders with nine other African nations. Plant your stake in its turf, and there was the possibility of spreading out across the whole region. Congo was a strategic prize without equal. For Russia it would be a first foothold in African soil, a prospect that was scaring the living daylights out of the cold warriors in Washington. The decolonization of the continent was the beginning of a second 'scramble for Africa', and the American objective was simple: keep the Russians out. Lumumba had put himself very much on the wrong side of the wire as far as the US was concerned. Not only had he alienated himself from the West, but his high-handed and capricious manner meant that he had burned his bridges with Kasavubu too, a relationship whose demise was helped along by the interference of Western intelligence agencies. In short, Lumumba was becoming dangerously isolated.

His friend Colonel Mobutu, on the other hand, was being actively courted by the same Western spies.

Since Larry Devlin first met Mobutu at the round-table discussions in Brussels, their relationship had quietly grown. Devlin had been poisoning Mobutu's mind against his old friend Lumumba, and promising whatever the young colonel desired in return for a Congo friendly to the US. We know that by the middle of August 1960, just six weeks after independence, Devlin received clearance for an operation aimed at 'replacing Lumumba with a pro-Western group'.[10] It included the option of assassination.

CIA agents were keeping watch at the airport. They noticed the arrival of several Russian transport planes, carrying military trucks and several hundred military advisors. Urgent radio messages were sent to their bosses holed up at the US embassy who believed that what they were witnessing was the start of a Russian takeover, at the invitation of Lumumba.[11] 'Congo's Castro', as they liked to call him, was about to gift the country to the Soviets, tilting the whole balance of Cold War regional power. The Soviet planes unloading their equipment at the airport demonstrated that Lumumba needed to be neutralized urgently. The CIA had a plan, but were keen to avoid any traceable involvement if they could rely on their Congolese assets to do the job for them. For their new friend, Colonel Joe Mobutu, the time for a momentous decision was fast approaching.

In Leopoldville, the streets were quiet, save for the occasional burning car. Soliders patrolled anxiously at the entrance to each government building. UN troops had begun to arrive, but were still hardly visible. The armed units that swept through the streets, machine guns trained on potential troublemakers, were Belgian. Mobutu considered his options: to remain loyal to his friend and supporter, the man who was rowing with President Kasavubu even now as the country slid into flames, or act on behalf of the US, which required Lumumba out of the way.

On the evening of 5 September 1960, President Kasavubu headed for the national radio station in Leopoldville. Just after 8 p.m., listeners heard his high-pitched, hesitant voice explain that he had removed the prime minister from power. If that were not extraordinary enough, an hour later, they heard the voice of Patrice Lumumba announcing that he had sacked President Kasavubu.

At that critical moment, in the midst of a military, ethnic and economic crisis, when a unified and determined position was paramount, the two elected leaders had placed personal politics above national interests. There would be no speedy resolution to the new crisis. Parliament declared it was unconstitutional for Kasavubu to displace Lumumba in such a fashion. In a fit of pique, Kasavubu put parliament into recess for a month. Both men were adamant they would prevail, and began casting around for heavyweight support. It seems they both had the same idea at the same time.

Colonel Mobutu was in his grand military office, on the hillside above Stanley Pool a week after the suspension of parliament, when he received a telephone call. It was Kasavubu. 'Colonel,' he gabbled, 'I order you to go and arrest ex-Prime Minister Lumumba.' Next on the line was Lumumba, furious and in a state of panic. 'Colonel,' he said, 'I order you to detain ex-President of the Republic Kasavubu.'[12]

It didn't take long for Mobutu to make a decision. He would obey them both.

Now it was his turn to make an announcement. The army would take charge of Congo until the year's end, allowing the politicians time to cool off. And he, Colonel Mobutu… well, he was head of the army. What choice did he have? Mobutu, still not thirty years old, was effectively the new leader of this vast young republic. The fact his quiet coup had happened so quickly may have come as a surprise, even to Mobutu, but that it had happened at all was anything but. Larry Devlin, the CIA station chief in Leopoldville, had put Mobutu on his payroll the week before.[13]

Later, Mobutu would allow President Kasavubu to return to office, but only under his stewardship, not with any real power. In the meantime, there was the awkward question of what to do with Lumumba. His many opponents didn't want him hanging around, stirring the crowds and causing trouble. Even the US ambassador, who was certainly no admirer, is reported to have said that if Lumumba walked into a gathering of Congolese politicians as a waiter with a tray on his head he would come out as prime minister. Mobutu needed him out of the picture, permanently, and there were already several plans afoot. The Belgians were actively plotting Lumumba's assassination, but the Americans were in the most advanced stage of preparation, ready to go whenever Larry Devlin chose. The CIA had sent him a phial of poison to be slipped into Lumumba's food or toothpaste. Devlin was just waiting for the moment. President Eisenhower had been briefed, and the scheme signed off. Over in Katanga, Moise Tshombe, once a member of the holy trinity with Lumumba, also wanted him dead, blaming him for blocking the secessionist republic, and the subsequent tribal fighting that had left so many dead.[14]

Aware that his life was under threat, Lumumba appealed to the UN for protection, and a group of Ghanaian Blue Helmets were quickly despatched to form a protective ring around his residence in Leopoldville. Then Mobutu sent 200 soldiers to have his old friend arrested. They were held back by the UN, and set up a second, outer ring, thus leaving Lumumba under a bizarre two-tier siege.

As Lumumba's closest allies began to flee Leopoldville for their stronghold in Stanleyville, the former prime minister had little choice but to wait in his besieged home for the result of a vote on the other side of the world. In New York, the UN General Assembly would stand in judgement as to whether Kasavubu's dismissal of Lumumba had been lawful. Faceless politicians with barely concealed agendas would decide the fate of Congo. A vote in favour of Kasavubu would be a vote against Lumumba and all he was perceived to stand for. The rows of suited men in New York could have had no idea what consequences their decision would bring. Under intensive American lobbying, they made the pro-Washington choice. Ten thousand kilometres away, Lumumba knew the game was up – the UN would no longer be prepared to protect him.

A tropical storm of rare ferocity descended on Leopoldville five days later on 27 November 1960. It was night-time, and Lumumba knew this was his chance. Noticing that Mobutu's soldiers and the UN Blue Helmets had taken refuge from the rain in a small shelter outside his house, he crept onto the driveway and crawled into the back of a Chevrolet station wagon, where his chauffeur was waiting at the wheel. As they drove slowly out of the drive, the chauffeur lowered his window to explain to the troops that he was on his way to buy cigarettes. Lumumba was curled up on the floor behind him.

The former prime minister and his remaining aides fled Leopoldville in a convoy of three cars and a truck. Ahead of them lay a two-day drive along rain-soaked roads to Stanleyville, where his supporters would protect him. But instead of hurrying along, Lumumba stopped to address cheering crowds by the side of the road. News of these impromptu rallies reached Mobutu and the CIA's Larry Devlin in the capital, and allowed them to guess his intended route. Mobutu sent up a spotter plane.

A convoy of army jeeps intercepted Lumumba and his aides as they attempted to cross the Sankuru River close to Mweka, still a day's drive from safety. Mobutu's troops pulled him from the Chevrolet and subjected him to a beating before flying him on a DC-3 to Camp Hardy in Thysville, the very military base where, four months earlier, the rebellion against Belgium's Lieutenant-General Émile Janssens had first broken out.

Waiting for him there was Mobutu. He watched impassively as the man he had ridden pillion with, whose speeches he had cheered, who had ultimately raised him to a position of power, was slapped and abused in the back of a military truck. At one point, a soldier found a speech in one of Lumumba's pockets, and read it out, mockingly, to the mob. It was a statement declaring that he was still Congo's prime minister. The soldier screwed it into a ball, and stuffed it into Lumumba's mouth.

My dear companion,

I write you these words without knowing if they will reach you, when they will reach you, or if I will still be living when you read them.

So began Patrice Lumumba's last letter to his wife, scrawled on a piece of paper whilst in captivity.

...what we wish for our country – its right to an honourable life, to a spotless dignity, to an independence without restrictions – Belgian colonialists and their Western allies have not wished for.

> History will one day have its say, but it will not be the history that
> Brussels, Paris, Washington or the United Nations will teach, but that
> which they will teach in the countries emancipated from colonialism
> and its puppets.

Mobutu couldn't detain his former friend at Camp Hardy indefinitely. There was always a chance his presence might inspire a rescue
effort. They needed him far away, somewhere he could muster no
support. What about Katanga? Lumumba was despised there. They
could send him to the secessionist leader, Moise Tshombe, and let
him decide what to do. And so it was that Lumumba was loaded
onto an aircraft bound for the Katangan capital on 17 January 1961.
Mobutu and his new American friends would have known there was
little likelihood of him ever returning.

On the tarmac at Elizabethville, outside the Belle Epoque airport
buildings, 100 soldiers were waiting, led by a Belgian captain, Julien
Gat. Lumumba and two of his closest allies, Joseph Okito – the
former vice-president of the senate – and Maurice Mpolo – who had
briefly been head of the army – were already suffering, having been
beaten again during the three-hour flight. They were bundled into
waiting lorries and driven to a low white house, Villa Brouwez, which
had been requisitioned from its Belgian owner earlier in the day.
There, they received a visit from three Katangan cabinet ministers
who gave the captives another beating. Among them was the second
most senior politician in Katanga, Godefroid Munongo. He and the
others emerged from the house tired and thirsty, and stood around
smoking and chatting in the warm evening air. Lumumba was
already in a bad way, his hands bound and face bleeding heavily.
But they couldn't just leave him there, they needed a plan of action.
It was decided nothing more could be done until they had consulted
the republic's president, Moise Tshombe. Only a year had passed,
almost to the day, since Tshombe had been sitting beside Lumumba
in those Brussels talks, debating independence, and now he was to
decide his old colleague's fate.

Tshombe was watching a film at Elizabethville's Cinéma Palace when his aides tracked him down and informed him that Lumumba was under armed guard. He waited until the film ended, and then called a meeting of ministers at his home. Fuelled by whisky, they worked themselves into a fury, and left the residence at eight o'clock in convoy.

At Villa Brouwez, they loaded the prisoners into the back of a car, and drove off in jeeps and military vehicles into the moonlit savannah. Forty-five minutes out of town, the vehicles pulled off the main road onto a rough track, and sped off cross-country through a landscape of soft red earth and stunted bushes. Waiting for them, lit by the yellow beams of car headlights, was a group of gendarmes digging a hole.

Looking on that evening, as night insects whirred in the torchlight, were President Moise Tshombe, two of his ministers, an assortment of military personnel, and four senior Belgian officials, including Captain Gat and Police Commissioner Frans Verscheure. A firing squad was assembled from among the Katangan soldiers. Three volleys of machine-gun fire pierced the night air. Lumumba was last to be shot. He was finished off, with a bullet to the head, by Captain Gat.

And there he lay, beneath the loose orange earth, Congo's great hope, dead at the age of thirty-five.

Someone was bound to have heard the gunshots. A shepherd might notice those fresh tyre tracks across the desert, or choose to examine the rough rectangle of disturbed earth. Lumumba was almost as much trouble dead as he was alive. Discovery of his corpse would cause wave upon wave of civil unrest. Tshombe and the others needed a clean-up plan.

The following day, they instructed the Belgian deputy inspector general of Katangan police, Gerard Soete, to dispose of the evidence. Soete took a group of Katangan policemen, equipped with two jars of sulphuric acid and an empty barrel, to the grave site. They exhumed the bodies, sawed them into pieces, and dissolved the remains. Soete used a pair of pliers to extract two of Lumumba's teeth. It is said he placed them in a matchbox, which he kept for years at his house in Bruges, occasionally getting them out to show visitors.[15]

Africa will write its own history and in both north and south it will be
a history of glory and dignity.

Long live the Congo! Long live Africa![16]

That was how Lumumba signed off his last letter to his wife.

In the rainy season, the mountain roads along the Congo-Rwanda
border were cloaked in thin, warm drizzle. The steamy conditions
made roads slippery and rendered every sound vague and indistinct.
Approaching vehicles sounded like distant tugboats. Only the crack
of gunfire was sharp enough to penetrate the damp.

It was into this environment that Colonel Joseph Mobutu stepped
in 1963, from the lead car of a motorized column, and grabbed his
rifle. The 'politicos', as he liked to call them, were still squabbling
back in Leopoldville. Since the death of Lumumba, the country had
sunk ever deeper into violence, stirred by Cold War paranoia. The
Katanga secession had finally been defeated, but at an enormous
human cost, with UN troops fighting Katangan soldiers, tribesmen
fighting the UN, and Belgian, South African and German mercenaries
fighting the tribesmen. To cap it all, the secretary general of the UN,
Dag Hammarskjold, had been killed in a suspicious plane crash near
the Congolese border on his way to broker a ceasefire. It seemed
almost certain to be the work of separatists. The whole world was
now watching as Congo's war moved into a new phase, the superpowers lining up behind opposing sides.

Mobutu had allowed President Kasavubu to continue in his role,
while he headed the army, but the government had lost control
of more than half of Congo to rebel fighters, despite the backing of
the US.

Marauding gangs were looting and killing their way across
the eastern half of the country, claiming to be Marxists loyal to the
memory of Lumumba. China and Russian were supplying them
with weapons and at one point, the rebels even declared their own
independent republic with its capital in Stanleyville. The Argentine

revolutionary Che Guevara joined them, hoping to assist in what he hoped was Africa's first proletarian uprising, but he found the rebel groups disorganized, apolitical and corrupt, and left Congo despondent, writing to Fidal Castro, 'We can't liberate by ourselves a country that does not want to fight.'[17] As he had discovered, the Congo crisis was more about banditry than politics. Nevertheless, Mobutu found himself on that misty hillside near the Rwanda border leading his men into combat against the most feared of enemies.

As his convoy approached a bridge over the river Sange, the still afternoon air was torn apart by mortars and machine gun fire. Down the hillside ran an army of half-naked men screaming 'Mulele Mayi!' – it was the Simba tribe, the 'lions' as they called themselves, rebels with a particular loathing for Mobutu, and their shout was intended as a magic spell that they believed turned their bodies into water. Confident a bullet would pass right through them, the Simbas were used to charging the Cogolese army, and watching its members flee in horror. But Mobutu was out of the vehicle and screaming for his men to gather their composure. He grabbed an assault rifle and ran towards the advancing Simba shouting for his men to follow. 'A bullet went through my képi without hitting me,' he would later say, 'while in front, the bodies started to pile up. All of a sudden the tables were turned... the poor fellows facing us suddenly lost faith in their magic.'[18]

For five years war raged in Congo. One hundred thousand people are thought to have lost their lives. Out of that chaos, shaking the dust from his hair, strode Colonel Joseph Mobutu, stronger and more popular than ever. It was Mobutu who still represented America's best hope of keeping the Russians at bay.

There was only one man standing between him and his formal acquisition of the top job – the quarrelsome Joseph Kasavubu – and Mobutu had had enough. Confident he could rely on the support of his army, and that of the CIA, on the evening of 24 November 1965 he called his most senior officers to his home. Over beer and a fish supper, prepared by Mrs Mobutu, he dictated a communiqué to be read over the radio. A major was despatched to cut the telephone lines of President Kasavubu.[19] The First Republic had been a disaster, he declared, and within hours the Second Republic would begin. Colonel Mobutu would be its president.

To the beleaguered civilians of Congo, the rise to power of the brave, single-minded soldier over the corrupt squabblers represented a moment of great optimism. When he stood before parliament and declared he could no longer trust them, and that he was transferring law-making powers to himself, the public was behind him. They would also tolerate his temporary banning of political parties, and his use of military courts in the civilian domain. These were extreme measures, no doubt, but a price worth paying to end the bloody cycle of secession and rebellion. Mobutu promised unity, order and peace, and if these were the tools he required, he must be given a chance. But seven months later, an astonishing scene began unfolding in front of a fearful crowd on a stretch of Kinshasa wasteland beside the Stade des Martyrs.

In 2016, on that same patch of wasteland, I watched as rows of brightly coloured plastic chairs were lined up to face a makeshift stage. Women swayed and sang in front of an immaculately suited man who began proceedings with a benevolent smile and a wave of the Bible. The women responded by singing more loudly, a warm mellifluous current drifting from speakers the size of wardrobes. The pastor stabbed the air and dabbed his brow with a white cotton hanky, and soon the women were trembling and reaching for the sky. As the singing turned from spiritual chant to hypnotic incantation a few of the women dropped to their knees, wailing and sobbing as the pastor placed a hand on each of their brows and shouted to the crowds that he was in the process of expelling whatever malevolent spirit hid inside.

The pastor's choice of location for his ritual on the wasteland had not been made arbitrarily. There is special meaning attributed to the Stade des Martyrs, and to the men who gave it its name. The ground is believed, by locals, to be a spiritual corridor to the other side, because of an event that took place here half a century ago, at the behest of the young Mobutu.

Push aside the pastor and the colourful plastic chairs. Close the shops and the puckered tarmac road. Silence the car horns and the singing, and let the dust swirl high from the wasteland into a clear sky. It is 1966, six years since Mobutu assumed temporary military control, and now he is president. The crowds have turned out for a spectacle, but they are not singing and swaying. They are whispering and creeping, tens of thousands of them, across the wasteland towards a stage surrounded by soldiers. John Matadi, the sparring taxi driver, is among them, just nineteen years of age and unsure what he has come to see. Professor-Monk Jacques Libelu is there too, a man I would meet years later in Kinshasa to hear how the Belgians under King Leopold had stripped and beaten his father. It is all a piece of theatre, he thinks; Mobutu is a populist, he would never actually *do* anything like this.

John Matadi was with his elder brother and a couple of friends. He was wearing the wrong footwear for this: a pair of slippers. He saw a physician waiting at the side of the stage. It must be a physician, he thought, only physicians wear white coats.

Jacques Libelu was surprised by how quiet a crowd of 100,000 people could be. It wasn't like any gathering he had seen before. No one moved forward to fill the gaps. When the first army vehicle appeared, the crowd seemed to draw a simultaneous breath. 'Isn't that Évariste Kimba, the former prime minister?' they whispered. Kimba had once been a minister in the separatist state of Katanga, but had been promoted to his role of prime minister in central government to satisfy regionalist agendas. Mobutu viewed him as nothing but trouble. He had dismissed him from his post on the day of the coup, and Kimba was now in the back of a pick-up truck being driven into the middle of the crowd where a wooden scaffold had been hastily erected. It consisted of a square timber platform about four strides across, and an inverted L-shaped pole from which hung a noose. Kimba climbed a short ladder, awkwardly, because his wrists were bound, and was met at the top by a man in a black hood. The man tied a blindfold around the former prime minister's eyes. There were no last words, at least none the almost-silent crowd could hear. When the trapdoor opened they lowered their heads as if the scaffold were a pulpit and Kimba was delivering his blessing.

The former prime minister struggled at the end of the rope for twenty minutes. When he was finally still, the man in the white coat examined his body and lifted him free. The other three condemned politicians had been watching, awaiting their turn.[20]

All were government ministers, accused of high treason for plotting against Mobutu. In truth, they had been the victims of a cruel trap. Several factions in parliament had been enraged by Mobutu's decision to sideline the legislature. Some had even expressed their views openly. They wanted a provisional government put in place while a new constitution was sorted out, followed by elections. Faced with so many dissenting voices when his grip on power was still weak, Mobutu set his military officers to work, asking them to compile a list of troublesome adversaries. The officers took to their task a little too enthusiastically. They became agent provocateurs, arranging meetings at their own homes during which they pushed Mobutu's opponents from being mere discontents into plotters. On a May night in 1966, the officers called four of the president's opponents to a meeting at the home of Colonel Alphonse Bangala. In the garden of his villa, the conspirators were encouraged to put the finishing touches to a coup plot which the officers themselves had dreamed up. The four politicians, including Évariste Kimba, are said to have agreed on the condition that no one was to be killed. They had no idea that the waiters serving them beer that night were actually commandos, or that soldiers lurked in the bushes. At one o'clock in the morning the trap was sprung. Mobutu's military men leapt from their hiding places around the villa and the four men were arrested.

It is said that even Mobutu's wife tried to persuade him against the executions. But the president's mind was set. He had posed himself the old Machiavellian question – 'whether it be better to be loved than feared or feared than loved' – and reached a conclusion from which he would never waver.

Last onto the gallows that day was former defence minister, Jerome Anany. As he fell through the trapdoor, Jacques Libelu felt a fierce wind sweep across the wasteland. It came from nowhere, a gale born in a moment out of a clear sky. People began running.

John Matadi didn't feel a wind, but an earthquake. He could sense it rising through the soles of his slippers.

The whole crowd was running away, feet pounding in the dust, tripping and treading on those who had already fallen. Even the executioner fled. Someone caught the heels of Matadi's slippers, tearing them from his feet. He didn't dare turn back. No one did. They were too scared. It seemed to them that the spirits were running riot.

The executions that June day in 1966 were a watershed moment. From then on the apparatus of Mobutu's authoritarian state began to reach more deeply into people's lives. Parliament was reduced to a rubber stamp. Mobutu organized a youth movement called the Volunteer Corps of the Republic, designed to mobilize mass support on his behalf, which quickly turned into a band of roving vigilantes. He took control of the press and used shameless propaganda to harness the popularity that still persisted for Patrice Lumumba, claiming he was the natural successor to his 'martyred' compatriot. He demanded complete obedience to the official ideology of his newly created party, the Mouvement Populaire de la Révolution, or MPR, which was hurriedly joined by all politicians who valued their safety. But what was his political philosophy? It was difficult to pin down: generally liberal in economic matters but almost Maoist in his social control. Anti-communist, but at the same time anti-capitalist. There were bits and pieces of everything in there, a political stew into which Mobutu tossed whatever ingredient he chose. He welcomed the continued support of the US, while at the same time travelling to Beijing for inspiration. Why not call it Mobutuism and be done with it? And so it was, and just like other personality cults, he needed to strip the country of all that went before in order to start rebuilding it in his own image, a process that would require even Mobutu himself to completely change his identity.

*

It was not an ideal time to be a student. Just as Florentin Mokonda Bonza found himself in the capital, studying for a degree in economics and contemplating the pleasures of being away from his parents for the first time, Mobutuism began marching through the campus corridors. Bonza was a softly spoken, irreverent intellectual, more comfortable in the company of books than people, and everywhere he looked his fellow students were dressed in military uniform. It was Mobutu's punishment for a student demonstration that had ended in a massacre, with government troops shooting dozens of young people dead. If Bonza was joyful at the reintroduction of civilian clothing, he was less so with what was to follow. The harsh winds of Mobutu's cultural revolution swept across campus while he was sitting in an exam hall. He had entered the room wearing a European-style suit and skinny tie, and three hours later, after handing in his paper, the same clothing was deemed so contentious it could attract a visit from the secret police. 'What are you doing?' people were shouting, 'Take it off. Did you not hear the announcement on the radio? Mobutu has banned ties.'

Medical student Gérard Kabamba would later become a vocal critic of Mobutu, but during his first academic year there was still some reluctance to classify their new leader as a dictator. It would be like starting a book with a full stop, he told himself. These were early days, Mobutu was a patriot trying to build a new system from the scraps left behind by the Belgians. There were bound to be casualties. But as the year drew on, the signs became more persistent. 'You watch him,' the senior students warned. 'He is turning.'

By 1971, the signals were too glaring to ignore. Mobutu changed the name of the country to Zaire, an ancient tribal word meaning *the river that swallows all rivers*. The great river itself became Zaire too. So did the currency.

Leopoldville had already become Kinshasa. Stanleyville, Kisangani. Even the people had to be rechristened. They were instructed to write their new names in the university register. Mobutu wanted an authentic African nation, not one stained by reminders of European oppression. They were instructed to choose names that sounded tribal. Gérard Kabamba had no clue what to call himself and so he phoned his family for advice. 'What about Mbwebwe?' said his father. 'It means a rock that is resistant in the path of running water.' Since the medical student had turned into a secret Mobutu opponent, his new name seemed suitable. Gérard became Mbewbwe. Florentin became Mokonda. Joseph Désiré Mobutu became Mobutu Sese Seko Kuku Ngbendu Wa Za Banga. It was said to mean 'the all-conquering warrior who, because of his endurance, will go from conquest to conquest leaving fire in his wake', although many say it can just as easily be translated as 'the cock who jumps on everything that moves'.

Buoyed by the soaring copper prices of the late 1960s, a run of good fortune that gave the illusion Mobutu had somehow mastered the running of his economy, the previously self-conscious leader was starting to become more assertive. The 'Zairianization' of his country – Mobutu called it his 'authenticity programme' – was ostensibly designed to return his people to some idealized version of their past before the arrival of Leopold, king of the Belgians. But it was really just a series of populist decrees designed to distract from the more pressing concern about where all the money was going. Most of the population were not impressed. The Zairianization of Congo became a cobbled-together African Disneyland animated by Mobutu's own idiosyncrasies. The inspiration for his leopard-skin hat came from some of Zaire's 450 tribal chiefs, but Mobutu chose a westernized version, wearing it at a permanently rakish angle, and establishing it as his trademark. Then there was the high-collared jacket, or 'abacost'. It became a uniform for Mobutu supporters, but it was most likely inspired by a visit he made to Chairman Mao. The ubiquitous Mobutu cravat was a sixteenth-century European fashion accessory, part of the very heritage he was trying to banish. Mobutu was embroidering an image for himself, a shorthand for his new nation: the hat and the thick-framed glasses, a stylist's dream, a brand that prefigured social media and went viral.

While forcing his subjects back in time, Mobutu was striding back through history himself, supposedly searching for an authentic heritage, though not of the African variety. He preferred that of the French Renaissance. The colonial heritage that he railed so fiercely against in public, had cast a spell over Mobutu that he found just too potent to resist.

In the jungle of the equatorial region, the home of his ancestors, 1,000 kilometres north of Kinshasa, acres of trees were felled and builders arrived. Mobutu constructed a palace in the village of Gbadolite, which became his jungle seat, founded on the proceeds of copper, diamonds and gold. Italianate fountains threw jets of scarce water into the air. Stone columns supported high ornate ceilings and shimmering Venetian chandeliers. In the ballroom, guests could skate across marble as smooth as frozen lakes. Artists set to work on frescoes of rainforests and brightly coloured birds. Architects designed a system of interlocking pools. The building's first incarnation was judged too big, and another was constructed, with cosier gold-embossed rooms and shaded Japanese pagodas where Mobutu could enjoy his favourite pink champagne. Soon statesmen and celebrities were being entertained at his 'Versailles in the jungle' where they were showered with gifts of diamonds, vintage wines and finely carved ivory. The procession of partygoers need not have worried about accessing such a remote spot. Mobutu had a runway built which was so long that it could accommodate the supersonic Concorde.

If people felt that the authenticity programme laid bare Mobutu's megalomaniac tendencies, the next step caused even greater alarm. When Mokonda Bonza heard what was happening, he hardly needed his degree in economics to understand that its effects would be uniquely destructive.

In 1973, Mobutu returned from a state visit to China with the words of Chairman Mao whirring in his head. 'All you are doing in Zaire is good,' Mao had told him, 'but if Zaire is not *economically* independent, it is nothing.' The conversation had resurrected in Mobutu a feeling of inadequacy that he had not experienced since the round-table talks in Brussels in 1960, when he had been so comprehensively outmanoeuvred by the Belgians. Back then he had been little more than a boy with no hope of fighting back; now the Congolese economy was his own to mould in any shape he saw fit.

Mobutu announced that all foreign-owned businesses would be seized and handed over to local people, irrespective of their education or skills. Shelf-stackers were given the shops they worked in. Shopkeepers were given the factories that produced their goods. A friend of the taxi driver Pierre Mambele, a man who was a musician by trade, was given a shopping mall. Overnight the governor of Katanga is said to have become the owner of nearly all the businesses in his province. It appeared that the American-backed Mobutu had experienced a communist epiphany and begun redistributing wealth at breakneck speed, but Mobutu's broadside against what he perceived as the agents of colonialism was pure clientelism, the creation of a sprawling structure of patronage. The country's economy was given away like goody bags at a children's party, and only Mobutu's most faithful supporters were invited. It was, he said, 'a decisive turning point in our history', justified because Zaire 'has been the most heavily exploited country in the world'. Mobutu would require a special gift. He treated himself to fourteen plantations and dipped into the country's mining industry as he pleased. Soon he was estimated to be the world's eighth-richest man.[21] Even today it irks Mokanda Bonza, now a professor of economics and a senator. 'These things should not come from heaven,' he despairs. 'They should come from hard work.' But Bonza was soon to surprise everyone by becoming Mobutu's chief of cabinet.

On the little finger of Glenn Kendrick's left hand is a ring adorned with a tiny nest the size of a peanut, and in that nest sits a diamond. He wears a similar ring two fingers along. Kendrick is a diamond prospector, but not the suited type, more like the nineteenth-century fortune-hunters who first rushed to Kimberley. He's lived in shipping containers in the bush while searching for elusive diamondiferous volcanoes, and had AK-47s poked in his face as he's chased rumours to the next big find. In Liberia during the rule of Charles Taylor, he insisted his armed guard stop at a dry river bed which had caught his attention. The rest of the party wandered off, but Kendrick examined the boulders and igneous rock and when he pushed a branch into the sand he saw fragments of kimberlite. A few centimetres down, he found two diamonds weighing half a carat each. A week later they had discovered another ninety. The spot is now marked on the Ordnance Survey map as 'Glenn Pit', and ever since, Glenn Kendrick has been known as 'The Man Who Can Smell Diamonds'.

If Glenn Kendrick could smell diamonds beneath the earth, he could certainly smell them hidden in the pockets of government officials when he arrived in Mobutu's Congo.

The sorting room in Kinshasa was on the eighteenth floor of a bank, a cleanish room with the look of an ill-equipped school laboratory. Trestle tables were arranged in lines and behind them stood local men handpicked by the ministry. They leaned intently over reefs of assorted stones, examining them with magnifying glasses before separating them delicately into heaps of high and low quality, some as large as peas, others speck-small, each lifted and examined with a pair of delicate tweezers.

The operation was being run by Kendrick's employer, the biggest diamond producer in Zaire at the time, a British company called IDC, which had managed to muscle the South African corporation de Beers out of the picture, and was now in control of 17 million Zairian carats each year, worth around $340 million ($1.4 billion in today's money). Most of the diamonds were of a very distinct shape and type. Drop one into the hand of an expert and they would be able to identify the region and even the mine it came from, as surely as a sommelier can identify a wine. And the odds, in Zaire, were on South Kasai, the short-lived independent republic, and home to the MIBA mine that once produced more than half the industrial diamonds in the world. They had the appearance of tiny grey translucent cubes, perfectly formed with crisp edges and sharp corners, and they handled like damp gravel. But no one cared much about their appearance because these were industrial diamonds, known as boart, and when

Kendrick was in Zaire, world demand for them was booming. The reason was oil exploration. Boart was studded into the heads of oil-industry drills, and was so hard it could cut through kilometres of solid rock. Zaire produced more boart than any other country in the world, and it was used in Saudi Arabia, Kuwait and Romania, home of Mobutu's good friend, President Nicolae Ceauşescu.

Zaire, however, had gem-quality diamonds too, worth many times more than the industrial variety. They were always somewhere in the mix, and it was the sorters' job to identify them and put them to one side.

The precise nature of the mix, and even the total quantity of diamonds being mined, was something of a mystery. Kendrick would refer to the number of carats that 'arrived in the building' as distinct from the unknown number that had actually been taken from the ground. When a team from London arrived at the MIBA mine to investigate the leakage, they found officials plucking stones from the conveyor belts to sell on the black market. There was worse to come. As the diamonds passed through the shaker to size them ready for transfer to Kinshasa, workers were happily flicking out handfuls at a time. After that the London team tried to shore up their defences, installing security guards to keep watch on the extraction process. But Kendrick faced an altogether more challenging problem in his very own office.

The sorters on the eighteenth floor were a curious lot. They were paid $100 a month by the ministry, and yet several proudly showed off expensive watches, and arrived at work each morning in brand-new foreign cars. Kendrick kept an eye on them. They were good at this. He decided to weigh the stones before and after sorting and discovered that, whereas each had started the day with 2,000 carats, they had finished with forty or so less. Kendrick did some quick mental arithmetic. He imagined a coffee cup being slowly filled by a spout of tiny stolen diamonds, and reckoned it would be overflowing at the end of each month. The quantities being spirited away equated to a loss of around $10,000 every day.

Kendrick called the boss at the ministry, a small man who dressed in a Mobutu abacost, and carried himself with a regal air, just like his president. The official was disinterested. It was simply 'a sorting loss', he declared, there was nothing anyone could do. Kendrick should stop making trouble.

The before-and-after weights gradually fell into line, but now there was a problem with the mix of stones. Gem-quality diamonds were suddenly fewer, the amount of boart was growing. Kendrick strode through the sorting room like Sherlock Holmes observing a convention of magicians. It was a tricky scheme to fathom. They were handing in the right *weight* of stones, but the wrong *types*. Kendrick arrived early one morning and doctored each of their portions by placing large gemstones among the boart. When he collected the sorted piles in the evening, the weight was the same but the gemstones had vanished. They were bringing in their own cheap stones and surreptitiously switching them with the gems.

Mobutu's official was called back. This time he had just one comment. 'You are wrong,' he said to Kendrick, before standing and leaving the room. Glenn Kendrick had just wandered into the foothills of Mobutu's mountainous system of patronage. It wasn't only diamonds, of course, but copper, gold, cobalt, uranium: larceny on a grand scale making Mobutu's officials wealthy and compliant. Millions of dollars were being syphoned out of the country or squandered on ministerial excesses. Mobutu was spending uncontrollably, not just on Gbadolite and acquiring a property empire for himself in exclusive Mediterranean resorts, but also on his grand MPR party headquarters, and his obsessive drive for military equipment. In 1970 the IMF estimated that Mobutu's pilfering from the national budget amounted to $60 million – equivalent to a quarter of a billion today. But what about those outside of his circle of patronage? How could he keep control of them?

The darkness was so ripe with petrol fumes that Joseph Nkoyi knew they could have ended it all with the strike of a single match. But his captors didn't want him dead, he kept telling himself, not yet anyway, just terrified at the prospect of remaining alive. His knees were jammed into his chest, his ear bumping against a metal floor, and a few feet away was the low growl of an engine. He was in the back of a car, not the back *seat* of a car, the very back of the car. Joseph Nkoyi was in the trunk. He had even managed to glimpse the model as they bundled him inside. It was a Mercedes W123, an exclusive vehicle driven only by Zaire's top officials. His captors had made a big show of stripping out the trunk's plastic lining, removing the thin carpet and slinging away the spare wheel so that the rivets and the sharp angles were all exposed. His body slipped slightly as the car rounded a corner. Then there was a jolt. The tarmac road had ended and he knew they were heading away from the Avenue des Trois 'Z', where the prison was located, and out of town on one of Kinshasa's many mud-track roads.

Nkoyi cursed. He should have stayed in America. He might have even been a lawyer one day. But there was something about his ancestral homeland that drew him back.

When he had flown into Kinshasa that first time he had taken great care to sanitize his luggage, clearing out pamphlets, videos, audio-tapes, all describing Mobutu's torture of political opponents. Nkoyi was part of the opposition movement in exile, and even though he was a risk-taker by nature, some might even say reckless, he wasn't going to get caught with anti-Mobutu material in Zaire.

He blazed through the airport, broad-chested, beaming. 'The passport? Yes, sir… The visa? Of course… The luggage? Feel free.'

One of the security officers pointed to his Walkman.

Nkoyi had nothing to hide. The Walkman, protruding from his crumpled suitcase. The Walkman he was lifting and handing to the security team. The Walkman with the little Perspex window which showed a cassette tape had been left, mistakenly, inside. One of the security officers put on the little orange headphones and pressed play. He was treated to a fiery anti-Mobutu speech recorded in the US, with particular emphasis on the president's use of torture in his secret prisons.

Later that same day, Joseph Nkoyi was able to experience Zaire's prison conditions first-hand. The jail he was taken to, after being arrested for sedition, was run by the misleadingly named Agence Nationale de Documentation (AND), whose business reached far deeper than the straightforward analyses of paperwork. It was the main civilian intelligence agency in Zaire, and its prison, 'The Three Zeds', was the place where all political detainees were taken first. There were no trials. The word of an AND official was sufficient to land a man in prison.

At least 'The Three Zeds' was an official prison. There were plenty of others that were not. These had sprung up all over towns and cities and were controlled by any number of agencies or even individuals favoured by Mobutu. Each section of the military had its own jails and hellholes. There was the Special Presidential Division (Mobutu's much-feared personal guard), the Service for Military Action, the Special Brigade and the elite Civil Guard, which was run by one of Mobutu's own relatives and which controlled the notorious underground cells known as OAU2.[22] Soldiers could be incarcerated there for any number of imagined offences, 'plotting against the president' being the catch-all favourite.

Internal power struggles crackled between rival interests in the judicial system. A colonel called Felix Mbayi Kalombo was released by one court, but some of Mobutu's agents were still certain he was a plotter. They visited his house and shot the place up. When they discovered that the colonel had survived with merely a bullet wound to the leg, they visited the clinic where he was being treated, and shot him again in his hospital bed.[23]

For civilians, even a casual anti-Mobutu remark could land them in custody. A young man called Jean-Claude Bahati was in a taxi criticizing Mobutu to friends when a fellow passenger drew a revolver and redirected the taxi to a military prison. It turned out he was working for one of Zaire's security services. Bahati was stripped, beaten, placed in a cell and shaved with a broken bottle.[24]

Detention was in the hands of Officers of the Judicial Police, known as OPJs. But being an OPJ was no normal job. There were no desks or files or pay packets at the end of the month. It was simply a status handed out to Mobutu's most loyal supporters, including all regional officials, and all intelligence officers. In the hierarchy of the single-party state, OPJs had more power than the actual judicial authorities, allowing detentions to become a political tool beyond the influence of judges and courts. Pretty much anyone with an 'official' job – in other words a senior position in the party – could put a metal door on a room in their basement and call it a jail.

Some commentators have suggested there were even cells beneath the 20th May Stadium where the Rumble in the Jungle was held and that, during the Ali–Foreman fight, hundreds were detained and tortured, their screams drowned out by the noise of the cheering crowd. The writer Norman Mailer, who covered the fight, talked of a thousand criminals held in detention pens beneath the ring, of whom a hundred were killed as a warning to the others. There has never been any proof, but the rumours reflect a broader fear about the savagery of Zaire's informal prison system.

The most dangerous places to be incarcerated, however, were those run by the security services, and that included 'The Three Zeds' prison where Joseph Nkoyi was being held.

The monsoon had torn potholes and trenches in the surface of the road, and the driver of the Mercedes W123 was attacking it with speed. Nkoyi's head slammed repeatedly into the floor of the trunk, his roped arms were smashed and his back pummelled by rivets. It was like falling through a tree in an oil drum. And this, he realized, was the point. They weren't actually taking him anywhere. They were simply testing out a new form of punishment.

It was a struggle to try to convince anyone outside the country that Mobutu's despotic regime was torturing and murdering its own citizens, as Amnesty International and Human Rights Watch regularly attempted to do. Wasn't Mobutu the natty dresser with the high collars and the leopard-skin hat, the one who hosted the boxing and flew 200 of his friends and family to visit Disneyland in Florida? Didn't he welcome the Miss Universe competition to Kinshasa? That didn't sound like the behaviour of a tyrant.

Mobutu was a master of carefully chosen distractions, often creating eccentric and spectacular events to shield his deeds from the outside world. He even launched an African Space Programme in which his role was that of valiant pioneer trying to reach Zaire into the stars and advance African science. In fact, the enterprise was owned by a German rocket company which paid Mobutu $150 million to locate its programme in his country because its activities were prohibited back home. At the inaugural launch of OTRAG-1 Mobutu stood proudly on a remote mountainside to observe lift-off. The rocket soared skywards, and then arced right back down again and exploded in a valley just beneath the president's feet.

The US had supported Mobutu from the start, assisting his 1960 coup in order to ensure the demise of Lumumba, and then helping him seize the presidency in 1965, while generously financing his army against the Soviet and Cuban-backed rebels during the Congo Crisis. In the early 1970s, Washington was still behind him, even though the destructive nature of his totalitarian regime was by now very obvious. The local alternatives were just too grim to consider. At least Mobutu was holding the line against Moscow.

Although he had no clue how to manage Zaire's economy, when it came to international political strategy he was a master. With Washington's foreign affairs in the hands of Secretary of State Henry Kissinger, the US was particularly sensitive to a Red threat, a position that played invitingly into Mobutu's hands.

By 1974 Zaire was broke. The mainstay of its economy was copper, and world prices had collapsed. Instead of reining in his own state theft, and that of his cronies, Mobutu borrowed heavily from American and European banks in the hope of riding out the crisis. But Zaire was experiencing the first murmurings of public discontent, and when the US became hesitant about bailing him out further, Mobutu devised an audacious plan.

Seven thousand kilometres away, in Lisbon, Portugal, the Carnation Revolution had swept away the country's authoritarian right-wing regime, the Estado Novo. It had also thrown Portugal's creaking empire into a deepening crisis, particularly in Angola, just across

Mobutu's southern border. An independence war had been raging there for more than a decade, drawing in a multitude of different factions. Now, with the country adrift, it was crucial for Mobutu to help install a regime of his choice.

He had thrown his weight behind the Western-supporting FNLA, the National Liberation Front of Angola, and given sanctuary in Kinshasa to its leader, Holden Roberto, with whom he had familial ties. At considerable expense, and with his reputation on the line, he had despatched battalions from Zaire's army, the Forces Armées Zairoises or FAZ, across the border to fight alongside them. If they helped secure victory, it would confirm Mobutu as a major world player. But his adventure in Angola was draining the last remaining dollars from his near-lifeless national budget.

The FNLA/FAZ forces were fighting the Marxist–Leninist MPLA, the People's Movement for the Liberation of Angola. Mobutu's problem was that if the MPLA triumphed in Angola, they might spill over his border and attempt to unseat him. It wasn't simply because they viewed him as America's puppet in the region. MPLA fighters had more personal reasons to want Mobutu dead. Among their ranks were former Katangan fighters whom Mobutu had ejected from Zaire during the secession crisis. They were impatient to get back in and retake the territory.

In the first few months of 1975, the Mobutu-backed FNLA seemed to have the upper hand, but the MPLA's strength was boosted by an air drop of military supplies from Moscow. Mobutu was in trouble. He simply couldn't take the risk that the Soviets might begin seriously funding his enemy. It was then he pulled off his masterstroke.

In Kinshasa, Mobutu had his state-controlled newspapers run a story accusing the American ambassador, Dean R. Hinton, of colluding in a plot to have him assassinated. He put on a display of furious indignation, kicking Hinton out of the country, and giving the impression that his relationship with Washington was all but over.

Suddenly the White House was facing the possibility of losing its bulwark against the communist threat in Angola. If Mobutu wanted money, responded a near-hysterical Henry Kissinger, give it to him. 'We are in the process of installing a communist regime [in Angola] by total default!' he shouted at his advisors. He then despatched the former US ambassador Sheldon Vance, who had got along well with Mobutu during his tenure in Kinshasa, to try to salvage the situation, exclaiming 'I want to hear what he [Mobutu] wants us to do there. He must think we are out of our damn minds... to have the whole country go communist without doing anything.'[25]

And thus it was that Mobutu drew America into a conflict which became one of the bloodiest in Cold War history. He had fabricated the assassination plot in order to help him through his own local difficulties. The whole thing was a self-serving charade. As a conduit for US funds, he could pilfer what he liked. But US covert involvement in Angola soon became too obvious to hide, and the Soviet Union responded by increasing its own support for the MPLA.

Kissinger's military backing for Mobutu was a terrible misjudgement. Angola became America's most humiliating Cold War defeat. The Soviet- and Cuban-backed MPLA installed itself in Angola's capital, Luanda, in November 1975, but the fighting dragged on for another three decades, and claimed more than half a million civilian lives. Throughout, Washington's support for its chief regional ally remained steadfast. Not only did successive presidents continue to finance Mobutu's floundering economy, they pressurized other world leaders to do the same.

If Erwin Blumenthal was optimistic about his financial mission when he first arrived in Kinshasa, he would be less so a few months later when he took to sleeping with a shotgun beneath his bed. Blumenthal was a senior banker with the West German Bundesbank, a man whose forensic banking skills and passion for Africa had convinced the International Monetary Fund (IMF) that he was a perfect choice for the job. It was 1978 and Mobutu was in search of another enormous loan. The IMF had just given him $305 million, in return for a promise of reform in his banking institutions (after more pressure from the US), but Mobutu wanted even more. The IMF was a little uneasy. Where was all this money going? Blumenthal's mission was to wade into Zaire's financial swamplands and find out. He would, effectively, take control of Zaire's central bank, and Mobutu had no choice but to allow him in, or he wouldn't get another penny.

Blumenthal set to work on the brimming filing cabinets and mountains of incoherent paperwork, and quickly discovered that plummeting copper prices were not the primary source of Zaire's problems.

There was a 'professor' on the books who was receiving a monthly payment of $300,000. Officials reassured him that it was 'honorary… for his studies contributing to the bettering of Zairian people's condition'. What invaluable contributions could he possibly be making? Later Blumenthal discovered the professor was the guardian of one of Mobutu's sons.[26] That set the tone for what was to come: millions of dollars slipping away into bank accounts controlled by Mobutu's family, government ministers, police chiefs, military officers, and anyone else whose support he deemed useful to keep him in power.

Some of Mobutu's senior officials would pop into the bank now and then and help themselves to state money. 'At the end of January 1979, at 7 o'clock in the evening,' wrote Blumenthal, 'I was in the central bank when the soldiers of General Tukuzu entered. They threatened me with their machine guns because I refused to provide them with money from the foreign exchange which they wanted for their general.'[27]

'Who is going to shout THIEF!' Blumenthal wrote furiously in one report. 'All control of financial transactions in the president's office has proved impossible. One cannot make a difference between the expenses of the State and the president's personal needs.'[28]

It all fitted in with what Glenn Kendrick was finding. Whenever fresh diamond fields were discovered, their location was kept secret. But the mining officials were instructed to deliver one copy of the geological report to the president's office. On each occasion, submission of the report would be followed, just days later by the arrival of armed gangs at the secret location exactly where the diamonds had been located. They would begin digging before the mining companies could secure the area. Kendrick calculated the overall theft at around 3 million carats a year – that is close to twenty per cent of all Zaire's diamonds: $250,000,000 in today's money.

Erwin Blumenthal's final warning to Western governments and the IMF was that 'control of fraud was impossible', the vast scale of Congo's debt was 'first and foremost due to Mobutu's government', and that any loan made by the international community was unlikely ever to be repaid. But Mobutu's strategic importance was just too great.

In the 1980s, Western governments gave him an another $3 billion.[29] On top of that, $700 million was donated by the International Monetary Fund, and $650 million from the World Bank. Mobutu took it, and looted unashamedly, not just from the loans, but from the humanitarian aid he received. Nothing was sacrosanct.

He stole from the US 'Food for Peace Programme' and distributed it among five of his associates. He took millions in US food subsidies intended to tackle malnutrition. Even his own refugee crisis offered an opportunity for plunder: UN transportation trucks were stolen, apparently by Mobutu's own troops.[30]

By the mid-1980s, while regularly appealing for loans, Mobutu's personal wealth had grown to around $4 billion. He had a weakness for grand homes in Europe, of which he had accumulated around twenty. There were nine in Belgium, including Château Fond'Roy, a famous Brussels landmark built by the original Congo-looter himself: Leopold, king of the Belgians. There was a villa in Savigny, Switzerland, overlooking Lake Geneva, a seaside home at Cap-Martin on the French Riviera, and properties in Italy, Spain and Portugal.[31] In Paris he owned an apartment on the prestigious Avenue Foch, close to the Arc de Triomphe, the favourite address of several African dictators, including Omar Bongo of Gabon, and Teodorin Obiang, the criminal playboy son of the president of Equatorial Guinea.

★

In the Binza district of Kinshasa, a gardener wheeled cut flowers through a pair of electric gates. Land Cruisers swept through quiet shady lanes. Behind pristine white walls could be seen several French-style villas with rose-tiled roofs. A woman sold cool drinks from beneath a parasol. If you awoke here from some deep sleep you would imagine you were in a residential neighbourhood of Aix-en-Provence. But Binza is the district of Kinshasa traditionally inhabited by those who were Mobutu's most loyal supporters.

When we reached the home of Florentin Mokonda Bonza, a security guard slid open the heavy metal gate and waved us onto a driveway beside a veranda. Bonza was working outside behind a large desk, dressed casually in a tropical-print shirt. Inside there was clutter and family photographs and some tribal trinkets. It was what the French might call *haut bohème*, more like the home of a successful artist than a man who was gatekeeper and chief of cabinet to Mobutu.

'Mobutu had many personalities,' Bonza explained. 'One was Christian. He would attend church every Sunday. But another side of him could be pitiless.' And then he added, quickly, 'I never came across that side.'

I suggested that Bonza must have known that countless people were being tortured and killed, and asked him if he ever raised objections with Mobutu.

'I was frank with him,' he said coolly. 'I sometimes learned things that had happened and when I raised them with him, he would respond, "Those things are just sayings".'

But he must have known about the disappearances and the political prisons; everyone did. Would he come home to his wife and confide in her that he was troubled?

'No, never,' Bonza responded edgily, addressing just the translator now.

But was there ever a voice inside his head, saying, 'This is unacceptable, I am part of a murderous regime,' did he ever—

'These are the wrong questions,' he snapped. 'You are asking the wrong questions.'

There was quiet for a while. The interpreter stared at his notepad. Mokonda Bonza stared at him. A cool breeze blew in through the patio door beside the swimming pool.

After a while, Bonza spoke again. 'You in Europe see him only as a devil, but that is too simplistic. Apart from embezzling money he also brought peace. He fought and ended tribalism, he united the country, he made a state into a nation.' I sensed that Mokonda Bonza hadn't intended to defend Mobutu quite so stoutly, but now he had begun, he might as well continue. 'Mobutu was like one of your European kings,' he smiled. 'You did it first. Building big monuments, executing people, living a rich life while the people were poor. That was him. He was like a European king.'

Then he went on to tell an extraordinary story.

The date was 24 December 1989.

The footage was bleak, ghostly, as if shot through a lens made of ice. An elderly couple were dressed against the snow. They were seated behind a wooden table. Fragile electricity, stick furniture, acned walls. The scene was a military base in Eastern Europe. Facing the couple were a dozen or so uniformed officers. The couple appeared ill-fed, desperate. They were remonstrating. Pale young soldiers covered them with AK-47s. A prosecutor spoke. 'It is very difficult for us to pass a verdict on these people who do not want to admit to the criminal offences they have committed during the past 25 years.'

'I do not recognize this court!' the elderly man shouted back, his finger wagging threateningly at his accusers. He seemed to think he was still in charge.

The man's name was Nicolae Ceauşescu, president of Romania. He had been a friend of Mobutu's since the early days. Both men had been in power more than two decades, and saw themselves as kindred spirits, members of the Non-Aligned Movement which, in theory, meant they were not formally partnered with either Cold War bloc. Both were also unapologetic leaders of monolithic single-party states.

Four days earlier, Nicolae Ceaușescu had been making another marathon speech alongside his wife, Elena, from the balcony of the Central Committee building in Bucharest when the mood had turned ugly. For the first time, a crowd had dared jeer him. After years of forced labour, food queues and random imprisonments, the people had turned. Ceaușescu attempted to flee that very day, but was arrested by his own army and was now facing a hurried court hearing in a cramped room at a military base.

'You not only deprived the people of heating, electricity and food, you also tyrannized the soul of the people,' declared the prosecutor.

Ceaușescu waved his hand dismissively.

'You have bank accounts in Switzerland... grand palaces where you eat from gold plates... parties and feasts while the people starve.'

'You killed children, young people and adults... you were so impertinent as to cut off oxygen lines in hospitals and to shoot people in their hospital beds.'

Mobutu was watching.

There on the television screen in front of him was Ceaușescu, being manhandled out of the room and into a corridor. The two leaders had dined together, drunk together, admired each other's palaces together, and now the pale young soldiers were tying both Ceaușescu's hands with twine as Elena loudly objected. 'I brought you up as a mother,' she told the paratroopers. Many Romanians still believe Ceaușescu's trademark hat was inspired by Mobutu, and now it was taken from his bound hands and placed, crookedly, comically, on his head. Ceaușescu and his wife were pushed along a corridor, shouting and protesting and out into a courtyard, cold and barren. The winter light was thin. They were led out through a door and placed against a wall. Automatic gunfire followed. A Mobutu-style hat lay beside a leafless tree.

Mobutu rushed to his phone. At the other end was his minister of information, Dominique Sakombi Inongo. He could not hear what Mobutu was saying, the volume of the president's voice was distorting the earpiece. The minister soon got the gist though. Mobutu wanted the news footage taken off the air. But it was far too late for that.

The next day, Mobutu summoned his head of cabinet, Mokonda Bonza.

The president had benefited from a night's sleep. He was calmer now, but still numbed. The image remained with him: Ceaușescu's haggard face, dead eyes staring, and blood pooling around the body. In a Hollywood version there would undoubtedly have been a slow focus-pull to Mobutu's own face staring back from his sofa, transposing his features onto those of his friend, until it was he lying on the floor of a military barracks, his hat near his feet.

Mobutu looked up at Mokonda Bonza.'It could happen to me,' he said. Then he retreated into his palace for two weeks.

'He absented himself,' says Mokonda Bonza. 'He needed to reflect.' On his return he had a plan. He, the president, would put himself at the mercy of ordinary citizens. He would host events up and down the country where people could tell him exactly what they thought of him. He would make a vague promise of reform, there would be some mutual clearing of the air, and they could all move on. And, in the spirit of open debate, there would be no punishment for the critics. No one would go to jail. It was to be called the National Consultation and would begin right away. But it wouldn't go quite as Mobutu planned.

Mobutu peered out of his plane window over a carpet of tropical rainforest as far as he could see. It was the great, rich heartland of Zaire, almost five times the size of France, and so fertile! Bananas, coffee, corn, pineapples, enough produce to feed the whole of Africa. The climate and soil were just right, but not the organization, not the infrastructure, not just yet. And that tiny village, how similar to the one where he was raised. But Mobutu was flying too high. If his small plane had landed on a bald patch of earth, of which there were many, this is what he would have seen: trees cleared and burned because there was no power, no fuel. The village cut off from its neighbours, and from its nearest town because the roads had actually deteriorated since the days of the Belgians. The inhabitants drinking rainwater, because there were no wells. Children wandering around with swollen bellies because malnutrition had reached fifty per cent in many areas, while the state had all but withdrawn from providing healthcare. And, outside the village, a graveyard where one in five inhabitants would be buried before they were old enough to walk, and most others would follow them into the ground before they reached fifty.

The airstrip at Goma must have appeared modest in comparison with his own immense runway at Gbadolite and, indeed, it was too short to receive airlifted medical supplies. Still, Mobutu stepped from the plane in optimistic spirit. This listening exercise should head off any Ceaușescu-style ending, even though some had already begun calling him Mobutu *Sesescu*.[32]

Alongside him at the event was Mokonda Bonza. 'Mobutu expected some reproaches,' he tells me, 'but assumed people would be too afraid to accuse him of anything directly.'

The president gave an opening address. The crowd listened patiently. He explained he wanted all civil society to express their views on the management of the country. They had not been consulted about anything for twenty-five years. Even during the grotesquely rigged elections they were always faced with just one party and one candidate. It was a red card for 'no', a green card for 'yes', all under the watchful eye of Mobutu officials. Now he wanted to hear their opinion. There must be security personnel recording the whole event.

'We are in Goma,' called out an early contributor. 'The roads are bad. The president repairs the route he takes to his palaces and his parks, but he leaves the rest like this.'

Mobutu was expressionless. Mokonda Bonza saw him stiffen. 'He was making a big effort to contain himself,' he tells me.

The crowd became increasingly emboldened.

'You and your family and friends do nothing,' called out another attendee, directly to Mobutu this time, 'but you are all wealthy.'

'You all have a good life while most of us suffer!' shouted someone else. 'And your money comes from corruption.'

There it was. The word had finally slipped out, and now it hung in the air of the auditorium, defiant and proud, and not at all out of place, waiting for other contributors to pick it up and throw it at the president. And so they did. Corruption! Corruption! Until it was the word that attracted all the other words like a magnet.

When Mobutu left the stage he turned to Mokonda Bonza. 'Can you believe it?' he said. 'After all I have done? This is how my people repay me. They are so ungrateful.'

In the evening he went into a kind of mourning, withdrawing to his room and refusing to eat. The other consultations went ahead as planned but Mobutu was not going to be caught like that again. He would give an introductory speech, and then leave the arena. Nevertheless, the public responses were collated and analysed, and change suddenly became a real possibility: momentous change.

On 24 April 1990 Mobutu stood in front of a lectern and a bank of microphones to address a handpicked audience of politicians, military officials and foreign journalists. The images were flashed around the world. Mobutu was wearing a ceremonial military costume, all epaulettes and gold braid. His acolytes were in the front row: men in identical abacosts, women in floral dresses. He had an historic announcement: there would be free elections, and an end to single-party rule.

The crowd was not sure how to react: to cheer and sing, or weep because that is what Mobutu appeared to be doing. 'I will oversee it all,' he said, jaw quivering. 'I will be the pacifier, the unifier... but I hereby announce that I am taking leave from the Mouvement Populaire de la Revolution, to allow a new chief to be chosen.' Mobutu lowered his head. There was silence in the hall. Just the shuffling of papers on the lectern. It was the end of Mobutu's rule. A transition period would begin right away.

Mobutu removed his thick glasses and theatrically dabbed at each eye. 'Forgive me for being emotional!' he said, and the crowd burst into song. There could be no greater expression of sincerity than the tears of their leader.

But no one could quite pin him down on a timescale for the transition.

In the meantime, Mobutu had some derailing to do. The process of democratization which he had rashly sanctioned was to be overseen by the Sovereign National Conference, where the great and the good would sit in committees and agree a way forward for the country. It was a tortuous and acrimonious affair that would drag on for many months, but just as it seemed to be making progress, a spree of looting and rioting began. How could this happen, when there was the promise of renewal and an end to tyranny?

Even the family of Professor-Monk Jacques Libelu took to the streets. 'On day one,' his grandson Emery told me, 'we said "No, we are Christian, we don't do this kind of thing."' From their window they saw neighbours returning with every kind of domestic appliance. 'Scales looted from supermarkets, kitchen sinks, some even carried toilets on their heads. 'They didn't think they might need plumbing,' chuckles Emery. On day two his family held a meeting. 'Now everyone's doing it,' a relative said, 'even the people who are supposed to prevent the looting are looting. We will go hungry. We will end up having to buy things from the looters.' One of Emery's uncles was a police officer. 'No,' he said, 'we should stay at home.' On day three, a family rebellion was under way. 'There will be nothing left,' they said to the uncle-police officer. 'No food in the stores. We will all blame you when we starve.' They watched more neighbours come and go. The pickings seemed to be getting thinner. Some were now struggling along with the fabric of dismantled buildings, metal rods and steel girders, which would lie outside their homes until the weeds grew over them. It was 2 p.m. A decision had to be taken. 'Let's do it,' said the uncle. They dressed twelve-year-old Emery in a gendarmerie helmet and set off for town in a truck. The uncle-police officer stood on top of the cockpit firing a gun in the air and ordering the mob to help load up the back. 'We weren't looting, we were loading,' smiles Emery. 'When we got home I tasted fresh milk for the first time. Before that I thought it came just as powder.'

As the country slipped into anarchy, Mobutu was quietly delighted. What further proof could his people need that he was the chief, that only he could hold Zaire together?

Mokonda Bonza was in no doubt how the unrest came about.

'I was still directing Mobutu's office,' he says, as he feeds his pet monkey on the back lawn of his home in Binza. 'I know that Mobutu organized the rioting, to prove the country would slip into anarchy without him.' Mokonda Bonza resigned shortly afterwards. 'By that time, I realized his bad side outweighed his good,' he says. But Mobutu just carried on and on.

'You want to see the torture marks?'

In Joseph Nkoyi's office the lights have gone out, and we are waiting for his generator to kick in. It is many years since he was driven around in the trunk of a Mercedes W123 by Mobutu's thugs. Today he is a bear of a man who carries the scars of Mobutu's regime all over his body. I ask him why he is still alive. 'We have our own destiny,' he replies elliptically. 'I was jailed forty-six times in all.' He swings around in his leopard-skin chair and reaches for a packet of biscuits beside a leopard-skin rug. The skins are all fake, Nkoyi has seen too many dead bodies to want one adorning the floor of his office. 'It is important to have God on your side in Congolese politics,' he says, munching away. 'The killer kills all who need to be killed.'

After his first stint in prison, instead of returning home to his privileged life in America, Nkoyi became the envoy of one of the leading opponents of Mobutu, veteran politician Etienne Tshisekedi, who had once been advisor to Patrice Lumumba. Nkoyi's new role began during the time the Sovereign National Conference was at work, trying to establish the democratic change Mobutu had promised. But progress was painfully slow, and Mobutu was still rounding up political opponents.

From Amnesty International:
UA 146/93 Legal concern/Fear of torture   7th May 1993
Zaire:
Joseph OLENGA Nkoyi
Joseph Olenga Nkoyi, an envoy (chargé de mission) of opposition Prime Minister Etienne Tshisekedi, was arrested on 29 April 1993 and is being

held at the Kinshasa headquarters of the National Gendarmerie, known as "CIRCO" (circonscription militaire). There are reports that he has been subjected to torture.

The jail Joseph Nkoyi found himself in this time was supposed to be run by a general who was married to Mobutu's elder sister. But no one was actually running anything anymore. The system was breaking down. Across the country, prison staff had sold everything they could find, machinery from the workshops, cooking utensils, tools and even the seeds intended to feed the inmates. Fights were breaking out over a piece of burnt crust and banana skin.[33]

Such desperate looting wasn't restricted to prison staff. Government officials had abandoned their desks after not being paid for months. Their salaries had hardly been worth collecting: inflation had reached almost 10,000 per cent. People needed bricks of Zairian bank notes just to buy bread. Mobutu was happily stirring the chaos, appointing prime ministers and jealously dismissing them before they had the chance to win public support. Tshisekedi was prime minister twice, once just for three weeks. So unpredictable had politics become that when Joseph Nkoyi was released from jail he ended up at a negotiating table with Mobutu, and in typically surreal Zairian style, the two men actually got along well.

'He was very curious, because I was so young,' says Nkoyi, 'but I found him a very civilized person. He had the manner of a real chief.'

The illusion did not last long. Mobutu had a death squad dispatched to neutralize Nkoyi. 'They came to the parliament building, but we had already been tipped off,' says Nkoyi. 'My colleagues went into the cellars and found a military uniform and a beret. They dressed me like a soldier, and even gave me a pair of sunglasses. I walked outside and the military guard actually saluted me,' he laughs, throwing his palm to the side of his head. 'There was a car waiting, then a boat, and I fled across the river to Congo-Brazzaville, where the American ambassador came to help.'

★

At Mobutu's palace in Gbadolite the fountains squirted water into the heavy tropical air. Peacocks strutted across neatly trimmed turf. The president was high on his sandstone terrace and when he looked out across the forest, the clouds were lower than his feet. Zaire was somewhere out there, but he was hardly part of it anymore. He had been forced to dabble in democratization for a while, reluctantly taking on eight different prime ministers, but had managed to pour so much glue into the machinery of the Sovereign National Conference that it had jammed up without resolution. When its members finally won the power to elect a new prime minister (they voted for Tshisekedi again), Mobutu simply appointed his own, and set up a second, competing government. Six years after announcing his tearful non-exit from politics, he sat in his pagoda, sipping pink champagne and allowing his favourites to run the country. They squabbled between themselves and looted whatever was left. Mobutu was out of ideas, sinking into sloth amid the abundance of his stolen wealth, indulging in whatever small pleasures were left beneath the dimming chandeliers of his castle in the sky. Rumour had it he regularly procured a new fourteen-year-old virgin for himself from the flattered mothers living in nearby villages.[34] But over to the east, beyond his own borders, belligerent forces were gathering. He must have thought them of little consequence at first. How could events in tiny Rwanda affect its giant, well-armed neighbour? However, a chill breeze blew into a storm, and a humanitarian disaster was unleashed: the Rwandan genocide, in which an extremist Hutu government massacred its Tutsi citizens, claimed a million lives.

For one last time, the orchestra played, the curtains opened and Mobutu was prodded back onto the stage at the behest of the West, balding a little now, his cheeks slack, his body less mobile, but still happy to don the leopard-skin hat and the thick glasses, and try to make himself a significant player. He accepted a million and a half displaced Hutus who had fled Rwanda and made their way across his border and it seemed he might, once again, help stabilize the region. But some of the refugees were part of the ousted Hutu government that had launched the genocide, and the new Tutsi leaders wanted to make sure that they, and all of their kind, would never return.

The Tutsis couldn't simply pour into Zaire, a sovereign state, and attack their enemy. They needed pre-existing armed groups on the other side of the border, groups hostile to Mobutu's Hutu refugee camps and, preferably, hostile to Mobutu himself. One of those who stepped forward was a gangster and gun-runner named Laurent Kabila. He had attempted to mount rebellions against Mobutu before, even assisting Che Guevara on his failed Congo adventure in 1965, during which Kabila had failed to impress. Now the Rwandan civil war seemed like an ideal vehicle upon which he could hitch a ride. He and the leaders of several other armed groups, assisted by the new Tutsi-led government in Rwanda, set up the Alliance de Forces Démocratiques pour la Libération (AFDL) and when the Tutsi army swept across the border into Zaire, they joined forces, chasing the Hutu first from camp to camp along the border, and then westwards into the interior. The waves of AFDL soldiers may have had different priorities, but they shared unstoppable momentum. On they came, wiping out entire communities during a frenzy of ethnic cleansing in which machetes and hammers were the instruments of choice. Mobutu was out of the country during much of the advance, receiving treatment for prostate cancer in Europe, but he returned to Kinshasa for the denouement, seemingly unconcerned that his troops were melting away, offering almost no resistance. Major cities fell as soldiers from the rebel alliance swept 1,500 miles across Zaire to the capital for a showdown with what remained of Mobutu's rabble army.

In the fragile morning light of 16 May 1997, a few SUV's and pimped-up jeeps began appearing on the roads adjacent to the river in the smart Gombe district of Kinshasa where the embassies and top hotels are located. Well-heeled women clutching Gucci bags picked their way through the undergrowth down the steep banks to the water's edge and into waiting motor launches. Other boats carried soldiers from Mobutu's own personal guard. Laurent Kabila's AFDL were at the city gates, and those who had done well under Mobutu's regime were fleeing for their lives, across the river to Congo-Brazzaville.

A convoy hurried through the emptying streets, carrying the president to the airport. Racked with cancer, and gravely ill, he boarded a plane for Gbadolite, and his palace.

When AFDL fighters began streaming into the city the following day, they encountered little resistance. Rag-tag government soldiers, who had spent their last hours of service looting, hastily destroyed their uniforms and slipped into civilian clothes. AFDL fighters, many of them children dressed in wellington boots and carrying AK-47s, went from house to house searching for stray members of Mobutu's clan. People cheered them, handing out food and water for the 'liberators'. The death toll was mercifully low: just 200 people lost their lives in a few hours of score-settling. By the time Laurent Kabila declared himself president, and renamed Zaire the Democratic Republic of Congo, Mobutu was in his Gbadolite palace, collecting the possessions he had been able to save. He had the bones of his mother and a few other family members exhumed, so he could take them with him. A regime that had endured thirty-two years had, in a matter of hours, evaporated into the damp Kinshasa sunshine.

The monsoon came. Warm rain dripped through the broken windows of Gbadolite and spread puddles across the marble floors. Peacocks sheltered beneath wrecked pagodas. Young rebel soldiers crunched through the crockery and dried their clothes on makeshift fires in the gold-embossed rooms. Mobutu had fled within hours of Kabila's victory, flying via Togo to Morocco, into permanent exile. He had amassed a fortune of $5 billion during his three decades in office, much of it hidden in Swiss, Belgian, and American bank accounts. But he had little time to enjoy it. Four months later, he died at his villa in a residential district of Rabat at the age of sixty-six.

Much of the money has never been recovered. Some disappeared quietly into the crepuscular world of lawyers, bankers and offshore shell companies. A proportion found its way into the hands of his dozen or so children.

CHAPTER TWO

Zimbabwe

ZIMBABWE

You have inherited a jewel, keep it that way.

PRESIDENT JULIUS NYERERE OF TANZANIA,
TO ROBERT MUGABE ON INDEPENDENCE DAY

MOST BOYS OF his age hated such a chore. They simply lacked
the patience, the self-discipline that Robert possessed. They would
interpret the task as punishment, whereas for him it was a gift. It
took him away from the punch-ups and the football and the childish
conversations, and allowed him to pursue a path that his mother
believed was preordained.

He wandered through the tall grass, collecting short, malleable
branches, and headed for the river. Red sand, cracked mud, the
creak of insects; it required ingenuity to find food on the flatlands
of Kutama in Southern Rhodesia. He was a tiny, birdy boy, brittle in
body and temperament, with a face serious beyond its thirteen years.
It gave him a manner that was easy to mock, an old man's head
on a buttonquail's body, a ripe corn cob sprouting from a stunted
stalk. Since the death of his elder brother from mistakenly drinking
locust poison, and his carpenter father's disappearance into the arms
of another woman, Robert's academic self-confidence had turned
into stubborn loftiness. His pious mother saw him as the saviour
of the family.

The river was low, the sand soft beneath Robert's feet. He pressed
the sticks in, just above the waterline, so they formed a ring as high
as his waist, tying the tops together with grass, so he had what
looked like an upside-down basket. Inside he placed soft leaves, and
scattered a handful of seed. Then he retired into the undergrowth
and hid. With him he took a book from school, so he could read
the day away, undistracted by scornful classmates or the cramped
conditions at home.

When the doves came, they scratched around for a time, nodding
and cooing at the edge of the water. It could take hours before one
inspected the wicker trap. When it wandered inside, Robert burst
from his den, thrust in his hand, grabbed the bird, and killed it.

It was a technique he used to catch many dinners, but the doves were not the most important sustenance from those outings, not for Robert anyway. It was the books, always the books.

His academic potential was spotted by local Jesuit priests, who invited him to attend the elite St Francis Xavier College, which they ran and funded. Sometime in the late 1930s, the headmaster of the school, Father Jerome O'Hea, informed Robert's mother, Bona, that her child would, one day, become an important person, a leader. Because the message had been relayed to her by a man of such an elevated position in the Catholic Church, she believed it must have come from God.[1]

The country that Bona Mugabe was born into at the end of the nineteenth century, Mashonaland, a dry and sandy plateau where British prospectors were digging for gold, diamonds and copper, was ruled by a private company based in London. The few tribal chiefs who remained had been reduced to ceremonial duties, having signed away their mineral rights to clever lawyers and agents working on behalf of Cecil Rhodes's British South Africa Company (BSAC). The less compliant among them had been driven out or killed by the company's private army. After one notorious episode, when the Ndebele king, Lobengula, was chased from his Matabeleland capital, Bulawayo, Rhodes's pioneers had divided the spoils among themselves on the spot: 600,000 acres to their chief of staff, 640,000 acres to the company's surveyor-general, smaller parcels to the foot soldiers. The hillsides for sixty miles around were pegged out as white-owned land.

Rhodes had made his fortune during the diamond rush at Kimberley, and had expanded into precious metals when the world's richest deposits of gold were discovered nearby in the Witwatersrand Mountains. He used his immense wealth to secure a royal charter, allowing him to create the BSAC, and with it press northwards, acquiring mineral-rich territory as he went. He named his capital Salisbury, after the British prime minister, the 3rd Marquess of Salisbury, and from there swept across the Zambezi River, securing more land at the expense of local chiefs. His men intended to extend company territory into the copper-rich kingdom of Katanga in Congo, but were narrowly beaten to the prize by Leopold, king of the Belgians. Still, his territory was immense. Company-owned Mashonaland, the former tribal territory of the Shona people to whom Bona belonged, was joined with Matabeleland, the home of the Ndebele, and together they formed what would later be Southern Rhodesia. Land owned by the company north of the Zambezi became Northern Rhodesia. By the time Bona Mugabe married in 1918, the BSAC controlled more than 400,000 square miles of landlocked central southern Africa, an area of land five times that of Great Britain.

When Robert was born, in 1924, the influx of white settlers, attracted by what turned out to be abundant reserves of copper, meant that the governance of the company's territory had shifted. Whereas the majority in the Southern Rhodesian legislature had once been unelected company men, they were now overtaken by elected white settlers, making the territory effectively self-governing. As a result, the British Crown decided to revoke the BSAC's charter. Both Northern and Southern Rhodesia were transferred into the hands of the British Empire. Soon, the indigenous black population, numbering 2 million, was restricted to specially demarcated 'Native Reserves', that quickly became overcrowded. Many of them were simply evicted from their land, and forcibly moved into the communal areas. Before Robert Mugabe was of school age, the 44,000 white settlers had awarded themselves four times more territory than the black population, including all that was most fertile, accessible and mineral-rich.

As Bona Mugabe sank into deep depression with the double loss of her eldest son and her husband, all her affection and hope were vested in Robert. He would attend mass with her every day, and twice on Sundays: she dressed in austere ankle-length dresses; he in his college uniform, with a book tucked beneath his arm. Such was his mother's fanatical Catholicism, that on the rare occasions he was smacked, Robert was expected to thank her for correcting him. Her lonely and serious young boy, eager to please his emotionally fragile mother, focused all his attention on fulfilling her expectations. He was mocked as a 'mummy's boy', and for preferring the company of his teachers over that of other children. Father O'Hea became his surrogate father, and when Mugabe left school after six years of elementary education, the priest invited him to study at the teacher-training college he had established in Kutama, even helping to pay the fees. It was Mugabe's privileged English-style education that gave him a lifelong affection for the British royal family and for Savile Row suits. But it was the aristocratic Irishmen, Father O'Hea, with his teachings on Ireland's struggle for independence, who gave Mugabe a taste for revolution.

Itinerant teaching positions followed through the early 1950s. Mugabe was drifting, searching for purpose. Southern Rhodesia, under British control, was a land of few opportunities for blacks. Its white-minority government ran the territory along strict racial lines. If the young Mugabe had wanted to drink coffee in a restaurant overlooking Cecil Square, the beautiful gardens named after the colony's founder in Salisbury, he would have found his way barred. The indigenous black population was not allowed into restaurants or hotels unless they were waiters or servants. They were barred from drinking European beer, attending white-only cinemas or swimming in white-only pools. Mugabe would have needed a folder of permits and paperwork wherever he went: a pass to move from a rural location into a town, a permit to look for work, a Certificate of Service to prove he had found work. Before his father ran away, Bona Mugabe would have required a Certificate of Recognition of an Approved Wife.

The white settlers, most of them British, lived in a parallel universe. Many simply transposed their home counties' lives into the dusty African heat. There were weekend rugby matches and dinner dances at the Women's Institute Hall. Landowners met at the Farmer's Association or the River Club, while their wives sipped tea at the

Garden Society or the local theatre group. Middle-class households had black servants who would cook them English breakfasts and wash their Ford Zephyrs parked in the drive. They might wince when blacks had parcels thrown at them in the post office, or were forced to wait outside the butcher's in the midday sun, but many whites thought that their presence in Southern Rhodesia was needed to civilize the African population under paternalistic European control.

For more than forty years, certainly since the end of governance by Rhodes's British South Africa Company, the black population had passively accepted white domination. But a new generation was coming of age, young Africans who had been educated, like Mugabe, in the few educational establishments available to them, the missionary schools, and who now wanted a say in the running of their country.

Mugabe, who at one stage had considered entering the priesthood, was still unsure of his own future. At the age of twenty-five he won a scholarship to Fort Hare University College in South Africa's Eastern Cape, an elite establishment that would ignite the political senses of several future African nationalist leaders. The ANC's Nelson Mandela and Oliver Tambo had studied there ten years earlier, and when Mugabe arrived, he was plunged into a campus burning with anti-imperialist fervour. He devoured Marxist literature and became captivated by Mahatma Ghandi and Jawaharlal Nehru's campaign of nonviolence in India.

But Mugabe was still deeply conservative. When he returned to Rhodesia in 1955, he took no part in the growing protests over British rule in what had become the Federation of Rhodesia and Nyasaland, an uneasy grouping of three territories – Northern and Southern Rhodesia and the tiny protectorate of Nyasaland – governed as a unit by a knight from Kent, Sir Godfrey Huggins. Instead, he drifted again, teaching for a time while studying for another degree, a correspondence course at London University. His first steps into political activism were taken three years later in 1958, when he arrived in the ecstatic, self-appointed capital of African nationalism.

*

At a conference hall in the Ghanaian capital of Accra, beneath a banner which read 'Hands off Africa, Africa must be free!', sat a combative intellectual who had attained near-prophetic status among the leaders of independence movements across the continent. The previous year, on 6 March 1957, Kwame Nkrumah had wrestled the Gold Coast from the hands of the British to become the first prime minister of the newly named Republic of Ghana, one of the earliest of the former European colonies to achieve independence. His struggle had been a nonviolent, attritional campaign, punctuated by spells in prison during which his popularity had grown. His success made Ghana a blueprint for others. Delegates gathered for the first All-African Peoples' Conference, to exchange ideas about defeating stubborn colonial regimes. Among them, captivated by Nkrumah's speech about scientific socialism, was Patrice Lumumba, equipping himself for the seemingly hopeless struggle against the Belgians in Congo.

Accra was announced as the permanent headquarters of the conference's secretariat, and many more aspiring African leaders rushed there. This was the heady atmosphere of revolutionary possibility into which the thirty-four-year-old Robert Mugabe stepped the same year. He had won a teaching position at a school along the coast in Takoradi, where he would witness ordinary people rejoicing in their hard-won freedom. For the first time, Mugabe saw for himself that direct political action could provoke momentous change. He also accepted the general principles of Marxism as espoused by Nkrumah, although Mugabe's methods of achieving liberation would follow a different path from that of his pacifist Ghanaian mentor.

It was in the warm sea air of Takoradi that he met a local teacher called Sally Heyfron. Self-assured and infectiously warm, she had qualities Mugabe lacked, a charm and openness that unlocked something in the withdrawn, unemotional visitor. While her friends were out partying, the two would discuss politics deep into the night, enraptured by each other's views. Mugabe couldn't wait to take her to Rhodesia, to receive the blessing of his mother for their marriage. But when he landed at Salisbury airport in 1960, his homeland was beginning its inexorable slide into turmoil.

Where Ghana had led the way, a flurry of other African nations had followed in 1960. In the Cape Town parliament where Rhodes had served as prime minister six decades earlier, British Prime Minister Harold Macmillan made his historic 'winds of change' speech signalling Britain's shift in attitudes. The tricolour was lowered across French West Africa, and even the Belgians in Congo seemed to be bowing to the inevitable. But the British were in no hurry to relinquish their elaborately structured, copper-rich Rhodesian Federation. Particularly unappealing was the prospect of a speedy withdrawal from Southern Rhodesia. It was self-governing, but not independent, and Britain didn't want to relinquish the territory, and with it the power to restrain Southern Rhodesia's conservative whites and their home-grown system of apartheid.

When protests broke out in Nyasaland, the white authorities responded by declaring a state of emergency. Instead of trying to establish a dialogue with the nationalist leaders of each federal state, they banned their primary vehicle of opposition, the African National Congress (ANC), and its many offshoots. It is worth pausing to note the identity of their leaders at that moment, a triumvirate of nationalist colossi: in Nyasaland, Dr Hastings Banda – a medical doctor, trained in Edinburgh, who had been jailed during the state of emergency; in Northern Rhodesia, Kenneth Kuanda – a teacher and relative moderate, jailed at the same time; and in Southern Rhodesia, Joshua Nkomo – a trade unionist who had escaped arrest by flying to America to raise support for the ANC. In the circumstances, it seemed like outright provocation when the Southern Rhodesian prime minister, Sir Edgar Whitehead, boasted publicly that his was the most peaceful state in Africa. Mugabe, who had been intending to return to Ghana and settle down with Sally, would soon be caught up in the drama.

After taking Sally to his mother's home in Kutama, he was persuaded to join a protest march in the township of Highfield, just outside Salisbury. The nationalists had formed a new movement, the National Democratic Party (NDP) to supersede the banned ANC, but almost immediately three of the NDP's leaders had been arrested. The protest Mugabe joined was intending to march on the home of

Sir Edgar Whitehead to demand their release. As they walked the eight miles into Salisbury, their numbers swelled to 40,000. Planes buzzed overhead. Police jeeps sped through the crowds. Five hundred officers stood by in riot gear. At some point, Mugabe was hoisted onto a podium, nervous and unprepared. He was introduced as a distinguished scholar who had travelled in Africa and had obtained three university degrees. After a halting start, he managed to find his rhythm, addressing the crowd about his vision for an independent Rhodesia, 'Zimbabwe' as he called it – a name derived from a fourteenth-century city built by the Shona, Mugabe's ancestral people. Filling the stage beside him was the bear-like, beaming figure of the NDP's soon-to-be president, Joshua Nkomo, fresh back from the US and delighted to have discovered such a promising newcomer. Mugabe would have felt somewhat overawed in the presence of such a confident, garrulous and physically imposing politician. His self-deprecation wouldn't last long.

In the smothering heat that afternoon, the police, already on edge, fired tear gas into the crowd. Three people suffered gunshot wounds. Sporadic violence continued through the night. Whitehead responded by sending troops to the townships around Salisbury, shutting down schools, and imposing a three-month ban on political meetings and processions. But, days later, trouble flared again, this time in Southern Rhodesia's second city, Bulawayo. Tens of thousands rioted in the streets. Police and white-owned vehicles were stoned, shops looted and burned. Steel sleepers were piled onto a rail line in an attempt to derail a train. Most significantly, twelve Africans were killed by government forces, the first to meet such a fate since 1896, when Cecil Rhodes's British South Africa Company put down an uprising. As police battled with demonstrators on the sticky, dusty streets of Bulawayo that day in July 1960, everything changed. The civilizing whites were resisting their black subjects with bullets and death. With an eye on the unfolding crisis in Congo, the anxious government in Salisbury acted swiftly to block further dissent. They imposed the notorious Law and Order Maintenance Act, which gave police sweeping powers to arrest and detain suspects at whim, a piece of legislation that would later be adopted and strengthened by the country's future dictator.

Robert Mugabe could suppress his instincts no longer. In the midst of the chaos, the shy and normally cautious teacher made an impetuous decision. He would abandon his teaching career and became a full-time politician. The leadership of the NDP was delighted. Straight away, they elected him to the position of publicity secretary. Mugabe's ascent had begun.

In the following months, the white leadership tinkered with the system of apartheid, rather than dismantle it. They amended the Liquor Act to allow blacks to consume European beer, they relaxed the rules on cinemas, and opened public pools to the locals. 'We don't want to swim in your swimming pools,' responded a typically ebullient Joshua Nkomo. 'We want to swim with you in parliament.' Whitehead and his government had imagined that a paternalistic racial 'partnership' would solve the federation's problems, but the NDP wanted black self-rule, no half-measures. After further outbreaks of violence, and British-brokered talks, it was announced that self-rule would indeed be granted, but only in Nyasaland and Northern Rhodesia, not in Mugabe's Southern Rhodesia, the dominant territory of the federation. Nyasaland would become Malawi under the presidency of Dr Hastings Banda; Northern Rhodesia would be renamed Zambia, and led by Kenneth Kuanda. But Southern Rhodesia's fate would be decided in lengthy constitutional negotiations that would take place in London and Salisbury in 1961. They were rancorous and highly charged, with secret meetings and many cloak-and-dagger conspiracies, and they ended in compromise: only if the territory's white leaders were to guarantee black seats in parliament would Britain consider granting independence – a proposal that the more right-wing elements in the Rhodesian government furiously denounced as 'compulsory integration'. But their leaders, who were relative moderates in the circumstances, saw this as an opportunity. If they accepted Britain's proposals, allowing seats for a few token black representatives, they would secure virtual autonomy while preserving white-minority rule. They agreed to put the proposal to a national referendum. As with all votes in Southern Rhodesia, it would be rigged. The only people allowed to vote would be those who met strict criteria: an annual income of £240 or more, and a satisfactory grade in a literacy test. These were stipulations that ruled out the vast majority of the black population.

A 'Yes' vote would give Southern Rhodesia a complicated parliamentary formula that would deliver fifty seats to the whites, and fifteen to the blacks, the theory being that, as the 'backward' indigenous population progressed, by increasing their incomes and improving their education, their access to the vote would grow and a more representative parliament prevail. But that would take many years. For the foreseeable future, the deal on the table at the Salisbury leg of the conference was a watered-down version of white rule, with a commitment to the dissolution of racial laws. It was assumed the black nationalist leaders would reject such tepid change out of hand.

Leading the NDP delegation was Joshua Nkomo. His publicity secretary, Mugabe, stalked the corridors outside, frustrated with his lack of involvement, and relying on Nkomo to do the right thing. Nkomo dithered. This was a chance for his party to take a few seats in the legislature. Blacks would finally have a voice, a faint one, for sure, but a voice all the same. He agreed to the proposal, and signed the paperwork accepting the new constitution.

When Mugabe heard the news he erupted. His leader had just surrendered to a racist state. Southern Rhodesia was a colonial anachronism that must end. For Nkomo to agree anything other than an immediate transfer of power meant failure. It was black-majority rule or nothing, and nothing meant a ceaseless escalation of violence. A humiliated Nkomo hurriedly tried to backtrack on his decision, telling the conference he had been misinterpreted. He withdrew his support for the new constitution, and urged all blacks to boycott the referendum. But it was too late.

In a hopeless attempt to halt its implementation, and with no coherent plan in mind, Nkomo called on his followers to extend their boycott to the upcoming parliamentary elections in 1962, thus abandoning the nationalists' chances of winning a seat. There were sit-ins, marches and arrests. It seemed the spiral of violence was beginning again. The white-minority government responded in a way that could only inflame the situation: the NDP was banned. Predictably, Nkomo simply formed a successor party, the Zimbabwe African People's Union (ZAPU), reserving a senior role for his increasingly disaffected colleague, Robert Mugabe. As Nkomo toured sympathetic neighbouring countries, toying with the idea of setting up a ZAPU-led government in exile, Mugabe was increasingly of the view that armed struggle was the only way forward.

On the green, Westminster-style benches of the legislative assembly in Salisbury, the normally inscrutable, socially awkward Ian Smith was whispering tea invitations to anyone who would listen. Traditionally the assembly had met for just three months of the year, breaking regularly for refreshments on the lawn. It was an arrangement that had suited Smith well, allowing him to indulge his passion for farming at his ranch in Selukwe, a gold-mining region 200 miles south of Salisbury. But the events of 1962 required his full attention. The prime minister, Sir Edgar Whitehead, was the leader of Smith's party, but he seemed to be going soft, encouraging blacks to vote and offering them ring-fenced parliamentary seats. As far as Smith was concerned, this 'mad idea of a handover', no matter how long it took, was 'a sell-out of the European and his civilization', and would inevitably lead to a Congo-style implosion. The violence and looting in Salisbury and Bulawayo, he warned, were evidence of that.

Smith had been a fighter pilot with the RAF during the Second World War, and had famously bailed out behind enemy lines in northern Italy, from where he escaped by crossing the Alps barefoot on the ice and snow. Despite being born in Rhodesia, he saw himself as 'more British than the British', and felt that his spiritual homeland had abandoned him with its refusal to grant independence to the white-minority government. Exploiting fears of the escalating violence, in March 1962 Smith broke with the governing group and, along with other right-wingers, created a hard-line white supremacist party, the

Rhodesian Front (RF). It was entirely out of step with prevailing world opinion – aside from the National Party over the border in South Africa – and seemed likely to attract only lukewarm support. But the night before the December 1962 parliamentary elections, Prime Minister Whitehead made an announcement that frightened even the moderates in Rhodesia. If he won the election, he told a public meeting, he was looking forward to appointing his first black cabinet minister. White voters took flight, turning to Smith's RF instead. On its first electoral outing, the new party swept the board, and Smith, the epitome of the white Rhodesian ascendency class, became deputy prime minister. He always said that he wasn't racist, that educated blacks had the same right to stand for election as he did, but that he objected to guaranteeing them a certain number of parliamentary seats, as the other parties wanted to do, because it was a distortion of democratic principles. His virulent opposition to Mugabe, and less so to Nkomo, was not their black nationalism, he said, but their communism. Fifteen months later, Smith had secured the top job. He was Rhodesia's prime minister, and would use his position to pursue a singular purpose; to achieve independence, at any cost, from Britain.

Rekayi Tangwena had everything in life he desired. His people's land was a fertile patchwork of terraces and high fields in Southern Rhodesia's eastern mountains. He would watch the rainclouds drift in from the plains of neighbouring Mozambique, leaving in their wake glinting tin roofs and jewelled trees, rising up the Nyanga mountains like a steaming surf. Tangwena could plan his day by the rain, planting maize in the weak morning sun, feeding cattle as the heat gathered, chopping the firewood and moving it indoors before the deluge struck. It had been this way since his childhood, and would continue so after his death.

But that day in 1963 was to mark a great change. The chief had died, and Rekayi Tangwena, a distinguished-looking fifty-five-year-old with clipped white beard and watery brown eyes, was to be his successor. He had to register the fact at the district commissioner's office in Nyanga. As he set off, wearing his woollen hat decorated with cowrie shells, he shook hands with his supporters, and promised to be back before dark. Paperwork relating to such matters was held at the colonial bungalow that served as headquarters for the local administration. Young white men wearing khaki shorts and long white socks milled around outside, smoking and chatting. Land Rovers came and went. Tangwena's confirmation as chief was a formality, a simple amendment to the file, but there was a problem. He had no rights to the land, they said. Generations of his people had mistakenly assumed it was theirs, he was told. In fact, it belonged to the British South Africa Company from the moment Cecil Rhodes vanquished the old Ndebele leader, Chief Lobengula. The company had then sold it on, to two European brothers. Since the law stated it was illegal for blacks to live on 'European land', and Tangwena had no tenancy agreement, he and his people were squatters. They must, he was told, leave immediately.

The territory from which Chief Tangwena was being evicted comprised 6,400 acres, about ten square miles. The white settlers whose government wanted to evict him, owned more than two-thirds of Rhodesia's land, despite the fact that, by this time, they numbered just 200,000, a mere seven per cent of the population. The country's 3 million blacks were being squeezed into ever-more-overcrowded plots, often disease-ridden, with infertile land from which they could hardly scrape a living. Even if they had been able to join together and save up to purchase land outside the Native Reserves, they were barred, unless by special agreement. They could only step on white-owned soil if they were employed as labourers. The restrictions, which Chief Tangwena had fallen foul of, were provided for in the draconian Land Apportionment Act. For the nationalists and many liberal whites, it was a hated symbol of racial segregation that must be torn down. For Ian Smith and his Rhodesian Front, it was a cornerstone of white survival, and must be protected at all costs. Later, the repossession of white-owned land would become Robert Mugabe's most potent weapon. He would use it to punish opponents and reward supporters whenever he chose, an activity he viewed as simply returning stolen property to its rightful owner. But for now, Mugabe and his colleagues were about to embark on a new, and unwelcome chapter in their lives.

It was the period before the elections in 1962. ZAPU, like all its predecessors, had been banned. An increasingly sure-footed Mugabe climbed onto a stage in Salisbury and accused the 'gangster' government of 'planning murder', a speech for which he was arrested and charged with subversion. While awaiting trial, Sally, who was also facing jail for a speech of her own, discovered she was pregnant. Mugabe's priorities quickly changed. He needed to get his wife to safety. But if they left the country, they would both be breaking bail. On the other hand, many of ZAPU's leadership were relocating to Dar es Salaam, the capital of newly independent Tanganyika (later Tanzania) to regroup and decide their next move. The pair decided to join them, slipping off to the coastal city where they met up with the ZAPU executive. But Mugabe soon became disaffected. The struggle, for him, had to be waged from inside Rhodesia, not by a group of distant, suited politicians, radioing their instructions to hot and sticky townships from their sun-loungers on the beach. After Sally gave birth to their son, Mugabe insisted she return to Ghana to avoid prison, while he caught a plane to Salisbury to face the music.

A guard observing Robert Mugabe through a crack in the cell door at his jungle detention centre in Sikombela would have found a scene of quiet discipline and intellectual endeavour more akin to a don's study than a top-security prison. Mugabe perched on his bed, surrounded by books, young prisoners at his feet, transfixed by his lectures on African nationalism. They treated him as their headmaster. 'These months, these years, however long it takes,' he told them, 'must not be wasted.'

Mugabe had been arrested immediately on his return to Salisbury in December 1963, and later sentenced to twenty-one months in prison, but in reality he would remain in custody at Prime Minister Ian Smith's pleasure. He wasn't alone. The entire former executive of ZAPU, and dozens more influential nationalists, were rounded up and detained in Rhodesia's jails over the following months. The movement, domestically at least, had been neutered by the powers of the Law and Order Maintenance Act. But Mugabe himself was no longer part of ZAPU. He had taken a decisive step, or rather, it had been taken for him.

While he was still away in Dar es Salaam the others politicians had begun drifting back to Salisbury. Dissatisfaction with Nkomo's leadership had been brewing for some time among a hard-line group concentrated around Mugabe. They were tired of their leader's obsessive quest for foreign backing, and impatient with his lack of direction. In an effort to revitalize the movement, they set up a rival to ZAPU. It was to be called ZANU, the Zimbabwe African National Union, and Mugabe, in his absence, was chosen as its secretary general. As ZANU and ZAPU tried to assert themselves, new battle lines were drawn. Instead of fighting the symbols of white government, they turned on each other. By the time Mugabe stepped off the plane in Salisbury, gang violence had spilled onto the streets. That is how most of the political leaders had ended up in jail in the closing months of 1963.

Sikombela detention camp was so remote that its disorientated inmates had no hope of escape. Beyond the corrugated metal huts where they ate and slept was a wall of endless trees and all manner of wild animals, as effective as any barbed wire and gun towers. Circulating through the prison system at the same time as Mugabe, and often sharing the same communal cell, was the entire top-tier of his new party. On an adjacent bunk sat Edgar '2-boy' Tekere, named as such by those who assumed his violent outbursts were the result of a split personality. Tekere could trace his lineage to a fight against the British colonialists in Rhodes's time, and was out for revenge. His propensity for violence had always been encouraged by his mother. In later years, on hearing that her son had shot dead a white landowner, the elderly lady is said to have fallen to her knees and kissed his feet.

On another bed nearby was Enos Nkala, in whose house ZANU had been created. He nursed an obsessive hatred of Joshua Nkomo, and his appetite for casual violence would lead to him becoming ZANU's enforcer.

Also among them was ZANU's leader, Ndabaningi Sithole. He had the battered features of a failed boxer, but he was actually a mission-educated preacher, who had travelled widely and whose intellect compared with that of Mugabe. His 1960 book *African Nationalism* had been the first in Rhodesia to express the philosophy underlying the movement's cause. But, in the company of political fanatics locked up in a jungle jail, he was fatally ill-equipped.

On 25 October 1965 prison guards took Sithole away, and drove him the 110 miles through the bush to Salisbury, where he was taken to a government building. There he found Joshua Nkomo, brought from another jail to the same waiting room. After a short while, they were both bundled into the presence of a British man wearing a dark suit and tie, and puffing a pipe. On seeing them, hungry, tired and dehydrated, the man exploded. If food and drink were not brought for them immediately, he shouted, he would go into town and purchase them himself. The man was British Prime Minister Harold Wilson. By his own admission, it was the first time he had ever 'seen red'.[2]

Wilson had become prime minister twelve months earlier, and Rhodesia was his first major international challenge. At stake was the real possibility of war. Ian Smith was pushing stridently towards declaring independence without British approval. Britain still had legal responsibility for the country. If Smith pursued a Unilateral Declaration of Independence (UDI) it would be tantamount to a coup, and Wilson would be expected to retaliate. The Labour leader was strongly supportive of black majority rule, and Smith had no intention of conceding an inch. Talks in London made absolutely no headway, and ended with Smith expressing his faux surprise to the media, when in truth it was he who wanted them to fail. Throughout 1965 the deadlock remained. It ended with a staggering diplomatic blunder in London. Smith's team was told, unofficially, that the Labour government in Westminster would not respond to UDI with military force, that it wasn't considered 'practical politics'. The path to white-minority rule in an independent Rhodesia was wide open.

It was after Smith returned home, visibly relieved by the news, and preparing to declare UDI within days, that Wilson flew to Salisbury in a final desperate attempt to change his mind in October 1965. Things didn't begin well. By insisting on seeing Nkomo and Sithole he had made the point that Britain viewed them as legitimate leaders and would refuse to abandon them. His fury over their mistreatment, which his advisors put down to his fierce anti-racism, continued when he arrived at the office of the governor of Rhodesia, Sir Humphrey Gibbs, where Wilson later recalled, 'On going in to harangue the governor, I was unable to see him because of the red flashes before my eyes.'[3]

That evening, as Sithole and Nkomo were driven back to their cells under darkening skies, Wilson found himself at a dinner in Salisbury being mocked by Smith's ministers. Throughout the year-long negotiations, Smith had always presented himself as a relative moderate, reluctantly trying to accommodate the ill-mannered right-wingers in his party who were pushing him further to the right. Now Wilson got to see them for himself. One, the old Etonian Lord Graham, a minister in Smith's government, told a lewd story and then illustrated it by belly-dancing and 'brushing his capacious frame' against Wilson's face. The others were boorish and drunk, and taunted Wilson as he squirmed with discomfort. He finished the night feeling physically sick. In the circumstances, with such a momentous decision looming, their behaviour did not bode well.

On his return home, deflated but still hopeful, Wilson threw away any small advantage he might have had by confirming in a radio broadcast what Smith suspected but couldn't, until now, have known for certain. 'If there are those in this country who are thinking in terms of a thunderbolt hurtling from the sky, and destroying their enemies,' announced Wilson, 'a thunderbolt in the shape of the Royal Air Force, let me say that thunderbolt will not be coming.' It made absolute practical sense that Britain would not try to salvage control by force. British soldiers would have been reluctant to fight their Rhodesian counterparts, viewing them as colleagues rather than enemies. Europeans would undoubtedly have been killed, as would many of the very Africans they were trying to protect. Not only that, the chaos might invite allcomers into a Cold War conflict not unlike Congo. It was the fact that Wilson had openly declared his hand that was so astonishing.

Three weeks later, on a cold November morning in London, Wilson received a telephone call. It was Ian Smith. After he had finished, Wilson called his cabinet together and described the Rhodesian president's call as 'astonishingly calm – almost friendly – the calm of a madman'.[4] Smith was declaring UDI, the first rebellion by a British dependency since the eighteenth century.

In their cramped shared cell in Rhodesia, Sithole described to Robert Mugabe his bizarre encounter with the British leader. He explained that London would not be intervening over Smith's UDI. Mugabe felt bitterly betrayed. The message was soon passed to the outside in secret notes by sympathetic black warders from both ZANU and ZAPU, that more guerrillas were needed to join the forces gathering in the borderlands of newly independent Zambia.

Before dawn on 18 September 1969 a bulldozer arrived at Chief Tangwena's village. For three years, he and his tribe had refused to vacate their land after being given notice by the local administrators. Now a convoy of Land Rovers disgorged several dozen armed security personnel. As women grabbed their babies and fled, the white men crushed and torched their homes, and impounded their cattle. Those who resisted were beaten. As Chief Tangwena watched helplessly from a nearby hillside, he gave an interview to a white journalist from a radical magazine. 'It is the Europeans who have come to disturb us, to destroy our property, to deprive us of the wealth of this land,' he said. 'Where was the African living when the European first came? They found us here. Should we live in trees today? Where can we go?[5] After publication of the article, Chief Tangwena was charged with making subversive statements. The white reporter, a former university lecturer, fled abroad.

The chief and hundreds of his people took refuge in the thick mountain forests above the village. For several years, they would return by cover of night to rebuild their old homes and replant and hoe the land. Each time, the security services would respond with another slash-and-burn operation. It only served to politicize the chief more deeply.

He began frequenting a co-operative farm at Nyafaru, high in the mountains, a hotbed for dissidents and young black activists, where he was treated as an icon of the resistance movement.

Cold water was regularly pumped across the concrete cell floors of the communal blocks in Salisbury Prison where Mugabe and the ZANU executive had been relocated. It was 1966, and the water was ostensibly for the purposes of hygiene, but it gave the place a cave-like smell and left the walls and beds constantly damp. The passing of notes to activists outside, using trusted warders, became ever more important. Smith's declaration of UDI had galvanized cells of hard-line nationalists into guerrilla units awaiting orders. They gathered over the border in Zambia, ready for lightening raids into Rhodesia, and established separate camps according to their loyalties. Joshua Nkomo's ZAPU fighters were known as the Zimbabwe People's Revolutionary Army (ZIPRA), while those of ZANU, the movement led by Sithole and Mugabe, were the Zimbabwe African National Liberation Army, ZANLA.

Both sets of fighters were short of food, clothes and weapons. They wore T-shirts and flip-flops, and begged meat and eggs from local villages. A few had AK-47s, but many were armed with old hunting rifles. There were few concrete military plans. They crossed into Rhodesia, expecting to be welcomed by enthusiastic villagers, and were surprised when they encountered only suspicion. Rhodesia had no history of armed struggle. People were unaccustomed to having armed men in their midst. They would call the Rhodesian security services, who turned up in armoured vehicles and shot the guerrillas on sight. On one occasion in April 1966, the Rhodesian security forces engaged ZANLA fighters in Sinoia in the north of the country. It was seen as the opening skirmish of the Bush War. Seven ZANLA fighters ended up dead. In retaliation, ZANLA arrived at a white farm in Hartley nearby and killed two white civilians. The pattern was set.

Both groups of nationalist fighters soon realized they needed foreign assistance. For Nkomo's ZIPRA it came from the Soviet Union; for Mugabe's ZANLA, from China. Instructors were flown in from Beijing. They brought with them Chinese weapons and Chinese tactics. ZANLA launched a Maoist-style people's war. 'Blending with the people, you are like fish,' the Chinese told them. 'Away from them you are like a fish out of water.'

ZANLA began slipping back into Rhodesia at dusk, mingling with villagers. They would organize all-night meetings with singing and dancing, and provide free food and entertainment for the peasant communities, interspersed with lectures on Marxist ideology. The gradual radicalization of villages hardly registered in Salisbury's white neighbourhoods. They continued to enjoy waterskiing on Lake McIlwaine, and gathered for barbecues and cocktail parties at the weekends. Fashionable young women walked their pampered dogs in Cecil Square. Housemaids bought flame lilies and sprays of blue orchids for European villas. Purple blossoms fell from the jacaranda trees and settled on the Minis and Morris Minors that lined every neatly kept avenue, and all seemed well.

Inside Salisbury Prison, however, Robert Mugabe had just received devastating news. It was December 1966, and he had been called from his cell and led to an interview room. Waiting for him was his sister, Sabina, accompanied by a Rhodesian Special Branch Officer. She told him that his three-year-old son, Nhamodzenyika, had died at Sally's parent's house in Ghana. Mugabe broke down and wept uncontrollably. Sabina, tears streaming down her face, explained that the child had been suffering from encephalitis. Mugabe was inconsolable. He requested permission to travel to Ghana right away to comfort his wife and mourn the child. It would not have been unusual for political prisoners to be granted temporary release. Mugabe was committed to the struggle, and would have undoubtedly returned to Rhodesia. But Smith's government rejected the request. It was a decision that Mugabe would never forgive.

As the years passed, with the nationalist leaders still shut away, Ian Smith's illegal regime, proudly isolated from the rest of the world, began a series of grim and defiant executions. Anyone caught with a firearm, or even in some cases a knife or axe, could face a mandatory death sentence, on the grounds that they were involved in terrorism. Some were hanged with just one hour's notice. Young men living close to guerrilla battlegrounds were picked up by security forces and convicted of terrorism under 'joint enterprise' laws, just for being in the vicinity.

By 1974, ZANU's executive council had been in jail for a decade, and cracks were beginning to appear. Their leader, Ndabaningi Sithole had been receiving visits from a young woman at Salisbury Prison. He had given her instructions about arms and ammunition for use in a plot to assassinate Ian Smith. Unfortunately for Sithole, it turned out the woman was a plant from the Rhodesian security services. A trial followed, where Sithole feared he might receive the death penalty. In order to save his life, he publicly renounced the armed struggle. It didn't go down well with Edgar '2-boy' Tekere and Enos Nkala. They scurried from cell to cell organizing a prison election so that the six members of ZANU's executive could decide whether he was still fit to be their leader.

The vote was split: two for Sithole to stay, three for him to go. Robert Mugabe decided to abstain. It was wrong in principle, he explained, to oust a sitting president.

Quickly, the conspirators cornered him in his cell. The scholarly, physically vulnerable Mugabe experienced his first taste of the gangster tactics that would come to dominate his own methodology. 'Here's the picture,' they told him. 'If you vote for Sithole, we three are going to carry the vote against him anyhow. Once that happens you will know that you are at political war with us. We will throw you in the same dustbin we are now throwing him.'[6]

Mugabe capitulated. The 'jailhouse coup' had succeeded. The next leader of ZANU was Mugabe himself.

From his cell, he soon had a new battle front to organize, along the border to Rhodesia's east. The Carnation Revolution in Portugal, which had seen the overthrow of the country's right-wing regime in 1974, had effectively ended Portuguese rule in Angola and Mozambique, and the latter was key for Mugabe. Mozambique would now be run by a friendly regime. The Mozambique Liberation Front (FRELIMO), had fought for years against the Portuguese colonizers, using similar guerrilla tactics to that of Mugabe's ZANLA, and the group had a similar Marxist–Leninist political philosophy. Now its leader, Samora Machel, a beret-wearing socialist who would later become an admirer of Margaret Thatcher, had dispensed with his military fatigues, and was sitting behind the presidential desk in the capital, Maputo. He promised far more than simply moral support for Mugabe. Rhodesia shared an 800-mile border with Mozambique, which passed through high mountains and uninhabited savannah, ideal for concealing arms and personnel. Machel would allow ZANLA to set up guerrilla camps for thousands of fighters, allowing deadly hit-and-run strikes into Rhodesia. It would prove almost impossible for the Rhodesians to control.

On a stormy March night in 1975, Chief Tangwena was at his mountain hideaway at Nyafaru farm near to the Mozambique border when two fugitives arrived. The pair had travelled the first leg of their journey, from Salisbury, in a Volkswagen Beetle, driven by a sympathetic European nun. Hiding in the undergrowth were members of the Rhodesian security forces. They regularly kept the farm under surveillance, as it was a staging post for ZANLA recruits on their way to the camps. Tonight they had been issued with a photograph of one of the fugitives, and instructed to prevent him from leaving the county.

The tropical cyclone was intensifying. The deluge was so severe that one military vehicle had skewed off the narrow mountain road. Visibility was a matter of metres. Spotting a 'gook', as the soldiers called black activists, would be challenging.

Chief Tangwena greeted the two fugitives enthusiastically and took them in from the rain. He warned them that the building was being watched and urged them to leave at first light. The following morning, after a breakfast of tea and buns, the men clambered through a small window at the rear of the farm and spirited themselves away across the border into Mozambique.

One of them was Edgar '2-boy' Tekere. Behind him, stumbling through the high grass, was Robert Gabriel Mugabe. The ZANU leader had been released from prison after serving eleven years, and had begun secretly recruiting fighters for ZANLA around Salisbury. Realizing that the net was closing in, and that he would face another lengthy detention if caught, he had decided to take flight.

The Rhodesian pilot would never have noticed it, but for a gap in the clouds. A series of angular shapes caught his eye, rows of rectangles and intersecting lines in the elbow of a river. He was flying over Mozambique, just twenty-five miles from the Rhodesian border. The rest of the reconnaissance had provided endless vistas of rust-coloured farmland and a few stunted trees, but whatever was down there now seemed man-made. He hardly had time to take it in. Long afternoon shadows. A flash of something metallic. Movement. Lots of movement. The navigator clicked the camera. Then it was gone.

At the HQ of the Selous Scouts, the elite Rhodesian counter-insurgency unit, Lt-Col. Ron Reid-Daly took charge. He asked for the photograph to be enlarged. With his rocking-chair manner and his almost priestly appearance, 'Uncle Ron' didn't fit the mould of Rhodesian Special Forces. His skills were in covert operations, not brute force. He leaned across the photograph and began counting. 'Eight hundred gooks,' he said. Their shapes were easily visible in high-resolution. They were lined up on a parade ground. Nearby he could make out vehicles and living quarters. Reid-Daly identified it as a ZANLA camp.

Over the following weeks, the Selous Scouts monitored the location and watched it grow. The number of rebel fighters stationed there swelled to around 5,000. It seemed a major offensive was imminent. Reid-Daly called over his commander-in-chief, General Peter Walls, and asked for permission to launch an elaborate clandestine operation. As the two men squatted on the floor over dozens of maps, Walls whistled through his teeth. 'It's a hell of a risk, Ron,' he said. Reid-Daly smiled reassuringly. 'It'll work,' he said, 'because it's the last thing they will expect.'

On 9 August 1976, a convoy of four Rhodesian Ferret armoured cars and seven armoured trucks crossed the border into Mozambique by cover of night. Their number plates had been changed to those of Mozambican vehicles so that they could pass for FRELIMO forces – former Mozambique Marxist guerrillas whose vehicles would arouse little suspicion now they were running the country. The convoy carried eighty-four Selous Scouts, several of them Portuguese-speaking blacks.

It always seemed an anomaly to Europeans that the scouts had any African fighters at all. In fact, they represented between fifty and eighty per cent of the unit. The need for them was obvious; they could be passed off as guerrillas during covert operations. But their recruitment was time-consuming. The scouts became experts at 'turning' those they captured. 'Turned-terrs' were often injured fighters, picked up on the battlefield and given life-saving medical care. They would be offered a good salary and a comfortable, safe home for their family. If that failed, the final tool of persuasion was employed: if they refused to fight loyally for the scouts, the Law and Order Maintenance Act would see them to the gallows.

That night in the summer of 1976, the black soldiers were riding in the front of the vehicles to deal with any unexpected checkpoints. The whites were in the back, wearing balaclavas and black greasepaint to cover any exposed white skin. A ZANLA defector directed the convoy over the border, through a timber plantation, and towards the camp. An advance party had already cut the telephone lines.

It was dawn by the time they reached their destination. Through the trees, the scouts observed thousands of guerrillas milling around a parade ground. The timing of the mission had been chosen to coincide with a national holiday, and the soldiers were still recovering from the festivities. Some were drinking. Among them were fifty or so FRELIMO troops, supplied by the Mozambique government. At the entrance the scouts were stopped briefly by a pair of sentries, who took a look inside, and then waved them through. The Selous Scouts were outnumbered sixty to one. Instead of discretely parking behind the living accommodation, they drove their trucks right into the centre of the parade ground and formed a semi-circle. On board they had two 20mm cannons. The four armoured cars peeled off to cover escape routes. With engines still running, a black Portuguese-speaking member of the team called for everyone's attention. The guerrillas, still half-asleep, gathered round. The scout shouted out, triumphantly, that the white-minority government in Rhodesia had been defeated, that the country was liberated and under black control. The guerrillas cheered, and swarmed the vehicles, shouting and whistling. They were carrying training rifles, which were made from wood. Then one of them noticed that a hooded fighter in one truck was actually white.

Most of the guerrillas were still celebrating when the order to fire was given by Captain Rob Warracker.

There was no immediate cover for those caught in the middle of the parade ground. Each of the scout's machine guns fired at a rate of almost a thousand rounds per minute, sixteen bullets a second. It was, as Reid-Daly later said, like a scythe cutting through a corn-field. With the vehicles carefully positioned in a crescent shape, the guerrillas were half-surrounded, and fled in the only direction available to them. That took them right into the firing line of the four Ferret armoured cars. The roar of machine guns continued. Bloodied bodies lay thick across the ground. Men ran across corpses to try to escape. Belts of ammunition flew through the Scouts' weapons at such a rate that the ground was layered with a carpet of spent shell casings. They continued firing until all visible movement had ceased.

Then they employed the cannons, launching mortars into the remaining escape routes and destroying buildings where survivors were still hiding out. The scouts swept quickly through the camp, ostensibly hoping to capture senior officers for intelligence-gathering purposes, but instead killing them in the chaos. The main hospital building, a crude, thatched construction, caught fire, burning to death those who were unable to evacuate. The scouts later claimed the blaze was started inadvertently, probably by a tracer round, others say they torched it on purpose. The flames quickly spread, engulfing other buildings. Those on the outskirts of the camp, who had managed to escape the machine guns, tried to swim to safety across the fast-flowing river which ran around its perimeter. Many drowned. Others tried to hide in the reeds, and were dragged out and shot.

An estimated 1,026 ZANU guerrillas lost their lives that day, another 2,000 were wounded. Worldwide condemnation swiftly followed. Ian Smith, already internationally isolated, hardly cared. But the reaction of South Africa, Rhodesia's only ally, was cause for some concern. Prime Minister John Vorster was so sickened by what he'd heard, he temporarily suspended crucial supplies of weapons and military support to his neighbour.

Robert Mugabe was in the Mozambique capital when he heard about the operation. What Reid-Daly called 'a good hit' was to him a ruthless massacre that would inspire a storm of attacks against Rhodesian targets.

LANCASTER HOUSE, LONDON, 10 SEPTEMBER 1979

Mugabe's body language was striking: all rolling shoulders and nervous ticks, like a man with bees beneath his skin. When he was first invited to the conference, aimed at finding a solution to the Rhodesian problem, Mugabe had had no intention of attending. He felt he was on the brink of military victory anyway. The fighting had intensified since he'd taken command of ZANLA, spreading into every region of Rhodesia, with white farmers having to barricade themselves into their own ranches to escape the frequent attacks. The frontline states – those dedicated to defeating apartheid in Rhodesia and South Africa – had implored him to join together with Nkomo to form a more coherent and powerful single movement. Mugabe had done so, under the banner of the Patriotic Front, even though the rancour between the two men remained. He was in no mood for further compromise. At first he had dismissed the idea of attending the Lancaster House talks as a 'sell-out', but Mozambique's Samora Machel had stepped in with a stern ultimatum: negotiate with the others in London, or lose your guerrilla bases in Mozambique. Mugabe stalked the corridors, making it plain he was in London under duress.

The conference brought together leaders whose entourages would have shot each other on sight a few days before. Now they were sitting around a polished wooden table beneath grand stucco ceilings in a neoclassical building around the corner from Buckingham Palace.

Joshua Nkomo, tired and in ill health, seemed relieved to be in civilized surroundings after so long as an itinerant exile. To the British he was the welcome face of moderate nationalism; good-humoured, flexible, always looking for solutions. He still had his eye on the presidency, and was London's preferred choice.

Ian Smith, his ruddy skin paled by the onset of London's autumn, was a distant, uneasy and querulous figure. Like Mugabe, he didn't want to be there, and for similar reasons; he didn't trust the British. Their running of the conference, he said, was like 'no-holds-barred, all-in wrestling' under the guise of extravagant and ornate hospitality. His suspicion was that they wanted to orchestrate the final act – some form of nationalist solution – so that they could claim the credit.

Mugabe, attired in Mao-style suit and oversized glasses, arrived flanked by warlords and bristling Marxist intellectuals. He was caustic in his meetings with the British, but his keen intellect and grasp of history impressed officials. Mugabe still thought the whole thing a con designed to bring an end to fighting, while leaving the whites in overall control. He would have preferred to be back in Rhodesia, carried through the streets of Salisbury by triumphant ZANLA guerrillas, victorious in battle and beyond the reaching hands of London.

The conference chair was the urbane Conservative Party grandee, Peter Carrington, 6th Baron, and holder of the military cross. He remarked that he had never shared a room with so many thugs and murderers in his life. Driven by his new boss, Margaret Thatcher, who was eager to resolve an intractable crisis that had plagued the last five prime ministers, Carrington's tactic was to bully and caress in equal measure. He gave the impression to each delegate that, if they remained at the table and saw the conference through, they would be the one returning to Salisbury as favourite to lead a new Rhodesia. All he needed was for them to agree a constitution that included majority rule, sort out the land issue with a guarantee that white farms would not be seized if a black government took control, and then send the whole lot of them packing to face British-brokered free and fair elections in Rhodesia.

Two months of talks passed. Mugabe's entourage detected foul play at every turn, even accusing the British of intentionally giving them inferior hotel rooms, and of having them bugged. Smith was similarly suspicious, claiming the British gave him beautiful and over-indulgent hospitality as a 'kind of compensation in advance for what was to come later'.[7]

At one point Mugabe stormed out of the talks altogether saying there were too few concessions on the table to offer his fighters after two decades of war. He made it as far as Heathrow Airport before Carrington phoned Samora Machel who had his ambassador intercept the ZANU leader and return him to Lancaster House.

Then, in December, before the talks had even concluded, Carrington took a gamble He sent his friend, the Conservative peer Baron Christopher Soames, to Rhodesia in full regalia, and had him installed in Government House. Soames, a man with zero experience of Rhodesia or anywhere else on the continent, was to become temporary governor, Britain's last potentate in Africa. The plan was for him to oversee elections and impose a ceasefire, on the assumption that Lancaster House would conclude in a way acceptable to all. Mugabe was livid. One of his entourage announced to the press that if Britain thought it could blithely resume its imperialist role, the

Patriotic Front would escalate the fighting and Soames would be trapped in an all-out war.

As the season's first snow fell on London, the Lancaster House Agreement was finally signed on 21 December 1979.

Nkomo descended the steps of the plane into a sea of chanting exuberant faces. Palm leaves waved in the air. The father of nationalism was home. It seemed certain that victory would be his. Even Ian Smith might do business with the former trade unionist; he certainly preferred him over the unforgivable 'communist devil' Mugabe. Nkomo set to work fulfilling the ceasefire agreement so that the election could go ahead. He confined his guerrilla fighters to specially created demobilization camps, as agreed in London, and then set off for a grand tour of the country.

Mugabe was banned. Soames could simply not let him back into the country while his guerrillas were still on the rampage, killing and intimidating opponents. But when the restrictions were lifted a fortnight later, the crowds that gathered to greet him were even larger than those for Nkomo. Mugabe leapt onto a wooden stage, a Marxist theoretician transformed into a dancing, irrepressible leader. Like Nkomo, he took ownership of the name Patriotic Front, and attached it to his own party, ZANU-PF. In interviews he spoke in cut-glass English almost as aristocratic as that of Lord Soames, but he also used the temporary governor as a symbol of all he stood against. 'We are Lord Soames's number-one enemy,' he declared to the rapturous crowds. Some of them wore T-shirts displaying Kalashnikov rifles.

There was another candidate, a moderate black African nationalist who Ian Smith believed would win, and who, if he did, would be likely to offer Smith a prominent role. He was Bishop Abel Muzorewa, previously the only legal black party leader in the country, on account of his rejection of violence. In a smoothly executed pretence at compromise, Smith had given way to Muzorewa and his United African National Congress (UANC), allowing him to become prime minister a few months before. In reality, Smith had still been in control, but with Muzorewa formally at the wheel, the so-called 'internal settlement' had allowed them to argue for an end to international sanctions on the grounds that they had a black-led government. Now, with independence set to happen immediately after the election, victory for Muzorewa would be the least worse result for Smith.

As election day approached, all parties were involved in intimidation. The whites were no exception. Rhodesian security forces tried to assassinate Mugabe by placing a bomb beneath his convoy. But ZANU-PF were by far the worst offenders. They murdered canvassers working for Muzorewa and Nkomo, and buried some of them alive. It meant there was considerable pressure on Soames to disqualify Mugabe from standing. But, deprived of a voice, his supporters would surely just continue the civil war. When Soames's advisors pointed out that ZANU-PF guerrillas were touring villages and beating suspected opponents, the Tory peer, with typical theatrical flourish told them, 'This is Africa, not Little Puddletown-on-the-marsh. They behave differently. They think nothing of sticking tent poles up each other's whatnots.'

ELECTION RESULTS, 4–5 MARCH 1980

At 4 p.m. on Tuesday 4 March 1980, Ian Smith was summoned to the house of the deputy head of Rhodesia's intelligence services, Derrick Robinson. When he walked into the living room, there waiting to meet him was Joshua Nkomo. The two bitter rivals had decided to bury the hatchet in order to defeat their common enemy, Robert Mugabe. In the past few days, Nkomo, Smith and Bishop Muzorewa had been frantically trying to make sense of the early voting data, in the hope that they might win enough seats between them to create an all-inclusive government of national unity – inclusive, that is, apart from Mugabe. Initially it had looked promising. Out of 100 seats, Smith's Rhodesian Front had a guaranteed twenty, Nkomo was expected to collect twenty, and Muzorwea another twenty. That would give them a clear majority, enough to keep Mugabe out. But now that the results were pouring in, their expectations had been radically downgraded. It seemed Mugabe might win significantly more than forty seats.

At 7 p.m. on Wednesday 5 March, Smith received a phone call from Mugabe inviting him to his home in Mount Pleasant. 'I was welcomed most courteously,' he said, and ushered to a seat in the lounge. Mugabe told him that the results now indicated ZANU-PF had won a clear majority and that Smith was the first person he had called for an exchange of views. Mugabe was right, he had won sixty-three per cent of the vote, giving him fifty-seven seats. Smith and Nkomo had won twenty each, as predicted, but the moderate Bishop Muzorewa, the compromise candidate favoured by liberal whites, had won just three. And then came the surprise. Instead of the belligerent Marxist 'devil' he had come to expect, Mugabe presented himself as generous, warm and modest in victory. He said he could not get over his good fortune at inheriting 'this jewel of Africa', and wanted to assure Smith that he wished to retain Rhodesia's system of free-enterprise. There would be no Marxist state, and while there needed to be change, it would happen gradually and in a realistic manner. Smith could barely believe what he was hearing. Mugabe spoke of the white farmers favourably, saying that they would be encouraged to continue their 'wonderful record of production'. At the end of the meeting, Mugabe politely escorted Smith to his car. 'When I got back home,' wrote Smith later, 'I said to Janet I hoped it was not an hallucination. He behaved like a balanced, civilized Westerner, the antithesis of the communist gangster I had expected. If this were a true picture, then there could be hope instead of despair.'[8]

There was a surprise, too, for the former head of the Central Intelligence Organisation, Cornishman Ken Flower, whose men had tried to assassinate Mugabe only days before and on several previous occasions. Flower was invited to visit Mugabe's office for an informal chat, and was keen to explain his various attempts to kill the new leader. Mugabe listened patiently. 'Yes, but they all failed, otherwise we would not be here together,' he laughed. 'As far as I have realized the position, we were trying to kill each other; that's what the war was about.'[9] Several air-clearing meetings followed and Mugabe invited Flower to keep his job as security chief for the new administration, a proposal Flower accepted. It was all a long way from the white purges and civil war that so many had predicted.

Mugabe's spirits of reconciliation didn't end there. Next on his list was Lord Soames, the man who confessed he had viewed Mugabe as 'something of a Marxist ogre' who would 'slit your throat as soon as look at you'. Mugabe met Soames at Government House and spoke of national unity and the preservation of law and order. He was articulate, moderate and hungry for advice on the mechanics of government. Soames was amazed. Mugabe asked him to stay on in the newly named Zimbabwe after independence. Soames declined because of other commitments, but Mugabe later became a man he admired. It was a spectacular turn around. When Soames died in 1987, Mugabe dropped everything and flew to London to attend his funeral.

For the white farmers who had been expecting crop-burning and farm seizures, the sleepless nights of the Bush War were over. They returned to their fields, and enjoyed one of the country's best harvests for many years. It seemed Mugabe had confounded them all.

Martin Olds was a bear of a man: broad, hirsute, with spade-carrying arms and a fitness born of years on the hot Rhodesian veld. He spoke Ndebele as if it were his native tongue. Olds was a white farmer, but he hardly felt it. Just 'a farmer', he would say, not 'white'. Such titles were for the 'long socks and shorts' brigade, the whites who swanned around Bulawayo like little princes, and slapped their black labourers for the smallest infraction. Olds was Rhodesian born and bred. He preferred the Ndebele's company. When sacks of animal feed were delivered to his ranch, he insisted on carrying more than his staff. 'The Ndebele are strong men,' he would say. 'I can manage.'

Like all young white men, Olds had been conscripted to the armed forces during the Bush War. He had chosen a mounted infantry division, Grey's Scouts, enabling him to indulge his love of horses. He never spoke of it, but after the elections, former guerrilla leaders would visit the butchery at his farm and Olds would embrace them, like long-lost friends. 'One of Nkomo's lot,' he would smile to his daughter through his thatch of black beard.

Soon after independence, Mugabe announced that no white farmers were allowed to provide charity to the poor, a tradition that Olds valued dearly, handing out food to the most needy in his workforce every Friday. If he gave them extra cash, the men would often just spend it on beer. Food parcels ensured they fed their children. But with what seemed like misplaced Marxist purity, Mugabe announced the practice humiliating: a regression into a patriarchal society, a way of subjugating the masses. Olds ignored him. He did things the way he wanted.

'They have invented tractors, you know?' neighbours would shout, but Olds preferred oxen and a cart. He trained six of them to pull him on a grader, which would slice through the orange earth to carve fire-breaks between the crops. One day, his two young children rode along with him, accompanied by a couple of farmhands. There was nothing like it: the taught muscles of the oxen, the deep baritone voices of the workers singing and swaying, loose grass blowing into their hair. Olds stood and leaned over to check the blade. Something made him slip. Amidst the children's screams and the unstoppable momentum of the cart, one of the Ndebele launched a flying tackle, sending Olds and himself spinning into the dirt away from the blade. They rolled on top of each other, laughing with the relief of it, and when they stood up, head-to-toe in mud and dust, the children couldn't tell who was black and who white. Both had turned orange.

It was soon afterwards, on a cloudless summer day, that two young Ndebele children wandered onto the farm. They were lost, having run beyond the boundary of their village. As Olds took them in, they shuffled bare-foot across the ranch's wooden floors, leaving a trail of tears in the dust. He knew straight away they had narrowly escaped a terror that was spreading across Zimbabwe.

It was hardly surprising that after almost two decades of Bush War, thousands of guerrillas from both sides eschewed a peaceful, peasant existence in their home villages, and chose instead the thrill of banditry. Violence swept towns and villages in the first years after independence, and both whites and blacks patiently awaited their new leader's response. When it came, it was the old partisan Mugabe that had re-emerged.

He chose to ignore the actions of his own fighters, and concentrate instead on those of Joshua Nkomo's men, accusing them of being sore losers after the election. They, and by implication his people, the Ndebele, were trying to undermine Mugabe's sovereignty, said the new leader, and were intent on provoking a tribal war. Mugabe's old ZANU cellmate, Enos Nkala, weighed in too, announcing wildly that Nkomo was 'a self-appointed Ndebele king' and needed to be 'crushed'.[10] Long-buried tribal differences were being forced to the surface.

Mugabe's ZANU-PF had always relied heavily on the Shona for support, an ancient agricultural people representing the largest ethnic group in Zimbabwe. Their ancestral territory, Mashonaland, was the region first occupied by Cecil Rhodes's British South Africa Company in his quest for gold.

Nkomo's ZAPU, on the other hand, were mainly Ndebele, from the neighbouring region of Matabeleland, the territory which Rhodes had moved into next, tricking Chief Lobengula into signing away his mineral rights, and chasing him out of Bulawayo. In truth, the two tribes had far more to bind them together than tear them apart. But rivalry during the Bush War had left many scores to be settled, and Mugabe and his supporters seemed bent on punishing their erstwhile foes.

At first, the clashes were between ZANLA and ZIPRA fighters who were supposed to be joining forces to form a Zimbabwean national army. But the fighting soon spread from military camps onto the streets, and hundreds were killed. Instead of calling for unity, Mugabe chose to punish Nkomo. The two men were supposed to be sharing security responsibilities, but in January 1981, Mugabe sacked him from his ministerial post, and hid him away in a minor job in charge of the public service. It was a deeply wounding humiliation for the man who was runner-up in the country's first elections, and who still represented a sizeable proportion of the population.

Having removed Nkomo, and with Smith's Rhodesian Front powerless, the way was open for Mugabe to begin his construction of a one-party state, and he set about it with zeal and cunning.

First, he created an elite and secretive armed unit called '5 Brigade'. Its members were recruited almost entirely from Shona areas and trained by instructors flown in from communist North Korea. It was to be outside the normal chain of command, a unit of ideologically motivated killers controlled by Mugabe's most loyal lieutenants. 5 Brigade's remit was to crush 'dissidents', by which Mugabe meant anyone perceived to be armed opposition. But the term was broad enough to condemn former ZIPRA guerrillas, peaceful ZAPU supporters and, indeed, entire Ndebele villages. Then he pulled a stunt that Nkomo should have seen coming.

Set among the hardy mopane trees on flat savannah north of Bulawayo in the heart of Nedeble country, was Ascot Farm, close to the racecourse of the same name. It was a large, ranch-style build-ing bought by ZAPU after the war with money from its guerrillas' demobilization payments. Ascot was a resettlement home, a place for veterans to live quietly while they tried to rebuild their lives. But ZAPU needed storage for military hardware. A substantial arsenal ended up hidden at Ascot Farm. Mugabe would have known that former ZAPU guerrillas were holding on to their guns. In such unpre-dictable times, it made sense. Former ZANU fighters were doing the same. It's likely Mugabe's security services had known about the location of the arms dump for several months, and had been waiting for the right moment to expose it. In February 1982, his men raided Ascot Farm and emerged carrying chests of AK-47s, missiles and mortars. Mugabe made an angry speech, full of fake indignation.

Proof, he declared, that a coup attempt was afoot, that Nkomo was trying to topple him. Mugabe's recriminations turned into a storm of ethnic cleansing against the Ndebele that raged for several years. Led by 5 Brigade, Mugabe justified it on the continuing pretext of neutralizing the 'dissidents', who, he said, were trying to overthrow his regime. It became known as *Gukurahundi*, a Shona word meaning *the early rain that washes away the chaff before the spring rains*, but in Matabelaland, where the pogroms were carried out, it simply meant *the sweeping away of the rubbish*. No one knows exactly how many died, but 30,000 deaths were estimated by 1987.

Beginning in January 1983, 5 Brigade swept through villages in Matabeleland North, under the command of Perence Shiri, known as 'Black Jesus' because 'he could determine your life like Jesus Christ'. Rape, torture, executions: the horror of 5 Brigade's operations became blunted by numbers too large to comprehend, actions repeated until their meaning wore thin.

On 3 February 1983, 5 Brigade arrived in trucks at a row of thatched huts beside a remote airstrip in savannah northeast of Bulawayo, known as Neshango Line. It was warm and humid, with a little rain in the air. They ordered everyone from their homes, and began a systematic beating that left some permanently disabled. There were two young girls in particular who caught the soldiers' attention. Both were pregnant. The pair were rape victims, from an earlier visit by the Zimbabwean National Army. 5 Brigade would not normally leave a village without isolating at least one individual for some gruesome performance, and today was the turn of the two young girls. Both were shot. Then soldiers stood over the dead bodies, pressed their bayonets into the rounded bellies, and cut the girls open to expose the foetuses still moving in their stomachs.[11]

The soldiers then moved southwards. Nine days later they arrived at the village of Gulakabili, where they abducted the entire population. They took them to a nearby mission, where the beatings began. At some point, 5 Brigade instructed a group of men to start digging. They were then told to climb into the pit and were shot. While some were still moving, villagers were forced to bury them.

After the job was complete, they were made to dance on top of the grave and sing songs in praise of ZANU-PF.[12]

Feeding the spiralling violence was a group of agents working covertly for both sides simultaneously. South Africa's white-minority government was under pressure to end apartheid, and needed an unstable Zimbabwe next door to show that majority rule would only end in terror. It recruited ex-Rhodesian army, police and spies from the Central Intelligence Organisation, and used them to stage 'black ops' atrocities. They attacked Mugabe's main air force base, kidnapped European tourists and attempted to assassinate Mugabe himself, knowing that each side would always blame the other. By constantly 'stirring the pot', they increased ethnic tensions, and provoked 5 Brigade into ever more sickening tactics. The unit began using hunger as a weapon, imposing a food embargo on Matabeleland South, another mainly Ndebele region. No shopkeepers were allowed to restock their shelves. Sacks of grain were destroyed. Anyone discovered sharing food with their neighbour was beaten and sometimes killed. Starvation set in. People began to eat the roots of trees.

During one 5 Brigade raid, two children managed to hide themselves away and escape. They ran, terrified, across the savannah, and come upon a farm. It was owned by a young white man with a thatch of black beard, who took them in, dried them down, fed them, and gave them a safe place to sleep. His name was Martin Olds.

And so it continued, threads of paint in a quiet corner of Mugabe's sinister mural, brush marks on Zimbabwe's *Guernica*. Rarely did a day go by without 5 Brigade committing atrocities.

Independence had come with a condition that land, the most precious of Zimbabwe's resources, would only change hands between 'willing seller' and 'willing buyer'. In other words, it could not be seized. Land had been fiercely contested at Lancaster House, but Mugabe had reluctantly agreed there would be no expropriation for a period of ten years. The British government had even offered to help him by purchasing land on the government's behalf from 'willing buyers'. Mugabe kept his word, and the land issue was shunted off the political landscape.

Ten years later, he reintroduced the question for the elections of 1990. 'It makes absolute nonsense of our history as an African country that most of our arable and ranching land is still in the hands of our erstwhile colonizers,' he announced, 'while the majority of our peasant community still live like squatters in their God-given land.' He was right, of course, but the question remained, how would he achieve the necessary redistribution? White farmers braced themselves. Mugabe had massacred his own people, what respect would he have for the original sinners? They were right to be anxious. The Zimbabwean parliament passed a programme of 'revolutionary' land reform, enabling the state to take its pick of whichever farms it fancied, at whatever price. There were celebrations in parliament. An ebullient Mugabe was not going to be restrained by international opinion, particularly the sort that came from Westminster. The aim, he said, was to acquire 13 million acres, almost half the white-owned farmland in Zimbabwe. A few weeks later, in January 1991, 4,000 white farmers marched on Harare, formerly Salisbury, to protest. It was a remarkable spectacle, the biggest gathering of whites since independence, and it secured their leaders an audience with the bullish agriculture minister, Witness Mangwende.

Mangwende was a passionate Marxist, very hostile to Britain and its legacy in the country, who had gained his PhD at the London School of Economics. He had been a political activist since junior school, achieving teenage notoriety by challenging his white teachers on their bowdlerized versions of colonial history, an approach that had won him multiple expulsions. Now, with the farmers' leaders in his ministry, he was faced with a roomful of white faces appealing for reason.

The government already had access to half a million acres that it had failed to redistribute, they argued; shouldn't that be the priority, not evictions? Then they took Mangwende through the economic arguments for maintaining the status quo. Agriculture, they said, was by far the largest provider of tax receipts, and white farmers were responsible for three-quarters of it. Where was the sense in forcing land into decline? Mangwende nodded and smiled, and then waved them impatiently away. 'The land question is a time-bomb which must be solved now,' he told them. The time for energy-consuming debates on the desirability or otherwise of this programme has run out; only tangible action is required.'[13]

Cries of foul play came from Britain, the United States, the World Bank and the IMF in 1991. They served only to invigorate Mugabe. Mangwende, on the other hand, adopted an uncharacteristically conciliatory tone, promising that his main target would be land that was underutilized, or was the property of absentee landlords or 'people with more farms than are considered necessary'.[14] The first tranche of functioning farms to be 'designated' numbered just thirteen; the second wave, seventy. But they accounted for almost half a million acres of Zimbabwean soil.

New owners began to move in. But they had no farming skills and no inclination to learn. They wanted trophy properties, and let them fall into disrepair, tearing up irrigation pipes to sell the lead, abandoning farm machinery, allowing the fields to revert to wilderness. Mugabe, with his degree in economics, knew that rendering fertile farmland unproductive made no economic sense, but this wasn't about that; it was about rewarding the loyal, and punishing the old enemy.

It wasn't just white farmers who were targeted. Mugabe used his Land Acquisition Act to punish political opponents, some of whom had bought their farms legitimately, at least in the sense that they had paid some money, if not the full market price. Among them was his old cellmate, Ndabaningi Sithole, the former ZANU leader who Mugabe had ousted in the notorious 'jail-house coup'. Mugabe viewed him as a traitor who had tried to make deals with Ian Smith. As such, Sithole was evicted and his land was awarded to someone thought more deserving.

When newspapers dug into the identity of those living in the scores of redistributed farms, they found among them a former commander of 5 Brigade and the head of Mugabe's own private office.

More embarrassing was the new resident of an enormous 3,000-acre property in a fertile tobacco-growing region south of Harare. The property was ten times the size of an average British farm, and had been designated for settlement by dozens of landless peasants. Instead, the new leaseholder had kept it entirely for himself. His name was Witness Mangwende, the minister for agriculture.

For the time being, the land issue was shepherded away again and hidden in the shadows.

A funeral was the last place Robert Mugabe expected it to happen, particularly that of a war veteran and popular guerrilla fighter. Mukoma Musa had been a Mugabe loyalist until the day he died. He had never been an officer. Mugabe had never heard of him. If the president had witnessed the former soldier's final moments, he might have felt some shame. Musa was cripplingly poor. We can picture him lying on the mud floor of a tin-roofed shack, a pouch of maize by his side, no medicine, no fresh water, filthy, hungry and ill. He passed away, like many other former fighters, having never enjoyed the fruits of independence promised during the struggle. His family couldn't even find the money to bury him.

But Mukoma Musa had an influential friend. His name was Gibson Mashingaidze, and he was a brigadier, the commander of Mugabe's Fourth Brigade. The two men had served together in the Bush War, and when Mashingaidze learned of his comrade's death, he was grief-stricken. The brigadier decided to pay for a proper funeral, giving Z$10,000 (about £100) to the organizers, and insisting on making the eulogy himself. The brigadier took the opportunity to launch a remarkable attack against his own governing party. It was absent of names but packed with recognizable figures. 'Some people now have ten farms and luxury yachts and have developed fat stomachs,' he told mourners, 'while ex-combatants like Comrade Musa live in poverty.' Standing beside his friend's coffin in December 1996, he demanded to know, 'Is this the ZANU-PF I trusted with my life? The party that promised to take care of us in our old age?'

It was a sensation. In the months that followed, officials decided it was time to examine the War Victims Compensation Fund, the money set aside for veterans. They discovered it had been systematically looted over several years. The money was supposed to be awarded according to the severity of injuries suffered during the war, as assessed by a supposedly independent medical examiner, who turned out to be anything but. An independent inquiry found the money had gone mainly to ZANU-PF loyalists with a range of manufactured complaints, from loss of appetite to skin allergies. On closer inspection they discovered several recipients were well-known figures who had helped drain the fund of Z$1.5 billion. Mugabe's brother-in-law, the aptly named Reward Marufu, was among them, having received Z$822,000 for 'a scar on his left knee' and 'ulcers'.[15] Mugabe's future head of intelligence had claimed to be 98 per cent disabled, but somehow managed to continue staggering into work. The former head of 5 Brigade, Perence 'Black Jesus' Shiri, was on the list, along with several government ministers and their wives. The medical assessor himself had claimed that his war injuries amounted to a disability of 117 per cent, meaning that, by rights, he should be dead.

Genuine war veterans took to the streets to protest. Mugabe dismissed them at first as 'rebels' and 'bandits', but the more contemptuous he became, the more they demanded. They crashed his appearance at Heroes' Day, heckling and banging drums, and then with jubilant defiance, they set Mugabe a deadline. If they didn't receive assistance soon, they would 'occupy white man's land', they declared, 'because the white man did not buy the land'.

Mugabe had painted himself into a corner, and he responded in the only way left to him. These remaining white farmers were Britain's 'children' he announced in October 1997, during a feverish round of addresses, 'the colonial exercise of robbery' must be 'corrected once and for all'. This time, 12 million acres would be expropriated from 1,500 farmers, and handed to the 'war veterans'. It represented almost half of Zimbabwe's productive agricultural land. Mugabe knew his decision defied economic sense, but this was now a visceral crusade and he was ecstatic with his own recklessness. 'We are going to take the land,' he declared', 'and we are not going to pay a cent to any soul.'

But it was hard cash his government required to quieten the war veterans, and for that he needed loans from the IMF and World Bank. The trouble was, they weren't willing to help while the land-grab threat hung over white farmers. Mugabe was forced to put the entire programme on hold, if he hoped to acquire any external help. In the meantime, still desperate for funds, he proposed raising taxes. There was a national outcry. The majority of people had become poorer during the 1990s, with most now classified as living in extreme poverty. Life expectancy was lower than during the Bush War, largely due to AIDS: forty-six years and falling. Newly unproductive farms and economic mismanagement meant spiralling food prices. This was no time for tax rises. Suddenly, Mugabe was faced with mass protests. Strikes paralysed the country. Out of the din, a single voice rose above all others. It was that of the first serious contender for Mugabe's crown, Morgan Tsvangirai and his Movement for Democratic Change.

It was as if Mugabe's instincts followed the same pathways as those of Cecil Rhodes. Northwards, beyond Zambia, in the tropical jungles of Democratic Republic of Congo (DRC), lay the largest diamond fields and gold mines in central Africa, and they were up for grabs. In 1998, DRC was in the midst of a catastrophic war involving nine different countries and countless armed factions. It was effectively a continuation of the conflict that had toppled Mobutu and replaced him with Laurent-Désiré Kabila. Several of Kabila's original backers had refused to leave, and now the Great War of Africa was upon them, the deadliest since the Second World War, which would last for a decade and claim the lives of between 3 and 5.4 million people.

Despite having no money, Mugabe decided it was a shrewd strategic investment to commit 11,000 troops to help keep Kabila in power, at a cost of US$1 million a day. There was no conceivable benefit to his own people, and he was risking further disruption at home, but the allure of gaining access to Congo's mineral resources was just too powerful to resist.

Mugabe's military began to take over the diamond mines of Mbuji-Mayi, the largest source of industrial diamonds in the world, once controlled by De Beers. It was all done in the utmost secrecy, with the Zimbabwean defence minister, Sidney Sekeramayi, warning Mugabe, 'Your excellency would be aware of the wave of negative publicity that the DRC–Zimbabwe joint-ventures have attracted... which tends to inform the current UN panel's investigation into our commercial activities.' Nevertheless, the Zimbabwean Defence Forces (ZDF) set up a company called OSLEG, an abbreviation of its military campaign, Operation Sovereign Legitimacy, to concentrate on mineral extraction. The commander of the Zimbabwean Defence Force became a director, as did the permanent secretary of the Defence Ministry.

While the Great War of Africa raged around them, an elite network of Zimbabwean and Congolese began to divide the country's mineral wealth between them. Putting their military obligations to one side, they began to educate themselves about diamonds. Senior Zimbabwean officers were sent for lessons with a convicted criminal in Johannesburg. They learned how to distinguish gems from industrial diamonds, and acquired skills in valuation. The key strategist for the Zimbabweans was the speaker of parliament, and former national security minister, Emmerson Mnangagwa, nicknamed 'The Crocodile'. He was supported by the former commander of 5 Brigade, Perence Shiri. Both men were part of the inner circle of ZDF diamond traders who turned Harare into a significant illicit diamond trading centre.

The sums of money involved were enormous. The network of political, military and commercial interests from both countries transferred at least US$5 billion of assets from the Congo state mining sector to private companies they controlled during a three-year period.[16]

*

On a clear summer afternoon in April 2000, Martin Olds stood in front of his ranch cradling a huge ginger wildcat in his arms, and waved goodbye to his wife and two children. It was safer if they stayed in Bulawayo, he said, just for a few days, until all this blew over. The war veterans were on the rampage, seizing any land they chose, with the blessing of Mugabe. Of course, most weren't 'veterans' at all, it was just a convenient title. Mugabe used them as a score-settling army which would 'spontaneously' mete out their own brand of justice.

As Martin Olds's family climbed into the car, he gave his wife a number on a slip of paper. It was the reference for a 'fear for life' statement he'd made to the police.

That evening, Olds inspected the ranch, which was built within a triangle of trees around their 1950s-style chalet home. All was quiet. Tomorrow was Independence Day.

He awoke as normal at 5.30 a.m. At 6 a.m., some of his workers reported seeing a convoy of four mini buses moving along the road towards his ranch, carrying a hundred young men. Witnesses later saw the same men on the road inspecting Olds's perimeter fence. They were carrying with them bags that clinked with the sound of bottles. Over their shoulders were slung AK-47s.

Olds was alerted and called a neighbour, asking him to go and check on his mother, Gloria, who lived on the adjacent farm. The neighbour took a motorbike and drove cross-country to avoid the growing crowd on the road. When he arrived at Gloria Olds's farm, Silverstreams, he found she was well, and remained there to protect her just in case the situation turned violent. At 6.15 a.m., Martin Olds decided the situation was serious enough to radio the Commercial Farmers Union, who contacted the emergency services and put word round that he needed help. 'They are cutting through my fence,' he said. He was anxious. It looked like things might 'turn ugly'.

A number of farmers heard the news over their radios, and headed to Olds's farm in pickup trucks. They found a police checkpoint on the road outside. These were the same police to whom Olds had made his statement. Their vehicles were parked across the road, and they were letting no one through. By now, the armed men had broken through the fence, and were fanning out around the grounds of his property. Olds grabbed whatever guns he could find and positioned himself beside a window. The radio was on the kitchen table. He needed it close by.

The first Molotov cocktails began falling soon after. One crashed into Martin Olds's Datsun truck, setting it ablaze. Another smashed through a window, setting light to furnishings. From behind the trees, men began firing at the house.

The gunshots could be heard down at the roadblock. Olds's neighbours again tried to get through to help him, but the police pushed them away.

By this time, the 'vets' had reached the front door, and a gunfight was under way. Olds's army training, and years of hunting, meant he was a crack shot, but these men were firing AK-47s from all directions. Farm buildings were burning, chunks were flying out of the brickwork. Olds turned on the taps in the bath and began filling buckets. His next call to the Farmers Union was brief. 'I've been shot!' he shouted above the din. 'Call an ambulance.'

Olds hobbled into a bedroom looking for sheets to bind his wounded leg. He was losing blood. The ambulance would take time, half an hour maybe. He repositioned himself at a window, and picked off at least one attacker. The incoming fire was overwhelming. He retreated to the bathroom. The tub was positioned beside the window. From there he could throw water on the encroaching flames, while keeping his gun trained on the bushes. Down on the road, the ambulance was turned away by the police.

A local farmer flew a plane overhead and saw ribbons of black smoke rising from every building.

Olds took one of the shotguns he had with him, and placed it carefully beneath the bathmat. It was a family heirloom that he had promised to his teenage son, and he didn't want it damaged. He then took up position in the tub for his last stand.

The mob had reached the bathroom window. Their arms were reaching inside trying to grab him.

Martin Olds's funeral was held in a pretty, modern chapel full of African flowers, the sound of birdsong floating in through tall arched windows. Several Ndebele attended, some of them his former farm workers, others were people he had helped with food parcels or loans. No one bothered occupying Olds's farm after his death, that had never been the purpose. Ballistic experts said the assault was that of a drunken and spontaneous mob. It was likely the work of 5 Brigade – a political assassination to mark Independence Day. Olds was not only a white landowner, but a friend of the Ndebele. In Mugabe's eyes, he was guilty twice over.

Eleven months later, Olds's 68-year-old mother, Gloria, was leaving her farm one morning when she saw something moving in the bushes. As she opened the gates, a gang of three men approached her, armed with AK-47 assault rifles, and shot her fifteen times.

The soil gusted like sand across the plains of Chiadzwa in the Marange district, gathering in soft drifts on the windward side of primitive brick homes, stiffening the hair of goats and colouring the chickens red. Children would often find pea-sized stones on that land, close to the Mozambique border, grey and strangely oily in texture. They were good for sling-shots, and for killing birds.

In the early 2000s, a subsidiary of De Beers set up camp close to a riverbed. They found a few rough stones, broke away the opaque gum-like coating, and found diamonds. There were plenty of them, but distributed unevenly, and largely of industrial quality, rather than gems. De Beers lost interest and left. A UK-registered company, African Consolidated Resources (ACR), was then awarded the rights to take over. They cut deep trenches through the sandy soil, and discovered the world's largest deposits of alluvial diamonds.

ACR was obliged, by company law in London, to publish the find. Three weeks later, a convoy of vehicles arrived outside their offices and disgorged a group of men from Mugabe's security forces. They explained that if ACR didn't leave the site immediately, they would force them out at gunpoint. ZANU-PF then made an announcement.

The diamonds belonged to everyone, the fields would be open to the public.

Thousands of men, women and children arrived in buses from all over the country. Many were civil servants whose salaries had been wiped out by spiralling inflation. There were teachers and engineers from Bulawayo, accountants from Harare, police officers and subsistence farmers from the fern-covered hillsides around Mutare, buying up buckets and spades in local hardware shops, and organizing themselves into gangs. All the stones were supposed to be sold to the Reserve Bank of Zimbabwe, so that the state could take its cut. But the opportunity for corruption was just too good to miss.

Unofficial middlemen set up sorting tables on the edge of digs. Black-market dealers took up residence in cheap hostels. They came from South Africa, Mozambique, Congo and Botswana, and paid the diggers far more than the official government rate. Soon, diamonds were being smuggled across the border in toothpaste and shaving cream. They were hidden in shoes and seat belts, and sewn into car tyres. More valuable stones were swallowed and retrieved later. Camps were built. Diggers drank, gambled and paid prostitutes in rough stones. By November 2006, Mugabe had had enough.

On a narrow asphalt road leading from the city of Mutare to the diamond fields, eleven police checkpoints were set up. The diggers were anxious that this would mean the end of their income. They offered the officers cigarettes and beer and pleaded with them to be allowed access. Police pay was so low, even small bonuses were welcome. The diggers were waved through. Unofficial entry fees rose quickly. The checkpoint furthest from the dig was soon charging US$5, the closest was demanding US$100. If a digger didn't have the required fee, he could pay per minute.

By late 2006, the officers had devised a more business-like strategy. They would manage the diggers themselves, in syndicates, employing gangs of thirty men at a time. Police divided the takings, fifty-fifty. Some ran several syndicates simultaneously, becoming wealthy within a matter of weeks. Two members of a police-support unit later admitted employing 102 diggers. Their government salary for three months, they claimed, was the equivalent of US$5, while their takings from the Marange diamond fields in the same period topped US$10,000.[17]

'VIP syndicates' stood to benefit most. The diggers began to recognize when a minister or senior Mugabe official had arrived at the fields, because police 'reaction teams' cleared the site, and trucks brought in men from out of town. They took over the best digs for days at a time. One diamond-rich hillock became known as *Zamu ramai Mujuru*, Mrs. Joice Mujuru's breast. Mrs. Mujuru was the vice-president of Zimbabwe. She and her husband were the most feared and powerful couple in the land after Mugabe himself. During the Bush War, Mrs. Mujuru had taken the *nom-de-guerre* 'Spill Blood' and remained a physically formidable woman well into her fifties – despite claiming Z$389,000 for battle injuries from the discredited War Victims Compensation Fund. Her husband, Solomon Mujuru, was the former leader of Mugabe's guerrillas. The couple had a sense of entitlement few dared challenge. Shortly after the murder of Martin Olds, during the so-called Land Reform Programme, they seized a white-owned farm themselves, 5,000 hectares of prime tobacco and maize-growing land, and gave the owner just an hour to leave. When the diamond rush began, Joice Mujuru was swept away in the excitement, treating the hillock as her own tract of diamondiferous real estate.

The chief of Mugabe's own office also took a share. William Nhara, nicknamed 'Diamond Geezer', was on his way out of Harare airport with a Lebanese business associate in March 2007, when the pair were pulled over. Nhara tried to bribe immigration officials with US$700. In the circumstances it was hardly enough. His colleague was found to be smuggling 10,700 carats of Marange diamonds, around half a bucketful, with a market value of US$1 million. Forty-six-year-old Nhara died while awaiting his court case, giving rise to rumours he had been poisoned to stop the possible incrimination of other government officials, and those even closer to the president himself.

*

When Robert Mugabe's wife, Sally, passed away, the seventy-two-year-old married his former secretary, Grace, forty-one years his junior. Gone was the quiet restraint, the gentle tug on the sleeve that counselled 'no' to his wildest schemes, the homely feasts of custard and tea on the veranda. In marched a princess who thought she was entitled to whatever she wished. Grace Mugabe's marriage to the Zimbabwean president in 1996 was billed, by state-controlled Zimbabwe papers, as the 'wedding of the century'. Six thousand guests arrived in Harare from across the world, including Nelson Mandela. It wasn't long before the new First Lady began taking advantage of her position.

Mugabe himself had toured the country searching for land for his new wife even before the wedding. Now she joined him. First to catch her eye was a 1,000-acre estate called Highfields, which she bought from a willing seller. But it wasn't enough. Grace wanted the country's largest dairy farm, and, after violent intimidation, the white owners were forced out. A fee was paid but it was a fraction of the market price. Grace Mugabe then set to work as an unlikely milk baroness, snapping up other dairy farms and becoming the country's biggest producer of milk. International buyers stepped forward, but had to pay in cash to avoid the scandal of doing open business with the Mugabes, both of whom were under international sanctions. At the last count, the couple had twelve farms, but Grace was looking for more, egged on by obsequious state governors. 'The land is no longer sufficient to sustain the projects the first lady has up her sleeves,' said the governor of Mashonaland Central, Martin Dinha. 'Some might say she is greedy... but we are saying it is justified for her to have more land.'[18]

At the same time, the first lady was gaining a reputation for heroic shopping trips abroad, and needed somewhere to store her long rows of shoes and Gucci handbags. She grew tired of her first palace, nicknamed Gracelands, and sold it to Colonel Muammar Gaddafi. The Libyan leader operated a series of front companies in Zimbabwe, where it is said he hid some of his $200 billion fortune. He bought Gracelands from the Mugabes in 2002, and many people assumed he would flee there during the Libyan civil war. Mugabe would certainly have offered him sanctuary. He was already hosting Ethiopia's tyrant Mengistu Haile Mariam, who fled his country in 1991, and who still lives on a farm outside Harare.

With Gracelands in the hands of the Libyans (today it is used as the Libyan embassy), Grace Mugabe began construction of her 'Blue Roof' mansion in Harare's leafy suburb of Borrowdale, so called because of its distinctive 'midnight-blue' tiled roof. That was all people could see of it. The rest of the large house was hidden. No photographs existed. Mugabe, always socially awkward, rarely invited guests. Rumours spread of a US$10 million property with two lakes, swimming pools, sunken baths hewn from Italian marble, bronze Chinese dragons guarding the gates, and a sixty-acre perimeter fitted with a complex system of gas detectors to stop chemical weapons attacks.

Questions about how it was financed appeared to cause Mugabe more embarrassment than those concerning his massacres in Matabeleland. He seemed stung by the notion that 'Blue Roof' might not fit with his socialist credentials. But his young officials were on hand with a story. 'Blue Roof', they said, was paid for with donations from wealthy supporters and from ZANU-PF in recognition of a lifetime of duty. Even if it were true, it all came from the same pot. 'Wealthy supporters' meant cronies whom Mugabe had rewarded with illicit deals from the country's triumvirate of looting schemes: land grabs, Congo mining and the Marange diamond fields. As the Mugabes filled 'Blue Roof' with French antiques, the rest of the country was living through the worst financial crisis in Africa's history.

At the start of 2008, Zimbabwe's prices were rising at an annual rate of 100,580.16 per cent. Let the camera zoom into Mabvuku, a suburb of Harare 17 kilometres out of town: neat tin-roofed homes, two rooms per family, gardens – some with grass – carports, tarmac roads. There is water and electricity, although both are currently switched off. Rubble from a barber's shop is half-blocking the main road, a casualty of Mugabe's demolition teams punishing businesses that operate without permits. A teacher waits for a bus, one hand over his mouth because of the stagnant sewage on the street. There is a cholera outbreak; he needs to take care. He skips over the pool of refuse and faeces, and onto the bus. It is something of an indulgence. His salary sounds astronomical, at Z$400 million a year, but it is hardly enough to cover a week's expenses. He has just received his pay for March, and he needs to find a money dealer with hard currency, preferably US dollars. On the way into town, he passes the market. People are panic-buying maize and flour, piling sacks into pickups. His wife has instructed him to buy bread, but a loaf costs Z$10 million. As he tries to negotiate, he is observed by a group of middle-class men prowling like a gang of hoodlums. If he gets a deal, they will rush in and try to buy everything on the stall, so they can sell it on for an immediate profit. Everyone has become a commodity broker.

He finds a currency dealer in the local bank – the manager, in fact – running an illicit exchange alongside the official one. But there's nothing left. Clients have already deposited wheelbarrows containing bricks of notes, and left with a few dollar bills. The teacher gives up and heads home.

By the time he reaches the bus stop, fares have risen fourfold. It is beyond his budget. Instead he walks. Worthless bank notes blow through the streets. In the old days, he might have stopped for a beer, which now costs Z$120 million a bottle. The printers can't keep pace. The latest denomination is a Z$100 trillion note, but it's only the equivalent of US$30.

By the end of 2008, even the money-manufacturers have given up. Inflation has hit a rate of 89 followed by twenty-three zeros per cent. What better time for a presidential election?

The right eye of Morgan Tsvangirai was swollen shut, stitches sewn into a deep gash on the side of his head. He rocked in the back of a truck, alongside fifty of his supporters from the Movement for Democratic Change (MDC), singing songs of defiance against Mugabe's regime. The women had bruises all over their legs. Men were lying in blood-stained rags, some were semi-conscious. The truck came to a halt outside the Harare courtroom, and the procession of broken and injured made their way gingerly inside. Tsvangirai staggered after them. These were the accused. Their alleged crime was to have attended a political gathering.

In truth, it had been a prayer meeting, upon which Mugabe's police descended with guns and iron bars. The president later claimed his officers had been beaten and were simply defending themselves, but he couldn't produce evidence of a single injury. One of the worshippers, on the other hand, had been shot dead.

All this was nothing new to Tsvangirai. He had been charged with treason on three occasions and received regular beatings. One evening a group of men had broken into his office, hit him over the head with an iron bar, and tried to throw him from a window. With attacks against his supporters commonplace, including torture and murder, much of 2007 had been spent trying to bandage the MDC into a functioning organization.

The presidential election was scheduled for March 2008, and promised to be closer than any since independence. But the hyper-inflation was a problem for the incumbent. Mugabe had, long ago, conflated the finances of ZANU-PF with those of the state, meaning that his people's taxes ended up funding his election rigging. But now, even with cash flows from Marange diamonds, his party was almost as hard up as the MDC. Twenty-eight years into his presidency, with a crippled economy and eighty per cent unemployment, even Mugabe's private opinion polls were showing his popularity at an all-time low. But he was not going to be defeated by something as tiresome as public opinion.

A recruitment drive was launched to get ZANU-PF supporters into the civil service. No qualifications were required, because they were never expected to work. These were 'ghost jobs' – positions that didn't exist but could be put through the books. It was large-scale and systematic. Out of 188,000 civil servants, a commission

later discovered, 75,273 were 'ghosts'.[19] Almost half Zimbabwe's
state apparatus was made up of dead souls.

Mugabe's next step was to deprive expatriate Zimbabweans of
their vote. In most countries, exiled voters would hardly be significant
in a national election, but where you have hundreds of thousands of
opposition supporters fleeing government crackdowns, it's a potential
game-changer. Three million Zimbabweans lived outside the country,
almost a quarter of the population. It would be reasonable to assume
that most were supporters of the MDC.

Then there was food. Zimbabwe was reliant on food aid, largely
supplied by the UK. The distribution was controlled by the government. In other words, ZANU-PF decided who should receive it.

In the months leading up to the poll, there was pressure on
Tsvangirai, from his own advisors, to boycott the elections in protest
over the rigging and violence that such a campaign was certain to
inspire. Their logic was sound. No election held under Mugabe's rules
could be won by anyone other than Mugabe. On the other hand, the
leader's support was so exceptionally thin that there had never been
a better chance to beat him. Tsvangirai decided, on balance, that the
contest should go ahead.

Polling day arrived, blisteringly warm and hopeful. There was less
violence than normal, but the queues were agonizingly slow around
many government-run polling stations. By lunchtime, they had
hardly budged. In army towns, which were overwhelmingly ZANU-
PF, the voting procedure seemed far more efficient. When the polls
closed that night, everyone who wanted to cast a vote had done so.
In non-army towns tens of thousands were turned away.

It was three days before the Electoral Commission began releasing
results, starting with the parliamentary elections, which were being
held at the same time. The figures were drip-fed over forty-eight
hours, almost as if they dare not release them in full. There was
good reason. The general secretary of the MDC, working on his
party's own figures, had calculated a clear Tsvangirai victory, and
had announced the result to the press. He was promptly charged
with treason.

The Electoral Commission fell silent. For three weeks. Zimbabweans assumed Mugabe must have scored less than the fifty per cent required for outright victory, and was frantically plotting his next move. Either that, or Tsvangirai had won outright. Then, still without a result, the violence began.

MDC supporters in villages were attacked and killed, their homes torched. Thousand fled the countryside to lodge with friends in the cities. One group built a camp in the grounds of MDC headquarters in Harare. It was soon broken up.

Police raided MDC offices and those of the only NGO, which had carried out its own analysis of voting patterns. Computers were smashed, hard drives destroyed, and with them any evidence that might contradict figures from the Electoral Commission. On 2 May, five weeks after the vote, a nation tuned in to hear the result. Crowds gathered around communal television sets at roadside bars, villagers squatted in the dust around battery-powered radios.

Morgan Tsvangirai had won. But he had failed to cross the 50 per cent line, which would have given him the presidency. With Tsvangirai on 47.9 per cent, and a humiliated Mugabe on 43.2 per cent, there would be a run-off.

The eruption of violence was unprecedented for an election campaign. Mobs of ZANU-PF youths attacked schools, forcing teachers to lie on the ground and whipping their buttocks. White families, all of them accused of being 'British puppets', were set upon. One elderly couple were given two minutes to leave their farm. The mob stamped on the husband's head and beat the wife until she was unconscious. In villages, ZANU-PF youths ran wild, systematically raping women believed to be MDC supporters in front of their terrified families. Tens of thousands fled. Even if they dared attempt to vote, they were now homeless and without identification papers, and wouldn't be eligible.

There was no pretence at civilized campaigning. 'We are looking forward for every Zimbabwean, not only to pledge their votes, but to cast them for Robert Mugabe,' announced the head of the war veterans. 'People should know that each vote is no longer secret, but a responsibility put in the hands of each Zimbabwean by pain of death.'[20]

In order to save the lives of his supporters, Morgan Tsvangirai felt he had no choice but to withdraw from the election. Mugabe won it unopposed.

A helicopter buzzed in low, churning the sandy soil. Men squatted, turtle-style, shielding their faces from the ochre blizzard. It was dawn on 27 October 2008, six months after the election results, and the Marange diamond fields were packed with thousands of half-naked diggers. They assumed the helicopters signalled the arrival of some big-money buyers, agents representing a government minister or team of foreign businessmen. Some people were underground in shallow tunnels when the machine guns opened fire. Diggers scattered in all directions. More helicopters dipped in from the hills, firing indiscriminately. They were supported by more than 800 soldiers on the ground. Each time a man was shot, the troops searched his pockets for diamonds and continued firing.

During the elections, when Mugabe's fate had hung very much in the balance, his army had been all that stood between him and a popular coup. Never had his position been so fragile. Now he was rewarding them for their loyalty.

Soldiers took over the diamond fields. Their syndicates replaced those of the police, rotating through Marange to ensure a succession of key frontline units had a chance to profit. Instead of sharing the diamonds with the diggers, they began operating a system of forced labour. Men who refused to dig were beaten and sometimes shot. Over time, soldiers discovered that children were more compliant than adults. Several hundred were kidnapped and made to dig. Since the schools in the area had long-since stopped functioning, teachers were captured and forced to work alongside them.

Much of the illicit distribution system remained in the same hands, the richest rewards going to key Mugabe loyalists, with diamonds smuggled out to the UAE, India, Israel, Congo and South Africa under the radar of the Kimberley Process. But there was a parallel system of legitimate mining ventures too, large international companies that won their prospecting rights through auctions held by the Zimbabwean government. Whether they liked it or not, most ended up in joint ventures with companies run by ZANU-PF.

Again, just like in Congo, senior military officers held pivotal and lucrative positions. A government procurement business called ZDI, Zimbabwean Defence Industries, was at the heart of it, but it was no longer reliant on Kinshasa. Mugabe's attention had turned to China. Money, personnel and equipment began flooding into Marange from Shanghai, with countless millions of carats moving in the other direction.

The most sought-after position in the land was that of Marange's gatekeeper, and that fell within the brief of Zimbabwe's minister of mines. The incumbent, Obert Mpofu, became wildly and conspicuously rich almost overnight. He was unable to explain how he managed to purchase the Ascot Race Course and Casino in Bulawayo, safari lodges in Victoria Falls, farms and business premises, a newspaper, and even a bank, all on a ministerial salary. Soon he was one of the top five landholders in Zimbabwe, and began referring to himself as the king of Matabeleland.[21]

During Mpofu's tenure, it is estimated that US$2 billion worth of diamonds were plundered from Marange.[22] That doesn't include the mining revenue, in taxes and other charges, lost to the government. Robert Mugabe himself put that figure at US$13 billion, equivalent to Zimbabwe's entire gross domestic profit.

'Blue Roofs' glinted in the cloudless Harare sky. It was 1 March 2014, a month after Mugabe's ninetieth birthday, and he was entertaining guests at the wedding of his only daughter, Bona, in a lavish ceremony at his home. White silk marquees were positioned among the pagodas and terraces. Guests arrived in bulletproof Rolls-Royces and Mercedes. Mugabe stood proudly, sipping tea – he rarely touched alcohol – and brushing the lapels of his tuxedo. There was no sign of frailty as he shook hands and posed for pictures, against a backdrop of silver-sprayed trees adorned with purple orchids. Officials were on hand to ensure all mobile phones were switched off, preventing any photographs of the mansion leaking out. After thirty-four years of plunder and merciless ethnic cleansing, Mugabe was still sensitive about how 'Blue Roofs' had been paid for. 'You might recall,' chirped one of his advisors to the few official journalists at the gates, 'that the land on which the home stands was bought by the party, ZANU-PF, for their leader. Not a single cent came from the state.' No one cared. Outside the grounds of his beautiful Chinese-designed home, the average salary was less than it had been when Mugabe came to power, US$50 a month. A reputable international think-tank had just announced it would take 190 years for the country's salaries to catch up with the rest of Africa.

The line of VIPs waiting to shake Mugabe's hand was long. Near the front stood a bespectacled pensioner, immaculate in gun-grey suit and lilac tie. He took Mugabe's hand confidently, and gave a half-smile to the camera. The pair had been in power a similar length of time. This was the African dictator Teodoro Obiang Nguema, president of Equatorial Guinea, a man usually surrounded by armed guards. Obiang's family had killed many more thousands than Mugabe, and his resource-theft had been of a different scale, though in oil not diamonds. He nodded regally at his Zimbabwean host, and was swept away by his entourage.

Billionaire businessmen passed by, mining magnates, heads of state from Congo and Ghana. Somewhere in this silk marquee was Mugabe's successor.

Emmerson 'The Crocodile' Mnangagwa arrived, Mugabe's key strategist during the diamond-looting operation in Congo, and one of his most loyal henchmen. A former Mugabe spy chief, he was solemn, unreadable, and gave the impression of being ill-at-ease at a party. It was Mnangagwa who had overseen Mugabe's bloody 2008 election victory against Morgan Tsvangirai, a job for which, he told friends, Mugabe had promised him the presidency when he retired.

Nearby, seated on a white leather sofa, was a beaming Grace Mugabe. She too had a promise. Her ninety-year-old husband had told her he would carry on governing from beyond the grave, communicating all his instructions through her. It was she who would be president, he said, a prospect one opponent called 'a coup by marriage certificate'.

She and Mnangagwa greeted each other like siblings, not rivals, sharing canapés and champagne. But both knew that the power struggle fast approaching would be played out between themselves and no-one else. Mnangagwa could rely on the powerful war veterans and army chiefs of the liberation wars. Grace's support came from the new business elite, but only via the bribes paid by her husband.

Mnangagwa waited, and played the game. He was promoted to vice-president shortly after the wedding. He still required Mugabe's goodwill. But not for long.

In November 2017, Mugabe made an uncharacteristic blunder. He sacked Mnangagwa to clear the way for Grace to become his successor. It was all Mnangagwa and his supporters needed.

At ninety-three years old, Robert Mugabe suddenly found himself a prisoner in Blue Roofs, surrounded by armoured units loyal to Mnangagwa. The old man had been reluctant to sort out a successor, as if he doubted even his own mortality. Mnangagwa had waited long enough.

PART TWO

Oil

CHAPTER THREE

Before the Dictators

Oil Discoveries in Sub-Saharan Africa

MENTION THE ROVER Boys to an old-school oil prospector and he will shake his head in awe. 'The Rover Boys?' he will say. 'Those guys were out there at the start, parachuted into the most dangerous territories with guns and supplies... off they'd go, searching for oil.' One frontier oil explorer gazed sadly into his wine glass. 'They'll all be dead now,' he said, reminiscing about the group's early days in Africa. 'That was my ambition, you know. They were hand-picked. It was like being chosen for the SAS. You had to be so clever, so resilient. They lived in the wilderness for months. If there was oil to be found, nobody would beat them to it.'

What followed was several days of phone calls and email exchanges between oil archivists and retired geologists who remembered the Rover Boys as if they were comic-book heroes, doggedly exploring the jungles and deserts for oil in a continent much of the world insisted was dry. 'Dave Kingston,' said one source in the US. 'I think that was the leader's name, but we are talking about the 1950s here, even before.' 'I never met Kingston,' lamented another. 'My stories about him come from an old paperback book.' The leads were scant. Membership of the Rover Boys had changed over the years, but it was the final combination of three guerrilla geologists and a mechanic that had acquired a romantic cachet similar to that of the great American oil pioneers of the nineteenth century. I was lucky enough to find an old photograph of the four posing in Mali with hunting rifles. One of them has his weapon cocked and is aiming somewhere into the African bush. Another is bare from the waist up and shielding his face from the sun. Seated in the middle on a camping chair is an imposing figure in gnarled boots and trekking fatigues, staring defiantly from behind a pair of dark lenses: a wild-man adventurer with a handgun and a bramble of beard. That man is Dave Kingston.

Eventually the internet yielded the inevitable obituaries. They had been born during the Great Depression, fought in Korea, climbed mountains and swigged whisky together on remote desert rocks. 'He never conformed to norms and routines,' read a tribute to one. 'He heard a different drummer.'

But there was one obituary I could never find, that of Dave Kingston. It turned out he was still alive.

At eighty-nine years old, Dave Kingston has the barrel chest of an adventurer: a man who's cut his way through rainforests, shot antelopes in the remote savannah, and slept in tiger territory beneath the stars. His hair is cotton-white now, and the wildman beard of his youth was shaved off many years ago. At his home in the rose-coloured desert of New Mexico he examines the latest geological charts, tracing his finger along Africa's west coast. He's still got the bug, still lusts after that first clue, that eureka moment when the puzzle finally snaps into place. He pauses at the Gulf of Guinea, then again at Nigeria and Angola. A complex grid of oblongs and squares covers the coastline. It shows where oil companies are looking for crude or already pumping it from the ground. When Dr Kingston first studied a map like this in the 1940s, the whole continent was blank. African oil, in commercial quantities, had not yet been discovered. And so began some geological detective work that would take him back to a period when Africa was still attached to the Americas, when the northern coastlines of Libya and Algeria lay deep beneath a tropical ocean and the great West African rivers were first pouring their waters into a prehistoric sea.

It was a world empty of humankind, but in his imagination Dr Kingston has explored its rainforests many times, searching for clues, testing the land and water for conditions that would lead to the creation of oil. There he stands, beneath an equatorial sun in a forest teeming with life. There are apes, ants and brightly coloured birds, and through the trees and the muddy hillsides flows a wide, brown river. Dr Kingston reaches down and feels the soil. It is rich, fertile and warm with life. Clods of earth are being washed from the banks. There are giant ferns riding the currents, trees uprooted by electric storms, vast garden rafts of vines and grass, all of it flowing westward.

In a region of swampland the flow divides into creeks and channels, spreading its load of silt through mangroves and deep sedimentary pools, before fanning out into thousands of square miles of braided rivers. The jungle's endless cycle of birth and decay washes through this vast region, and there stands Dr Kingston, the only man on earth, watching the creation of Africa's Niger Delta, a river system so powerful it flushes its sediment 100 miles out into a prehistoric sea.

Over millennia the sediment settles, becoming more than a mile deep. The weight and pressure cause the lower levels to become hotter than boiling water. There is more pressure, more heat, until the earth buckles and folds, and out of the carbon furnace bursts oil and gas, pushing upwards through the layers of rock until something so solid lies in its way, it can travel no further. And there it waits, trapped beneath a seal for millions of years, waiting for someone like Dr Kingston to discover it.

The Rover Boys will come together later, but for the moment, Dave Kingston is a young boy growing up in the North Woods near Lake Michigan, trapping wild animals and eating fish fresh from the river. Each summer during the late 1930s he could be found helping his grandfather at the sawmill. There was still no electricity, just kerosene lamps. His grandfather's generation had used whale oil, and thought this new fuel nothing more than a dangerous novelty. They still hadn't mastered its volatility, and thought it a filthy, bothersome liquid that could never compete with coal. It was coal that powered the steam engines in ships and trains on both sides of the Atlantic, coal that powered the factories and created electricity, and there was no reason for anyone to look for an alternative.

But at the turn of the century everything changed. The age of the automobile dawned. Now oil was urgently required to refine into petrol in great quantities. Demand for cars and oil followed the same giddy curve.

By the time Dave Kingston was of school age, even in remote villages people had ditched their horses. Petrol pumps appeared with clock-face dials and luminous globes: 'ESSO', 'SHELL', 'GULF', art deco columns in the brightest enamel. In east Texas there was jubilation when an oilfield called The Black Giant was struck. It produced half a million barrels every day. No one needed to worry that car engines were the size of wardrobes, and drank petrol as fast as you could pour it; they seemed to hit oil every time they dropped a well.

By the time Dave Kingston was ten years old, however, the 'oil fever' nation seemed to be running dry. The discovery rate simply couldn't keep up with the runaway demand for cars. An historic shift was under way. The search for oil needed to move beyond Texas and beyond the shores of the US, to geologically uncharted lands.

America had only one competitor in the international search for oil, and that was the British Empire.

Hanging on the wall of Edgar Lloyd's study in South Wales is a photograph showing him and a dozen African officials looking out over a tropical river. A gleaming American stretch car is waiting on the mud road beside them. There are other shots of Lloyd in white shorts and knee-high socks exploring a mangrove swamp, and slashing through forests with a cutlass. Lloyd was working for BP in colonial Africa just as the search for oil began to extend to other parts of the world, away from the petroleum heartlands of America and the Middle East. He still mocks what he calls the 'Somerset Maugham types', with their 'drawling English accents and ladies in straw hats', and winces at being referred to as an old colonial himself. For him it was a chance to experience an exotic new land, but Britain's goal was to find and exploit natural resources across its empire, and time was running out. It was the mid-1950s and independence movements were gathering momentum. If Britain was to find oil in Africa, the window of opportunity would be slim.

Lloyd is ninety-three now, and one of the last living links to that period. Ironically, he was raised in a town that would have been happier if the new fuel had never been discovered.

The pastures and woodlands of the Welsh valleys were once the site of Britain's own 'Black Giant' discovery, beneath the remote hillsides of Rhonda Valley. Coal lay in bands so thick it broke the surface and turned the streams black. When Lloyd was a boy, the shaft wheels turned day and night, throwing dust as fine as fire-smoke over Ferndale. It was coal that heated the terraced cottages against the long valley winters and lit the gas lamps that threw haunting shapes across Edgar Lloyd's bedroom walls. But even then, coal was losing its place in the world, thanks in part to an audacious gamble by an aristocratic war correspondent and soldier who had turned his hand to politics.

Winston Churchill, First Lord of the Admiralty, was faced with a momentous decision at the start of the First World War. The British fleet ran on coal, but Churchill wanted it to be faster and more efficient. Oil was the answer, he said; it was the fuel of the future, a strategic necessity. Colleagues cautioned against spending such considerable sums on an unproven and potentially combustible renovation, but Churchill had made up his mind. He called it his 'fateful plunge'; once the shipyards had started building new oil-fired vessels and converting existing battleships and cruisers, there was no going back. From now on the British navy would depend on oil. Of course, the refit, and with it Britain's entire maritime capabilities, was reliant on a regular and reliable supply of oil. With nothing suitable in the UK, Churchill knew he would need to look further afield.

He turned to Persia, a British protectorate in the Middle East, where huge oilfields had already been discovered. Helpfully they were under the control of a British company, Anglo-Persian, which was struggling to find the money to exploit its discoveries fully. Churchill offered to help with the necessary investment in return for a controlling stake. Unable to progress without the funds, Anglo-Persian had little choice. The deal meant that Anglo-Persian would come under the authority of the British government.

With Churchill's new oil-powered naval fleet under construction, Britain could pipe as much oil as it required out of Persia, and even help set the price that it was charging itself. Anglo-Persian would become an indispensable arm of government, the official supplier of energy for wartime Britain and for the empire's industrial future. It would soon be renamed British Petroleum, or BP.

Relying on a single supplier so far from home, however, was still a strategic risk; no one was sure how long Persia could be kept inside Britain's imperial orbit, and so the search needed to move on, just like it had in the United States. And when it came to combing the world for resources Britain enjoyed a head start over all its rivals.

The British Empire, at its peak, held sway over one-fifth of the world's population and almost a quarter of its land. Britain was able to call upon its territories for exclusive and generous exploration rights. In Africa, the early favourites for an oil discovery of commercial value were Nigeria, Ghana, Egypt and Sudan. Other European nations had their own contenders; the Portuguese had high hopes for Angola, the French were already drilling in the Algerian desert, and Spain anticipated that Equatorial Guinea would prove fruitful. But for the moment, the whole of the African continent remained near the foot of the geologists' list. There was far more interest in a string of tiny and impoverished desert states over in the Persian Gulf.

By the 1920s, oil seepages were regularly being discovered along the coastlines of Bahrain and Kuwait. Tar had been observed bubbling out of the sand, and there were often traces of oil in the water. In the past, such signs had been the prelude to significant discoveries, and private companies in America were becoming excited. There was talk in Washington of asking the sheiks for permission to drill. Britain stood back from the fuss. If anything came of it, they were confident of taking control: both Bahrain and Kuwait were British protectorates.

With oil, just as with diamonds and gold in the past, the world's largest empire could hope to extract from its subordinates pretty much whatever it wanted, irrespective of what was best for the indigenous population. When the American concession-hunters, in the shape of Gulf Oil and Standard of California, finally decided they were ready to drill in Kuwait and Bahrain in 1928, the British government moved quickly to block them. Officials in Whitehall invoked the 'nationality clause', which meant concessions could only be operated by British nationals working for British companies. London calmly reminded the sheiks of the agreement. They were desperately poor at the time, with economies based on little more than pearl-diving and fishing, and Britain had become a crucial source of funds. Fearful of jeopardizing the relationship, their leaders agreed to the terms of the nationality clause and shut the furious Americans out.[1]

Only temporarily, though. After a full-blown diplomatic row, Britain grudgingly climbed down – not all the way down, but almost. On this occasion, it would wave the nationality clause, allowing the Americans to start exploratory drilling in Bahrain, but only on condition London was kept abreast of developments.

The US must hand over all its communications with the sheiks: every note, every telegram, every geological report. At the first sniff of oil, London needed to be in the loop so that British officials could be first in line for an extraction deal.

The tiny Gulf states erupted with oil. Bahrain first in 1932, then Kuwait, and finally Saudi Arabia six years later. World leaders poured in, their private planes landing on makeshift runways constructed from sand mixed with oil, and began showering the sheiks with dollars and gifts. Japan, Germany, Italy, all tried to gain a foothold in the Middle East, but America and Britain dominated the arena. The chasing pack just couldn't challenge. Both countries exploited London's influence to win generous exploration rights that stretched into the next century. In Abu Dhabi, one contract was struck that would last beyond the lifetime of anyone who negotiated it: seventy-five years.

Britain now had access to richer reserves than ever before, but the geographical spread remained worryingly narrow, confined to Iran and the new discoveries in the Middle East. The risks were obvious, particularly when the Second World War intervened, leaving Britain's oil-producing assets on the other side of the world, across several thousand miles of potentially hostile seas. The Allied governments ordered that all the wells in Kuwait be sealed with cement for the duration, to prevent them from falling into enemy hands. The Gulf went quietly into shutdown.

In an unprecedentedly mechanized and mobile war, secure and plentiful supplies of oil would be the critical strategic commodity. America provided ninety per cent of the Allies' supply. Fifty US tankers were switched from transporting crude along the eastern seaboard and reassigned to the perilous Atlantic crossing instead. The successful targeting of the route by 'wolf packs' of German U-boats led to dangerously depleted stocks in the UK, a looming catastrophe that Churchill described as 'the blackest cloud which we had to face'. At one point, in 1941, the Royal Navy had just two months of fuel in reserve, when seven months' supply was considered the rock-bottom minimum for safety.[2] With America almost single-handedly fuelling the Allied war effort, strain on US domestic reserves began taking its toll. Washington was completely reappraising its view of oil security. US economists were no longer talking about *if* domestic oil fields might one day be exhausted, but *when*.

By 1945, a new world order was beginning to establish itself around the oilfields of the Middle East. Helped by unprecedented investment from the US and Britain, oil production in the Gulf rose spectacularly. But an historic crisis was looming that threatened to dim the lights from London to Edinburgh, and undermine Britain's still-ailing economy as it struggled to rebuild after the war.

Mohammed Mossadegh was a tall, rudder-nosed lawyer, an aristocrat with a whiff of menace, whose theatrical manner and impassioned dislike of the British had won him much support among the Iranian public. As the country's prime minster, he railed against British oilmen meddling in his land. The deal cut by Anglo-Iranian back in 1933 (this was the company's second incarnation before it became BP) had, according to Mossadegh, been grossly unfair. The British were getting Iran's oil on the cheap, while the Iranian population was struggling with disease and poverty. Mossadegh told his followers he would fight the 'dreadful and savage system' and would risk his life to evict the 'world's greatest empire'.

Even the Americans warned Britain that the price it was paying for Iranian oil was unreasonably low, but London wouldn't have it. Clement Attlee's government argued that British investment had led to the discovery in the first place. Without British expertise and capital, he said, the oil would still be in the ground. Mossadegh disagreed. In March 1951, he'd had enough. He nationalized Britain's oil company, seizing its refinery in Abadan, the largest in the world at the time, and kicking out its 2,500 personnel. High drama ensued, with Britain and America sponsoring a coup d'état in Tehran that brought about the downfall of Mossadegh's government and his replacement by the Shah of Iran, effectively as punishment for having had the temerity to stand up to colonial bullying. Mossadegh himself was put on trial and ended his days under house arrest. His foreign minister was less fortunate. He was sentenced do death.

The flow of oil to Britain was soon resumed, but London had learned an important geopolitical lesson. The race was now on to find an alternative source, more secure and more firmly within London's sphere of influence. Africa was beginning to look like a distinct possibility.

'*For Rex*,' reads the inscription in neat blue ink, '*on the occasion of his departure for Darkest Africa, from his fellow BP traders. October, 1955*'. Rex Brown looks up and releases a long, nostalgic sigh. In front of him, on his kitchen table in Hampstead, is an old hardback book stained with tropical damp. Scattered around are photos of men with pencil moustaches, dressed in crisp white shorts. Land Rovers and Morris Minors are parked outside lush art deco villas. Trays of drinks rest on shaded verandas. 'I took this with me, when I left for Nigeria,' says Brown, handing me the book. He's eighty-three now, a little unsteady on his feet, but formidably bright, with an old-school correctness that's easy to steer towards a conspiratorial chuckle.

In golden letters on the spine of the volume is written 'Our Industry'. It's the old handbook for BP employees, first published in 1947. I leaf through the index, and discover that out of 400 pages, there are only four paragraphs on Africa, one of which I begin reading aloud. '*The continent of Africa as a whole offers less hope of finding great oil reserves than almost any other land area of the same extent.*'[3] Rex Brown looks uncomfortable. The fact that Britain's oil giant had mistakenly been so dismissive of Africa's prospects shortly before a series of game-changing discoveries is still a source of embarrassment to him more than sixty years on. 'Am I going to get in trouble for letting you see that?' he asks. 'It's not really something you should publicize.' But it was the prevailing view among geologists at the time. There had been seepages here and there, thick tar leaking from the coast of Nigeria, mysterious slicks in the deep-water wells of Libya, but no one believed Africa could possess reserves of any significance. When Brown headed off to Nigeria, Africa was still a low priority for BP. Even if they struck oil, the expense of drilling in the sodden wilderness of the Niger Delta would be astronomical.

Dr Dave Kingston and his Rover Boys travelled to Africa soon after, but didn't choose Nigeria. Their bosses were wary of trying to compete in a British colony, particularly after what had happened in the Gulf, and preferred to take their chances on the territory of almost any other European power. On this occasion, it was the Portuguese. The country was Guinea Bissau, on the coast of Africa's western bulge, with the extensive mangrove swamps of the mighty Geba River pouring sediment into the Atlantic in similar quantities to that which created the delta in Nigeria.

A new and controversial hypothesis had attracted the attention of the Rover Boys. It was the work of the German explorer and geophysicist Alfred Wegener, and it concerned his theory of continental drift. By Wegener's reckoning, the continents were all constantly on the move, by just a few millimetres every decade, but enough so that over millions of years, they would have migrated halfway around the planet. He argued that Africa had once been attached to the Americas, and as the two had gradually separated, the gap was filled by the Atlantic Ocean. Wegener was treated by many geologists as a crank during his lifetime – he died in 1930 – but by the early 1950s his theory was being taken very seriously indeed.

The idea of continental drift was of great interest to the Rover Boys because oil had been discovered along the coast of Brazil. All they needed to do was trace the corresponding piece of land over the other side of the Atlantic, in West Africa, and if Wegener was right, his theory would transform the race for African oil.

The Rover Boys were run by Esso, if they were run by anyone at all. Their only contact with 30 Rockefeller Plaza, the company's art deco skyscraper in New York, was when they submitted their irregular field reports, containing their most recent geological finds and pleading for another crate of whisky. If they thought the geology seemed promising, they would call in their colleagues, who would fly in seismic equipment to peer deeper beneath the surface. If that looked good, Esso might send in the drills and drop a well or two.

And so it was that Kingston and his colleagues ended up in Guinea Bissau. The desert landscape of the Middle East had been inhospitable, but the jungles of West Africa provided a unique set of challenges. The only way of penetrating the remote regions they needed to explore was on foot through mosquito-ravaged forests and fast-flowing rivers. They ended up hiring a line of porters, in the style of Henry Morton Stanley six decades before; Kingston at the front, his long, wild beard tucked into his shirt, rifle resting on his shoulder, behind him came translators, cooks, guides, all of them scrambling through the mud and undergrowth. In the evenings they would pitch tents, and, if they were lucky, roast an antelope over the fire. The villagers in those steaming, remote forests thought they looked like a gang of armed white men up to no good. 'CIA!' they would shout, 'CIA!' even there, in the late 1950s, they had heard rumours regarding America's Cold War interests in Africa. Kingston would send in the translator to reassure them while he headed off into the bush to shoot a guinea fowl or two for supper. At nightfall they would gather around the fire, chewing charcoaled meat and drinking palm wine, as Kingston told them about the black liquid that was likely to be hidden beneath their feet.

'They didn't really know what oil was,' he recalls. 'We saw them looking for gold, or even diamonds, because they were alluvial: they could pick them out of riverbanks or off the jungle floor; but oil? That was different. That required drills and teams of experts and large sums of money and, even then, the whole thing was a gamble.'

It was the expense, wildly unpredictable but always considerable, that restricted the number of competitors in the field. Aside from

Dave Kingston's Esso, and Rex Brown's BP, the only other significant player in Africa at the start was Dutch company Shell. The costs were just too high for smaller speculators to take the risk. Even if they could afford to drop a well, it would likely be dry on the first attempt, and the second. Six holes were required, on average, before a strike. Drilling at sea was even more demanding, but it seemed to be where much of the geology was pointing. Along the West African coast, where mighty rivers formed ancient deltas that feed into the Atlantic Ocean, was an ideal hunting ground.

Oil and gas are created, mostly, from the rapid burial of dead micro-organisms in an environment where oxygen is so scarce that they cannot decompose. The continent of Africa is split by a series of rift faults – one of which splays out into the Gulf of Guinea near to Nigeria – and mobile tectonic belts where ancient continental collisions have occurred, one curving around the Cape, another looping around the coast of North Africa and down to Guinea-Bissau. Both these geological structures lead to gulleys and open basins forming on the sea floor which are shielded from the normal circulation of Atlantic currents, and thus have lower oxygen levels – anoxic water. These created the trap points for organic sediment flowing from West Africa's rivers over many millions of years, where it compressed itself into vast reservoirs of oil, which the Rover Boys needed to find. Their hope was that these structures had migrated, which they often do, so that they were beneath terra firma, and more easily exploitable. A sea discovery entailed sailing heavy equipment miles into the Atlantic, and drilling at depths of several hundred metres. It was a mammoth task. Each attempt had to be considered at the very highest level in the company. Money would drain away like the monsoon rain off the villages' tin roofs. Offshore exploration would cost five times more than the equivalent on land.

Dave Kingston's men found a promising geological structure in Guinea-Bissau, where the mathematics of the rock pointed to a dipping seam further to the west. They called in the seismic boys, who bounced sound waves through the earth and found a pattern that agreed with Kingston's visual assessment. The drills were brought in and a couple of test holes made. The problem was that west of where they were standing lay the Atlantic Ocean. It seemed the structure's oil-producing rock lay more than a mile offshore.

The company's board in Rockefeller Plaza was consulted, and a drilling platform despatched. The geological structure was thankfully not far beneath the sand. As they broke through there was a surge of hot, good-quality oil. But everyone knew that they had to treat the initial discovery with caution. Countless geological events could have corrupted it over the millennia. Suddenly, through the pumps came a tremendous gush of salt water. The oil was just a thin layer floating on an ancient column of water. For the moment that was the end of Guinea's hopes.

'Beware, beware, the bight of Benin,' Rex Brown recited to himself as he climbed from the plane in the northern Nigerian city of Kano in January 1956, 'where few come out but many go in.' Packed into his case beside his BP handbook was a copy of *Four Guineas*, a guide to Africa by the British writer Elspeth Huxley. As an introduction to the continent, it could hardly have been darker. 'Tiny skulls of monkeys,' wrote Huxley, 'wings of bats and small crows, the antlers of baby deer, dog paws, bundles of feathers, all exactly like the witches' brew in *Macbeth*.'[4] Huxley was describing a witchdoctor's stall on a Lagos market, but it all added to the impression that Brown was entering some primordial and hostile land, rather than a country on the cusp of independence.

Kano was a baked-mud labyrinth of flat-roofed homes and smooth clay walls. Buildings tumbled into each other like spilt bricks. Women drifted across its hot squares carrying water in tall earthenware pots, as men squatted in the road selling groundnuts from wicker buckets. 'Sometimes people would float in from the plateau,' chuckled Brown, 'naked but for leaves fore and aft.' He took lodgings in a large, breezy apartment above a bank with two other BP employees. Their British Morris Minor car was parked outside, and at night the houseboys would drop by to blow out the kerosene lamps.

Kano seemed an-out-of-the-way place and yet, even here, the British were turning on the colonial charm. The year Rex Brown arrived in the city, Buckingham Palace despatched the Duchess of Kent to parade along its mud avenues in a Rolls-Royce. Curious crowds turned out from across the city, and that evening she stayed in the residence of the senior district officer. What the residents of Kano made of such a conspicuous display of wealth has not been recorded, but the growing nationalist movement viewed such visits as a useful tool of recruitment. Among the residents of Kano that day was a thirteen-year-old schoolboy named Sani Abacha, no doubt intrigued by the arrival of a British duchess in his sprawling largely Muslim city. Quiet and withdrawn to the point of being assumed intellectually slow, Abacha would later acquire more wealth than the British Royal family, and more power. After multiple coups, and driven by the theft of oil money, he would become Nigeria's tenth leader after independence.

A British oil company, the D'Arcy Exploration Company, had begun searching for oil in Nigeria in 1918, almost half a century before the duchess's visit. D'Arcy was a wholly owned subsidiary of the Anglo-Persian Oil Company (BP), and would lead the company's drive for diversification outside of Persia. In the early days its exploration teams discovered frequent seepages around the Niger Delta, but D'Arcy's geologists classified it as 'dead oil', and recommended pulling out of the country altogether. The company's most prolific discoverer, the geologist E. H. Cunningham Craig, had assessed the potential of South Nigeria in 1922 and advised, 'It is not worth spending another cent on the concession.'[5] Now, with Britain's supply confined to unpredictable regions of the Middle East, D'Arcy was keen to take another look. The fact they were on friendly soil, in British colonial territory, promised to give them the run of the land. But when their interest had first been renewed in 1938, there had been a problem. D'Arcy wanted to enter the race in a joint venture with Shell, and Shell was a Dutch concern.

The British authorities were not enthusiastic. They dragged out the 'nationality clause' once again, banning Shell from setting foot in Nigeria. But the Colonial Office pointed out that, working alone, D'Arcy would not have the resources to engage in a pioneering exploration of such a vast and geologically unexplored territory. Success was more likely in partnership. A face-saving solution was required. British officials suggested that Shell might want to change the composition of its board, filling it with British nationals. Afterwards, the freshly Anglicized company was welcomed in and given exclusive rights to explore Nigeria in partnership with D'Arcy.

Shell-D'Arcy, which was renamed Shell-BP in 1956, soon enjoyed all the privileges of a British-run company working under a British colonial regime. Not only was the joint venture charged very favourable rents to explore on Crown Land, it was openly supported by the government in the face of growing local opposition.

The exploration side of the business was the job of Shell, which was permitted to drill wherever its geologists wished. There was no need to seek permission from landowners. If locals objected and tried to resist, it was they who risked going to jail. Shell-BP's bulldozers and rigs moved from one tribal land to another after the Second World War, brushing away protestors and calling in the police at the first hint of trouble. A token sum of compensation was paid to those whose land was used for drilling, but there was little concern for the rights of local communities. The growing excitement among British officials about potential oil discoveries, and the assumption that it belonged to the British Crown, played right into the hands of the independence movement.

Nnamdi Azikiwe, or Zik as he became known, was an Igbo born into a privileged family in the mainly Muslim north of Nigeria. His father, a clerk in the British administration, travelled extensively, and was worldly enough to realize that his son's education would best be served in the United States. Zic attended four different US universities, including Columbia in New York, and spent his holidays working as a journalist for the pioneering Associated Negro Press in Chicago. He returned to West Africa newly politicized, and energetically anti-colonial. His wish was to be involved in politics, but there was no meaningful role that he could find in Nigeria. Instead, in 1934, he accepted an offer to edit a newspaper, the *African Morning Post*, based in British Gold Coast – what was later to become Ghana.

His pungent, incisive writing in a column called 'Inside Stuff by Zik' established his reputation as a radical nationalist, and, although alarm was caused among the British administrators in Accra, it gathered Zik a following. While he was giving a speech, a shy, young student teacher plucked up the courage to introduce himself. His name, he said, was Kwame Nkrumah, and he wanted to know more about Zik's vision of 'New Africa', a place where both ethnic affiliations and European imperialism would be erased. The two men became friends and it is said that Zik inspired Nkrumah on the journey that would see him become the first leader of post-independence Ghana.

Zik's real ambition, however, was to light the nationalist fuse in Nigeria. He returned and established the famous *West African Pilot* in Lagos in 1937. Its masthead read 'Show the light, and the people will find the way', and Zik continued his often artful denunciation of colonialism, with plenty of new ammunition. Among his most deadly assaults was a campaign that targeted Britain's obsessive search for oil.

In 1945, Nigeria's governor, Sir Arthur Richards, later the 1st Baron Milverton, implemented a banal-sounding set of regulations and ordinances, some of which concerned mineral deposits. They gave ownership of all Nigeria's resources to the British Crown; oil, diamonds, gold, anything found in Nigeria was hers, whether 'in, under, or upon, any land in Nigeria and of all rivers, streams and watercourses throughout Nigeria'. With the accession of Queen Elizabeth to the throne, the wording seemed to suggest that all Nigeria's natural assets would be passed to 'her heirs' and 'her successors' in perpetuity. Coming at a moment when Nigerians expected the colonial grip to be loosening rather than tightening, the ordinances provided a golden opportunity for Zik and his nationalist supporters.

He rechristened the regulations *The Obnoxious Ordinances*, and had a field day writing furious articles for *The Pilot*. Shell-BP, he

told his readers, was exploring the Niger delta not to help benefit
a future independent Nigeria, but so that the country's riches, even
after independence, would continue flowing to London.

Dave Kingston and his Rover Boys were still pursuing the theory
of continental drift, and had found themselves in the lifeless moonscape of the Anti-Atlas Mountains in southwest Morocco. A few
half-hearted holes had been drilled by French colonizers back in the
1930s, but only a trickle of oil had been discovered: not enough
to hold the interest of officials in Paris. By 1956, the French had
relinquished their protectorate – their interests in Morocco were
far less deep-rooted than in neighbouring Algeria – but the sultan,
Mohammed V, did not have the financing or the expertise to explore
for oil properly on his own. Just like other African states would
discover on achieving independence, Morocco had no choice but to
call in the oil giants from the US and Britain. Among them were Esso
and Dave Kingston's Rover Boys.

They were hoping to find Jurassic reefs deep beneath the foothills
of the Anti-Atlas near to the Atlantic Ocean. 'It was like studying a
history book,' Kingston recalled, 'only some of the pages had been
torn out, and those are the ones we had to find.' Unfortunately,
when they did find them, they indicated that, once again, the oil
lay far out beneath the waves. A drilling platform was sailed in at
enormous expense, and for several weeks the world's oil industry
held its breath. Kingston was in Esso's London office when the
telex arrived.

'STRUCK OIL!' it read.

Soon he was in a helicopter flying low over the Atlantic on his
way to Esso's offshore rig. They had drilled almost a mile and half
through a fold in the rock, and had been rewarded with a taste of
light oil. The drilling manager was ready for the last push through
the rock seal – a Jurassic limestone trapdoor from which the hot oil
should shoot to the surface. Kingston returned to London a happy
man. The next telex was less good.

'Shoe polish,' it read.

'Shoe polish' was the industry's nickname for sticky bitumen. It meant water had bled through a fracture and bacteria had eaten the oil over millions of years. Nothing was left but a substance similar to tar.

The race for Africa's first oil moved seamlessly on, this time along the North African coast, to a kingdom where Britain and America held political sway.

'Do You Play Bridge?' the advert had enquired of its readers in January 1956. Edgar Lloyd had seen it in *The Guardian* and *The Telegraph* and was intrigued enough to apply. The job was for a construction engineer. Why, he wondered, did an oil company like BP want to know if prospective employees enjoyed a game of cards? The interview passed without the subject being raised and Lloyd secured the position. He left the Welsh valleys for oil's hopeful new frontier, the Kingdom of Libya, three months later, in the spring of 1956.

A barren, sun-blasted land, whose tiny population lived mainly on a fringe of fertile coastline, Libya had featured little in previous explorations. There had once been a suggestion that it might share similar geological features with parts of the Arabian Gulf, but that had been roundly ridiculed by mainstream geologists. Even if they had wanted to explore in Libya, the country was so disorganized there was no prospect of getting permission. It was one of the poorest countries in the world, dependent on the sale of scrap metal left behind when Rommel's army was driven out, along with the Italian colonizers, by the British in 1943. Burnt-out tanks and engine parts were Libya's currency. The idea of prospecting for oil there, with ninety per cent of the country taken up by Saharan desert, seemed fantastical. Any company wanting to take the African gamble would concentrate on West Africa first. Libya was right at the bottom of the pile.

But there was a reason BP had flown Edgar Lloyd into Tripoli.

The Suez Canal was the main artery of oil for Europe, carrying two-thirds of its supply, more than a million barrels from the Gulf every day. So dependent was Europe on the waterway that tankers had evolved to fit its width and depth. The canal had originally served as the gateway to British India, the jewel in the colonial crown, but had later become an oil superhighway, a 120-mile shortcut across the Egyptian desert from the Gulf to the Med. Without it, tankers had to embark on a four-week voyage around the South African Cape. The canal cut the journey time, and the fuel bills, in half. But the fact that it carried such strategically important supplies made the canal, and the land adjacent to it, a stew of competing interests.

Britain controlled a broad corridor of territory along the banks of the canal that stretched along two-thirds of its length. The 'Canal Zone' amounted to 9,000 square miles of British territory, a huge complex of warehouses, airfields and barracks that was then the largest overseas military base in the world. To Britain it was an indispensable strategic territory at the crossroads of Europe, Africa and Asia. To the Arab nationalists it was an obscene display of colonialism that required immediate liquidation.

In July 1952, a clandestine group of dissident officers in the Egyptian army launched a coup to overthrow the debauched and corrupt King Farouk, a leader who had meekly capitulated to the British occupation and who spent most of his time at his coastal retreat in Alexandria, seemingly unaware of the competing forces trying to establish a new political order in his country. Late on 22 July 1952, the Society of Free Officers, led by Lt-Col. Gamal Abdel Nasser, cornered Farouk's entire army command in military headquarters, and seized power with minimal resistance. The initial aim was simply to depose the monarchy and introduce a series of loosely socialist reforms, but it became a rolling revolution, with opponents supressed and imprisoned and with the Free Officers taking control of the country, under the newly formed Revolutionary Command Council (RCC). Nasser, a taciturn, bookish and hitherto secretive man, became the organization's secretary general and seized complete control of the government in October 1954. He wanted a new world order, an Arab North Africa that fused organically with the Middle

East, creating a pan-Arab wedge of land starting at the Atlantic coast of Morocco and taking in Algeria, Tunisia, Libya and Egypt, with himself as leader. The last thing he needed was such a visible symbol of European imperialism cutting right across his territory. Evicting the 80,000 British troops was a priority. Even for Britain, grudgingly mindful that these were the closing days of empire, it had become an unwieldy and expensive operation. They agreed a deal with Nasser in October 1954, promising to withdraw from the Canal Zone in twenty months' time, while leaving just a few civilian technicians to wind things down over a seven-year period. That should have been the end of the matter, but instead Britain responded to an increasingly hot-headed Nasser with a series of reckless acts that precipitated the biggest international crisis since the end of the Second World War.

It began with the Egyptian leader's hugely ambitious plans to build a three-mile-long dam at Aswan on the Nile. The enormous expense and expertise required for such a project meant that he would need foreign assistance, and both Britain and America stepped forward to signal their support and keep Nasser relatively sweet. Relations were edgy but functioning. There was an undertow, though, a constant finger-pointing from Nasser about 'imperialist regimes' and 'foreign occupation' and the rallying of his people against the West. In turn, Britain and the US doubted Nasser's insistence that he was a neutral in the Cold War, preferring to believe he was a communist sympathizer bent on destabilizing the region.

It was a military strike by Israel that triggered the descent, a raid on Egyptian army camps in the Gaza Strip in March 1955. As a result, Nasser became convinced that he needed to undertake a rapid and massive expansion of his army. He chose to shop for his military hardware in Moscow, buying fighter aircraft, bombers and tanks. London and Washington were incredulous. As far as they were concerned, Nasser was inviting the Soviet Bloc to establish a foothold in the Middle East. They promptly rescinded their offer of help with the Aswan Dam. A livid Nasser responded on 26 July 1956 with a move that stunned the world. He nationalized the Suez Canal. Its ownership had been in the hands of Britain and France since its

construction in 1866, but now it would belong to the Egyptian state
and the tolls would help pay for his dam.

London's main concern was the passage of oil. Instead of respond-
ing with artful international diplomacy to try to isolate Nasser and
force him to back down, Prime Minister Anthony Eden, burning
with imperialist indignation that bordered on hysteria, decided to
teach 'the upstart dictator' a lesson. His plan would involve the
French, who were furious with the Egyptian leader for supporting
the Algerian nationalists of the *Front de Libération Nationale* (FLN)
fighting French forces in their war of independence.

Britain and France secretly met with Israeli officials just outside
Paris to plot a military assault that would become the last, strang-
ulated gasp of empire. Nasser's threats of war against the Israelis
had reached a crescendo, and the Israelis were itching to flex
some military muscle. Wouldn't it appear justifiable, suggested the
European officials, if Israel were to invade Egypt across the virtually
uninhabited Sinai Peninsula, driving towards the Suez Canal?
Wouldn't it also appear reasonable for Britain, on the pretext of
separating the combatants, to insist that Egypt withdraw from the
canal? If Nasser refused, wouldn't it be acceptable for Britain and
France to launch military action to take the canal back?

And so it was. The Israelis invaded on 29 October 1956, as agreed.
Britain and France came crashing in behind them less than a week
later, their paratroopers landing in the Canal Zone and their aircraft
bombing Egyptian positions. They deployed marines at the canal's
entrance into the Mediterranean. But instead of the world thanking
Europe for stepping into the crisis, there was global condemnation.

In Moscow, Khrushchev threatened to retaliate on behalf of Nasser
by launching a nuclear attack. Saudi Arabia, the source of Europe's
oil in the first place, imposed an embargo on London and Paris,
stopping shipments through the canal. But it was Nasser himself
who performed the *coup de grâce*. Though his forces had been swept
aside by the invaders, he ordered that ships currently queuing along
the waterway should be scuttled, thus blocking it irretrievably for
the foreseeable future.

Britain and France had been outfoxed. They were now in a worse position than they had been before their invasion. No oil whatsoever could come through the canal. Even the Americans thought Europe's behaviour disgraceful. President Eisenhower refused to provide his allies with emergency supplies of oil, threatened to sell US holdings of sterling bonds and demanded that the British withdraw. Eden had disastrously underestimated the American opposition to his adventure. He was publicly humiliated and resigned in early January 1957.

The lights in Europe just about stayed on, but Britain was forced to sail its oil the long way round – via the Cape and along the West African coast. It had been an oil calamity worse than the shutdown in Iran. European minds were now focused more intently on Africa than before. Nigeria would be good, just halfway down the coast, but Libya would be even better. It was just a short hop across the Mediterranean Sea, and the country was in the hands of a staunch Western ally. There would be no risk of becoming entangled with Arab revolutionaries ever again: and against this backdrop BP's Edgar Lloyd arrived in Libya.

He landed at Tripoli International Airport six months after the Suez Crisis, with a wave of other BP staff, all hoping this would be the scene of the African breakthrough.

The Libyan monarch, King Idris, was a pushover for London. A frail and bespectacled Muslim scholar, he was entirely out of step with the rest of North Africa. While other leaders saw a future riding the glittering coat-tails of Colonel Nasser and the guerrillas fighting the French in Algeria, King Idris couldn't have been more repulsed by the thought. He had always looked westwards, and would continue to do so. Not only was his country receiving financial aid from Britain and America, it was Britain that had installed him on his throne in the first place. Idris had helped the Allies fight the Italians in North Africa during the Second World War and, in return, they had offered him his own kingdom. If Britain and America wanted to explore his desert for oil, Idris had no objections.

His kowtowing to the West was bitterly opposed by many young Libyans, among them a fifteen-year-old Bedouin schoolboy named Muammar al-Gaddafi. He was the son of a goatherd, but was already shining at school and taking an interest in nationalist politics. Gaddafi and his friends were passionate admirers of Nasser. The sooner King Idris was out of the way – and they could take part in Nasser's exciting Pan-Arab vision – the better.

'Look out for the bullet holes in the airport,' Edgar Lloyd's manager had told him as he left BP's London office. 'I put them there in 1942, flying my Spitfire!' Soon he was speeding along an Italian-built highway in his BP Land Rover, past olive and lemon groves and through a tall corridor of poplar trees south of Tripoli to a large concession BP had just won from the king. After some hours he came to a barren plain of dust and scrubland, across which a series of wooden pegs had been laid. The pegs marked the intended route of a road BP was building to carry heavy drilling equipment to a remote desert spot where seismic tests had suggested the presence of oil. The work had already been agonizingly slow, because of the care taken to avoid any of the estimated 3 million unexploded land mines left over from the Second World War.

Sitting on the floor in the middle of the pegs was a young school-master.

'You cannot build your road here,' said the man, 'unless you pay them.' He motioned towards a group of squatting Bedouin.

'For what?' asked Lloyd.

The man nodded towards a group of tents. 'For their damaged crops,' he said, 'and the cattle that will miscarry because of the noise, and the graves you will desecrate.'

Lloyd could see only thorns and boulders.

The following day he returned with a renowned Palestinian fixer, an immaculate businessman with a hypnotic charm and a huge American Lincoln that paddled through the desert like a glinting alien spaceship. The fixer took the Bedouin chief by the arm and led him away behind the tents. When the pair emerged, he announced BP had a new representative who would make sure the work suffered no more delays. The Bedouin leader put a hand on his heart and saluted Edgar Lloyd, the British government and BP. No oil had yet been found, but these private companies possessed greater wealth than their host country's entire exchequer. The impoverished tribes of Libya were already spotting opportunities.

The workmen on that BP road used limestone blocks and quarry-fill, 'just like in ancient Rome', constructing the surface with their bare hands and primitive wooden tools. At lunchtime they ate cat food mixed with nuts, which they happily washed down with cans of a drink called Kitty Cola. Lloyd had never witnessed such poverty. Even the king himself was in dire straits. Idris had recently sent a begging letter to London asking for £4.5 million of emergency aid, the latest in a long line of requests. Britain had grudgingly obliged, but made it clear it was losing patience. It had already asked the Americans to do the charitable thing next time it was needed.

During the long winter evenings Lloyd and his BP colleagues sampled the bars and cafés of Tripoli and pondered the months they would have to spend together in a shared apartment with no television, no telephone and only sporadic electricity. That was why the job advertisement had asked if they could play bridge. But the arrival of the young oil men had made a strong impression on Idris and his officials. If the Europeans were investing so heavily, the evidence must be building that Libya was a likely source of petroleum. Idris was no fool. He realized that these wealthy Western companies would be willing to pay a lot simply for the possibility of striking oil, and a new system of charging for exploration rights was born.

Instead of awarding a single concession across his entire kingdom, he divided it into multiple concessions of different sizes to suit all budgets. Onto the market came a promising slice of anticline in northern Cyrenaica, portions of a desolate shale desert in the Sirte Basin, and an option to drill beneath the Great Sand Sea. All oil companies were welcome, but they would need to bid against their rivals for each concession. Even then, successful bidders couldn't hold on to their acquisitions indefinitely. There had been a tiresome tactic in the past, where companies would rent a concession with no intention of drilling simply to block their competitors. Idris wanted to hurry things along. Every five years they would need to select which territory they were least keen on, and toss it back in the pot for another round of bidding. That way, the oil companies would need to keep exploring, and Idris's government would keep the dollars pouring in, whether oil was discovered or not.

Among Libyans the strategy seemed like a piece of financial wizardry, with twenty-two rich Western companies scrapping over eighty-five plots of barren and inhospitable desert. A feverish territorial competition began, which promised to transform the fortunes of North Africa's poorest country. The system needed to be beyond reproach. Everything relied on the transparency and honesty of the king's men because it was they, in the shape of the Libyan Petroleum Commission, who would choose the winning bids.

The corruption of these officials was not long in coming.

While Libya was opening its doors to allcomers, hopes of an oil breakthrough in Nigeria were entirely in the hands of the colonial government's sole guest, Shell-BP. Above Port Harcourt small planes buzzed through the coastal thermals, conducting aerial surveys of the vast swamplands of the Niger Delta, a sprawling hothouse of creeks and tangled mangrove covering an area of land the size of Belgium. Teams of surveyors paddled the insect-infested waterways, trying to make geological sense of sedimentary deposits that had been building for millions of years.

Fifty miles west of Port Harcourt, perched on dry ground between two looping arms of the Niger Delta, sat a small fishing community called Oloibiri. Each morning the men would paddle their tree-scooped canoes into the slow-moving river, returning with fish for their wives to smoke over an open fire. They had lived like that for generations, steadily struggling through the seasons like any other delta village, more or less untouched by modernity, unaffected by governance from Lagos or by the race for oil.

Sunday Inengite was a confident and inquisitive nineteen-year-old, born and raised in the village. In the summer of 1955, he spotted several Europeans exploring the waterways and wandered over to strike up conversation. He had never seen white men this deep in the delta before. It turned out they were from Britain, Holland and Germany, all living in houseboats with food supplies and equipment. The party was accompanied by district officers from the British Colonial Authority who, mindful of previous protests against Shell-BP, instructed the locals not to disturb them. Sunday and his friends watched from a distance, and assumed they were searching for palm oil.[6] It was only when the white men stumbled from the forest covered in 'black stuff', shouting and waving, that they knew something else was going on.

In the spring of 1956, Shell-BP finally struck oil. Nigeria had won the African oil race.

Exhilaration, exhaustion, soaked shirts and hugs. All they had were buckets of hot black sludge and grit, but the geologists knew what it signified. The problem was that the site was several days walk into the swamps. Extraction was going to be more technically challenging, and costly, than anything the oil industry had attempted before. The loading point for the tankers would need to be the mouth of the Bonny River – fifty miles away. It was the equivalent of scrambling and wading from Piccadilly Circus to the Kent Coast, through dust storms and perpetual rain, felling mangroves as thick as lighthouses with nothing but machetes. The pipeline alone would take two years to build.

Today, maps of the Niger Delta show a thick latticework of wells and pipes. Oil fields are so plentiful it is as if someone flicked a paintbrush from Warri to Calabar, spraying red dots across the region and out into the sea.

A series of new discoveries followed hot on the heels of Oloibiri, and BP staff were flown in from around the world. Edgar Lloyd was transferred out of Libya into Nigeria's Port Harcourt as a new golden age dawned for the company. The town, once a small colonial export facility for coal, was transformed. There were chalk-white bungalows, billiards and tennis courts down at the club and even a golf course where a group of Irish priests would compete after travelling from their remote presbytery in the bush. Traditional rural communities began relocating with the promise of European money. People who had previously made a living from the fertile soil of the delta, from cocoa, palm oil, rubber, timber, pineapples, began migrating into town. The crops that had sustained the country were gradually abandoned. Nigeria had once been the world's biggest exporter of cocoa, but the allure of crude oil would see thousands leave their farms for a room beneath a tin roof and a job laying roads, cutting forests or running errands for the Europeans. Nigeria was beginning a journey that would gradually make its economy entirely dependent on oil.

'Master! Master!' shouted Lloyd's head-boy, running terrified from the bush. They were cutting a route for the pipeline through a section of forest. 'Big ju-ju, Master! Big ju-ju!' Before he could reason with the man, the whole work gang had retreated into the clearing, waving their cutlasses and shouting. Nothing could persuade them to return to work and so Lloyd went to fetch the village chief. He, along with a medicine man and a couple of elders, climbed into the BP Land Rover to investigate. Back at the cutting-front they found a collection of beads and sacrificial animal bones in an earthenware bowl on the floor. Next to them was an empty bottle of de Kuyper's gin. Someone had been using black magic.

The chief explained to Lloyd that a few years earlier the daughter of a village elder had been banished into the forest for refusing to marry the man chosen by her father. Later, a farmer had found the girl hanging from a tree. This was the spot BP had stumbled upon. The medicine man would need to placate the ju-ju, so that the men could return to work. That would, of course, require a fee, just a bit of 'dash'. It was trifling, really, but the culture of irregular payments and backhanders quickly spread and would soon reach far deeper into Nigerian society. Next it was the Nigerian planning officer who required 'compensation' in order for the pipeline to progress. 'You've stolen our sand,' he said, and when Lloyd pointed out it had merely been shifted from one river to another, he quickly realized he wasn't addressing the official's overriding requirement.

After the strike at Oloibiri the Europeans held a party on their houseboat and invited everyone to see what they had discovered. It couldn't have looked like much – dollops of tar veined with stones and sand – but the white men were ecstatic and erected long wooden tables on the banks of the river where they served beer and food. 'They made us be happy,' remembered Sunday Inengite. 'They made us clap like fools, and dance as if we were trained monkeys.'[7]

A journalist who spent time with Sunday Inengite years later, when he had become chief of the village, described how he had kept the original contract signed with Shell. It was a remarkable agreement, awarding the oil company the right to the two-acre plot for a period of five years. The rental fee was £1 per acre, per year: £10 for the duration.[8] Not bad for the rights to extract millions of barrels of oil.

In Oloibiri today, conditions are still primitive. There is only sporadic electricity. Oil companies drained the site and moved on, taking the pipes with them and sealing the well. It stopped producing in 1972. All that is left is a rusty Christmas tree of plumbing beside a weathered sign that reads 'OLOIBIRI WELL No 1, Drilled June 1956'.

The history books will always record Oloibiri as the winner of Africa's oil race, but a quiet discovery of huge commercial value had in fact been made six months earlier. The reason it is rarely mentioned, however, is because it happened in the middle of an African war zone.

The scorched village of Edjeleh lay on a plain of grit and gravel where sandstorms sometimes a mile high blew in from the Sahara, smothering the sun for days on end. Although the village was close to some promising Libyan concessions, the oil companies were never much interested in Edjeleh itself. A twitch of the cartographer's pen had left it on the other side of the border, not in Western-friendly Libya but in Algeria.

The country was a French possession, but rebellion had exploded in 1954, and had become a fierce war of independence characterized by massacres and torture on both sides. The main reason Paris doggedly clung on while the death toll soared was the possibility of discovering gas and oil. Algeria was the French empire's best hope. As fighting raged in the more populous regions on the coast, a French oil consortium was able, in 1955, to move unhindered into the sparsely populated southern desert. Protected by an armed unit, the exploration team managed to wheel drilling equipment to the edges of Edjeleh, almost in sight of the Libyan concessions on the other side of the border. Canvas tents were erected, and a 100-foot rig winched into place. It looked like a tower made from Meccano, but its drill penetrated hundreds of metres through solid rock. After several weeks, it broke through an ancient seal, sending a column of hot oil shooting into the sky. The French had, technically, won the race. But how could they make it pay? There was no chance of building a pipeline while the war was going on. Neither were they prepared to give it up to the Algerians.

France quickly realized that all it really required of Algeria was the empty southern desert quarter. The populated coastal region was worth nothing, though it contained a million *pieds-noirs*, non-Muslim settlers of European origin. Paris came up with idea of dividing the country, splitting it between a self-governing north and a French-governed south. There was no point in trying to disguise their motives. The French began to turn on the charm. If only the Algerians would trust them, they would extract the oil and share it fairly with the impoverished desert tribes. The Algerians chose not to. It seemed to them like this was a fading colonial power – France had already lost its Indo-Chinese colonies after a disastrous war – making a desperate last grasp at cheap oil. The war dragged on for eight years, putting Edjeleh out of play.

But what about the corresponding piece of land over the border? It was possible they could drill into the same geological structure from the Libyan side.

Oil companies stampeded to pay court to King Idris. They

purchased forty-five concessions in just two months, and a spree of urgent drilling began.[9] The borderlands around Edjeleh yielded nothing of value, and the whole circus departed as quickly as it had arrived. The next destination was Libya's Sirte Basin, where Esso, the most prolific of drillers, was about to become involved in one of the oil industry's luckiest-ever steals, a discovery that would make Libya the hottest property in Africa.

There was a vacant strip of land in the scorched moonscape of the Sirte Basin. It lay between two concessions, and remained unclaimed because it seemed to have no potential. On one side was Esso, on the other, Mobil. The Libyans were unhappy about dead acreage in the middle of their quilt-work of expensive desert. They offered it to Mobil, but Mobil said no. Esso was minded to do the same, but the Libyans badgered the company until it agreed to take the concession. Esso called in its seismic team to carry out a quick survey of the neglected plot.

When the first data began arriving at their tented base in the desert, they thought it must be a mistake. The figures seemed to indicate that, right beneath their feet, was an oilfield of spectacular proportions. They quietly rolled in the rig and began drilling. It was the spring of 1959. A mile beneath the Libyan desert, Esso hit the jackpot.

It was a staggering find. There were 2 billion barrels of oil down there, with several interconnecting reservoirs that promised more. It became known as the Zelten Field and heralded an unseemly Libyan oil rush.

One summer evening in West London I was sitting in a cramped Indian Restaurant with an oilman who holds the secrets to some of North Africa's most contentious early deals. David Orser is an American who cut his teeth in the Libyan desert, swept up in that first wave of exploration fever.

'They used to call him "straight-arrow",' chuckled his wife across the table. She was a pretty ex-hippy, all bangles and ashrams. 'He wanted to play everything by the book, didn't you, David?' Orser

nodded and smiled and pecked at his chicken korma. He was
wearing an oversized Hawaiian shirt and a pair of crumpled canvas
shorts. On one of his legs was a long strawberry-coloured scar where
his 83-year-old kneecap had just been replaced with a plastic one.
'His ex-wife thought he must have had a Swiss bank account, didn't
she, David, and the lawyers searched high and low for it, didn't they,
when the divorce happened, but nothing.' Orser nodded along and
sipped his beer. 'He was a straight-shooter, always have been, haven't
you, David?... pity, really... you should have taken the money when
you could!' and the two of them crumpled into laughter and clasped
each other's hands across the paper tablecloth.

David Orser wasn't just a straight-arrow, he was the voice of reason
who refused to get drawn into the madness. Orser was a problem-
solver. While everyone else was looking for a route through the Libyan
maze, he was constructing his own ladder to climb right over it.

When he arrived in Tripoli on behalf of US giant Mobil in February
1960, it was shortly after that first Esso strike, and the oilmen were
taking over. There were geologists, engineers, salesmen, negotiators,
intermediaries and dealmakers. Golf courses were under construction.
They dined at chicken shacks, and drank Budweiser in US-style bars.
So many Americans had arrived that they even established their own
baseball league. The industry was 'following the oil' – wherever a big
strike occurred, it was always assumed more would follow – and now
Libya was that place and Tripoli was a boom town.

Orser and his family settled into the city's expat community,
living at first in a primitive duplex with no cupboards and only
wood-burning stoves against the winter chill. The country remained
desperately poor. The Esso discovery had been in a remote spot, far
out in the Sahara Desert. A pipeline would be needed to link it to
a port and that could take years to build. Even then, there was no
refinery; the infrastructure just didn't exist. Although Idris promised
that the Zelten Field would revolutionize the country's fortunes, it
was going to take time to work its way through the economy. But
there were signs already that the money was being diverted into the
pockets of the king's men.

In a flash, Idris had gone from being an impoverished hermit, writing begging letters to Britain and the US, to a king whose country was awash with dollars, able to make rich men of whomever he chose. The opportunity for personal enrichment came at the point of auction. The oilmen were prepared to be extremely generous to whomever put them in pole position. 'There were kickbacks galore,' says Orser, 'and many greedy hands.' One new boy on the block, a small independent American company, learned how to fill those greedy hands like no other. Its name was Occidental Petroleum.

On an autumn day in 1967, David Orser was sitting in his Mobil office when news reached him that seemed to suck the air from the room.

It had all begun when Mobil was forced to surrender one of its least-promising concessions at the end of the five-year cycle imposed by Idris. There was to be an auction. As usual, one of the big seven oil companies was expected to win. This tiny outfit from California, Occidental, or Oxy as it was known, was sniffing around, and no one could understand why. It had no expertise in oil exploration outside the US, no experience of running concessions, and anyway, Idris's prices were too high, way out of Oxy's league.

But, despite competitive bids from the other players, Oxy somehow walked away with Mobil's former concession: blocks 102 and 103, 2,000 square miles of bleak, gravelly desert in the Sirte Basin, more than 100 miles from the coast. The others scoffed from the sidelines. Oxy would have no idea where or how to drill, and no chance of riding out the inevitable dry holes. They'd be bankrupt before the concession was up.

Then came the news that had so alarmed David Orser's office in the autumn of 1966. Oxy had struck oil, first at block 102, and then at 103, not just a few drops but a spectacular field. It dwarfed the first Libyan discovery. There were 3 billion barrels down there, making it one of the most prolific deposits in the world. Sweet Libyan crude came shooting straight from the ground. To make matters worse it had happened right beneath an abandoned Mobil desert camp. The ageing seismic apparatus that Mobil used meant they had missed it.

The discovery required an appropriate celebration. There was to be a party for the king. A vast marquee was erected in the desert, its floors laid with fine Persian carpets, rose petals scattered along its walkways. Oxy presented Idris with a Fabergé cigarette case, and his wife with a Fabergé beauty box. In the middle of the celebrations, the company's ecstatic bosses announced they would rename the block. From now on, it was to be called 'The Idris Field'. Of course, the Mobil team only heard about all this second-hand. They had not been invited to the party.

But the question remained: how did an unknown oil company manage to leap the rest of the field?

Occidental Petroleum was run by an American industrialist named Dr Armand Hammer, or simply 'the Doctor'. He was a dealmaker extraordinaire, a tireless schmoozer who was already in his sixties when Occidental arrived in Libya but had lost none of his appetite for moneymaking, or his knack of knowing who to pay off. His Libyan contact book was empty. The country had been in the business deep-freeze so long, he had no connections there. When the Doctor heard about that first Esso strike, he had sent out a speculative team with a brief to bring him back a piece of the action.

It was said that the route to oil success in Libya passed through the bank accounts of a man called Omar Shelhi.[10] Shelhi was a short, bullish man who had spent time in exile with King Idris during the war and was now treated as his adopted son. Idris had needed someone to oversee the bidding process, and Shelhi seemed the obvious choice.

It hadn't taken the Doctor long to realize that Shelhi was his target. As it turned out, the king's most trusted lieutenant was so well insulated by layers of dealmakers and officials that the Doctor needed intermediaries just to introduce him to the intermediaries.

As the deadline for bids approached, he finally managed to secure a meeting with a facilitator called Hans Kunz, a Swiss citizen who had begun his working life as a lowly fixer in the oil industry. Kunz passed the Doctor to his business partner, a man called Kemal Zade, a Soviet who had graduated from the London School of Economics. Zade didn't actually know Shelhi, and so couldn't organize the introduction personally, but he did know Shelhi's brother. He could pass the Doctor to him. It was a maddeningly circuitous route, but with just days to go until the deadline for bids, the Doctor had no better option.

Even that plan had a hitch. The two intermediaries didn't want to recommend the Doctor without getting to know him personally. They needed to make sure he wasn't a time-waster. The Doctor was invited to a hastily arranged dinner in Germany, for no other reason that that was where Zade lived, and it was Zade who was calling the shots. The Doctor flew out the next day to meet the two intermediaries. They drank and ate while a belly-dancer gyrated around their table, and the Doctor impressed them so much, they made the call to Shelhi's brother that same night.

A week later, the Doctor met Shelhi himself in another German hotel. The king's representative was not impressed by what he saw. The Doctor looked like a crumpled pensioner and seemed to have no idea about oil. He had no concept of prices or how the bidding system worked, and Shelhi had the world's seven biggest producers waiting to wine and dine him back in Tripoli. But slowly the Doctor worked his charms. He had no board of directors, he said, no auditors and no shareholders. There was no one making sure that he followed company rules because he *was* Occidental. He *set* the rules. As Shelhi visibly warmed to him that night, the Doctor announced that, should he win the concession, he would make Shelhi 'the richest man in all Europe'.

What followed was the most crooked oil deal of the era.

Shelhi and the two facilitators would require $2.8 million in cash from the Doctor as a thank-you for being awarded the concession. The Doctor agreed, but it was just the start. If they struck oil, they would then require a cut of the money from every barrel sold. They set the figure at a modest-sounding 3 per cent, which was to be paid into their Swiss bank accounts. That was before Oxy struck oil, of course, so no one knew quite how that 3 per cent would translate into cash.

In the event, with a forecast of 3 billion barrels, at a price equivalent of $22 per barrel in today's money, the lowly oil-fixer and his mate were set to become wildly rich. At the rate the oil was shooting from the ground, they stood to earn $4 million each, annually. The payments were set to continue for the life of the oilfield. And they would all have done very well indeed, if it weren't for an unexpected event.

A young Libyan army officer had just returned from a British military training school, and had begun organizing a clandestine revolutionary group called the Free Officers Movement, named after his hero Nasser's original organization. He hadn't enjoyed England much, with its noisy traffic and rowdy bars, and was pleased to be back home. But he arrived in the middle of the oil rush, and saw where the king's corruption was leading the country. He couldn't sit back and watch while Libya's natural resources were being drained into the pockets of a privileged few, particularly when Colonel Nasser was inciting young Libyan nationalists to rise up and align themselves with the revolutionary Arab states in a display of Pan-Arab unity. The young Muammar Gaddafi had a plan.

CHAPTER FOUR

Libya

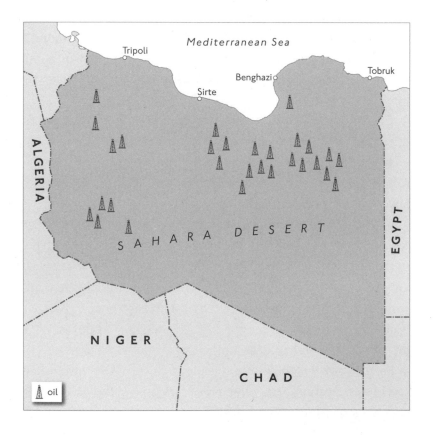

LIBYA

> *With a single stroke the Revolution has lightened*
> *the long dark night of this reactionary and decad-*
> *ent regime, which was no more than a hotbed of*
> *extortion, faction, treachery and treason.*

MUAMMAR GADDAFI,
REVOLUTION BROADCAST, 1969

IT'S SAND, MOST of this landscape, save for the lunar boulders and the towering basalt ridges, and the granite carved into jags and spikes, and when the Sahara wind blows, it sweeps that sand into mountainous drifts, and raises it higher, and moulds and shapes it into soft-razored edges. If you were down there, in the desert, you'd see it's not like any other sand, not the heavy clods of the public beaches, or the ribbed sands of the estuaries, or the windy dunes of northern Europe. This is sand that lies somewhere between solid and liquid, sand that flows.

But follow the wind. It is blowing in from the south, from the vast desert states of Niger, Chad and Sudan, across an ocean of steep and teetering sand peaks. There is an ancient town down there, a stone raft on a sea of sand, where goats and men endure the hot sun and a few papery palms lean over a dry well.

Now the sand's turning black, volcanic, with vast swirls of granite; sometimes you can't tell what's floating in the sky and what's fixed to the earth. There's a trail, a spindle thread across the canvas, where ancient caravans once crossed, taking spices and leather and precious metals. Fly higher, above the dust and the heat to where the air is clearer, and you can see the high, barren mountains of Algeria to the west, the scorched desert plains of Egypt to the east.

Further north is the isolated city of Sabha, with tents and nomads and huddled camels, and after a thousand miles the first dabs of green appear: thorn bushes and dry stick trees. Soon there is arable land clawed from the sand: patchwork farms, irrigation channels, a flat-roofed building. And then roads that link and cross, blaring horns, military vehicles, people moving quickly from shade to shadow.

This narrow band of coastal Libya is where ninety per cent of its population live, squeezed up against the gin-clear waters of the Mediterranean Sea.

Tripoli appears first, humble streets of whitewashed homes, crumbling Roman ruins, and sandy lanes clinging to the water's edge, and then, 400 miles to the east, Benghazi, on a spur of land pressing up towards southern Europe.

It's September 1969, and at a military barracks in Benghazi, a group of young army officers have been awake since the early hours. Some have already left their compound for the day, heading along the palm-fringed boulevards into town. The streets are quiet save for the fish carts and the bottle carriers, and the waves curling onto the beach, but the young officers are agitated, driving to their positions before light to set in motion a plan they've been working on for months.

Three hundred miles further east along the coastal highway is the king's Summer Palace in the port of Tobruk. The maids are polishing the marble floors, the gardeners beginning their daily battle against the sun, watering lemon trees, trying to grow lush green grass from unwilling soil. They think they can relax a little today because the boss is away.

Seventy-nine-year-old King Idris has been doing well out of his country's oil. After the first discovery by Esso in the Sirte Basin many more have followed, and by 1969 Libya is making astonishing strides, with 3 million barrels pumped from the ground every day: an achievement that takes its production for that year ahead of Saudi Arabia. Few Libyans have benefited, though, except for men like Omar Shelhi and other members of the king's inner circle.

The improvement in Idris's finances, however, have not been matched by an improvement in his personal health and, on the cusp of his eighth decade, he is in need of a complete medical overhaul. He has submitted himself to a strict regime of plunge pools and massages at a spa resort in Turkey for two months.

Close to the king's palace in Tobruk, out near Windy Corner where the cacti tumble across the road, are the low white buildings of the British garrison, which consists of NAAFI, guardroom, a barber's shop and a sick quarters. It's situated in an isolated corner of Tobruk, a desolate town still full of war debris, and containing little more than a post office, a church and the palace itself. The nearest restaurant is 300 miles away in Benghazi. For the 2,500 British troops stationed there, it is an unpopular posting. But the king still finds it reassuring to have the British close, although there are no guarantees they will step in if there is an attempt to unseat him. The parade ground is empty at this time in the morning; it's mainly used for football anyway, and the dust is so deep it's permanently puckered in wave patterns, like a holiday beach. At one end, a pair of salt-rusted goalposts lean slightly in the breeze.

The Americans are in Libya too, almost 5,000 of them at the Wheelus Airbase in Tripoli. It's a useful staging post for Cold War mock raids on the Soviet Union, and this morning, just like any other, the Phantom jet fighters are lined up at the side of the runway, ready for their aerial drills. The US ambassador has described Wheelus as 'a little America on the sparkling shores of the Mediterranean Sea' – a claim unlikely to impress the young and restless Arab nationalist movement, to whom the base symbolizes the neocolonialism that the king supports and which confirms to them that he has to go.

Brenda Whitney is sleeping at her gated home in Tripoli alongside her oil-worker husband and two sons. She's at the centre of the expat social scene concentrated around the oil industry, a 'Mobil wife' who organizes days out at the beach and picnics among the Roman ruins at Leptis Magna. But she's also savvy about security. Ever since the Arab–Israeli war in 1967, she has noticed increasing hostility towards the Americans and British because of their support for Israel. Their embassies have been targeted by protestors, as have the offices of Western oil companies, and Brenda thinks it's just a matter of time before young, armed Arab nationalists turn up on her own doorstep. Hidden inside her villa she has baseball bats and spears. 'If anyone tries to break in,' she tells her boys, 'we will go down fighting. I expect you to get five Mo's,' she says, 'and you to get three.' 'Mo' is expat shorthand for Mohammeds, or Arabs.

Across the border in Cairo the nationalist leader who has bewitched so many disaffected young Libyans, Egypt's President Nasser, may have already been informed of the historic events set to begin this morning. If they are executed properly, it will be the end for his neighbour King Idris, and the beginning of a new Arab republic. Even the British government, 2,000 miles away, can sense something ominous is going on. Urgent notes have been flashing between Whitehall and MI6, planning their response in the event of a Libyan coup.

The first hint that something's wrong comes from a British diplomat. He is taking an early morning stroll by the sea in Tripoli sometime before 7 a.m. on 1 September 1969, and sees a man running along the street in a balaclava. The wife of a BP worker notices a man climbing telegraph poles. He appears to be equipped with wire cutters.

In Tripoli, the oil executive David Orser receives a call from his security staff. They have heard reports of possible military movements but are unsure what is happening. They suggest Orser remains at home until things have become clearer. Orser ignores them and sets off for his office. As he enters the city he runs into a hurriedly erected road block. 'What's going on?' he asks the soldier in charge. There is no explanation, just an impatient order to 'Go home!' Orser attempts to reason with the man. 'I have work to do,' he insists, 'for Libya, for your country.' The soldier reaches to his holster and draws a pistol. 'Go home,' he repeats more firmly this time. Orser swings his car around and retreats back along the road.

At a military barracks in Benghazi, Lieutenant Muammar Gaddafi has overslept. His co-conspirators will, years later, complain he was in bed and only appeared when the operation was already under way. There are seventy of so of them from the Free Officers Movement and most have already begun seizing control of military and government buildings.

BP engineer Glen Mathias is on a flight touching down at Tripoli airport at the very moment the airport buildings are being seized. He watches as the steps roll into place and a group of nervy soldiers rush across the tarmac. They board the plane brandishing hand-guns, and announce that the entire flight is under arrest. Mathias and the others are led into the airport buildings and told they won't be leaving.

When Gaddafi finally gets out of bed, his mission is to seize the Berka Barracks, high in the Jebel Mountains. He goes straight to the sleeping quarters of the commanding officers and tells them that his men are taking over. The story has likely been embellished in its retelling, but one of the officers is said to have greeted Gaddafi with the words, 'Go away. You've got the wrong date. The coup is next month,' the point being that another group of officers had a similar plan. In fact, it is believed there were several other contenders within the military, all preparing to take advantage of the king's absence. After that, Gaddafi heads back to Benghazi, and to the radio station, where he has an announcement to make.

The streets are empty. At the BP club the shutters are closed, the swimming pool empty, the bar silent. The tom-tom drums of the expat oil community have ensured that everyone is in their homes. A 'BP wife' reports gunfire in the streets of Benghazi, her husband races back from an aborted meeting and reports artillery positioned on the airport road. An official has told him there is a coup going on.

'People of Libya,' begins Gaddafi, 'your armed forces have undertaken the overthrow of the reactionary and corrupt regime, the stench of which has sickened and horrified us all.' He talks of slaves becoming masters, of how he will champion unity and social justice, and the creation of a Libyan Arab Republic. And, later, when he walks languidly towards the camera flanked by his fellow officers, all faces are turned to him. His co-conspirators look like sombre mediocrities stuffed in uniforms.

In London, there is confusion over who has taken control, but cautious optimism that British interests seem unaffected. 'There has been no interruption in the flow of oil,' declares the British foreign secretary Michael Stewart to a cabinet meeting, 'and none is expected.' Idris has already contacted London to plead for an urgent military response, but they have no further use for their old ally and are already looking to protect their most valuable assets. 'It is important to be on good terms with whatever government controls Libya,' advises Stewart. 'BP and Shell have an investment in the country of about £100 million.'

The US is making similar calculations, but they're working in an information vacuum. In his first dispatch after the coup, the American ambassador in Tripoli, Joseph Palmer, can only tell Washington, 'The still-anonymous young men of the Revolutionary Command Council promise to protect all interests, including the pumping of oil.'

For Gaddafi and his colleagues the next few weeks are a post-revolutionary tornado of political speeches, socialist decrees and celebrations. There is Gaddafi dressed in sand-coloured fatigues on the back of a cantering horse, its tail twisting and mane flying before a wall of mesmerized faces. Officer's cap pulled low over his eyes, he stands before a crowd of thousands clambering onto rooftops, shinning up trees. One pretty young woman touches him and is so overcome she covers her mouth like she's going to weep. Gaddafi waves and flashes his smile. Later he is joined by Colonel Nasser, the two men standing in the back of a Land Rover as they are mobbed in Tripoli's Green Square, Gaddafi's face framed by outstretched hands like a messianic portrait wreathed in palm leaves.

And if the clocks had stopped there, in the winter of 1969, that image might have adorned a generation of students' walls. There could have been silk-screen prints by Andy Warhol, Gaddafi ballads from Joan Baez, revolutionary anthems from John Lennon. He had driven out the imperialists and begun redistributing the country's oil money. There were promises of modern hospitals and schools for all. But, for those who watched events more closely, there were already clues as to where all this was heading.

Having promoted himself to the rank of colonel, Gaddafi announced a drive for purity in public office. It sounded progressive but its execution was a fiasco. It centred around a decree requiring all judges, diplomats, government officers, soldiers and policemen to produce a full statement of their family possessions – money, shares, gold and jewels – for which they must explain the provenance.

On paper, in a student's textbook, it read well, but on the ground, from house to house, prying under mattresses, rifling through handbags, gangs of revolutionaries demanding explanations for the presence of trinkets and cash? It was an early taste of Gaddafi's jackboot reformism, where the state could burst into anyone's life and violently dismantle it.

The household of Abdul Atti was always a busy one. Whenever a new baby arrived in the family, friends would bring semolina cake with soft date filling and bags of baklava, and they would sit for hours chatting to Abdul's parents and sipping cool drinks in the salon. 'How do you have the stamina… and the space?' they would ask. 'The family is already the biggest in the neighbourhood.' And it seemed the cake was barely finished before Abdul's mother would announce another baby was on its way, and the celebrations would begin again. In the end there were eleven children, five boys and six girls, and Abdul was baby number four – 'the naughty one'.

He was three years old when Gaddafi seized power, and his parents were delighted their children would grow up in a brave new Arab republic. What had the king known about the lives of ordinary Libyans, with all his palaces and his motorcars? And what about those 'cousins' and 'assistants' with their baksheesh houses and baksheesh wives? They were filling their pots with oil while everyone else was lucky to fill theirs with fresh water. Now they had a leader who was going to stop all that, a 'saviour', an 'achiever', a 'People's Leader'.

Abdul spent much of his childhood in Tripoli's blazing outdoors, racing barefoot along the hot dusty lanes, hunting for locusts or watching the tortoises tumble over each other in the ruins of a local house. Sometimes he was joined by his older brother, Fuzi, baby number three, his closest sibling. Fuzi was quieter, more reflective than boisterous Abdul, and later, in middle age, Abdul would remember him as his spiritual guide, a boy who prayed with the conviction of a man, and gave away every sweet in his bag, leaving none for himself. One day the two brothers would try to save each other's lives during the most murderous episode of Gaddafi's rule, but for the moment their new leader had filled the household with optimism as he led Libya into a new decade.

In their seaside villas, the oilmen were anxious. Four months into the new regime and they were still unsure what Gaddafi was planning to do. The Libyan oil bonanza was barely a decade old, with fresh and startling finds still enticing the world's biggest players. Production had overtaken that of Kuwait and Saudi, and now their future was in the hands of a revolutionary socialist who wanted to cleanse his country of Western imperialism. It didn't look promising.

Gaddafi soon turned his guns on the industry that represented so much of what he loathed, while at the same time providing him with the dollars he needed for his revolution to prosper. He announced his regime required a far bigger slice of the pie and said the only way of achieving it was to raise the selling price and increase taxes on oil. Prices had been plummeting around the world between 1960 and 1969, and Gaddafi was intent on reversing the decline by force. If the oilmen refused, he would evict them from his country. Gaddafi called a series of meetings to let them know he would tolerate no dissent. First into his office was David Orser.

Orser had left Mobil for the newcomer Occidental shortly after its discovery of the massive Idris Field, and now Oxy was almost entirely dependent on Libyan oil. Such reliance on a single source made it the most vulnerable producer in the country and thus the easiest for the new leadership to manipulate. When Orser arrived at Gaddafi's Oil Ministry in January 1970, accompanied by two of his Oxy colleagues, he was shown straight to a boardroom to await the Colonel – as Gaddafi was now popularly known. An hour later, Gaddafi strolled in, flanked by an interpreter and a bodyguard who was cradling a machine gun. Immaculately dressed in a tailored military uniform, the Libyan leader negotiated with a kind of sinister charm.

'We Arabs have gone without oil for 5,000 years. We do not need any of you,' he began, pausing to allow the translation to settle. 'The Revolutionary Command Council is in charge now,' another pause.

'If you fail to do what we want, we will nationalize each company.'
The oilmen remained silent. 'You will hear from the ministry very
soon.' Gaddafi then got up to leave, and as he reached the door
turned and gave the men from Oxy a small smile.

Soon after, Oxy and the others were instructed by Gaddafi's
officials to increase their oil prices and raise the proportion paid to the
Revolutionary Command Council. They refused, complaining that it
might put them out of business, and precipitate a hike in prices around
the globe. Gaddafi responded by ordering Libyan oil production to
be slashed by forty per cent. Every oil company in Libya would lose
millions overnight, and would have to begin rationing supplies to
customers in Europe and the US. Then he sat back and waited. It was
he who held all the cards. The Suez Canal was still closed and Libya
was, by now, supplying thirty per cent of Europe's oil. If the oilmen
refused to increase prices, he would happily kick the lot of them out
of his country.

Oxy's Doctor Hammer was so alarmed, he contacted Gaddafi's
hero, Colonel Nasser, and asked him to intervene. Nasser warned
Gaddafi not to make the same mistakes he had made, nationalizing
foreign companies and evicting key technicians. But Gaddafi chose to
follow his own path, upping the pressure on the oil companies with
further threats. Oxy was the first to buckle. The others followed soon
after. But none had anticipated quite how far Gaddafi would push it.

He forced oil prices so high in his first year alone that his government secured an extra $1 billion of income.[1] With the oil majors on
the ropes, he repeated the same threats time and again, coercing them
into setting ever higher prices, and contributing more to his fledgling
Arab republic. The Middle East responded by raising its prices too,
as did Nigeria. The balance of power was tipping decisively away
from the oil companies, and towards the host nations, and Gaddafi
was about to use BP for a spectacular display of his readiness to
punish any company, or country, that failed to please him.

In late 1971, the British government went ahead with its plans to
withdraw military forces from the Persian Gulf, removing British protection from the nine little sheikhdoms. The Shah of Iran, a long-time

enemy of the surrounding Arab nations, took a close interest in Britain's withdrawal, keen to take advantage of the imminent power vacuum in the region. The Shah had his eyes on three tiny islands in the Straits of Hormuz, a strategic bottleneck through which much of the world's oil passed. In his eagerness to secure them before anyone else, he sent military units to seize control days before Britain had actually formerly withdrawn. The Arab world was incensed and looked to Britain for an immediate response. But London decided to turn a blind eye, allowing the islands to fall into Iran's hands. As punishment for what Libya called 'a plot mechanized by Britain, with the puppet government of Iran, against the Arab nation', Gaddafi chose to turn his guns on BP. He nationalized the company and seized its Libyan assets. It was a stark warning that oil companies would be treated as proxies for the perceived misdeeds of their governments. Further part-nationalizations followed, with Gaddafi justifying his takeover of one US-based company as 'a big hard blow... on (America's) cold insolent face.'[2]

The son of illiterate Bedouin parents had discovered how to plug into the world's political circuitry: he'd pulled a lever in Tripoli, and the lights had flickered from Africa to Westminster. Within six years he had forced oil prices six times higher than when he first seized power. His regime was receiving unprecedented revenues and taxes which, for a country of just 1.5 million people, should have promised undreamed-of riches. But Gaddafi had scores to settle, and grand foreign schemes on which to spend his people's money.

In Tripoli, Brenda Whitney received a telephone call from a girlfriend in Rome. Her name was Elizabeth and she was married to a successful Libyan businessman who had been an enthusiastic supporter of the former king. The husband had learned he was on Gaddafi's blacklist and had fled to Italy to escape, taking his wife and three children. When Elizabeth called Brenda Whitney it was to report that two Libyan assassins had broken into their house in Rome, smothering her with a pillow and beating her husband unconscious with a baseball bat. The couple were lucky to escape with their lives. It was early evidence that Gaddafi's regime was prepared to hunt its detractors beyond Libya's borders.

Others with links to the king were easier prey. Brenda Whitney had befriended an elderly Arab she liked to call her 'Palestinian Baba' and who had once been the chief citrus advisor to the royal family. He was arrested and beaten in Tripoli by a gang of thugs.

There was talk of bodies being found on the steps of government buildings. Some had had their throats slit. Soon expats were hearing the names of armed groups that were supposedly arriving in Tripoli to collect money and arms from Gaddafi; the Palestinian 'Black September' group, and the Popular Front for the Liberation of Palestine, along with other, more familiar paramilitary organizations.

In March 1973 an Irish freighter crawled discreetly into Tripoli's crescent-shaped harbour and docked alongside the cargo ships. Its crew disembarked, made their way to waiting cars, and were driven into the city. The group leader was in his early fifties, pug-faced, balding, and wearing oversized, thick-rimmed glasses that gave the impression they were part of a disguise. His name was Joe Cahill and he was chief of staff of the Irish Republican Army, the IRA.

When Cahill met Gaddafi the two men embraced and greeted each other as fellow revolutionaries whose common purpose was to defeat neocolonialism by whatever means. Cahill later said that Gaddafi possessed 'an awful hatred of England' and couldn't understand 'why we spoke in English, the language of our enemies' and not Irish.[3]

Cahill requested that Gaddafi supply them with military hardware. Gaddafi agreed. The Irishmen were told they could take as much as their boat, the *Claudia*, could carry. Five tonnes of weapons and ammunition were loaded on board before Cahill and his crew headed back to Ireland. They didn't realize they were being watched. The *Claudia* had been under surveillance by British intelligence for seven months.

On 23 March 1973, the British foreign secretary, Sir Alec Douglas-Home, sent an urgent telegram to the British ambassador in Dublin informing him that, 'The *Claudia* left North Africa a few days ago carrying... small arms and explosives reported to have been provided free by the Libyans for delivery to the IRA in the Republic. At least one senior member of the IRA is reported to be on board. *Claudia* is to be located and kept under discreet surveillance by British maritime forces... the interception should be a matter for the Irish government.'[4]

The first Cahill knew what was happening was when he felt a gun muzzle pressed against his temple and heard a young Irish naval officer say, 'Don't move.'[5] The *Claudia* was approaching the coast of County Waterford when it was apprehended.

That interception seriously undermined the IRA's operational ability for several years. But by the mid-1980s the arms shipments were larger and more sophisticated than before. During a fifteen-month period between 1985 and 1986, the IRA took delivery of more than 120 tonnes of weapons from Tripoli. One delivery was so large it took thirty Libyans two nights to load it on board: rocket-propelled grenades, SAM missiles, and around a tonne of Semtex, the almost undetectable explosive that was to transform the IRA's operational capability on mainland Britain.

Gaddafi's prime minister during that period was Abdul Ati al-Obeidi. When I met him in Tripoli in 2009, he bumbled into the room in an oversized stained shirt and creased trousers, and seemed so disorientated and disheveled I assumed he was a caretaker lost in the warren of grubby government offices. A whole roomful of sharp-suited security officials failed to notice him for several minutes. We were supposed to be talking about Gaddafi's relations with Europe but he seemed weary with the subject before we even began.

'Who do you support?' he asked.

'You mean in football?'

Obeidi nodded.

'Well, I was brought up in a town near Manchester, so—'

'Aha!' he leaned forward jubilantly. 'Manchester United! That's my team too!'

Later, I walked with him outside his ministry and asked why his regime had funded the IRA.

'For punishment,' he muttered. 'For Thatcher. We hated Thatcher. We were at war with Thatcher.'

'But before Thatcher, back in the 1970s?'

'It wasn't just the Irish, it was everyone,' he said, '… all the groups fighting imperialists, we supported them all.'

Obeidi was not exaggerating. The IRA was just one of many recipients of Gaddafi's largesse. Libya funded Egypt and Syria in their war against Israel, giving them around a billion dollars in 1973. It represented such a colossal sum that it wiped out the year's oil revenues and left Gaddafi 'stripping shops of food and hospitals of medicines, and piling them into lorries for despatch'.[6] Any armed groups fighting Israel were given generous assistance, the mainstream Palestinian Liberation Organization (PLO), Black September, the maverick Marxist Carlos the Jackal, and Abu Nidal, the most intransigent Palestinian terrorist leader. Then there were the Islamic revolutionary groups fighting their own governments, in Guinea, Chad and even the Philippines. Gaddafi was cementing his reputation as being 'the arsenal of Islam', and the leader of the Third World's struggle against colonialism. He was also proving that his home-grown revolution was moving from the defensive to the offensive.

The Libyan leader's military hardware was being sourced from the Soviet Union, but ideologically, Gaddafi always kept Moscow at arm's length, wary of giving it any leverage in his domestic affairs. This was strictly a financial relationship. Bristling with Soviet weapons, Tripoli became a centre of excellence for all sorts of would-be guerrillas. Gaddafi was soon hosting revolutionary groups from across the globe. Volunteers were told to apply at Libyan embassies for a place in his newly created guerrilla training school, the First Nasserite Volunteers Centre, which was opened in July 1972. In one training camp, an ambitious and wayward soldier called Charles Taylor acquired the skills that would later help him raise a children's army and seize the presidency of Liberia. Another, more established rebel leader – Robert Mugabe – felt he needed no in-country training, just funds. Gaddafi donated some of Libya's oil money for ZANU's fight against white-minority rule in Rhodesia and the pair became good friends.

'Everyone who needed our help, we supported them,' insisted Obeidi in his Tripoli office. 'All around the world we gave them money and weapons for fighting the oppressors.' He saw no irony in being part of a uniquely oppressive regime himself.

'How much is a ticket?' he enquired as I was preparing to leave.

'How do you mean? I asked.

'For Manchester United,' he grinned, 'for the season.'

When Abdul, 'the naughty one', was growing up he was dimly aware of the foreign 'freedom fighters' celebrated on state television, but the oil money had begun bringing social improvements too and people took little notice of international affairs. There was food on the table and goods in the shops and by the end of the 1970s average incomes had risen by 400 per cent. Some of Abdul's friends attended newly built schools, their parents worked in clean and well-functioning government departments, their grandparents were treated in state-of-the-art hospitals, and there was much excitement about what Gaddafi called his 'Eighth Wonder of the World'.

He had commissioned a project to bring fresh water from ancient reservoirs located deep beneath the Sahara Desert. The 'Great Man-Made River' would comprise 3,000 kilometres of pipes wide enough for a tanker to sail through. It was miraculous and Abdul's family, like most others, were proud of their president's feat of engineering. His socialist revolution was redistributing wealth and property, and taking power from the tiny elite that prospered during the monarchy. Private companies were virtually eliminated, their affairs placed under state ownership. Gaddafi challenged people to take control for themselves, to set up People's Committees in universities, hospitals, farms, even in the armed forces. Abdul's family hurried to take part. It was radical socialist theory reaching into the most trivial and inconsequential aspects of public life, anything from land use to cleaning rotas, and at first it tasted good. Gaddafi was so inspired he tried to elevate his practice to the status of grand political theory in his 'Green Book'. Inspired by Chairman Mao's 'Little Red Book', it detailed a baffling array of people's organizations and promised a happy solution to the problems of democracy. The book's grand tone and warped reasoning was met with amusement abroad, but in Libya it was deadly serious. Abdul and his brothers were forced to recite passages from the book at school. *The natural person has freedom to express himself even if, when he is mad, he behaves irrationally to express his madness.* Every day, there would be readings on state television. *If an instrument of governing is dictatorial, the society's vigilance towards deviation from the law will have only one way to gain re-adjustment. That is violence, which means revolution against the instrument of governing.* But for all his talk of purity in public office, Gaddafi had already begun gifting his oil money to random celebrities.

In 1974 he watched the Rumble in the Jungle, live from Kinshasa. Muhammad Ali was at the peak of his popularity: World Heavyweight Champion, social reformer, and voluble critic of Western hegemony. He was also a Muslim convert. Gaddafi couldn't wait to have him as a guest in Libya.

The boxer arrived in Benghazi just a few months after the fight. He was driven through town in a small Peugeot car, trying to squeeze his enormous frame through the windows to wave to ecstatic crowds. Here was an American icon visiting a Revolutionary Socialist Republic, criticizing his own country's imperialism and the Israeli state, and then sparring with the kids and posing for photographs. Gaddafi couldn't have asked for more. The Colonel kept in touch with Ali, and in 1980 made him a generous offer.

David Orser had left Libya and was back in the US by then. He told me the story during our meeting in London in 2015. One day he received a telephone call from an attorney in Chicago. 'We represent Ali,' said the man, who was a partner in the firm. 'You have been recommended to us to give advice on purchasing oil from Libya.' The first shots in the Iran–Iraq war had just been fired and supplies had been disrupted. Anyone with access to Libyan oil could make a killing. 'Ali has visited the Colonel,' Orser was told, 'and the Colonel has promised to sell him oil at below market price.'

Ali's legal team wanted Orser to make arrangements with Gaddafi's National Oil Corporation to take delivery of the knock-down consignment, and then help sell it at the going rate to a third party, thus making potentially millions of dollars on the deal. It was corrupt, and Orser tried to put them off.

Without an official contract from the Libyans, he told them, the deal was a non-starter. But the attorney insisted, explaining that Ali had a new partner, a Greek tanker owner, and they were keen to push ahead.

They met for lunch at the famous 21 Club in New York: five of Ali's lawyers and a sceptical David Orser. They explained that the idea was to take delivery, and then find a customer. 'It can't happen,' repeated Orser, 'not without a contract from the Libyans. They just won't release the oil.' He explained they would need to hire an agent in Tripoli if they wanted to take things further. The lawyers passed the news to their Greek shipping client and to Ali, who paid Orser's fee, but pursued his business proposal no further, at least not with Orser.

World oil prices rose in dramatic leaps through the 1970s, empowering Gaddafi to continue his ambitious and violent foreign policy objectives, while simultaneously funding his extravagant socialist reforms at home. In 1973 the Organization of Arab Petroleum Exporting Countries (OAPEC), which included Libya, proclaimed an oil embargo to punish America for its support of Israel during the Yom Kippur War. US allies were included in the ban: the UK, Canada, Japan and the Netherlands. Queues soon began forming outside petrol stations in the designated countries as prices shot up overnight, ultimately rising by 400 per cent in just six months. For Gaddafi and other OAPEC members it was a triumphant display of defiance. The oil-exporting nations had taken control of a vital commodity that had long been manipulated by the dominant industrial powers. They were becoming richer by the week. Exhilarated by his new-found wealth and the power he was able exert on the world stage, Gaddafi's behaviour became increasingly outlandish.

At a world summit for non-aligned countries in Colombo, Sri Lanka, in 1976, a high-ranking diplomat described his conduct as 'hair-raising'.[7] The Colonel's temperament had changed, he said, from being a 'hesitant, paradoxically self-effacing Arab zealot in army fatigues' to almost a 'demagogue, delighting in being surrounded by the trappings of power'. Gaddafi arrived in a 'startling' combination of slacks and a loud striped shirt, surrounded by 'huge gangs of thugs'. Fights broke out between his bodyguards and local security officials, and when Gaddafi appeared at the main debate, he was armed with a pistol in an open holster while his bodyguard brandished a machine gun.

The decade's second oil crisis came in 1979, with the Iranian Revolution. The disruption in supplies meant prices more than doubled in a year. By the end of the decade, a barrel of oil had increased from $3 to $34, a trajectory that necessitated much belt-tightening in America and Europe, leading to slowed economic growth and an era of energy conservation. But it was no longer all good news for the oil-exporting countries. They soon accumulated a glut of oil that they couldn't sell, and in 1980 the inevitable happened.

Gaddafi watched helplessly as the world chose nuclear power, coal and natural gas in preference to his overpriced oil. Prices began a six-year slide. The Libyan leader had to rein in his subsidies to foreign allies. The IRA, the PLO, all manner of revolutionary groups felt the pinch. At home, his building work on the Great Man-Made River was put on hold. The People's Committees were no longer seen as exciting experiments in direct democracy, but bureaucratic black holes swallowing his shrinking resources. Criticism of his authoritarian leadership grew, with Gaddafi's secret police crushing any hint of dissent. His terrified opponents began fleeing abroad.

The Libyan People's Bureau in London was a grand neo-Georgian town house situated in one of the most prestigious addresses in the capital. The pavements outside were bustling with men hurrying to lunch at The Athenaeum, or to enjoy whisky and cigars in the buttoned-leather library of the East India Club. The Libyan ambassador could watch them from behind his desk at 5 St James's Square. His name was Musa Kusa, ambitious, inscrutable and probably unstable. Kusa had overcome his ideological loathing of

America long enough to gain a master's degree at Michigan State University, where he had written a flattering portrait of Gaddafi for his thesis. It had impressed the Colonel so much that Kusa was invited into the regime's inner circle, and awarded the London job at the age of just thirty.

The name Muhammad Ramadan would have been familiar to Kusa. Ramadan, a shy, almost apologetic man, armed with a sharp journalistic instinct, was a news announcer at the BBC's Arabic Service in Bush House, central London. He had made a name for himself among Libyan émigrés for writing passionate anti-Gaddafi articles that were published in underground magazines, some of which had found their way back to Libya. A recent piece had concerned the murder of a Libyan living in Italy. His body had been found in the boot of a car and Ramadan was quick to point out that the chief suspects were connected to the Libyan embassy in Rome. Kusa and his officials in London would have been very aware of the article.

On 11 April 1980, Ramadan attended Friday prayers with his wife at the Regents Park Mosque, a short distance from his BBC office. On the pretty tree-lined avenue adjacent to the duck pond, men chatted or waited for friends. Many of them wore traditional Islamic clothing. Ramadan would have stood out in his Western suit and favourite skinny silk tie, making it easier for the two assassins to recognize him as they watched from their Vauxhall Carlton on the other side of the road.

He parted from his wife at the entrance, prayed for a while beneath the central chandelier of the mosque's golden dome, and then left the building. A few moments later there was a volley of gunfire.

Four police officers happened to be nearby and arrived in time to see an armed man running out of the mosque grounds. A crowd was already gathering around the dying body of Muhammad Ramadan.

Gaddafi had become obsessed with tracking down and neutralizing 'stray dogs', the term he used for political exiles. Their pamphlets and public events were drawing international attention to the short-comings of his regime. But the assassination of Ramadan only served to inflame the exiled community even further.

At Ramadan's funeral an agitated crowd gathered to chant anti-Gaddafi slogans as his coffin was loaded into a hearse. The plan was to drive the body to Heathrow Airport for repatriation to Libya. On arrival in Tripoli, officials seized the coffin and put it on the next flight back to the UK, declaring that Ramadan was unfit to be buried in Libyan soil.

Gaddafi followed up the Ramadan murder with a deadline and a warning: all 'stray dogs' must be back in Libya, he said, by 11 June 1980, or else they might be targeted next. On the day of the deadline, instead of boarding planes home, hundreds gathered noisily in St James's Square outside the Libyan People's Bureau. From inside the building, Kusa and his colleagues would have watched as the crowd chanted for Gaddafi's removal from power. We know there were firearms on the premises but, even for Kusa, shooting out of an embassy window was a step too far. In the end, he allowed the demonstration to pass peacefully. But his behaviour provoked fury in Tripoli. Officials, possibly Gaddafi himself, notified him that a gesture of merciless punishment had been required, and that at least one of the demonstrators should have been killed.[8]

Soon after, Kusa tried to remedy his misjudgement by announcing to a journalist from *The Times* newspaper that, 'The Revolutionary Committees have decided to kill two more people in the United Kingdom. I approve of this.' The British government responded by giving him forty-eight hours to leave the country.

Once back in Tripoli. Kusa's career really took off. He became head of the Libyan security service and was regularly seen at the dictator's side, the highest-ranking official from outside the Colonel's own tribe. It was a role which earned him the nickname 'Gaddafi's Envoy of Death', hunting down opponents at home and abroad.

The next incumbent at St James's Square had got the message. When an anti-Gaddafi demonstration was organized on 17 April 1984 he sent Tripoli a list of options: 1. To clash directly with the demonstrators outside the bureau. 2. To fire on them from inside the bureau. 3. To prevent the demonstration through diplomatic pressure.[9]

WPC Yvonne Fletcher was one of the police officers on duty that day as a small crowd gathered across the road from the building. Most of those attending wore hoods and sunglasses to prevent identification by officials inside. When they first arrived, Fletcher had greeted them with a smile; it was a bright spring morning, and she had directed them behind the metal barriers erected on the opposite side of the road. They waved placards and chanted, 'No to the Dictatorship in Libya', 'Yes to Freedom'. Yvonne Fletcher was standing in the road facing them; it was routine crowd control, police officers positioned every ten metres or so. The mood of the protestors was determined but peaceful and the officers expected it to fizzle out by mid-afternoon, allowing them to return to base.

Fletcher had her back to the embassy.

At 10.18 a.m., a witness saw two sash windows slide open on the first floor. Several bursts of machine-gun fire followed. Stone chips flew from the pavement. Some in the crowd sank to their knees. Fletcher fell onto her right side, clutching her stomach. The bullet had entered through her back. Police officers ran over and crouched beside her, unsure at first why she had collapsed. The crowd scattered. Fletcher, with her colleagues huddled helplessly around her, writhed beneath the open windows of the bureau. Her hat, which had rolled across the tarmac as she fell, lay alongside the helmets of male officers trying to administer first-aid. Their abandoned headwear on an empty London street became the lasting image of the day. It is believed Gaddafi personally sanctioned the shooting.

In Libya the hit squads, relentless round-ups and executions were breeding a new style of opposition: small cells of daring young men plotting to overthrow their leader, despite the certainty that if they were caught they would not be spared.

Yasser was a sensitive ten-year-old, more interested in ornithology and Latin bird names than the stories of disappearances that swirled around his school. He would travel with his parents to the wilderness south of Benghazi to look for golden eagles and the Egyptian nightjars which camouflaged themselves in the desert sand. His parents kept him protected from politics; it was his best hope of survival, as such innocent pastimes were for any young man growing up in Gaddafi's Libya.

In June 1984, Yasser walked to school as usual in the fierce Benghazi heat, but when he arrived the older children were already lined up ready for a trip to the city's basketball stadium. Yasser was deemed too young to go, and probably thought he was being deprived of a treat.

The next day he heard just fragments of the story. There had been no basketball. The stadium was full. Many of the spectators were schoolchildren. A man was led to the middle of the court with his hands tied behind his back. He was wearing a shirt and a jumper like a teacher or a foreigner. He had curly hair and a beard. A man with a microphone said that he was a spy. That he had lived in America. That he was a terrorist. That he had made plans against Gaddafi. The adults in the crowd were cheering. Some waved banners. The man in the centre of the basketball court was sitting by himself with his legs crossed. He was sobbing. He asked for his mother. He confessed to being a 'stray dog'. Then some men in white gowns lifted him from where he was sitting and took him over to a wooden frame that was shaped like tall goalposts and positioned near the scoreboard. There was a rope hanging from the frame. They put the man's head in the rope, and then they let go of him so he was hanging by his neck. The man wriggled and jerked spasmodically. The crowd cheered. The man still struggled. Then a woman in green fatigues came out of the crowd, wrapped her arms around the hanging man's legs and swung with him. She kept pulling on his legs until the man stopped moving. When she let go, the crowd cheered.

The dead man was 30-year-old Sadiq Hamid Shwehdi. He was suspected of having been involved in a coup attempt against Gaddafi the previous month, during which a group of armed men had tried to storm the leader's Bab al-Azizia compound in Tripoli. Several of the plotters had been killed at the scene, but Shwehdi, who had given up his studies in America to return to Libya, had the misfortune to survive, if indeed he had ever been involved in the first place.

Gaddafi is said to have watched the execution live on television and was so impressed with the woman who pulled on the struggling man's legs he made her Mayor of Benghazi. Huda 'The Hang-woman' Ben Amer as she became known, developed her own line in populist catchphrases, among the more memorable of which was 'We don't need talking, we need hangings'. Her flint-hearted demonstration of loyalty that day turned her into a Gaddafi icon, the living embodiment of how a true revolutionary should behave. The wealth poured in. She swapped her two-bedroom bungalow for a smart home in Benghazi overlooking the Mediterranean Sea and was welcomed into the fold by the country's political elite. There were foreign holidays, parties on the Med, jewellery from the best Western designers. She became a dollar millionaire many times over, one of Libya's richest women. In 2003 she was made head of the Ministry for Inspection and Popular Control. It was her job to investigate alleged corruption in the country's oil deals.

Many more public hangings followed that execution in Benghazi's basketball stadium. Others suspected of plotting against the revolution were simply thrown to lynch mobs and their houses bulldozed. That's why Yasser was raised in an environment that avoided any mention of politics.

'This is excellent music, isn't it, Paul?' he whispered to me one day as we thundered across the desert in a government 4x4 during the summer of 2009.

'Habibi!' shouted the driver, laughing and pointing through his mirror. He worked for Gaddafi's internal security, and so did everyone else accompanying us: the three drivers, the 'translator', the government 'cameraman' (many of whom were more used to filming torture and executions for propaganda than British journalists in the Sahara) and Mohammed from the media department. The only person who wasn't being paid to spy on me that day was Yasser.

'Very ancient music, Paul. It's called Maloof,' he raised his voice over the driver. 'You can hear the tambourines… and some of the words… they are actually poetry,' and he leaned his head back into the seat with a smile and shut his eyes.

'Habibi!' the driver shouted again. He was going faster now, close to the base of the dunes, throwing up sheets of powder sand with each turn of the wheel, left, right, swinging the car through an invisible slalom while whooping and gesturing to me in the mirror, 'Habibi, say you love Libya, Habibi!'

'It means darling,' said Yasser. 'He's being affectionate. Libyans have a good sense of humour, Paul.'

Later that evening I sat beneath a vast indigo sky, sharing goat stew with Gaddafi's men in a desert camp. Some wanted to practise their English, others larked around in the sand, pretending to be scorpions or desert dogs. It seemed a good opportunity to try to engage Yasser out of earshot of the rest.

'So, Libya must be a difficult place to live…' I suggested.

'Ahhhh, Paul,' he hummed, like he was still listening to the music we had heard earlier, 'you have seen how beautiful Libya is, how friendly the people are.'

I examined his face for the tiniest flicker of irony. I was hoping he would feel free to speak now the rest were distracted.

'So what about Gaddafi?' I persisted.

'Ah yes, Paul, we have many names for our Great Leader… Africa's King of Kings… The Keeper of Arab Nationalism… Brotherly Leader and Guide to the First of September Great Revolution.' Yasser was smiling and nodding along in apparent appreciation. It seemed I had misjudged him. 'The Supreme Leader… The Architect of the Great Man-Made River…' He paused and let a handful of sand drain through his fingers. 'But the thing is, Paul, we also call him The Farmer.'

'Why "The Farmer"?' I asked.

Yasser broadened his smile. 'Because we are his animals, Paul, and he can do what he wants with us.'

Gaddafi's treatment of opponents was, indeed, brutal. During the Libyan Civil War in 2011, I had the misfortune to be handed previously unseen footage filmed in one of his prisons. It showed blindfolded prisoners being led into a cell and seated on a mattress. A guard then entered with a whip, quietly, to surprise them. The horror wasn't just the ferocity of the attack, but the enthusiasm with which he and his colleagues undertook their work, and the fact it was being filmed at all. Another video continued for twenty minutes, with frantic soldiers swarming over a prisoner long after he was dead.

Europe and America were less interested in human rights abuses inside Libya than Gaddafi's campaign of terror outside the country. Even so, for the first fifteen years of the Colonel's leadership they refrained from saying too much about his sponsorship of attacks against Western targets, reluctant to jeopardize the flow of oil. Diplomatic overtures were made asking him to cease and desist, but the realpolitik of the situation was that the US was Libya's biggest oil customer, followed by Europe, and that any attempts to isolate the Libyan leader would risk pushing him into the arms of the Soviet Union. He had already been courted by Moscow to join the Warsaw Pact, and there were thousands of Soviet military advisors and many Soviet weapons in Tripoli. One more nudge might just tip him over the edge. The risk of an international belligerent gaining full Soviet backing was just too dangerous to contemplate. And then President Ronald Reagan stepped onto the stage.

Gaddafi greeted his new sparring partner with characteristic acidity, assuming he could maintain his anti-imperialist credentials publicly, while quietly keeping the petro-dollars flowing. 'How could he become president of the greatest state on earth?' mocked Gaddafi, 'What a comedy – the comedy of the twentieth century, the absurdity of the twentieth century, the triviality of the twentieth century.'[10]

Reagan was almost as ideologically unyielding as Gaddafi. He denounced the Libyan leader as a Soviet puppet, which he was not, and labelled him an international pariah. Unsurprisingly, an increasingly isolated Gaddafi was invited to Moscow, and offered more weapons, and financial assistance for the construction of a Libyan nuclear power plant, but Gaddafi still kept the Soviets at arm's length; his populist Arab nationalism had nothing in common with their atheistic Marxism. Gaddafi's presumed Soviet flirtations served to confirm and harden Reagan's attitude, and the Libyan leader basked in America's hostility. He needled Reagan with public declarations of assistance to armed groups operating on America's doorstep; the Sandinistas fighting the US-backed Contras in Nicaragua, and rebels fighting the US-backed junta in El Salvador. In turn, Reagan became more provocative. He personally took the decision to conduct military exercises in Libya's Gulf of Sirte, during which, on 19 August 1981, a US aircraft shot down two Libyan jets. It was a direct challenge to Gaddafi's sovereignty. The next line of attack from Reagan was financial. In 1982, he announced an embargo on Libyan oil and advised US oil companies to begin scaling down their operations, a move that posed a serious threat to the health of the Libyan economy. Gaddafi was furious, but still offered to engage in dialogue, even if in a typically caustic manner. 'He has changed a little, no doubt,' said Gaddafi of Reagan. 'At first he was a hundred per cent ignoramus as far as international relations are concerned. Today he grasps at least twenty-five per cent of the world's problems.'[11]

By this time, Gaddafi had been forced, by the falling price of oil, to curtail his revolutionary activities abroad. But for Reagan he was still the world's biggest sponsor of international terror. Gaddafi regularly countered that that accolade fell to the United States, through its intervention in the affairs of developing countries. And so the antagonism spiralled. When Reagan accused Gaddafi of sending a hit squad to assassinate him in Washington, an allegation for which no evidence was ever produced, Gaddafi declared, in May 1984, that it was Reagan's CIA that was plotting an assassination of him, financing groups like the Muslim Brotherhood to attack his compound in Tripoli. The following year, Reagan turned the screw tighter, terminating all direct US economic activities with Libya, freezing Libyan assets in the US and directing all US citizens working in Libya to leave. Events were moving inexorably towards conflict.

It began in West Berlin, at a night club called La Belle, on 5 April 1986. The establishment was frequented by American military personnel, and on that Saturday night it was packed. A bomb had been placed under a table close to the DJ's booth. At 1.45 a.m. it was detonated. The explosion blew the windows from the front of the club and brought the ceiling crashing down. Two people were killed instantly, one of them a US army sergeant, Kenneth T. Ford. Of the 200 people injured that night, 79 were US servicemen. US intelligence reports show that Gaddafi officials had planned and executed the attack through the Libyan embassy, just as they had the stray dogs campaign in London. The next morning their operatives in Berlin reported back to Gaddafi that the mission had been a 'great success'.

Within hours of receiving the intelligence, Reagan was on the phone to Margaret Thatcher. He requested permission to use UK airbases to launch an attack on Tripoli.

Gaddafi's compound, Bab al-Azizia, on the south side of Tripoli, was a self-contained, heavily protected fortress-town with a complex system of gateways and escape tunnels leading to the nearby airport. Behind its metre-thick walls was parkland where he sometimes kept camels, living quarters for members of his family, a mosque, football pitch, swimming pool, military barracks, and the famous Bedouin tent where Gaddafi himself resided. The tent's interior was consistent with his claims to live a simple life: there were throws and rugs, portable air-conditioning units, paperwork spread on tables, family clutter collecting on sofas.

In the early hours of 15 April 1986, Gaddafi received an urgent call from the Italian prime minister, Bettino Craxi. He told the Libyan leader that American jets had just been spotted flying along the Mediterranean coast. It was some time before 2 a.m. There was little time to digest the news. American F-111 fighters could cover the distance to North Africa in little more than five minutes.

Moments later, one shrieked low over the Bab al-Azizia compound, so low that the pilot could make out the poles around Gaddafi's tent.

There were thumping explosions at military installations and urban targets around Tripoli and Benghazi. Libyan gunners on the ground were taken by surprise, firing surface-to-air missiles wildly into the night. Phosphorescent beads of orange tracer fire sputtered pointlessly above the city while American F-111s dropped sixty tonnes of explosives. Buildings were reduced to sticks and rubble. Vehicles burned. The French embassy was hit. Then the sky went still. Thirteen minutes after the first bomb, the Americans were gone, the operation finished.

In the thin morning light, Libyan officials inspected the damage to Bab al-Azizia. It had received thirteen direct hits, destroying residential buildings as well as the military's Command Control Centre. Gaddafi had managed to scramble to safety along with most of his family, but two of his sons had been injured. His adopted fifteen-month-old daughter, Hana, was reported dead.

Later Gaddafi converted her room into a shrine, with glass casing placed over her damaged bed. On the rough ground in front of the bombed-out building, he erected a defiant memorial, a 15-foot golden arm with its fist crushing an F-111. It became a backdrop for countless speeches, photo-calls and visits from international statesmen, some more surprising than others.

After being released from a South African jail in 1990, Nelson Mandela was eager to visit Gaddafi to thank him personally for helping train and fund ANC fighters. Brushing aside a UN air ban on Libya, Mandela gained access by road, driving across the border from Tunisia. Gaddafi's international reputation was at an all-time low, and he seized the moment for a PR coup: the universally admired African leader meets the misunderstood outcast. He took Mandela to Bab al-Azizia and the two men were photographed holding hands and punching the air in front of the damage inflicted by the US Air Force. Mandela described Gaddafi as 'one of the revolutionary icons of our time'. Washington was appalled. 'Those who say I should not be here are without morals,' Mandela pointedly told reporters. 'I am not going to join them in their lack of morality.'[12]

The US bombing of Tripoli, supported by Britain, failed in its primary objective. Gaddafi continued his campaign of subversive activities abroad. There were more weapons for the IRA, with a huge shipment leaving Tripoli for Ireland on board a ship called the *Eksund* in October 1987. The consignment included SAM-7 missiles capable of bringing down British military helicopters, but the *Eksund*'s steering failed off the French coast, and the IRA crew decided to scuttle the ship and its cargo. There were attempts by Gaddafi to destabilize the governments of Kenya and Benin, and allegations from the CIA that he was building the largest chemical weapons plant in the world at Rabta, just outside Tripoli.

The tit-for-tat campaign of punishment and meaningless victories continued until, on the evening of 21 December 1988, Pan American flight 103 fell out of a winter sky into the Scottish town of Lockerbie.

In the spring of 1989 Gaddafi's secret police poured from vehicles outside the home of Abdul Atti, 'the naughty one'. He was twenty-two years old and living with his favourite brother, Fuzi, at the time. Fuzi had grown into a self-assured, open-faced young man dedicated to the Quran. Many of his friends wore beards and traditional Muslim clothes, but Fuzi was more cautious. He knew Islamist groups were hotbeds of opposition to Gaddafi and in the circumstances it seemed wise to remain clean-shaven and dress in T-shirts and jeans. But Gaddafi's men were watching Fuzi's more traditional friends and, when those friends visited Fuzi at home for mint tea and religious debates, the police assumed Fuzi was a Jihadist.

He was arrested and bundled into an unmarked car. No one knew where they had taken him.

In 2011, after the rebels toppled Benghazi, I went to the smouldering ruins of a secret Gaddafi cell block. The fleeing guards had set it alight, hoping to burn any evidence of what had taken place there. When the locals heard it was now clear of Gaddafi's men, they came rushing over in cars and pickup trucks to look for evidence of missing relatives. From cell to burnt-out cell they went, crying and praying, clutching photos of young men in 1970s suits with wide lapels and fat, patterned ties. Among the ruins of the main office, files were strewn across the floor, yellowing photos, surveillance reports, medical notes. One elderly man suddenly found a pink folder in the rubble that had his son's photograph attached. '*Allahu Akbar!*' he shouted. *Thanks be to God*. A crowd gathered around.

He leafed through the paperwork, hungry for clues. There were scribbled notes... a photo of his son staring uncomfortably into the lens...
more notes... the old man laughed through his tears, this was all new,
a life he was never sure had continued... more notes... a photo, this
time of his son standing against a white tiled wall with his shirt off...
'My son! There is hope'... but there was something odd about the
image... there were hands gripping each of his son's arms and legs...
and he was not standing after all, but lying, the tiles were on the
floor, he was being held to the floor... another photo, the same tiles,
the same hands holding him down... this time his stomach was wide
open. His organs and intestines were lying on the floor beside him.

Five months after they took Fuzi from his apartment, the secret
police returned. This time for Abdul.

On a bleached summer day in August 1989 he was driven through
the streets of Tripoli's south side, past a concrete gun tower in a
built-up part of town, through a pair of metal gates and into a quiet
sandy lane that ran between two high walls. The van followed the
road and turned through more gates into another parallel road,
before tracking back on itself. It was making its way through layers
of security in order to reach the main buildings.

Abdul was being taken to Gaddafi's Abu Salim prison.

It was set out in several blocks: low, windowless units with flat
roofs and cat-runs above each building allowing the guards to hurry
from one to the other. The narrow spaces between each block were
used as occasional exercise yards, with metal mesh ceilings which
armed guards would patrol, their guns trained on the men beneath.

Inside the reception block the corridors stretched away into
the distance, broad, white-washed passageways that had a faintly
medical feel about them. Abdul saw men in uniforms bashing away
at typewriters. There were pot plants and people walking briskly
with files. Two officers escorted him to an interview room. They
had questions to ask but their manner seemed reasonable enough.
They even took notes. 'Are you involved in a sleeping cell plotting
to overthrow the leader?' they asked. Abdul said that he wasn't. 'Do
you know anyone who is?' Abdul said not. The questions continued,

general in nature, calmly expressed, and in the end they seemed to lose interest.

'You'll be out of here in a day or two,' one of them reassured him, and Abdul was led out of the reception area into one of the main blocks.

It began like the rumble of distant traffic, a low, guttural vibration that he felt in the fabric of the building. A metal door was swung open and it hit him. Bellowing, praying, fists thumping metal doors, guards shouting, wooden clubs rapping on walls. Abdul was moved quickly along. On each side were heavy doors with slits the size of letterboxes through which eyes peered and arms reached. The floor crunched with discarded plastic bottles and tin plates. Beyond another door he saw prisoners being pushed along by men with guns, there was graffiti and spewed food, sweating walls, kettle-hot gates, and everywhere the stink of sick men's diarrhoea.

Above the pandemonium, in an air-conditioned office on the first floor, sat Musa Kusa, the former ambassador to London. As head of Libya's security services he had many places of work, but Abu Salim provided a particularly rich diet of dissidents from whom Kusa could extract information.

Abdul was led into one of the communal cells, and the door shut behind him. Propped against thin mattresses in the gloom were a dozen or so prisoners sleeping and praying. The only source of light was a small barred window, high up near the ceiling, and not wide enough for a head to poke through. A platform at the back of the cell held a sink and a bucket. A bed sheet had been spread across an alcove to lend some dignity to the toilet. Scattered on the floor were personal possessions such as notebooks made from food packaging, and cups cut from halved plastic bottles. The prisoners turned to greet the newcomer, some pulled themselves to their feet and wandered over. One shouted out Abdul's name.

It was not unusual for the prison authorities to put brothers or fathers and sons in the same cell. It made sense. If you beat one, the other would hurt too. And so Abdul found himself sharing a cell with Fuzi.

The promised stay of 'a day or two' turned into months, and then years. The reasons were never explained. The regime did not need reasons or explanations. Men were jailed on suspicion, rumour, whim. Sometimes it was to silence them, sometimes to scare them. Some were dressed in red boiler suits and told they were to die at an unspecified date in the future. Still no reasons were given.

Abdul and Fuzi shared a cell for five years until an annual reassessment committee decided Fuzi should be moved. He was taken one morning and led away to the Liquidation Block.

It was said every person in Tripoli knew someone who had been jailed in Abu Salim. Families would leave food packages outside the gates for collection each day without knowing their sons or fathers had been dead for years. There were similar detention blocks in all major towns.

It was no way for Gaddafi to maintain the popularity he won in the glorious early days of the revolution. He had been in power for two decades and a new generation were coming of age, youngsters who knew little of the fight against colonialism or the allure of Nasser, and who had become tired of Gaddafi's isolationism, the complete absence of new ideas, the public hangings and random purges, the flattening of hope. Coup attempts became more frequent. Several came from within the army itself, one so serious that Gaddafi had to scramble fighter jets to attack one of his own military barracks.

The police and military were not enough to stop the subversion. Businessmen were expected to pass on information about potential dissent, as were doctors, receptionists, garage mechanics, taxi drivers, everyone was watching everyone else. Even the most banal of activities would be reported in the hope of earning some perceived advantage. When my fixer, Yasser, invited a girlfriend to his apartment, a neighbour informed the police that he was involved in improper moral conduct.

Gaddafi's own internal security – the secret police – was of particular concern to the regime because of its access to information and weapons. Several alleged plots were thwarted and the service was divided into rival groups so that they could keep watch on each other.

It was an attempt to coup-proof the regime, but departments were working in such a hair-trigger environment that wild allegations and counter-allegations paralysed the service.

It was a section of fuselage still attached to the wings of Pan Am Flight 103 that hit the ground first, at 7.03 p.m. on 21 December 1988. Most of the residents of Sherwood Crescent, a quiet street of grey 1950s bungalows and modest houses adjacent to fields on the west side of Lockerbie, were settling down for an evening of television. An all-star pantomime had just begun on BBC1. Some were wrapping their Christmas gifts or putting up decorations. The temperature outside was below freezing. A strange noise was heard, a rising howl that seemed to be coming rapidly closer. Residents felt their homes were going to explode, like they were in a kettle under pressure. Then the roar abruptly stopped. The electricity had gone. People's living rooms were dark, televisions blank. One woman opened her door and saw a wall of flames 600 metres away. There was a smell of kerosene in the air. A child's body lay on the steps of her house. Just moments before, the boy had been flying at 31,000 feet in a plane on his way to New York. Other bodies lay alone or in groups, dotted through fields and gardens, beside telephone boxes and on people's roofs.

Two hundred and fifty-nine people fell from the sky that night. Eleven others were killed on the ground.

Three years later, in November 1991, Britain and the US issued indictments against two Libyans for the bombing, and demanded that Gaddafi hand over the suspects; something he refused to do. The wave of sanctions that followed cut Libya adrift from the rest of the world. The UN Security Council froze Libya's overseas assets, banned the sale of some oil equipment, and ended commercial air links. One hundred and eighty-four countries shut their doors on Gaddafi, leaving him more of an outsider than ever before, the de facto head of a rag-tag collection of anti-Western and anti-Zionist fanatics who made Tripoli their international hub. The terrorist mercenary Abu Nidal moved his headquarters there, and he and Gaddafi became great friends. Charles Taylor, who had trained in Tripoli in the 1980s, returned to receive arms and money to launch his war in Liberia.

As the sanctions began to bite, hampering oil production, shutting down factories, and disrupting agriculture, Gaddafi's eight children were flying around the world, enjoying rock-star lifestyles, studying at the most prestigious universities, and representing their father as Libyan diplomats. The two most high-profile sons were Saif al-Islam Gaddafi, the bespectacled, apparently Western-leaning politician tipped as his father's successor, and Saadi Gaddafi, the black sheep who oscillated between drug-binges and desperate attempts to win his father's respect.

Saif al-Islam was the soft face of the regime, a reformer within the narrow confines of the Great Jamahiriya – as Gaddafi called his country – who negotiated access for Amnesty International to visit prisons in Libya and showed apparent concern about the country's record on human rights. He was considered the second most powerful man in the land but met with resistance from the old guard determined to protect their own interests. His apparent liberalization came about after studying for an MSc in Philosophy, Policy and Social Value at the London School of Economics in 2002, and later for his PhD, during which time he lived in a £6 million mansion in Hampstead. One of his academic advisors, Professor David Held, says Saif al-Islam was a funny, witty man, who arrived 'very set in his opinions... struggling with himself and his place in the world', but who, over a period of time, 'showed every sign of being committed not just to opening up his country but reforming it on liberal democratic principles'.[13] But the LSE's links to Saif al-Islam were soon shown to be more than purely educational. It was revealed that, in June 2009, the Gaddafi International Charity and Development Foundation, which Saif al-Islam ran, had pledged £1.5 million to the university. In addition, the Libyan Economic Development Board, also led by Saif, awarded a £2.2 million contract to the LSE's commercial arm, with a view to educating members of Libya's elite. Obvious questions were raised about the propriety of accepting money from organizations run by a dictator's son, particularly just eight months after he had received his doctorate from the same institution. A media storm followed. It didn't end there. It turned out that an international businessman, Peter Sutherland, was chair of the LSE's council (which took the decision to accept the money), while simultaneously non-executive chairman of BP, one of Libya's biggest oil producers. That appeared to represent further uncomfortable links between the LSE and Libya. Sutherland declared a conflict of interest at the June 2009 meeting when the money was accepted, and took no part in proceedings.

Worse was to come. It was found that Saif had received extensive outside help to write his thesis. The humiliation for the LSE was complete when, caught between his father and his conscience at the start of the Libyan Civil War in 2011, Saif made an arrogant finger-jabbing speech on TV, railing against the Western media and predicting that if his father fell, there would be chaos and civil war: 'We will need forty years to reach an agreement on how to run the country.'

Saadi, the second most high-profile son, was a mumbling, awkward contrast, a man-child who raided the dictator's book of clichés for inspiration on how to conduct his private life. There were model girlfriends, yacht parties, A-list celebrities, suitcases stuffed with cash, private performances by rock bands, and an annual expenditure said to be in excess of $200 million. But it was Saadi's bizarre entry into professional sport, and the use of it as a weapon against dissenters, that really defined him. Saadi told his father he wanted to be a footballer. He was only moderately talented but it hardly mattered. Things were smoothed over with the Tripoli team, Al Ahli, and Saadi Gaddafi became captain. Of course the matches were delicate affairs for the referee, the opposition, and even his own team-mates who were said to have received rewards for passing him the ball. 'He was the son of the leader so you couldn't play with him as if he was anyone else,' said one former colleague. 'He wasn't what you would call a team player.'[14] Nevertheless he was elevated to captain of the national team, and head of the Libyan Football Federation. Saadi found it all a little parochial, and so set his sights on the world's most prestigious league, Serie A in Italy.

Before he went, he had a score to settle with a group of fans who had dared support a rival team. The crowd at Benghazi's biggest club had once booed Saadi when the two teams met, and had dressed a donkey in his team colours. Saadi responded swiftly and decisively, by sending in the bulldozers and having the whole stadium razed to the ground. When I visited in 2011, all that remained was an uneven field and half a teetering stand.

Nevertheless the offers came pouring in from Italy, where Saadi's father was busily investing in football. First came Perugia. The club's volcanic owner, Luciano Gaucci, says Italian Prime Minister Silvio Berlusconi telephoned him personally to encourage him to recruit Saadi for the sake of government relations.[15] As it turned out, the club's manager was less enthusiastic about his new acquisition. He selected Saadi just once, and allowed him no closer to the pitch than the subs bench. Shortly afterwards Saadi's urine was tested and showed traces of the performance-enhancing drug Nandrolene. He was banned. Next came Udinese, where he played for ten minutes, and finally Sampdoria, whose manager kept him off the pitch altogether.

At the start of the Libyan Civil War, Saadi was entrusted by his father with putting down protests in Benghazi. It is not clear what qualities Gaddafi felt his wayward son had to offer, but it turned out to be a serious misjudgement. Despite his rank of 'colonel', Saadi had little understanding of military tactics or of international law. As unarmed protestors gathered around the Benghazi barracks, he called his men together and told them to shoot at the crowd. Some used anti-aircraft guns which sliced people in half; others fired wildly from the walls. More than 200 civilians were killed. Shortly afterwards, I spoke to one of the soldiers who had been present. He described in detail how Saadi had given the order to shoot, in the middle of a throng of cheering soldiers and intelligence officials. And then, a few days later, I met with Saadi himself.

The war had been under way for several days and Saadi arrived at our rendezvous point, Tripoli's zoo, nervous and distracted. His mood quickly changed when he saw his pet lions. He cooed and whispered to them through the bars as a keeper fed them chickens. I asked him about the shooting in Benghazi and he reeled backwards. His answers were unconvincing. Sometimes he smirked, at other moments he pulled away trying to get back to the lions as his armed entourage patrolled in a tight circle around us. In the end he agreed he was present in the Benghazi barracks but said the protestors were armed and were trying to get inside to kill the soldiers. Apparently the soldiers were simply trying to defend themselves, with anti-aircraft guns. It wouldn't be a convincing defence when he was finally captured by opposition groups and detained in a Tripoli jail.

Abdul first knew something was wrong at Abu Salim prison when he heard the sound of people running in the corridor outside his cell. It was 1996, in the depths of Libya's international isolation. Normally the guards sauntered, but today they were in a hurry.

'Push it, push it!' one of them shouted. More footsteps, at the top end of the central corridor. 'Shut the door, quickly, shut the door.' The footsteps turned and ran the other way.

The men in Abdul's cell crowded around the feeding slit, but it provided just a narrow envelope of vision. More shouting. 'Shut it and get out, now!' Abdul went for his mirror and squeezed it through, rotating it carefully between his finger and thumb so he could see in both directions. A guard running... and another... a door slamming... prisoner's voices... 'God is Great'... unusual movements in the central corridor. He wasn't sure who was running from whom, but he sensed something momentous was underway.

It was two years since his brother Fuzi had been moved to the Liquidation Block, but Abdul knew he was still alive, through the messages shouted from cell to cell. The beatings had become more brutal after that, the food less frequent. A group of prisoners had tried to escape and the authorities had come down hard on the whole prison. Each day inmates were taken from their cells, made to face the wall, and whipped. When the food came, the guards trampled it in the floor or just slung it straight in the gutters. Some of the inmates wrote a letter to the head of the prison asking him to contact the People's Committee. They wanted proper food, they wrote: water, sanitation, an end to beatings. They wanted trials.

Negotiations were offered with a surprisingly senior figure: one of Gaddafi's favourite lieutenants, Abdullah Senussi, a stocky thug. He had risen to prominence after marrying Gaddafi's sister-in-law in the 1970s, and was now deputy chief of external security. Senussi lived in a mansion in the smartest district of Tripoli, close to other members of Gaddafi's inner circle. I visited the ruins, after it was bombed by NATO during the Libyan uprising. There were the splintered remains of a grand kitchen, jewellery boxes, designer clothes, torn oil paintings. Senussi had lived well. But to negotiate with him, in Abu Salim prison, would require a great deal of caution.

Senussi's boss was the urbane but ruthless Musa Kusa, who was by this time head of external security. Kusa had a large office in Abu Salim prison, where inmates would be brought after interrogation, broken men delivered to the feet of one of the most feared men in the land. It is difficult to conceive that any significant decisions in Abu Salim would not have passed across Musa Kusa's desk.

It was Senussi, however, who responded to the prisoner's complaints. 'Yes,' the message came down, 'with God's permission, we will provide you with all that you need, and will improve conditions.' It was shortly afterwards that Abdul heard the guards running down the corridor.

At 4 a.m. he and the others were removed from their cell and taken to a different block. At 10.30 a.m. they heard an explosion somewhere in the prison. Immediately afterwards there was gunfire. A burst here and there. Then something more sustained, dozens of weapons, firing on automatic. Senussi's men had begun improving conditions.

Later that afternoon, scattered in the courtyards among the plastic bottles and the weeds, lay the corpses of 1,270 men. The guards had rounded them up, climbed onto the metal grids above their heads and opened fire with machine guns. The job had taken two hours to complete. Among the dead was Fuzi.

Abdul had been saved by a sympathetic guard who had herded a small group of prisoners into a distant part of the complex away from the killing.

It was a remarkable series of events that enabled a reinvigorated Gaddafi to rise, shake himself down from nearly a decade in the wilderness, and triumphantly return to the world community. He had finally agreed to hand over the two Libyan suspects in the Lockerbie bombing and, as a result, tentative hands reached out into his isolated world and began to beckon him back to civilization. The UN suspended sanctions. The US began to do the same. African leaders welcomed him reverentially to their summits – Gaddafi was in his element, in control of pieces on his African chessboard once again: trying to resolve disputes between Eritrea and Ethiopia, dispatching a peacekeeping force to Uganda. There were roles for him too in Congo, Sudan, Sierra Leone. So buoyed was he by his popularity, he resurrected his old campaign for a United States of Africa.

Gaddafi was soon finding common purpose with the West too. After Al Qaeda's September 11 attacks against the United States in 2001, he was quick to condemn the massacre and co-operate with America's war on terror. The culprits, he knew, were the same Islamic fundamentalists who had, for years, threatened to overthrow his own regime. Libya and the West now had a shared enemy, and so began an extraordinary relationship between Gaddafi and the intelligence agencies of both the US and the UK.

At a Tripoli jail in the winter of 2004, two British spies were ushered into a room and asked politely to wait. A prisoner was delivered to them accompanied by Libyan officers. The man would later be dressed in a red uniform, to signify he was to be executed, but today he looked like all the other prisoners, blue overalls, pale and unwashed. He sat in front of the two visitors, a man and woman who introduced themselves as representatives of the British government. The Libyan officers sat down at the same table to listen to the conversation. The British spies asked the prisoner how he was being treated, how were his family. What could he say? He couldn't complain, in the presence of Libyan security, that he had been electrocuted with cattle prods. They talked a little about how to fight terrorism in the wake of 9/11. They then stood to leave, reassuring him that all would be well, and that someone from the British embassy would be along shortly. That never happened, and instead the prisoner was transferred to Abu Salim prison where he was kept in a solitary confinement cell little larger than a telephone box.

The prisoner's name was Sami al-Saadi, a man who had once lived in London, and become a member of an armed group opposed to Gaddafi. He was a small, wiry man, erudite and precisely spoken. A few weeks prior to the meeting in the Libyan jail he had been living with his family in the Far East, and had been lured to a meeting at Hong Kong airport with the promise of meeting with British officials about returning to live in the UK. The officials never turned up. That had not been the true purpose of the arrangement. Instead he and his family were handcuffed, hooded and bundled onto a plane to Libya. It was a setup, organized by the CIA and MI6, so that Sami al-Saadi could be kidnapped, a process known by the euphemism of 'rendition'. America and Britain had become unlikely allies of Gaddafi, and the Colonel had wanted Sami al-Saadi served up on a plate.

The key player for Libya was Gaddafi's spy chief, Musa Kusa. The letters between him and MI6's counter-terrorism boss, Mark Allen, read like old golfing buddies supping malt whisky by an open fire; they sent each other Christmas greetings, gifts of dates, and drank together at the Travellers Club in Pall Mall. The letters, which were discovered in the flattened wreckage of Musa Kusa's intelligence headquarters, contained references to Britain's role in the rendition of Sami Al-Saadi, and that of a second Libyan, Abdel Hakim Belhaj, who had been captured and jailed under similar circumstances. In the letters, Allen congratulates the Libyans for the safe arrival of their human 'cargo', when he must have known the men would end up in Abu Salim prison.

The close relationship did have its benefits. Mark Allen played a key role in persuading Gaddafi to surrender his weapons of mass destruction, although in truth this much-vaunted arsenal amounted to a paltry collection of parts and precursor agents. In return Britain allowed Libyan spies into the UK to help hunt jihadis.

It was all leading to a carefully choreographed finale where Gaddafi and British Prime Minister Tony Blair would meet and embrace in the desert in front of the world's press, signalling the final thawing of relations between Libya and the West. 'Number 10 are keen that the Prime Minister meet the Leader in his tent,' wrote Mark Allen to Musa Kusa before the meeting. 'I don't know why the English are fascinated by tents. The plain fact is that the journalists would love it.'[16] Allen was right. The photographs of a beaming Blair standing beside his host in a Bedouin tent in March 2004 were flashed around the world. The 'Deal in the Desert' as it became known, signified a new era, a friendship unthinkable during the Thatcher and Reagan years, and most importantly a reopening of Libya's oilfields to the West.

The resulting deal struck by BP in Libya was its biggest exploration commitment anywhere in the world. It was facilitated by a newcomer to the oil industry, a man with no business experience but with unique access to the Libyan regime. It was the soon-to-be-knighted Mark Allen. The former spy chief had left MI6 and become a special advisor to BP.

Gaddafi was now portrayed by Western governments as a tamed lion, still liable to roar if provoked, but more of an ageing and docile curiosity than the wild beast of old. As the oil companies poured back in, the Tripoli headquarters of Libya's National Oil Corporation (NOC) was soon busy once again. It was a return to the good old days, with huge sums of oil money quickly disappearing into the secret bank accounts of people close to the regime.

Najwa al Beshti was an unlikely Libyan oil official, elegant and petite, with tumbling raven hair and a catwalk wardrobe. She was clever too. A former petro-chemical analyst, Najwa rose to become head of crude oil contracts at the NOC in 2008 and took a seat on the committee that set Libya's oil price. It was during that period she noticed that some foreign companies were being sold Libyan oil for considerably less than the market price. In a country producing around 2 million barrels every day, even a tiny difference in price could be making someone, somewhere, extremely wealthy; either a rogue employee of the oil company who was pocketing the difference himself, or an official at the NOC, or, more likely, a combination of both. Najwa pointed out what was happening to the head of the NOC, the former prime minister Shukri Ghanem, who said he could do little about it, because the corruption usually involved those close to Gaddafi, and so no one could safely interfere.

The person overseeing NOC transparency at the time was Huda Ben Amer, the Benghazi 'hangwoman' from all those years before. Surprisingly, she agreed with Najwa's assessment that money was draining from the public purse into the hands of a few corrupt individuals. Her ministry had previously discovered that 5 million barrels of oil had gone missing in 2008, a consignment worth around half a billion dollars that had simply vanished from the books. Only someone close to the regime could carry off such an audacious theft. It required discreet and influential contacts prepared to shift the load, insiders sanctioned at the highest level.

Najwa had observed Saif al-Islam Gaddafi, hanging around the offices of the NOC on several occasions. She wrote to him, as the supposed political reformer of the Gaddafi family, and explained what was happening. He never replied. Libya's money was still being spirited away.

As head of the NOC, Shukri Ghanem had his own battles to fight. In 2008 he had complained to colleagues that several of Gaddafi's sons were using the National Oil Corporation as a 'personal bank'. One day in 2009, the Colonel's fourth son, Mutassim Gaddafi, a tall, defiant and sometimes violent man, turned up in Ghanem's office and demanded $1.2 billion of oil money. Mutassim said he wanted to create his own militia. Ghanem was uneasy. He decided to inform the president, to make sure it conformed with his wishes. When he explained to Gaddafi that his son wanted such a vast sum of money,

Gaddafi snorted at Mutassim's impertinence, and cheerfully told the head of the NOC to ignore the request. It placed Ghanem in an invidious position. Mutassim was a dangerous man. Ghanem knew that the confluence of Libyan politics and Libyan oil was a dangerous place to swim, and resigned his post shortly afterwards.

During the civil war, Ghanem chose to remain in Libya for the first three months but, as Gaddafi's forces lost ground, the new temporary administration, the National Transitional Council, began investigating him for 'wasting public funds, making illegal gains, and signing some oil contracts that had irregularities'. Interpol was also considering issuing a red-notice arrest warrant against him. Ghanem fled Libya in May 2011, at the height of the NATO bombing campaign, and travelled via Tunisia and Italy to Austria, taking with him his intimate knowledge of how millions of dollars from international oil deals ended up in the pockets of senior Libyan officials, including millions allegedly syphoned from an ExxonMobil contract.

He set up home with his wife and daughter in Vienna. But, eleven months later, at 5 a.m. on 29 April 2012, his body was found floating in the River Danube. There was no sign of violence, but the mysterious circumstances of his death inevitably led to rumours that it was no accident. Not only did Ghanem possess incriminating evidence against senior oil industry figures, he was also wanted back in Libya to give evidence against Saif al-Islam Gaddafi, who was by then in custody. Even today, the cause of Ghanem's death remains a mystery.

From: Yasser
To: Paul Kenyon

DEAR PAUL

I have finally managed to escape from Tripoli; I chose to stay there to document things secretly, but at some stage I had to give up all that since the situation was too bad and being caught with any material I filmed in the street was a matter of life and death!

Major defections have just happened and you should be ready to act at once!

I confirm the Liberation of some Abu Salim prisoners, not sure
about the numbers!

I have reached Benghazi city, and am now absolutely free.

YASSER

It was the start of the Libyan Civil War in February 2011.

I entered the country from Egypt and was soon speeding along
the empty coastal road on my way to Benghazi. Cars occasionally
raced by in the opposite direction, weighed down with luggage.
Checkpoints had been abandoned. Murals of Gaddafi were already
defaced with cartoon horns and scribbles, an act that would have
guaranteed prison or death just a few days before.

Along Benghazi's palm-lined boulevards hordes of youths fired
automatic weapons into the air. Some cantered into town on horse-
back, others drove pick-up trucks converted to carry artillery. One
group had found an anti-aircraft gun and were pumping rounds
wildly across the bay while a young man danced around wearing a
grotesque rubber Gaddafi mask.

Gangs of rebels were moving from house to house hunting for
Gaddafi loyalists. 'What's that building?' I asked the driver as we
passed the burnt-out remains of a grand property near to the sea
with licks of black soot reaching from every shattered window.

'That was the home of the most hated woman in Benghazi,' he
said. 'We called her Huda "the Hangwoman".'

In Tripoli, Gaddafi was still holding out against the rebels. He
whirred around town in a golf buggy, dressed in a dear-stalker hat
and waving an umbrella. He popped up in hotels where foreign
journalists were staying and then roared off in a 4x4 with his head
poking through the sun roof. He appeared on the ramparts of Green
Square to deliver a rambling speech about 'drug addicts' trying to
take over his country. 'Stray dogs', a phrase he hadn't used since the
1980s, resurfaced as a theme, as did British and American 'colonizers'.

Later, as NATO bombs fell around his Bab al-Azizia compound
in a co-ordinated attack with rebel fighters to seize Tripoli, Gaddafi
was spirited away by supporters to his home town of Sirte.

*

On a blustery summer afternoon a few days later I walked with Abdul, 'the naughty one', across wasteland behind Abu Salim prison. The guards had fled in the final days of fighting, leaving hundreds of inmates to break free. Some had been shut away for more than twenty years and had since brought their families back to the prison to see the ruined corridors and cells where they had spent so much of their lives. Abdul moved slowly, concentrating on what was beneath his feet. Mounds of sand and soil baked hard in the sun. Animal bones. Balls of discarded barbed wire. He didn't speak, he just stopped occasionally to push aside a pile of loose earth or stones and inspect what lay underneath. At some point he came across a flap of blue material poking from the ground and crouched beside it.

'This could be him,' he said without looking up, and began digging.

It was the remains of a prison jacket, stiff with dirt. This was the site reputedly used to dispose of the dead from the massacre.

Sami al-Saadi was there too. After his prison encounter with British intelligence officers, he had spent six years in Abu Salim, much of it on death row. Al-Saadi came over and embraced Abdul, and the two former prisoners stood silently for a while, holding on to each other, before wandering off to search for the remains of relatives and friends.

Abdul found some shoes near the blue jacket, the sort he and his brother used to make from prison blankets to keep their feet warm. He stood for a while, looking back at the concrete prison walls and the watchtowers, the place which had taken twelve years of his life without trial or explanation, and then he continued searching. Fuzi's body was never found.

Later, in his airy apartment drinking sweet mint tea, I asked Abdul about the leading figures involved in the Abu Salim massacre. He told me about the role of Abdullah Senussi.

'We could hear him through the window,' says Abdul, 'he was speaking with Gaddafi directly from his car. He was the one who gave the order to the officers to carry out the killings, and the officers ordered the soldiers.'

'Was Musa Kusa in the prison on the day of the massacre?' I asked.

'Yes', he said 'he was present on the night of the incident.'

Abdul was studying a faded photograph of his brother, taken when he was in his twenties, clean-shaven with dark, trusting eyes and a hesitant smile.

'So, are you saying Musa Kusa endorsed the massacre?' I asked.

Abdul looked up from the photo and smiled sadly, because I was still so innocent about the ways of Libya. 'I have no doubt about this,' he said. 'They were all competing to do such a thing just to gain Gaddafi's approval!'

'But if I track him down now, won't Musa Kusa simply deny he ever knew what was happening?'

Abdul nodded, then placed his brother's photo back on the tea tray and sat back in his chair. 'Libya,' he said, 'Libya is a world of wonders. In Libya you wouldn't be able to prove that I was in prison. Even I couldn't prove that I had been in prison if the government itself didn't admit that I was in prison.'

During the fall of Tripoli in August 2011, Abdullah Senussi fled south across the Sahara, to the small desert town of Ghat. From there he crossed the dunes to Niger led by Tuareg tribesman, before moving on to Casablanca, and finally Mauritania. In September 2012, while walking through the passport check at the international airport in Nouakchott, Senussi was apprehended. Within days, he was deported back to Libya to face justice under the newly elected General National Congress. As the helicopter doors opened in Tripoli, a small agitated crowd gathered and reached up to his gloved hands. At first he pulled away, then, tentatively, he let them touch him. The vinegar stare had been replaced with an unsure smile. Were they there to help, or to lynch him? He had no choice but to surrender himself to the crowd.

Later, he appeared in a courtroom, sitting in a metal cage dressed in blue prison uniform, similar to that worn by inmates of Abu Salim, his head shaved, stirrups of grey flesh beneath his eyes. The International Criminal Courts had wanted to put him on trial in The Hague for crimes against humanity, but the new authorities in Libya wanted him to face justice there. Beside him was the former prime minister, and Manchester United fan, Abdul Ati al-Obeidi. He had refused to flee after the revolution, saying he had nothing to fear. Also in custody was Saif al-Islam Gaddafi, caught trying to escape across the desert, and football-loving Saadi, extradited from Niger and facing allegations of war crimes for those orders he gave to shoot unarmed protestors in Benghazi.

Very much absent was Gaddafi's chief agent of repression and friend of MI6, Musa Kusa. During the uprising, Kusa had fled to the UK, where he was given protection by Special Branch. The British government announced that he was welcome in London, in the hope that their accommodating attitude might encourage others to abandon Gaddafi's crumbling regime. After a week, however, Kusa, who might have been expecting to face the International Criminal Court, was allowed to move on again.

I tracked him down to the Four Seasons Hotel in Qatar in 2011, where he was living in a penthouse suite. As he sat down for his breakfast of eggs and fruit in the hotel restaurant, I walked over. I tried to ask him about his role in the Abu Salim massacre and the regime of murder and torture which he had helped oversee. Kusa seemed surprised, not by the content of the questions, but that anyone had the impertinence to address him without being granted an audience first. As I outlined the case against him, he drew himself calmly from his chair without saying a word, wiped his lips with a napkin, and strolled away leaving his bodyguard to have me evicted from the hotel. Later he phoned a news agency to tell them the allegations were all untrue.

Colonel Muammar Gaddafi, Brotherly Leader and Guide to the First of September Great Revolution, spent the last few days of his life shifting between bombed-out apartment blocks in his besieged hometown of Sirte. With him was his driver, a contingent of bodyguards, a security official, and his son, Mutassim, the one who had wanted the billion dollars for his own militia and who was, by now, the regime's last national security advisor.

The rebels had quickly surrounded Sirte and were lobbing shells into the town, waiting patiently for their quarry to attempt an escape. As they pulled the drawstring tighter, moving closer to the city centre, Gaddafi and his entourage were forced to move on again into a more sparsely populated area, squatting in abandoned homes.

Africa's longest-serving dictator, reputedly worth $200 billion, was now living off scavenged food and rainwater collected in pots.

Muttasim was the person who designed the escape plan. It was simple enough: to leave Sirte by cover of night in a convoy while the rebels were asleep. They would almost certainly come under fire at some stage, but in the confusion and darkness, there was a chance some of them would escape. They were exhausted, their movements sluggish from poor diet, stress and lack of sleep. The process of preparing the vehicles and getting everyone on board took longer than expected. By the time they were ready to leave on the morning of 19 October 2011, the sun was already up. The convoy finally departed at 8 a.m., in the full glare of daylight.

As they turned into an open road on the outskirts of town there was a huge explosion. A missile had landed so close to Gaddafi's Land Cruiser it had inflated the airbags. The convoy swung around and retreated back into town. But the road was now blocked by rebel militia who spotted the leader's car and opened fire. Gaddafi's bodyguards fired back. The gunfight lasted several minutes, attracting attention from other militia nearby. The rebel units sent urgent radio messages asking for backup. NATO fighter jets observed the action on the ground, and dropped two laser-guided bombs that showered the convoy with shrapnel.

Some of Gaddafi's entourage were killed outright. The survivors, including Gaddafi himself, abandoned their vehicles and hid in an abandoned building. As more shells fell, he and a small contingent of bodyguards made the decision to run for it. They sprinted across an open field and hid in a drainage pipe.

There's something sickeningly compelling about the mobile phone footage of what happened next. A bewildered Gaddafi, bleeding and disorientated, can be seen standing beside the entrance to the pipe on a piece of wasteland that dips away to the side of the road. A couple of curious lads wander over. They don't seem to realize that they have stumbled upon Africa's 'King of Kings'. There is gunfire from up on the road. A few rebels run over to the see what their friends have discovered. The old man seems to be trying to reason with them. There is a pause. Gaddafi is bloated and terrified, swaying like a drunk. For a moment the rebels seem unsure what to do. Then a more purposeful youth approaches, and grabs hold of him.

'What have I done to you or your family?' Gaddafi pleads. A fist lands in the side of his head. The gunfire is continuous now. Gaddafi is propped against the back of a pickup truck and more men are running to see who has been caught. There is blood on his face, but he is still pleading, trying to reason with them. Then the mob descends.

The circumstances of Gaddafi's death are still disputed. He is seen being sodomized with a bayonet, and loaded onto the back of a pickup truck, surrounded by jubilant rebel fighters. Their leaders say he was killed while being transported across the desert to Misrata. Their convoy, they say, was caught in crossfire between rival rebel groups, and Gaddafi was hit by a stray bullet. The far more likely explanation is that his ecstatic captors executed him with a single shot to the head.

CHAPTER FIVE
Nigeria

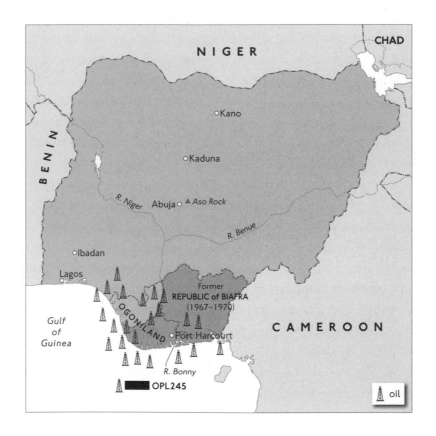

NIGERIA

I am unfortunate to be a Nigerian. I would rather
not be, but I am doing my level best to be one,
and a good one at that.

KEN SARO-WIWA

A HUNDRED MILES off the coast of Nigeria, the seabed plunges to the submariner's equivalent of outer space. Few people have ever travelled this far down. All our information is gleaned from robotic arms drilling into the grey ocean floor, and grainy spot-lit images. Yet every metre of this land belongs to someone. It is divided into hundreds of oil concessions, packed around the Nigerian coast in a tessellated crescent: smaller, more desirable pieces closer to the mouth of the delta; larger ones, some the size of Luxemburg, at the furthest limits of its territorial waters. Somewhere in the middle is an oblong-shaped concession that is one of the richest oil fields in the world. Its reserves are thought to amount to 9 billion barrels. That's enough to supply all of Nigeria's demands for almost a century, or the whole of Africa's for the next seven years. It is the continent's very own Black Giant, and it's called, simply, OPL245, Oil Prospecting License 245.

Choosing the private company to exploit OPL245 was a question of great national importance. Because of its 'ultra-deep' status it would be prohibitively expensive to develop. Only 'Big Oil' need apply: in other words, just a handful of huge corporations. The purchasers of OPL245 would need to pay at least $1.1 billion to the Nigerian state for control of the concession. Once oil started flowing, royalties and taxes would earn the federal government many billions more. It had the potential to be transformative for the Nigerian economy.

In the 1990s, OPL245 was much-coveted throughout the oil world, with Shell and the Italian supermajor Eni emerging as the two frontrunners. The person who would decide the allocation was the Nigerian oil minister. In a country where people joke that their leaders are 'professional fraudsters playing at being politicians', the oil job was open to abuse like no other. The Ministry of Environment, or Transport, were happy to skim off the conventional ten per cent, but the Oil Ministry had the potential to catapult its boss into the realms of the fabulously rich. Fees to middlemen alone could amount to tens of millions of dollars, and to the minister himself, hundreds of millions.

Dan Etete was a boisterous cannonball of a man, who ricocheted around social gatherings, glass of champagne in one hand, silver-tipped cane in the other, recounting tall stories about his shipping business or his connections in government, promising something to everyone and everything to someone. His tailor? Yes, he'd put you in touch. The wine? Always French, he had some properties there. The silk cravat? He knew a little shop in Abuja. Etete was a social whirligig, an honorary chief always looking for a deal, and precisely the kind of man who, in Nigeria, is destined to enter the political arena. He took a seat in the senate, representing an area right in the heart of the oil-producing delta, and soon began to attract the attention of the military chiefs who ran Nigeria, not just for his giant white-checked suits, but for his eagerness to take part in illicit schemes, and to keep his nose out of other people's. When the big job finally came his way in 1995, it was the gift of military dictator General Sani Abacha. Dan Etete was to become oil minister.

An application for OPL245 landed on Etete's desk at the Oil Ministry in Abuja sometime in April 1998, from a small start-up company no one had ever heard of. It was called Malabu, incorporated just days before specifically for the purpose. Malabu had no employees, no capital, no offices, just the names of three company directors on a sheet of paper. Its bid for what promised to be Nigeria's richest oilfield was just $20 million. It was like trying to buy a Rolls-Royce for the price of a hubcap. Dan Etete had numerous options, and might have wished to discount Malabu and its three aspirant directors without so much as an interview. But Etete knew something about the company no one else did. Within a matter of days, he had chosen Malabu for ownership of OPL245.

The whereabouts of Malabu's application letter was a mystery. Etete says he saw it at the time. Nigeria's federal government says no such application was ever received. All we are left with are the supposed names of the three shareholder-directors. For years, Etete would deny knowing who they were, caring little how it looked for the oil minister to be handing out a prize national asset for a knock-down price to three unidentified individuals. He preferred to appear incompetent than give Nigerians a glimpse behind the doors of his ministry. There were rumours, though, that an entire oilfield had been stolen from beneath the nose of the Nigerian state.

Sani Abacha was raised among the hot clay pathways of Kano, in the Muslim north of Nigeria, at the same time BP's Rex Brown was lodging above a bank in the city. While Brown was attending the British club at weekends, drinking beer and catching up on the papers, the teenage Abacha was playing with friends between the rows of windowless baked-mud houses, barefoot, in a pair of scruffy shorts. Nearby were women selling water from earthenware pots, and men dressed in starched Islamic gowns shepherding their goats, the whole scene wrapped in a soft-focus of grass-dust and Saharan sand. The only interruption to Abacha's street games would have been motorcars like Rex Brown's Morris Minor, driven by BP staff and colonial officers, or the water tankers that relieved the city during the regular droughts. Perhaps a thirteen-year-old Abacha was one of the children cleared from the road when the Duchess of Kent's Rolls-Royce passed through Kano in 1956. He would have been seventeen when Nigeria won its independence from Britain on 1 October 1960.

This was a vast country of 35 million people, home to 300 tribes jigsawed together by Britain to create an artificial nation. To many of its inhabitants, Nigeria didn't exist. There was no such country. The tribes themselves were the nations. The newly drawn borders were just an expression of imperialism. And now all these tribal groups, many of them hostile towards each other, were expected to govern themselves, peacefully and fairly, without the glue of national identity, in a federal republic.

The worry around the markets and coffee shops of Abacha's home city was that the mainly Muslim north would be subsumed by the better-educated Christian south, which is why many in the north were opposed to independence in the first place. The north was a huge region, twice the size of Britain, made up of wind-beaten savannah and high plains. But it was poor. The hand of modernity had barely touched it. Despite being home to more than half Nigeria's population, it only contained five per cent of the country's secondary schools. Tribally it was dominated by the Hausa-Fulani, who were mainly farmers and traders living in villages run as small fiefdoms by the Fulani ruling class. Many northerners harboured a fierce distrust of their Christian neighbours to the south, referring to them as pagans and infidels. When southerners migrated north into cities like Kano they were obliged to live in segregated housing and to attend separate schools.

The mainly Christian south of Nigeria was split into two, the eastern and western regions. The latter consisted of rich and fertile rainforests looking out over the Gulf of Guinea, with inland savannah that hosted several large conurbations, including the capital, Lagos. It was dominated by Yoruba people, often well-educated city-dwellers interested in trade and administration, and was divided into mini statelets run by kingly chiefs. The eastern region lay across the other side of the Niger River and included much of the swampland and mangrove of the Niger Delta, where the oil had been found. It was dominated by Igbo, whom British colonials described as 'the talented people'. The Igbo had enthusiastically embraced Christianity, and spread quickly from their homeland in search of work, settling across all of Nigeria. When their people ventured north, their arrival was viewed with distrust and sometimes violence. In Kano the local population had conducted pogroms against the Igbo in 1953.

It was these disparate and mutually suspicious tribes, each determined to ensure its own survival, and preferably dominance, that were expected to co-exist as a unified nation state once the British had left.

From the start, northerners like Sani Abacha were suspicious that the British had groomed southerners to take over the leadership, and that, once installed, they would slowly erase Islam from the north. Whoever secured the first foothold in power, it was argued, would seek to dominate for decades, rewarding those in their own ethnic group, and redirecting federal budgets to their own advantage. An Igbo would give a job to another Igbo, a Yoruba to another Yoruba. It was natural. Even if they didn't, everyone would assume that they did. But it was the north that had the advantage, in terms of territory and numbers of voters, with fifty-six per cent of the population.

The first election, held in 1959 just prior to independence, was fought by three main political parties, each representing a different region. The Northern People's Congress (NPC) triumphed, and was thus offered the first opportunity to lead a government. Without an overall majority, they agreed to run Nigeria as a coalition with the party representing the east, the National Council of Nigerian Citizens (NCNC). The opposition seats would be taken by members of the west's 'Action Group'. Splitting up representatives from the east and west seemed a sensible move. The arrangement ensured they didn't gang up to overthrow the new northern-dominated government. In addition, each of the three main parties had its own regions to run, with the creation of local assemblies to dilute the possibility of a single dominant party further.

But the ethnic cracks quickly started to show. A split among the leadership of the west's Action Group led to brawling in the local parliament, allowing the federal government to intervene gleefully, declaring a state of emergency, suspending the constitution and imposing its own hand-picked administrator instead. In the federal parliament in Lagos, easterners, who had hoped their power-sharing would bring a range of glittering privileges, soon realized that the northerners were allocating themselves vast chunks of development capital while keeping easterners firmly in the background.

As the three regions wrestled over state money and influence, it was the most banal of processes that turned into a fiasco of civic manipulation and corruption and began the slide into violence: the national census of 1962. Population numbers in each region really mattered. Whichever had the largest number of inhabitants would be likely to win an election, and could command a greater share of federal money. In the census, the north reported that its population had risen by thirty per cent in five years. The east managed to eclipse that, claiming rises in some areas of up to 200 per cent. Realizing they were being outmanoeuvred, the north hit back, managing to find another 8.5 million people almost overnight.

It all fed into a rancorous and bitterly disputed set of elections in December 1964. Ballot boxes went missing, bails of fraudulent votes were tossed into counting rooms, people bought and sold voting slips. Vast and unwieldy alliances fought it out, promising favours and plum positions in return for support. The sitting prime minister was the Muslim founder of the Northern People's Congress, Sir Abubakar Tafawa Balewa, knighted by Queen Elizabeth II at the time of independence, and it was he whose NPC-led alliance won the election. The federal government was going to remain in northern hands. Balewa simply had to request that the Nigerian president, the grandfather of Nigerian nationalism, Nnamdi Azikwe (Zik), reappoint him. It should have been a formality, but Zik had previously been the head of the rival eastern NCNC and, uneasy about further northern dominance, turned Balewa away. A constitutional crisis ensued and both men sought assistance from a state agency that had, thus far, stayed out of the political fray: the Nigerian army. For the first time, its commanders became aware of their potential to intervene in civilian affairs. In the end, Balewa was allowed to reclaim his prime ministerial post at the head of a corrupt and discredited government, but the army had smelled power.

From an early age, Major Patrick Nzeogwu was marked out by the Nigerian military for great things. An immaculately presented, articulate Igbo, he was a product of British military training, first at the Royal Military Academy at Sandhurst, and later at Hythe and Warminster, and once back in Nigeria was quickly elevated to a senior role in military intelligence. It was there that he witnessed first-hand the corruption of the country's elite and, in late 1965, began organizing Nigeria's first coup.

Nzeogwu was by this time stationed in Kaduna, the northern capital, where he was in charge of the military training school. His barracks was close to the home of the premier of the northern region, Sir Ahmadu Bello, a man with an almost fanatical following, who was known by the reverential Islamic title 'Sardauna of Sokoto'. In the early hours of 15 January 1966, Nzeogwu took his men, most of them Igbos, to the Sardauna's home. They were equipped with live ammunition and anti-tank weapons, and they came to a halt right outside the property. Nzeogwu instructed his men to begin shelling, and then ran inside where he found the terrified Sardauna hiding among his children and wives, and shot him dead. As flames licked the windows, Nzeogwu posed for a picture standing on the Sardauna's body.

At the same time, in a carefully co-ordinated attack in Lagos, a group of Igbo officers stormed the home of the federal prime minister, Sir Abubakar Balewa, arresting him and bundling him into a car. Balewa was tortured and killed. When his remains were found a week later, at mile 27 on the Lagos–Abeokuta road, he could only be identified by his frog-patterned white gown.

Another group of mutineers attacked the leadership in Ibadan, capital of the western region. The newly elected premier there, Samuel Akintola, was with his family when fifty mutinous soldiers stormed the house. He hid behind wardrobes to escape the bullets, shouting at the soldiers that he wanted to negotiate. When he walked outside to meet them, he was shot dead on his own front steps.

The January coup claimed the lives of twenty-one senior government and military officials, wiping out almost the entire upper layer of government, all from the northern and western regions. The coup had been carried out largely by Igbos.

Curiously, there had been one man who was slated for assassination that night who survived. His name was Major General Johnson Aguiyi-Ironsi, a rotund career soldier who carried a crocodile-head swagger stick wherever he went, and who had been equerry to Queen Elizabeth II during a state visit to Nigeria. Ironsi was of Igbo descent, but had been appointed commander of the Nigerian army by leaders of the ruling Northern People's Congress, and was thus seen by many as *one of them.*

It seems that the mutineers couldn't find Ironsi that night, or that he was being closely guarded by loyalist soldiers. Either way, he survived, and by sunrise on 15 January 1966, he was moving around army bases in Lagos, rallying his forces against Igbo-inspired attacks. Soon Lagos was secure, but rebellion was still raging in Kaduna and other northern cities. On 16 January, at 7.30 p.m., Ironsi called together federal ministers for a meeting in the Cabinet Office. He had an historic announcement to make.

As he began addressing them, Ironsi allowed the tears to run down his face. With great reluctance, he told them, he required them formally to pass the leadership to him. Only temporarily, of course. Just enough for him to put down the uprising.

With Ironsi's soldiers positioned at the office door, and surrounding all government buildings, the elected politicians felt they had little choice. If they had been in any doubt, Ironsi helped them focus: 'You either hand over as gentlemen, or you hand over by force.' With that, he instructed them to sign an agreement placing him in charge of Nigeria. But no one could find anything to write on, and the stationery cupboard was locked. They ended up jotting the terms of the handover on a piece of scrap paper. Nigeria's first experiment with democracy was over. Military rule had arrived. The country was in the hands of an Igbo.

Sani Abacha returned from military training school in Aldershot, England, a year before the January coup. He was a taciturn young officer, tribal scars down each cheek, unkempt hair poking from beneath his beret. As a Muslim from the north, he was incensed by the murder of the Sardauna and the Igbo-inspired coup. He and everyone else at the Kaduna barracks where he was based viewed the

Igbos with deep distrust. They kept an eye on them at all times. All Igbos were potential assassins.

In the meantime Ironsi and his supporters were terrified of a northern-inspired counter-coup. Ironsi banned the use of live ammunition among soldiers, even for target practice. One Nigerian diplomat at the time wrote in his diary, 'I do not blame the northern chaps for feeling sore since the events of the last few days. It must have been shocking, to say the least, for one to wake up one fine morning to find nearly all one's revered leaders gone overnight… I know the present state of affairs will not last long. I think the general [Ironsi] is sitting on a time bomb with the fuse almost burnt out.'[1]

Abacha was already part of a militant northern group of officers known as the 'Kaduna Group', who were organizing secret meetings to discuss revenge. The group had even sent a letter of protest to their chief-of-staff, General Yakubu Gowon, warning that if he didn't take action soon, then they would.

On 30 July 1966, the hockey pitch at the Kaduna military base was a patch of bald, sun-baked earth, pounded by marching boots so that in the moonlight it glistened like the surface of a jungle pool. It was four in the morning, an unusual hour to turn out a parade but, with events moving so rapidly elsewhere in the country, the commanding officers needed to check that everyone was present. Lieutenant Sani Abacha was one of those in charge. He had been at a party in the officers' mess a few hours earlier.

The messages pouring into the signal room at Kaduna had been confused. It seemed a group of Abacha's colleagues based at the Abeokuta Barracks in the western region, 100 kilometres north of Lagos, had suddenly begun a mutiny. The camp was two days' drive away. They couldn't be sure what was happening. There were at least four alternative coup plots being considered by northern officers at the time, but this was not one of them. It seemed to have happened spontaneously. Abeokuta Barracks was a mixture of ethnicities, as all camps were. It appeared that a group of Igbo officers stationed there had heard there was to be a counter-coup that night. Fearful they would be murdered in their beds, they tiptoed around the dorm

The newly-promoted Colonel Joseph Mobutu in his office in Leopoldville shortly after Congo won independence from Belgium in 1960. Within months, Mobutu would launch his coup.

Patrice Lumumba, the first democratically elected prime minister of Congo, is captured by Mobutu's soldiers in December 1960. He was executed six weeks later.

Mobutu with Muhammad Ali during the build up to the 'Rumble in the Jungle' fight against George Foreman in Kinshasa, 28 October 1974.

President Robert Mugabe celebrates his 93rd birthday with his wife Grace, February 2017. It was Grace – renowned for her Herculean spending sprees on shoes and handbags – who was his preferred successor, but events took a different turn.

Esso's legendary guerrilla geologists – the Rover Boys – in Africa in the 1960's. Dr Dave Kingston (*seated*) and his team (*left to right*): Dick Murphy, George Voutopoulos (mechanic) and Shelby Eddington made many important discoveries during the African oil race.

Libya's Colonel Muammar Gaddafi relaxing in Tripoli shortly after the revolution of 1969. Ordinary Libyans were ecstatic that a man of such principle and promise would lead the newly oil-rich country.

Gaddafi in 2008, forty years after his revolution, accompanied by his elite female protection unit – the Amazonian Guard. Known for their oaths of virginity and heavy mascara, they were also expected to take a bullet for their leader.

The author with Colonel Gaddafi's playboy son, Saadi, feeding his pet lions at Tripoli Zoo in March 2011 as rebel forces closed in. Saadi awaits trial on a variety of charges, including murder.

The military dictator of Nigeria, General Sani Abacha. Renowned for being a lazy, sadistic drunk, even his closest colleagues were shocked by his disregard for human rights and his blatant theft of oil money.

Dan Etete, former Nigerian Oil Minister and master of corruption. He hid his millions in tax havens around the world, and awarded himself a $1.2 billion oil field.

The Nigerian writer and environmentalist, Ken Saro-Wiwa, addressing supporters at Ogoni National Day in the oil producing region of Rivers State, January 1993. 'Ken will deliver us from trouble,' chanted the crowd.

The much-feared Macías, first president of Equatorial Guinea, said to be responsible for the death of a quarter of his population. Behind him walks his nephew and military governor, Obiang, who had Macías executed in 1979 before replacing him as president, a role he still holds today.

President Obiang of Equatorial
Guinea in 2016. His involvement
in torture and mass killing under
his uncle's regime are now largely
overlooked. Here he is holding
hands with his friend Robert
Mugabe.

Teodoro, vice president of Equatorial Guinea, and playboy son of President
Obiang. He is next in line to rule the oil-rich state.

Côte d'Ivoire's President Felix Houphouet-Boigny posing outside the monument he built to himself. Our Lady of Peace Basilica, completed in 1989, is a copy of St Peter's in Rome. The building is thirty-five storeys high, with grounds large enough to land a Boeing 747.

Eritrea's President Isaias Afwerki during a rare foreign trip, to Khartoum, Sudan, in 2015. Once a war hero, he presides over Africa's most secretive state, forcing the population into endless military conscription.

awakening Igbo soldiers, and telling them to prepare to defend themselves. At the same time, in true Keystone Kops style, northern officers noticed the Igbos rising quietly and assumed this was a continuation of the first coup: that the Igbos wanted to finish the job. The northerners responded swiftly.

They got word to the armoury to secure all weapons and to allow only northerners inside. The command was met. Northerners collected their assault rifles and ran into the officers' mess, executing any Igbo officers they could find. The August counter-coup of 1966 had stuttered into action through a complete misunderstanding.

The military radio was abuzz with incoherent messages. It was twenty-four hours later that Abacha and his colleagues in Kaduna were finally able to make sense of what was happening. They decided to join the coup.

Soldiers were lined up on the hockey pitch at Kaduna Camp and the register read out. All were present. Abacha and other officers stalked the lines, separating the Igbo soldiers from the rest, and locking them in the guardroom. Those who resisted were beaten. Some were shot. Land Rovers were then summoned, and the men drove through the early morning in search of Igbo officers still sleeping, either in Brigade HQ or at their homes. The mission was intended to round up the so-called 'jubilators'. These were the men who had conspicuously celebrated the first coup, and in particular the assassination of the Sardauna of Sokoto. After his murder back in January, the jubilators had taunted northerners, wearing graphic stickers of his dead body on their jackets, and even selling gramophone records of machine-gun fire that was supposedly a recording of his assassination. The Abacha group had compiled a list of their names.

When they found them, later that morning, most were executed on the spot. But six Igbo jubilators, were driven off in Land Rovers to the Sardauna's former residence.

The burnt-out shell had once been an elegant, whitewashed, Georgian-style mansion. The northern officers led their captives around, pointing to the licks of soot around the property's broken windows, and the charred timber remains of the roof. They then took them next door to the Sardauna's guest house, where food was prepared, and drinks handed round. Captors and captives sat down for a meal. The conversation was lively, but courteous. When they had finished, the Igbos were taken into the main house, and given a tour. They were shown the bullet holes from the machine-gun fire, and the cratered walls where the artillery shells had hit. Then they were led through the courtyard, to the place where the Sardauna was shot. The tour stopped beside a portrait of the former leader. The Igbos were instructed to kneel before him, among the broken glass and burnt furniture, and bow. When they had done so, they were led outside, into the warm afternoon air, and shot dead.[2]

Major-General Ironsi was on a tour of the country at the time, staying at Government House in the western regional capital of Ibadan, a rare event given his concerns over personal security. On the night the mutiny began, 28 July 1966, he tried to phone his chief-of-staff, General Gowon, but he was ominously uncontactable. At 8 a.m., the following morning, Ironsi requested a helicopter to fly him to safety. It never arrived. Instead he was arrested by soldiers from a rival brigade who kidnapped him, drove him to the outskirts of town and shot him dead. Ironsi had been right to be suspicious about his unanswered calls to Gowon. Gowon was the one taking over. It was he, a northerner, who was to become Nigeria's next head of state.

In the Delta, the rainy season was it its height. The afternoons brought large, oily drops that thundered against the metal roofs of Port Harcourt, and swilled into the open sewers, spilling litter and human waste onto the roads. In the villages that sat on the spongy ground between the rivers, pathways became brief streams, which the fishermen waded through to reach their canoes. Engineers from Shell-BP hurried out of the mangroves to shelter from the deluge beneath their tarpaulin tents. In the first six years of independence, oil production had soared by fifteen times, all of it around the delta in the south, and in particular the Igbo heartland of the eastern region. The rest of the country had quickly become dependent on this booming trade.

News of the August '66 counter-coup filtered through as easterners huddled around their radios beneath the crying skies. With it came terrible accounts of killing. They heard how Igbos living in northern cities had been rounded up and massacred by northerners. It was a free-for-all, said the reports, and the new federal military government wasn't doing anything to protect the victims. General Gowon's own soldiers were indulging in a frenzy of ethnic cleansing. In the four months up to November 1966, 100,000 Igbos were murdered.

In the eastern region, Igbos sought revenge, rooting out northerners from their homes and offices and killing them on the streets. By May 1967 Igbo leaders concluded that their people were unsafe anywhere else in Nigeria and that the eastern region should break away. They placed troops along their borders, and declared themselves the Independent Republic of Biafra. Beneath their land lay Africa's largest reserves of oil. The Biafran leaders were fortified by it, reassured that the very earth they walked on would provide their means of survival. The region had sixty-seven per cent of Nigeria's oil. But just as it fuelled their fight for independence, it convinced Gowon's federal military government that they could not let the eastern region go. The rest of Nigeria could simply not afford to lose Biafra.

The guns were starting to crackle across the delta's inky morning sky as Ken Saro-Wiwa and his new wife dressed themselves in the cramped bedroom of the home they shared with his parents in the heart of Biafra. The *crump* of mortar fire was drifting in from the direction of the Bonny River. Federal troops were firing into the darkness towards the sleeping villages. Saro-Wiwa rooted through the boxes of shoes and Western-style clothes he had worn as a PhD student over in Ibadan, and chose instead a pair of filthy shorts and a T-shirt, the sort a fisherman might wear. We can imagine the radio playing quietly, perhaps the station's favourite morale-boosting Igbo war songs, as the couple made their final preparations, a kerosene lamp on low burn so as not to attract the attention of federal binoculars. The waterways around the delta were obscured by mist at that time in the morning, but Saro-Wiwa knew the terrain well. This was his ancestral land. He was familiar with the course of every stream and braided river, with each fishing village that clung to the slippery banks, with the yam and cassava farms planted on the precious fertile ground. This was Ogoniland, and Saro-Wiwa was an Ogoni, a member of a little-known micro-minority that British rule had barely touched, other than in its pursuit of the area's hidden treasures. White men had cruised its waterways looking for oil, and had drilled so many holes across Ogoniland it was as if the clouds had opened and the monsoon delivered gunshot. Ogoniland was the area within Biafra where much of Nigeria's oil was concentrated. But because the Igbo were the region's dominant tribe, the rest of the country thought the oil discoveries were on Igbo soil. Few had heard of the impoverished Ogoni people. It was Igbo who shouted loudest, Igbo who conceived the state of Biafra, and Igbo politicians who were using oil to further their agenda. When the Igbo cut themselves adrift from the rest of Nigeria, they took the Ogoni with them, and Saro-Wiwa and his family wanted nothing to do with it.

He and his wife scrambled through the undergrowth and into a canoe. The river was narrow, the water clear. There were periwinkles and clams, healthy green weeds, mangrove trees where crabs hid among the roots. But soon they were paddling through slicks of oil that undulated glutinously as the canoe passed by. Fighting had ruptured the pipes that transported oil across Ogoniland, and the crude had begun to leak into the river. The source of drinking water, and of food nutrients, was already being poisoned, less than a decade after Shell-BP had made its first discovery.

Saro-Wiwa paddled downstream towards the fighting front. Many of the villages had been abandoned, but a few daring farmers remained to harvest what they could, working largely at night to avoid the guns. The federal government had blockaded Biafra, cutting off food supplies, fuel, and medicine. People trapped inside were dying of starvation. Saro-Wiwa was hunched in his canoe among heaps of fishing net, his wife perched on the rear, as he switched channels through the labyrinth of waterways, pressing on towards the gunfire. If federal troops suspected he was a Biafran soldier, they would shoot him dead. But Saro-Wiwa's cover story, that he was a fisherman simply going about his morning catch, convinced them to wave him through. The couple abandoned their canoe, and climbed up the harbour wall in Bonny. Once inside the federal-controlled town, they could mingle easily. From there, they took a ship up the coast to Lagos, and waited there until the war was over.

It was two and a half years before Saro-Wiwa returned home in January 1970, by which time Biafra was defeated, its population decimated. Around a million easterners had lost their lives through starvation, disease and warfare – more than total British losses in either of the World Wars.

In victory, Gowon was conciliatory. There were no medals awarded to his own federal troops, no demands for reparations, and an amnesty for former Biafran fighters. He made an effort to unify the country, announcing a massive programme of 'reconciliation, reconstructions and rehabilitation', much of which would be directed towards the ruined towns and cities of the eastern region, where Ken Saro-Wiwa had just landed a senior government position. The aspiring poet and activist was appointed a minister in Rivers State, the new regional government which covered Ogoniland. But he could hardly have been less suited to a career of compromise and quiet diplomacy. From his offices in Port Harcourt he hoped to create a counterbalance to the unchecked activities of Shell-BP, which had continued producing oil with skeleton staff through much of the war, and was now back at full strength. But Nigeria was becoming what academics term a 'rentier state', a country solely dependent on rents and taxes paid by foreign businesses – in this case, oil companies. Nigeria's military leaders didn't need their own economy to perform. Neither did they need to rely on an electorate. There was no electorate. The junta had no contract with its people, just opaque agreements with big oil. It was a heady and intoxicating brew that would corrupt the country's leaders for the next fifty years.

★

The letter which landed on the desk of an air-conditioned office in Shell-BP's Port Harcourt HQ was addressed to the regional director. He passed it straight to the lawyers. It was March 1970, three months after the end of the civil war, and already some Ogoni had serious grievances with the way their land was being used. The letter contained not just one or two complaints about Shell-BP, but a detailed and evidence-based list of twenty-one. The oil company's instinct was not to respond. Shell-BP was a guest of the federal government; the views of the Ogoni hardly mattered. If these tribesmen wanted to complain, their beef should be with the generals, not foreign businessmen. But there was something tantalizing about this letter. A little sport would be enjoyable. The Ogoni had attempted a legal tone: cautious language, numbered points and references, faux courtesy. Shell-BP decided to show the author how real lawyers play the game.

If the Ogoni believed their roadways were collapsing beneath the weight of oil machinery, then they should prove it, said the letter. Provide the evidence it was caused 'exclusively by use of company traffic'. If they claimed their land was being poisoned by oil leaks, again, prove it. Wasn't it the case that the Ogoni were 'exaggerating' in order that Shell-BP would have to provide a fresh source of drinking water, which would inevitably require them to drill an expensive well? If Shell-BP had paid too little for the land, why weren't the farmers themselves writing to complain?

The Ogoni were largely illiterate. They had no understanding of environmental laws or the standard of proof or the workings of a multinational company. When disaster befell them, they treated it as an act of god. Flooding, illness, crop failure, oil spills, they were all the same. There was no remedy other than prayer.

Two weeks after Shell-BP despatched its reply, there was a catastrophic blow-out in the heart of Ogoniland. It was 19 July 1970 at a site called Bomu II.

The wellhead exploded, hurling jets of fire and hot oil into the sky. One eyewitness described an 'ocean of crude oil... moving swiftly like a great river in a flood, successfully swallowing up anything that comes in its way'.[3] The ruptured equipment howled. Oil filled the streams, poisoning the water supply. People were barred from entering their own farmland, in case they carried a naked light. Those who managed to get to their fields had to wade knee-deep in crude. Some submerged themselves in the black gunk trying to uproot their rotting cassava and yams. Acrid black smoke billowed across all of Ogoniland and, beneath it, the people gathered to sing.

The flames of Shell are Hell
We bask beneath their light
None for us save the blight
Of cursed neglect and cursed Shell.[4]

The oil continued to pour from Bomu II for three weeks, and was still contaminating farmland and water twenty years later. The number of explosions and spillages rose steeply. By the 1990s several thousand such events had occurred, releasing 2.5 million barrels of oil onto farmland and into waterways.[5] Ken Saro-Wiwa was monitoring the spills from his offices on the busy Aggrey road in the Old Township district of Port Harcourt. By this time, he had left his government post to write books and start a business, and was spending more of his time campaigning for the Ogoni. He read and reread that first letter from Shell-BP, and one line in particular rankled. 'There can be no doubt,' wrote the oil company, 'that the incidental benefits accruing to the Ogoni... from Shell-BP's presence there greatly outweigh any disadvantages'.[6]

It seemed the whole of the Niger Delta was floating on oil. Agricultural communities abandoned their fields and migrated to cities like Port Harcourt, hoping to cash in on the bonanza. What had begun as a promising but unreliable sideshow to the rest of the economy was now the dazzling main event. The 1970s oil boom had sent prices soaring by 400 per cent in a matter of months. Nigeria, the new boy on the block, was overwhelmed. All other sectors of its economy were thrown under the juggernaut. Oil soon accounted for ninety per cent of the country's exports. Billions of dollars was flowing into the federal government's coffers. The junta took what they liked, and used it to bribe opponents and reward supporters. There were jobs with inflated salaries, bonuses, palaces, construction contracts, anything was possible. It was the dawning of the age of Nigerian patronage.

Sani Abacha still worked in the shadows, but his influence quickly grew. He had a hand in each of the many coups that followed. Gowon's leadership was literally sunk by corruption. Overwhelmed by the oil wealth available to them, military officials began ordering vast amounts of cement, ostensibly for construction projects. The Ministry of Defence needed 2.9 million tonnes, but its officials ordered 16 million, in return for multimillion-dollar kickbacks. Cargo ships began arriving from around the world. Nigeria's ports couldn't cope with the sheer quantity of cement. By April 1975, a queue of 105 ships had formed. Two months later it was 455, with vessels backed up across fifty miles of sea, all of them charging demurrage fees by the day to the Nigerian government. It became known as the 'cement armada' and was said to contain enough of the product to rebuild Lagos three times over. Gowon was overthrown soon after, while attending an Organization of African Unity (OAU) meeting in Kampala. His replacement, General Murtala Muhammed, announced plans for a speedy return to civilian rule, but on his way to work on 13 February 1976, Muhammed's Mercedes car was ambushed by a group of men who drew AK-47s from beneath their gowns and shot him dead. The assassins were all senior military officers, including Lt-Col. Buka Dimka. Dimka went straight to Radio Nigeria to announce news of his coup, warning listeners that 'any attempt to foil these plans from any quarters will be met with death'. As he was leaving the studios, forces loyal to the government turned up and Dimka fled for his life. He was arrested three days later and executed by firing squad. A pattern was beginning to emerge. This was no longer tribal politics; it was about access to oil money.

Several military dictators followed, many of them helping each other into power, only to launch another coup soon afterwards.

Aside from one brief window of democracy, under the civilian president Shehu Shagari in the early 1980s, the rest was a grizzly merry-go-round of military dictatorships.

Sani Abacha's rapid rise through the ranks was due almost entirely to his expertise in coup-making. Each successive military head of state since Gowon in 1966 had promoted him in exchange for helping them into the top job, and by 1983 he was a brigadier, at the age of thirty-seven. It wasn't because Abacha was popular. He was unemotional, often mute, always difficult to read. Some interpreted his personality as a sign he should be feared; others thought that he was just stupid. 'He might not be bright upstairs,' said General Babangida, a future head of state, 'but he knows how to overthrow governments and overpower coup plotters.'[7] In Nigeria, much could be achieved through backing the right horse.

When Shagari was overthrown, and military rule re-established in the person of General Muhammadu Buhari, it was Abacha who made the radio announcement on the morning of 31 December 1983. In a croaky, hesitant voice, he accused Nigeria's civilian government of 'squandamania, corruption and indiscipline'. Anyone who had been working for Shagari, he said, must report to their nearest police station. All political parties were banned, and their bank accounts frozen. Airports and ferry terminals were shut. No one was allowed in or out of the country. This was to be a corrective regime. Civilians had been given a chance to rule, and failed. Now the imposition of military discipline was required. But Abacha's support for the new leader was short-lived. Eighteen months later, he was working behind the scenes again, this time to oust Buhari and replace him with General Ibrahim Babangida, a leader who would later say he owed his life and his job to Sani Abacha.

Babangida spoke well, in gentle, polished English. His face was open, trustworthy, unlike other generals who hid behind sinister sunglasses. Sometimes, he even smiled. He, too, promised a speedy transition to civilian rule, and went as far as to name a date: October 1990. Preparations began straight away. His advisors needed to deconstruct the whole concept of democracy, and then reconstruct it again to suit Nigeria's particular ethnic and political needs. Perhaps Babangida had been a little hasty in announcing his original time-frame. The date slipped by a year, and then another.

When the time came to announce the legalization of political parties, Babangida didn't disappoint. All interested groups, he said, would be eligible to apply for registration. This was going to be a multi-party democracy, and Babangida bustled around his government offices in Lagos waiting for the applications to arrive. Bereft of legal political movements for much of the last three decades, his advisors predicted just a trickle of applications. In the event, there was a flood. Eighty-eight embryonic political parties wanted a chance at power.

Babangida scrubbed the idea. Such a plethora of choices could only lead to division. Instead, the military would create just two parties, one 'a little to the left', the other 'a little to the right'. If that weren't surreal enough, Babangida's men would also draft their manifestos, and design their flags and posters.

Nigerians launched enthusiastically into the campaign, eager to see the back of Babangida. Under his leadership, extra-judicial killings had increased. His mobile police force had become known as the 'Kill-and-Go' brigade. Its technique was to wave vehicles into a checkpoint, rob the passengers, shoot them, and then claim they were acting in self-defence. Hundreds had been ambushed. Gasoline drivers, whose tankers and contents were driven off and sold on the black market, were a favourite target.

The first step was to find leaders for the newly manufactured parties, and so in 1993, elections were held. But, when the results were announced, the losing candidates accused the winners of 'vote-buying', and the contest descended into an acrimonious farce. In the context of a military dictatorship that had attained power with no votes at all, it was hardly worth a blush. But Babangida, with his newly discovered democratic rigour, declared that this corruption of the election was a calamity. He cancelled the vote, sacked all party officials, and started the entire process over again.

All this was particularly frustrating for Sani Abacha, not because of its glacial pace, but because he was opposed to the whole idea of civilian elections in the first place. The next turn of the wheel, should the military have remained in power, would have seen Abacha himself installed as head of state. He had carried out his understudy role flawlessly; a king-maker quietly biding his time, and now Babangida was shutting the system down. Abacha was on the lookout for any chance to derail the process, and was particularly concerned when a successful and potentially unbribable businessman threw his hat into the ring to become leader of the party 'a little bit to the left': the Social Democratic Party (SDP).

Enter Moshood Abiola, in a private jet. Bright, popular and incalculably rich. Free from the military, free from the stain of oil money, and largely free from the horse-trading of Nigerian politics. After graduating from university in Scotland, Abiola (known as MKO Abiola) had made his fortune in business, spending so much time shuttling between boardrooms in the US and Middle East that he was almost a foreigner. But he never forgot his impoverished roots and, when he returned to Nigeria, he instructed his companies to sell necessities like soap and rice at knock-down prices. Abiola was a philanthropist, a fresh and relatively independent voice. His entrance into the rescheduled elections in the summer of 1993 was greeted with crowds lining the street. These polls were merely for the candidacy, for the right to stand in the presidential election, but still he rolled out an American-style campaign of TV adverts and merchandizing across the country. It wasn't just Sani Abacha who viewed him with suspicion. To most of the generals, MKO Abiola represented a potential disaster; although he was a Muslim, he was also a southerner. Worst still, if he became president he might cut off the flow of oil money to the military altogether. The junta would have to use all its creative flair to stop him from winning, particularly if they wanted to give the impression of free and fair elections.

A pristine tarmac road leads from the sticky chaos of the new capital city, Abuja, into open countryside. Manicured palm trees line the route, evenly spaced, hosed clean, pruned by an army of gardeners.

Behind them, porcelain-smooth, whitewashed walls follow the contours of the road all the way to the horizon. At the end of the road is a single smooth-rock mountain, a giant molar pushing through the jungle floor. In its shadow, a compound where mown lawns are fed by sprinklers, and men lounge beside swimming pools, chewing cigars with phones pressed to their ears. This is Aso Rock, the residence of the Nigerian president.

It was newly built for General Babangida when the capital moved from Lagos to Abuja in 1991, and became the location for frantic discussions on how to engineer the right result for candidacies in the presidential election. When Sani Abacha arrived in his armed convoy from the airport, he was in no mood to appreciate the bucolic setting. He didn't see Aso Rock as Babangida's residence, but his own future home, perilously close to being occupied by a pretender. Babangida had promoted him to defence minister, and everyone in the military knew that was the traditional role for the leader-in-waiting. He had even started referring to Abacha as *khalifa*, my successor.

We can imagine the scene when the two men met in Babangida's suite: cream leather sofas, waiters gliding across tiled floors, mint tea on silver trays, a television in the corner on which a reporter was babbling about MKO Abiola being mobbed by supporters. Abacha had already aired his concerns about the businessman. He had asked Babangida to ban Abiola from standing. Babangida reassured Abacha there was no need. Abiola would never win the candidacy for the SDP, let alone the presidency. But intelligence reports on voting intentions had been wrong in the past. What about 'vote-buying', suggested Abacha; couldn't they accuse him of that? There was no need, soothed General Babangida. Abiola could never win. Intelligence reports were unanimous on that. Even if he did win the candidacy, victory in the main event would go to the businessman's rival, a tame northern Muslim called Alhaji Bashir Tofa, an oil trader and industrialist, and a man who would be president only in name. Behind the scenes, the military would remain in control of oil contracts that, by 1993, made Nigeria the sixth-biggest producer in the world. One study found that in the final years of Babangida's leadership, he and his colleagues syphoned off $12.2 billion over a six-year period.[8] Bundles of notes were ferried in vans to the homes of supporters and influential businessmen. Paying for favours with suitcases of dollars was not unusual. The country's power-elite operated their own private economy, where the simplest deals were rounded up to the nearest million, while the rest of the country lived off $300 a year.

'Relax,' Babangida would have told his *khalifa*. 'You might never gain the top job, but it is you who will pull the strings. The oil money will fall under your control.' Abacha wasn't convinced.

The most popular TV sitcom of the era featured a small-time conman called Mr B, a resident of Lagos who dreamed of becoming rich without actually doing any work. The plot centred around Mr B's hair-brained schemes to trick people out of money, and convince his friends that millionaire status was waiting just around the corner. 'Basi and Company' was intended to lampoon the get-rich-quick attitude of Nigeria's political elite, particularly in relation to their brazen theft of oil money. The series became a fixture on Friday night TV for five years, with Nigerians wearing T-shirts emblazoned with Mr B's catchphrase, 'To be a millionaire, think like a millionaire'. It was written and produced by a man whose name was becoming well known, not just to TV viewers, but to the military junta too: Ken Saro-Wiwa.

Saro-Wiwa had spent the preceding decade busily establishing his writing career, with novels, poetry, and critical newspaper articles. By the time he was writing TV sitcoms he had also become the voice of the Ogoni people. His commitment to their cause had strengthened in pace with Shell-BP's dominance in the delta. Saro-Wiwa had awoken the Ogonis' sense of ethnic identity. Ironically, it was the presence of Shell-BP that was solidifying them into a tribal movement.

Sitting at a desk in his pastel-painted home in Port Harcourt in late 1990, Saro-Wiwa wrote a list of fundamental rights for his newly created pressure group, the Movement for the Survival of the Ogoni People, MOSOP. It was written in the tradition of the English Bill of Rights, composed after the Glorious Revolution of the seventeenth century. Historically, such a document would set out the rights and liberties of a people, to protect them from abuses by their own government. But Saro-Wiwa's people lived, in part, under a corporate regime. The military junta had, effectively, sub-contracted much of its role to Shell-BP, and so it was against their infringements Saro-Wiwa was seeking protection. The oil company had, he claimed, produced $30 billion dollars' worth of oil in Ogoniland, a sum from which the Ogoni people themselves had received 'NOTHING'. He sent a copy of his Bill of Rights to General Babangida.

Ken Saro-Wiwa's successful TV sitcom had earned him enough money to send his children to private schools in England. When they returned home each holiday, he was terrified they had gone soft, and insisted on toughening them up for two weeks. This routine consisted of a stay with aunts and uncles who had no electricity, running water or TV. The children would lie in bed late to avoid chores, and then slouch around in the sticky heat, praying it would soon be over. Sometimes he would drive them through the oil-producing areas, pointing out the bright-orange flares in disgust, while they sat in the back, too young to appreciate what was happening, and more interested in finding a bottle of authentic ice-cold cola. The family home was a modest three-bedroomed house with a palm forest to the rear and décor of unapologetic 1970s vintage, in a hullabaloo of mismatched colours. Saro-Wiwa's tiny study upstairs was all cluttered bookshelves, spilling manuscripts and the loamy smell of pipe tobacco. It was during those summer holidays that the children sensed a change in their father. His life had become entirely dominated by the Ogoni struggle and the business of alerting the world to the oil spills which were now happening at the rate of one a week. They would hear him raging down his study phone, or exploding with laughter about some mischief or another he had perpetrated to publicize the cause.[9]

We can imagine him grinning, and puffing away on his pipe as he typed a demand to oil producers in December 1993 that was both preposterous and inspired. Preposterous because there was no hope the companies would concede; inspired because it was so audacious that it whipped up a storm in the world's media. Saro-Wiwa demanded $4 billion in damages for the Ogoni people, and another $6 billion in unpaid rents and royalties, to be paid by Shell, Chevron and the Nigerian state oil company, within the next thirty days. And if the oil companies refused, then what? This was his problem. They held all the cards. Saro-Wiwa had nothing.

He awoke early on a humid morning in 1993, and drove towards a town in Ogoniland where he was due to address a crowd. It was 3 January, and as he approached a fork in the road it seemed as though a wave of vegetation was racing down the hill. Palm leaves, mango branches, tall ferns, all held high, swaying to the rhythm of drum beats and a low, tribal chant. Beneath them, boys blew whistles, men banged oil drums, women spun in circles with ancient wooden effigies strapped to their heads. Half-jogging, half-dancing, they swept onto the road in front of Saro-Wiwa. 'Who will deliver us from trouble?' they sang. 'Ken and MOSOP will deliver us from trouble.' Saro-Wiwa's fist-pumping speech that day was to become a defining image of the movement. The reception he received left him holding back tears. Three hundred thousand people turned out: a third of all the Ogoni people. The twigs and branches were Saro-Wiwa's suggestion. They were intended to symbolize peaceful protest.

A short while later, the women of a village called Biara gathered in vast numbers in front of a line of Nigerian soldiers. Without warning, one of Shell's contractors, Willbros, had begun digging up farmland to lay pipes, uprooting freshly planted crops and cutting deep trenches through the soil. They had requested an armed guard from the Nigerian government, the type of partnership that was to become so common, and then bribed and intimidated their way through village after village. The women waved their branches in the air, and chanted for it to stop. The Nigerian soldiers started firing indiscriminately into the crowd. It was a near-miracle that only eleven people were injured. A bullet caused a gaping wound to one woman's arm, and it needed to be amputated. But instead of retreating or running away, the crowds grew. The next day troops shot a protestor dead. More Ogoni arrived to replace him.

Suddenly, and unexpectedly, the oil rigs were switched to automatic. Shell personnel clambered into minibuses clutching their computers, and headed for the safety of Port Harcourt. The oil company was evacuating Ogoniland. It was April 1993, just two months before the planned presidential elections. The military junta were incensed. Not only were they faced with uncertainty over who would win the presidency, MOSOP had now driven away Shell, and their entire income stream was under threat. General Babangida was concerned the dissent would spread, perhaps tipping the east into another Biafra-style conflict. He quickly announced the infamous Decree No. 29 – the Treason and Treasonable Felony decree. It stipulated the death penalty for anyone 'uttering words', flying a flag or publishing material that was capable of causing violence, particularly if they were trying to encourage autonomy among an ethnic group. It was a broad, sweeping decree, designed to mop up any oilfield protestors in the run-up to the election. Shell seized on it. The company put out a briefing note accusing Saro-Wiwa of committing 'emotive and exaggerated attacks... with the objective of raising pressure on the federal government of Nigeria'.[10] The oil company was wading into the cauldron of Nigerian politics, planting itself firmly on the side of the military dictatorship. In the same publication it went further, accusing Saro-Wiwa of seeking 'political self-determination' – of encouraging secession. In the circumstances, it was tantamount to requesting Shell's friends in the junta do away with him.

ELECTION DAY, 12 JUNE 1993

They hung from balconies and shinned up telegraph poles. The business tycoon MKO Abiola had won the candidacy for the SDP and was now in a two-horse race to be president of Nigeria. When he stepped from his limousine in Lagos, the crowd wheeled around him, singing and dancing. As he left the polling booth after casting his vote, it was all the police could do to stop him being hoisted into the air and passed across uplifted hands all the way to the presidential villa.

The day began less promisingly for his opponent, and the presumed winner, Alhaji Bashir Tofa. The election was so poorly organized the authorities had failed to register him to vote. It hardly mattered. Military intelligence reassured the leaders that Tofa would be a shoo-in.

In Lagos and Abuja, television crews filed their reports from makeshift edit suites in the smartest hotels. On the rooftop of the Sheraton, TV anchormen stood among a forest of satellite dishes, welcoming the world to what international observers described as Nigeria's first free and fair elections.

In Ogoniland, Ken Saro-Wiwa had recommended that his people should boycott the election altogether. It wasn't a move universally supported by MOSOP. Saro-Wiwa's stance had prised open divisions among the leadership. Nevertheless, many still followed his advice, staying away from the polls. Whoever won the election would change little in Ogoniland.

And even on this historic day, there was a reminder of the impact of oil on Nigeria. In the tiny community of Bunu-Tai in Rivers State, a high-pressure pipeline close to a Shell flow-station ruptured. Hundreds of barrels of crude poured onto farmland and into neighbouring villages. It continued for forty days. Shell wouldn't fix it because the company feared its engineers would be attacked by the community.

Late that night, the ballot boxes were flown, under heavy armed escort, to Abuja for counting. Unofficial results began leaking out thirty-six hours later. A sensation was brewing. The underdog, MKO Abiola, had a strong lead in ten of thirteen states counted.

Then silence.

No one understood the ominous pause. Hours passed. Journalists gathered around the presidential compound at Aso Rock waiting for news. Had General Babangida already left? Were the military returning to their barracks?

The silence continued for several days. In Abuja, it emerged that a legal challenge was under way from a shadowy pressure group called the ABN, the Association for a Better Nigeria. The organization had been active throughout the campaign, putting up posters pleading for 'four more years' of military rule. Now it had secured a High Court order preventing the results from being released. The reasons were sketchy, to do with alleged conflicts of interests and money owed by the government to Abiola. It didn't really matter; it was all a charade anyway, and every savvy Nigerian knew it. The ABN was just a front for the military junta.

Violence broke out on the streets. General Babangida's closest military confidants convened an urgent secret meeting in his home town of Minna to decide their next move. Among them was Sani Abacha. There was unrestrained anger. If Babangida thought he could exploit the situation to extend his own presidency, he was going to be disappointed, they said. What was supposed to be an emergency council meeting turned into a near-hostage situation, with Babangida jostled and threatened by his own subordinates. He had promised them categorically that Abiola was not going to win. Babangida must either annul the election immediately, they warned, or step aside for one of his colleagues. If he refused, he would be killed, and so, too, would Abiola.

The 1993 Nigerian presidential election was declared void on 23 June. Ken Saro-Wiwa heard about it while in police custody answering charges of designing a flag, composing an anthem and holding a meeting in a village he had never visited. The only thing that surprised him was how unsurprised he was. A month later, on his release, the political landscape had changed once again.

General Babangida had thrust a bland, uncontentious and unelected civilian onto the stage: Ernest Shonekan. He would be chairman of a newly contrived artifice called the Interim National Government (ING), a body which would supposedly prepare the ground, all over again, for democratic elections. Babangida's credibility among his colleagues was irreparably damaged. His electoral blunder had almost gifted power to a popular, independent candidate. The military had been within a whisker of having to return to barracks. There was nowhere left for Babangida but the nursing home. He was forcibly retired. But in the final, febrile hours of his leadership, he made a parting gift to the man who had helped him into power. Babangida promoted Sani Abacha to the vice-chairmanship of the ING, effectively making him Nigeria's vice-president. He hoped, he said, that the appointment would be 'an insurance against coups'.[11]

It was as if Abacha was an idiot savant. Dull, even gormless, he filled his days with cowboy movies and sleeping off the previous night's indulgence in alcohol and prostitutes, but he was possessed of a prodigious flair when it came to coups. The Nigerian military dictators' club didn't know how to deal with him. Everyone seemed to owe him something: their positions, their wealth, even their lives, but no one really wanted him as a member. Even by their own standards of scandalous human rights abuses, Abacha was worryingly uninhibited in his use of violence. When protests erupted over the annulled presidential elections, he dispatched troops onto the streets of Lagos with orders to kill. Several hundred unarmed civilians were shot dead. There was disquiet among the ruling cadre. They had always felt the need to garner at least some public affection, but Abacha didn't care. More than that, he didn't know he *should* care. He was a blunt object. But he understood fear and he understood reward, and he knew that by banging the two noisily together he could separate his supporters from his enemies and get a clear view of the field.

Behind the curtain of civilian government, Abacha was hard at work. He began forcibly retiring service chiefs he knew to be against him, while resurrecting retirees he thought he could count on. Once he had packed the top jobs with his own supporters, he delivered his masterstroke. Abacha had his underlings dig out General Babangida's retirement papers, and change the dates, so it seemed the former leader had officially retired twenty-four hours earlier than he actually had. At first glance, it appeared an insignificant act, a heavy pen mark to disguise the original, a repunched typewriter key, perhaps. But it meant that all the important decrees Babangida had made on his final day in office, the ones ceding power to the interim government, were, legally, invalid. He had not been head of state at the time, and therefore had no authority to issue decrees. That's what the paperwork showed, and paperwork doesn't lie.

The interim civilian leader had no right to rule. Nor did his ministers or the regional administrators. Nigeria had been stripped of its governance by a simple piece of schoolboy skulduggery. Not only was the interim government without legal foundation, the country couldn't return to what had gone before because Babangida had resigned. Nigeria was leaderless. It was a brilliantly disguised chess move, a checkmate that reached from one board to another. Abacha had captured two kings for the price of one. His coup had been so un-coup-like, even today some still won't acknowledge it was a coup. They prefer to believe he stepped in to avert a constitutional crisis.

On 17 November 1993, Abacha's face appeared on television screens across Nigeria. He was sitting on a high-backed green leather chair, with a Nigerian flag hanging limply behind him. His face was almost without expression. His eyes swivelling from side to side to read the prepared script. The national and regional assemblies were dissolved once again. Political parties were banned. Any attempt to resist would be crushed. Then the picture cut out, and the military music began again.

Even among the expert plunderers of the Nigerian military elite, Abacha had always stood out as uniquely acquisitive. His modus operandi was to oversee the awarding of government contracts, and take a cut of each, often using a front company to give the transaction some semblance of legitimacy. The technique was hardly original, but when it came to oil, the sums involved were so enormous there was no need to flex his imagination any further. In fact, Abacha seemed incapable of flexing any muscle in any direction. He barely made foreign visits, had no clue about the economy, and left the enforcement of law and order to his favourite military chiefs. His singular expertise in coup-making had become largely redundant, but he was so finely attuned to risk he began examining his colleagues for telltale signs. In 1995, he accused his former head of state, Major-General Obasanjo, of trying to overthrow him and had him sentenced to death, a punishment that was later commuted to life in jail. He did the same to Obasanjo's deputy. It was probably a ruse, to allow him to clear out potential rivals, although when the Nigerian writer and publisher Christiana Anyanwu suggested this in her newspaper, she was jailed for treason. Later, Anyanwu wrote a book about her three years in confinement. A dedicated observer of Abacha, even she could think of few leadership duties he actually performed. She described a shambolic man with no sense of order or system, whose routine was on the opposite side of the clock to everyone else's. Abacha would head into town at 11 p.m. with his best friend, General Jerry Useni. The two men would visit brothels together, partying until 5 a.m., before leaving to attend Muslim prayers. He would return home to sleep at 6.30 a.m. and arrive at the office around midday. Gradually that slipped to 3 p.m., and then 4 p.m., and eventually he gave up altogether. When his staff managed to deliver paperwork to him, he would read no more than two pages. They tried to make it easier by marking the files Urgent, Most Urgent and IMMEDIATE PRIORITY.[12] But their relations with him were generally unhappy. Abacha fell out with his principal staff officer and had him sacked, and then sent into exile, and finally condemned to death by firing squad.

The scant attention Abacha managed to muster was rarely in the direction of his responsibilities as head of state, but rather his own financial interests. He was, from the start, intent on coaxing Shell back into Ogoniland, which would entail neutralizing the opposition in the delta, and in particular MOSOP. He knew just the man for the job.

Lieutenant-Colonel Dauda Komo was a hulking soldier with an eye for a business deal, and a fondness for bowler hats and Hawaiian shirts. He was probably good company – if, like Sani Abacha, you shared his taste in violence. The two men got on famously at the Nigerian Defence Academy together, and the next chapter of their relationship blossomed when Abacha chose his old friend for a job in Ogoniland. Komo was promised a share in the oil money if he could squash dissent and make the area safe for Shell to return. He arrived in Port Harcourt grimly determined to get things done. It was the week prior to Ogoni National Day, and he promptly placed Saro-Wiwa and his family under house arrest to prevent them from becoming the focal point of demonstrations. Komo then set up his own paramilitary force, which consisted of army, navy, air force, state security, and members of the 'Kill-and-Go' unit that had proved so effective in carrying out the checkpoint murders. This ragtag army was named the Rivers State Internal Security Task Force, and its specialism was in 'black ops', or covert operations.

The use of such tactics against the Ogoni was not new. They had started during General Babangida's time, when federal troops hit on the idea of stoking phoney tribal wars in Ogoniland, and using them as a cover for mass killings. Posing as Ogoni, they would ambush members of a neighbouring tribe, killing several of them, and incite a wave of escalating reciprocal attacks. It meant the Nigerian state could achieve high body counts, all deniable, using just a handful of men.

When Lieutenant-Colonel Komo arrived, he was keen to continue using these techniques against Saro-Wiwa and other members of the MOSOP leadership. His man on the ground was to be Lieutenant-Colonel Paul Okuntimo, a field-commander who idolized Shell. It was as if the oil company were his employer, his sovereign state, while the Nigerians who lived in Ogoniland represented the enemy. Human rights campaigners called Okuntimo a sadist, rapist and psychopath, but the phrase used by one of Shell's normally tip-toe-cautious former directors was more powerful. Okuntimo, he said, was 'a fairly brutal person'.[13]

Lieutenant-Colonel Komo was working in his Port Harcourt office one day when he received a memo from Okuntimo in the field. He was hardly able to comprehend the rush of information. The material was so sensitive, he reached across his desk and stamped the word 'RESTRICTED' across the top page. 'Shell operations still impossible,' it said, 'unless ruthless military operations are undertaken for smooth economic activities to advance.' He stamped the document again: 'RESTRICTED'. 'Wasting operations during MOSOP and other gatherings making constant military presence justifiable... deployment of 400 military personnel... wasting operations coupled with psychological tactics of displacement/wasting as noted above.'

By the end, the memo was stamped 'RESTRICTED' twelve times over. Wasting was American slang for killing.

But it was a particular piece of information about Saro-Wiwa's MOSOP that would prove the most valuable. 'Division between the elitist Ogoni leadership exists,' it read. A rift had appeared between Saro-Wiwa and some of the others. The question for Komo was how best to exploit it.

A group of Ogoni leaders visited Komo at his Port Harcourt office in May 1994, in the spirit of mutual co-operation. Ken Saro-Wiwa wasn't among them. There was, indeed, division among the MOSOP leadership – a schism – and those standing in front of Komo that day were the ones opposed to Saro-Wiwa's tactics. They thought him too militant, too intent on mobilizing the movement's unpredictable youth wing, while they preferred peaceful negotiation. The nature of their talk with Komo was sensitive. There had been a spate of killings, they said, and the Ogoni were scared. They planned to hold a meeting of elders the following day at an oil-producing village, and they wanted to make sure it wasn't targeted. Could they rely on Komo and his Task Force to protect them? 'Don't worry,' responded a bemused Komo. 'I will take care of the situation.'[14]

The Ogoni leaders met as planned the next morning, at an elders' palace in the village of Giokoo. The whole region was bristling with security forces. Local elections were under way and much of Rivers State was in lockdown. The palace was a cluster of interconnected huts, with concrete floors and tin roofs, each the size of a garage. Beside the building was a market and a patch of earth where youths played football. The elders sat around a table, discussing the possibility of forming a breakaway movement as an alternative to MOSOP. Ken Saro-Wiwa had been freed from house arrest, but was not in the vicinity. He was being stalked by security forces more than usual that day. He had intended to address a crowd in a village some distance away and then visit his mother, but had been turned back by soldiers, and eventually returned to his pastel-painted home in Port Harcourt.

A crowd gathered outside the elders' palace. Some say it emanated from the football pitch, others from the market. Several spoke of a mysterious vehicle appearing nearby, its number plates wrapped with leaves to obscure identification. Members of the crowd streamed into the palace, grabbing four of the elders, and dragging them outside where they were beaten and stoned by furious youths. At the same time, people trying to enter the town by road were turned away by the Task Force. Four of the bleeding Ogoni elders, all former MOSOP leaders, managed to crawl back inside. But the mob followed them, swinging clubs and machetes, and hacked them into pieces.

Later, their remains were packed into vehicles and taken away to be burnt. It was 21 May 1994.

In the early hours of the following morning, a military assault team broke down the door of the pastel-painted house in Port Harcourt. Armed with assault rifles, they stormed up the stairs. Moments later, a man was escorted out of the building, dressed in his pyjamas, and bundled into a vehicle. Ken Saro-Wiwa was on his way to a military prison on suspicion of having ordered the murder of the Ogoni elders.

Over the following weeks, under the pretext of tracking down more suspects, the Task Force went on the rampage. Soldiers burst into villages firing into the air, and shot anyone who tried to escape. At least fifty Ogonis were executed, and up to 2,000 detained. Girls as young as thirteen spoke of punitive gang rapes by soldiers in front of family members. There were allegations that Lt-Col. Okuntimo himself committed rapes.

The tycoon MKO Abiola was afraid, but what choice did he have? If he was going to declare himself the rightful president of Nigerian, it needed to be done now, on the first anniversary of the annulled elections. Dressed in a traditional gown, silver with handwoven braid, he climbed into his Land Cruiser and stretched out across the leather back seat to check his mobile phone for any hint that his plan might have leaked out. The journey to the slums of Lagos Island was uneventful. A small crowd had gathered by the time he arrived, but to his relief there was no sign of security agents. Abiola had hoped it would never come to this, that General Abacha would play fair. He'd even given interviews to the press describing the new leader as 'a man of reason', but that was when Abacha had promised elections. It was absurd, of course, a time-buying strategy employed by every military leader since independence, but Abiola had hoped on this occasion it would be different. The crowd milled around at a cautious distance. It had been a month since Ken Saro-Wiwa was arrested for murder, and lurid stories were emerging from the delta region of rampaging security forces. The crowds gathering in Lagos Island that morning would have known that open displays of support for Abiola would not be viewed kindly.

Abiola was ushered into a metal-panelled hangar, and onto a makeshift stage draped with the Nigerian flag. He tended to chuckle throatily when he was nervous. Of all the risks he had taken, buying football clubs, investing in Asian start-ups, starting his own airline, this was the biggest by far. From the moment he opened his mouth, his life would never be the same again. 'People of Nigeria,' he began, 'exactly one year ago, you turned out in your millions to vote for me, Chief MKO Abiola, as the president of the federal republic of Nigeria. But politicians in uniform, who call themselves soldiers but are more devious than any civilian would want to be, deprived you of your God-given right to be ruled by the president you had yourselves elected.' There was applause. Some glanced behind them at the high metal doors. 'Since that abominable act of naked political armed robbery occurred, I have been constantly urged… to put the matter back into the people's hands…' By now, the crowd was emboldened, spilling into the rabbit warrens of market stalls and corrugated shelters and clamouring for a glimpse of Abiola through the doors. 'It has been a long night. But the dawn is here!' he boomed, grinning widely. 'Today, people of Nigeria, I join you all in saying, "Enough is Enough!"'

With that, he demanded that 'the usurper, General Sani Abacha announce his resignation forthwith', and declared himself Chief Abiola, President of Nigeria.

It was twelve days before police trucks arrived at Abiola's Lagos residence. Two hundred armed men surrounded the place, crouching among the flower beds, training their guns on the door. The commissioner of Lagos Police was first inside. The villa was a grey functional building of angular balconies and few windows. The crowd strained for a better view. When the commissioner and the self-declared president exited, Abiola was pressing a mobile phone to his ear. He was speaking to BBC radio. Agitated. Jostled. 'They are arresting me for... er... treason... or something like that.' Uniformed arms parted the crowds. There was whistling and hollering. 'Please let me go,' he can be heard saying to the soldiers. Moments later he was in a vehicle, his own Land Cruiser in fact, the police commissioner seated beside him. Abiola was more sure-footed now, the statesman returning.

'Why are they allowing you to talk on your phone to the BBC when they are in the middle of arresting you?' asked the interviewer.

'They have come to arrest me, not to arrest my mouth,' he chuckled, gathering his thoughts. 'It's all part of democracy here. Any sacrifice is in order, if it will bring democracy to Nigeria. Mandela was in jail for twenty-seven years... Don't worry yourself, my friend...'

Life was looking good for Dan Etete. The oil minister's job was the most important in Abacha's cabinet, traditionally awarded to the ablest of swindlers, and Etete was a skilful and industrious practitioner. There was barely any need for even the pretence of legality. Who was going to prosecute him? He was doing it with the blessing of Abacha. The state expected it of him, demanded it. Grand theft was his job. The normal deterrent – the possibility of being caught – was absent. This was risk-free larceny on an enormous scale.

Still, Etete began using aliases just in case, particularly when his corruption took him abroad. For deals that required use of his offshore account in the British Virgin Islands, he used the name Omoni Amefegha. For his Swiss bank accounts, he sometimes used his brother's identity, or simply a name such as 'Papa'. Etete would talk about his aliases as if they actually existed, creating make-believe jobs for them, and even claiming to have met them. His companies, too, were disguised by code names. One was simply called 'Circus' and was provisioned by seven different petroleum companies. There was such a fog of false names that, in later years, even European investigators had trouble nailing down the real Dan Etete. Perhaps Dan Etete himself was fictitious. 'Chief Dauzia Loya Amefegha?' suggested one eminent British QC to him many years later. 'No, sorry,' responded Etete, beaming, 'that is completely an error from the judge. My actual name is Dauzia Loya Etete... they call me Dan Etete.'

Just to be safe, Etete would send intermediaries to withdraw money on his behalf. Sometimes they would travel to banks in France to collect millions of euros transferred from his accounts in Gibraltar, Geneva, Lichtenstein or the Middle East. The corporate firewalls he created were extravagant criminal confections, the sort that served no purpose other than hiding money. There were shareholders with aliases, directors with fictional addresses, beneficial owners hiding behind false beneficial owners.

His business dealings took place well away from the Oil Ministry, in fashionable hotels around the world, where he would meet a succession of go-betweens with links to the Italian Mafia or Russian oligarchs. There was no need for paperwork. Deals were sealed by handshakes in the presence of expensive lawyers. Paperwork meant leaving a trail. Etete didn't want to leave anything. All activities needed to be deniable.

The French supermajor ELF approached Etete in 1997, when he was still oil minister, to obtain the renewal of four exploration licences. Etete dealt with the request personally and informed the company's directors they would need to pay him a bonus of $5 million for each permit – a total of $20 million – or forfeit the deal. They paid the funds directly into his Swiss bank account. A similar sequence of events happened with Addax, a small independent oil company. Its directors explained in a French court some years later how it was impossible to obtain an oil concession in Nigeria without first bribing Etete. Their permits cost them $10 million.[15]

But Etete's personal life was anything but discreet. He bought a grand villa on the exclusive Boulevard D'Argenson in Paris for 28 million francs. One wasn't enough, so he bought another. And another. He filled his French homes with art deco furniture, and paintings paid for from Swiss bank accounts, and set to work updating the swimming pools, installing designer kitchens, and fitting acres of marble in the corridors and bathrooms. He joined the Ritz Club and developed a passion for the French Riviera. That whole coastline became his playground. He found the aristocratic charms of Nice much to his taste, and decided to buy property there too, before changing his mind and opting to rent in the tax haven of Monaco instead. He fell in love with boats, grand sailing yachts with helipads and pools, and would motor down to Cannes to see what was for sale. He moored his new purchases at the pretty resort of Golfe Juan. There was a twin-engine speedboat built in Miami, and an ocean-going yacht with four suites and a VIP stateroom. He named the yacht *King Amaran*, after one of his aliases, or his great-grandfather, or both, depending on who you believe.

Ken Saro-Wiwa was relieved to be moving to a civilian prison. He had been detained in Bori military camp for more than a year, often manacled and chained to the wall, and being back among normal prisoners and normal prison guards would, he hoped, improve his health. The order to pack his belongings had come first thing on the morning of 10 November 1995. He possessed little now, just his calabash pipe, which hung unlit from the corner of his mouth, and a large black leather wallet. The military guards kept an eye on him for any papers or pens he might have attempted to stash away. Before his trial he had regularly smuggled letters to his children filled with questions concerning reassuring family trivia: had they completed their homework, how was Aunt such-and-such, when were their exams? It was other, politically charged messages that had angered the military junta. At glittering ceremonies in Stockholm, London and the US, emissaries of Saro-Wiwa had accepted human rights awards on his behalf, reading out acceptance speeches he had composed in his prison cell. No, he wouldn't be able to attend personally, due to the murder charge, but he was humbled nevertheless. 'We are face to face with a modern slave trade,' he wrote to one, 'similar to the Atlantic slave trade in which European merchants armed African middlemen to decimate their people and destroy their societies... As in the Atlantic slave trade, the multinational companies reap huge profits.'

At 9.30 a.m., a Black Maria arrived at the Bori military camp, and Saro-Wiwa, together with his co-defendants, climbed inside. The streets were unusually quiet for that time in the morning. The melon-sellers and water-hawkers might have seen a speeding van splashing through the potholes.

The Black Maria arrived at Port Harcourt prison about an hour later. First out was Saro-Wiwa himself, pipe still clutched between his teeth. The others followed, and walked in single file, slowly on account of their leg-chains, into a hallway where they were told to sit on a long wooden bench and await further instructions. Saro-Wiwa was calm. He assumed they were waiting for cell assignment.

His murder trial had gone very much as expected, considering that one of the three judges was a friend and military colleague of General Sani Abacha, and had been handpicked by him to oversee proceedings. The prosecution alleged Saro-Wiwa had addressed a crowd of Ogoni youth on the morning of the murders, and ordered them to attack 'the vultures'. The youths had apparently taken off 'like bullets' to the palace of elders where the meeting was taking place, and hacked the four men to death. A succession of witnesses, mostly with long-standing grudges against Saro-Wiwa, claimed to have heard him give the instruction, although they all reported hearing different words, even in different languages. Two prosecution witnesses changed their evidence before the trial even commenced, signing an affidavit to say they were bribed by security agents to sign false statements. One swore he had been offered a new home anywhere in Nigeria if he would fabricate evidence. And so the trial had gone very much as expected. Saro-Wiwa and eight of his alleged accomplices were sentenced to death for murder.

Saro-Wiwa sat on the long wooden bench waiting for his new cell to be prepared. Elsewhere in the prison, Lt-Col. Komo, the recipient of the RESTRICTED 'wasting' memo had just arrived. His schedule had been busy, flying up to Abuja to brief General Abacha on the outcome of the trial and returning with the necessary paperwork. Only Abacha's signature would do. There hadn't been an event like this since before independence, and government officials were anxious that things should be done properly.

Saro-Wiwa's name was called from behind a closed door. He rose from the long wooden bench, and entered. Nigerian law provided thirty days to appeal, and although the trial had been conducted by a Special Tribunal sitting outside the standard legal structure, only ten days had passed since the verdict. There had been international outcry, with the British Commonwealth, the United States, the European Union and several African leaders, all imploring General Abacha not to carry out the sentence. Everyone, including Saro-Wiwa, believed there was breathing space.

When he walked through the door, he noticed a priest standing with a Bible. Alongside the priest were security officials, a government cameraman, one of the judges from the trial, and Lt-Col. Komo. The gallows had been erected hurriedly overnight, the carpenters using guesswork for the height of the drop, and the type of pulleys they should use.

It took five attempts to hang Ken Saro-Wiwa.

Sani Abacha had personally fast-tracked Saro-Wiwa's execution two days before. In the minutes of a meeting of his Provisional Ruling Council, the regime's highest decision-making body, Abacha announced that 'anyone who had killed his fellow citizens does not deserve to live', and that carrying out the death sentence was the only way of ending the Ogoni unrest 'once and for all'.

During the international outcry that followed, economic sanctions were placed on Nigeria by the European Union. Abacha was unrepentant. The following year he got to work on a plan to legitimize his leadership by making himself the elected president of Nigeria, while pretending to the electorate he had no such intention.

'George Washington?' Abacha would say to his staff. 'He was a general in the US military, wasn't he? Didn't he become civilian president? What about General Eisenhower? He did the same. General Nasser? No one seemed to mind. Why not in Nigeria?' Abacha had promised a transfer to civilian rule. Perhaps this was the answer. Whether he dressed in khaki or civilian clothing, why should it matter?

In the year after Saro-Wiwa's death, while Nigeria was considered a pariah state by many countries, posters began appearing around Abuja and Lagos showing an expressionless Abacha beside an image of General Eisenhower, both men in military uniforms, and then in mufti. There were variations on the theme: Abacha and Nasser; Abacha and Ghana's Jerry Rawlings. Some courageous journalists began to accuse him of a 'self-succession plot'. But Abacha's advisors denied it. 'Only the people of Nigeria can decide,' they would beam. Soon that changed to, 'Only God can decide.'

By 1997, the government had confirmed presidential elections would take place, but hadn't confirmed a date or who would be allowed to stand. The unofficial Abacha campaign became increasingly surreal. Aside from the normal badges and newspaper adverts from 'admirers', a new brand of television set appeared on the shelves, with Sani Abacha's face embossed on the side. Abacha, until now a semi-recluse, published a biography, *Abacha: the Man, the Myth*. He began doing interviews with foreign journalists, informing them he was 'consulting his constituency' about his next move. Several major companies began publishing rapturous birthday greetings in the press, addressed to Abacha's wife. 'Simply elegant, graceful, beautiful... a loving wife, caring mother and an exceptional first lady,' wrote one. 'For a special person who has warmed hearts by being near, who time and again made someone else's dreams come true,' wrote another.[16]

Fifteen new political parties applied for registration, but only five were granted. Still, it seemed more promising than 1993, when there were just two. The winner of that election, MKO Abiola, was still in prison. There was some speculation he might be allowed out to run again, but Abacha wasn't having it.

Then a date was announced. Nigerians were astonished. Abacha was going to go through with it. In August 1998, the country would go to the polls. It was just five months away. The five parties needed to choose their candidates quickly. Some were still convinced Abacha would distort the process. There were demonstrations in Ibadan where hundreds were arrested – 'not arrested', Abacha's government explained, just 'taken by security forces... prisoners of war'. The world was watching. Pope John Paul II made a visit to Abuja, appearing frail and uneasy with Abacha by his side. He had with him a list of sixty political prisoners he hoped the president would release. The first name was that of MKO Abiola. Abacha promised to do what he could. But when the pope left, he denied Abiola had ever been on the list.

Finally one of the parties was ready to announce its candidate for the presidency. It was to be General Sani Abacha. If he would accept, of course. The party's organizers said there had been no pressure to make him their leader, he just happened to be the most well qualified for the job. They appeared on television to announce that Abacha had 'ensured peace and stability, and the steady growth of the country's economy', and that he was favourite to win.

Shortly afterwards, a second party announced its choice. It, too, had selected Sani Abacha.

So had the remaining three.

Abacha would be the only candidate on the ballot paper.

It was twilight on the morning of 8 June 1998, two months before election day, when Professor Sadiq Sulieman Wali heard his telephone ring. Wali was a softly spoken man who wore his erudition lightly. His disinterest in politics, along with his legendary discretion, had earned him the trust of the last four heads of state, to whom he was personal physician. Today he was supposed to be accompanying General Abacha to an African Union summit in Burkina Faso. It wasn't that Abacha was ill. He was fifty-four, and in reasonable health; he just found it reassuring to travel with Professor Wali. But the nature of the telephone call suggested today's trip was unlikely to happen. There was hardly time to dress. A car pulled up outside his house, and Professor Wali climbed hurriedly onto the back seat.

Dan Etete was in Abuja that day. Later he would be guest of honour at an event organized by The Movement for National Stability discussing whether it was right for Abacha to contest the presidency. Etete would be arguing very much in favour. The same group had designated their 'mother of the day' as Abacha's wife, Maryam. At 6.30 that morning, as her husband's personal physician sped along the palm-lined boulevard to Aso Rock, Maryam Abacha was in her residential quarters, probably asleep. Her husband was not alongside her.

Professor Wali's car entered Aso Rock through the main gate, but then took a shortcut normally reserved only for the president. At this point, accounts differ as to what happened. It is possible that, before the professor even received his call, three young Indian prostitutes hurried out of the room where they had been entertaining General Abacha, and were driven at speed away from the presidential compound.

There was no sign of them by the time Professor Wali arrived. He was greeted by Abacha's chief of security and ushered into Abacha's sitting room. Another doctor was already present. Abacha was lying on a couch dressed in his work clothes. His eyes were shut, and there was foam coming out of his mouth. He wasn't breathing. The two men tried to resuscitate him, clearing his airways, and giving him CPR. When Abacha failed to respond, they injected him in the heart. They and the security chief were the only people in the room. After forty minutes of endeavour, Wali turned around to him and said, 'Sorry, there is nothing we can do.'[17]

The security chief left the room, and ordered an increased guard around the presidential complex. Service chiefs flew in from across Nigeria, demanding to see Abacha's body. Professor Wali was reluctant, but in a regime charged with such mutual suspicion, they needed to verify that Abacha was actually dead. No public announcement could be made yet, in case supporters of the jailed

MKO Abiola rose up demanding restitution of the 1993 election result. He was in solitary confinement, and had been for four years. There had been rumours of beatings and ill-health, but as long as he was still alive, he was a threat.

The official cause of Abacha's death was given as cardiac arrest, but his family refused to allow an autopsy, choosing burial the next day, in line with Islamic tradition. The presence of the Indian prostitutes would not have been out of character for Sani Abacha. It's alleged that he took three Viagra tablets in their presence, which could have interfered with the blood supply to his heart, and that the women, seeing him dead, fled the room. That would still be consistent with Professor Wali's testimony. Theories that the women fed him a poisoned apple pie are less plausible.

After Maryam Abacha buried her husband, she knew the family fortune was vulnerable – all new leaders made a show of establishing anti-corruption commissions, and throwing a few offenders in jail. She anticipated that her family properties would be targeted. Abacha's son, Mohammed, kept around $100 million in cash in his house. Abacha, too, preferred paper money, rather than relying on banks. Maryam Abacha was so anxious that she didn't wait for the end of the mourning period, but took off for Saudi Arabia with thirty-eight suitcases, travelling through Kano International Airport on the pretext she was going on a pilgrimage. Security officers thought the luggage excessive for a short break, and asked that they see inside. They discovered several million dollars in foreign currency. Her passport was seized and she was placed under house arrest.

At the same time, in his prison cell in Abuja, MKO Abiola was being prepared for release. The new military ruler, General Abdulsalami Abubakar – just a caretaker, of course – needed to smooth things over with the other service chiefs, but Abiola's freedom seemed certain. Despite being only sixty years old, he was not in the best of health. He had received messages of goodwill from Nelson Mandela and Desmond Tutu, and visitors were coming and going, scheduling meetings for him once he was back home. On the day of his expected release, 7 July 1998, a delegation of US diplomats arrived to see him.

They wanted to discuss his political future, but Abiola asked if he could pause for a while and take a cup of tea. He then requested cough medicine and painkillers, and was seen to be overheating. As they called for help, Abiola removed his shirt and asked for ventilation in the room. He then passed out. MKO Abiola died later that same day, having suffered a heart attack.

He had outlived his tormentor by just twenty-nine days.

'Would it be fair to describe you as utterly dishonest and corrupt?' began Mark Howard QC. It was December 2012, and a long cross-examination lay ahead in the Paris courtroom. He wanted to put down a marker with Dan Etete early on. Nigeria's former oil minister was sombrely dressed in dark suit and tie, but Howard found him a parody of an African crook. When he couldn't, or wouldn't answer, he pretended he had not heard the question or delivered an impromptu speech on an unrelated matter, smiling broadly at the female judge. Etete had debated his own name, corrected Howard's pronunciation of 'Abacha', and jousted over every wearisome detail. His confidence, thought Howard, was astonishing. He had paraded into court saying he was sorry for being late, but he'd had an audience with the pope.

'Would it be true that you are an inveterate liar with no respect for the truth?' continued Mark Howard.

'Absolutely not true,' replied Etete, glancing at the judge.

'Would it be true that you lie whenever it suits your interests?'

'Never. Never.'

It was that oilfield again, OPL245. Sani Abacha had died at a particularly inopportune moment. The mysterious men behind Malabu Oil and Gas Ltd were just about to clinch the biggest oil deal in Africa. During the decade since Abacha's death, the sale of OPL245 had been examined at hearings in the US, France and Nigeria, and Etete was still insisting he had no idea who was behind the company. No longer oil minister, he advertised himself simply as the company's consultant, but as to who had employed him, again, he could not help the court. Malabu, which existed only on paper, had intended to buy the field at a knock-down price, and sell it for around $1.2 billion to one of the oil majors. But Abacha's untimely death had left the company in a very different political landscape. Allegiances had changed. Etete was out of favour. The new government had decided to do its own deal, adopting the more orthodox approach of selling the concession to the highest bidder. Dan Etete, on behalf of Malabu, threatened to sue. It took seven years to sort out the mess, before the Nigerian government finally agreed to reinstate Malabu as the rightful owner. The problem was, Malabu couldn't sell it on, since no one was prepared to do business with the shadowy men behind the company.

'Would it, in your view, be honest or ethical for a minister to allocate an oil concession to a company in which he or the president was secretly interested?' asked Mark Howard QC.

Etete could hardly contain himself. 'That's not true,' he snapped back.

'I didn't ask whether it was true. I was asking whether that would be an honest and proper thing to do.'

Etete was not keen on questions of ethics. Even he could see where this was leading. 'I don't know,' he responded.

'You don't know whether it would be proper or not?'

'I don't know,' repeated Etete.

This was no normal Parisian court. London's High Court was sitting in the French capital because Etete was banned from entering the UK. This civil hearing was concerned with sorting out who owed what to whom in relation to OPL245. The UK was involved because more than $200 million from the deal had passed through a British bank, money that had been frozen until the legal issues were resolved.

Mr Howard had moved on. He was now trying to establish the identities of Malabu's shareholders, who Etete was clearly trying to shield from the court. The first name was Mohammed Sani, who owned 10 million Malabu shares. 'Mohammed Sani is, in fact, General Abacha's son, correct?' asked the QC. Etete frowned theatrically. 'I wouldn't know because there are two different names... Mohammed Sani and Mohammed Sani Abacha.'

Mr Howard tried again, 'Who appointed you as consultant to the company?'

Etete thought about it for a moment. 'The shareholder-directors,' he replied.

'Right. But who are they?'

He paused. 'Pardon?'

And on it wearisomely went. Mr Howard knew the men's identities, and so, too, did Dan Eteté, but he had told so many stories to so many different hearings, he couldn't recall what he had said to whom. It was safer to speak in riddles.

The uncomfortable truth was that Etete himself was the man behind Malabu. He was the beneficial owner. As oil minister he had awarded the richest oil concession in Nigeria to himself. General Abacha had been complicit in the deal and, when he died, his son had taken over the interest. But there was no point in owning the concession unless they could sell it on. Shell and Eni would not be prepared to do business with the disgraced Etete, not publicly at least. A way had to be found to sanitize the deal.

It was agreed Shell and Eni would pay the Nigerian government $1.3 billion, and the Nigerian government would pass the money on to Etete, minus their own fee. It was, as one expert observed, a 'safe-sex relationship' – the oil majors weren't required to have direct contact with the former oil minister at any time. But the result was the same: Etete got the money.

In the end, the $1.3 billion that should have gone to the Nigerian people found its way into the pockets of many go-betweens, dealmakers and government personnel, the bulk of it spirited away into offshore shell companies. The fees to the man who arranged the deal, alone, were a staggering $120 million. As for Etete, his reward was even bigger. As he explained, in an unguarded moment on a tape quoted in court, 'It is my block. I will fight. I will get the block. It's going nowhere. They can't do anything... as long as I am alive.' He received at least $250 million.

Etete is still alive. He went on the run for a short while in 2016, when the Nigerian Economic and Financial Crimes Commission charged him with fraud in connection with OPL245. He was eventually found, and is likely to spend the next few years winding his way through the Nigerian legal system, although judging from the country's recent history of corruption investigations, it seems unlikely he will ever lose his liberty.

His fortune is small in comparison with that amassed by his former boss. Abacha's wealth is estimated to have been between $3 and $5 billion at the time of his death, more than a billion of it handled by banks in London. But, unlike Mobutu in Congo, there were no extravagant palaces, no European villas or private jets. Unlike Houphouet-Boigny in Côte d'Ivoire, there was no self-reverential monument. It wasn't that he was abstemious in any way, or clung to some hidden moral code, just that his needs were more primitive. Sani Abacha needed oil money to pay off the ranks of officials, ministers, police commissioners and service chiefs who sustained him in power. But his purpose, once he had achieved it, seldom reached further than accumulating more wealth to keep the cycle going.

CHAPTER SIX
Equatorial Guinea

EQUATORIAL GUINEA

I have been considered as mad. When have I suffered from madness? The only madness I have shown has been the madness for freedom, and since freedom has now been achieved, my madness is over and done with.

FRANCISCO MACÍAS NGUEMA, FIRST PRESIDENT
OF EQUATORIAL GUINEA, 16 JANUARY 1969

FROM UP ON the volcanic rim, hanging among the towering tropical clouds over Equatorial Guinea, it's as if the capital doesn't exist, as if the slopes descend into a brief strip of lowland forest, which ends in a fringe of uninhabited bays and capes before the land is swallowed up by the Atlantic Ocean. It is night-time and it seems there is not a soul down there, not a car headlight or anxious bedside light, not a living thing to witness the beauty of a tropical island's rainforests cooling after another day in the heat of equatorial West Africa. But there are dark patches between the trees. Shapes begin to emerge: moon-glare on broken tin roofs; gouged strips of mud linking one scatter of shacks to another; silent Spanish churches thick with mould; the embers of a fire where soldiers sleep beside the high defensive walls of the Presidential Palace. Even here the electricity has gone and the soldiers are living off scavenged fruit or small animals snared in the forest.

At a Spanish villa to the east of the capital, Malabo, Raimundo Jnr dozes with his eleven brothers and sisters. Recent events in the country have been kept from him and so he sleeps peacefully, but in a room along the corridor his father is awake and restless. As a senior member of the regime, he has witnessed the activities of the president, and hiding it from his children and his four wives has meant living with constant anxiety. What he doesn't know is that his name, Raimundo Ela Nve, is on the *lista de asesinados*. There is no contradiction between being a member of the regime and being on its death list. Raimundo's name has been on the *lista* for three months.

Across Malabo, the shacks and the shanties are silent, the fountains of the Spanish Cathedral are muddied and clogged, its high doors have been padlocked for years, and there is no sound – not a car engine can be heard, not a radio, just silence and darkness. But, in a stained yellow building nearby, voices rise suddenly and dim light bulbs can be glimpsed against the darkness. This is Black Beach prison. People are moving quickly. Torches flashing, men running. Some in the jail do important work at night. From one block to another the shouts go up. A prisoner is propped between two others. His feet are lifted off the ground. He is naked. Another has fallen. His hands are bound behind his back. More men are being pulled from behind metal doors. A whole crowd of uniforms are gathering now, around the main block. There is life here in this one building, behind the barred windows and the high concrete walls. Some of the uniformed men have metal clubs, and inside they go, carrying the crying men, and there's a mêlée now as the captives try to buck and kick and stop themselves being taken into the room next to the office, because the room next to the office is the place no one wants to go.

Later, when silence resumes, a group of cleaners appear with brushes and buckets of water to mop the blood from the stone floor. The bodies have lost their human shape, and are dragged through a gate behind the prison and dumped in an open pit.

Often Obiang himself is here at Black Beach to ensure the job is done properly. His full name is Lt-Col. Teodoro Obiang Nguema M'ba N'Zogo, military governor of the island of Bioko, where the country's capital is located, and head of state security.

But tonight Commandant Obiang is not at the jail. It is 2 August 1979 and he has been busy in covert meetings. He is a short, strutting man with deep grin lines and a brow in the shape of a pinned black moth. Nothing happens in Black Beach without his word. Some say he likes to get physically involved himself while the rest of Malabo sleeps. He certainly comes to watch his men at work. Many witnesses can testify to that. For some, the face of Obiang is the last they will see. But tonight he has more important work to do. Obiang has business concerning his uncle, Francisco Macías Nguema, known more widely as Macías, the president of Equatorial Guinea since the country's independence in 1968. During the eleven years Macías has ruled the country, Obiang and other family members have formed his inner circle. Obiang is viewed as his number two. Almost all those left in senior roles are family members, although, in truth, there is no government to speak of; the ministries stand empty, officials haven't been paid for months and few can recall the last meeting of the national assembly.

Tonight Macías is away from his Presidential Palace and so the guards can sleep easily at their posts. The high walls are topped with electric wires. Macías is so afraid that he hasn't slept in his own palace for almost five years and has only rarely visited his capital. All the plotting means there has had to be a lot of killing: intellectuals, government officials, members of the assembly, even some of his closest ministerial colleagues and supporters. The numbers of deaths and disappearances are impossible to know for sure. Entire villages have been torched to eliminate a single perceived subversive. The militias have been out of control, drunkenly murdering people on the streets or burying them up to their necks in sand to be eaten by ants. There have been hurried mass executions and the prisons are regularly cleared overnight of the starved and diseased. The population of Equatorial Guinea is only 300,000, and the death count may be as high as a quarter of the population, greater proportionally than that of Stalin's regime.

Even Macías has been worried about his own mental health. At the start of his rule he made a secret visit to a psychiatrist in Barcelona, but now, several years on, he can hardly consult a local doctor, not just because news of his ill-health could lead to a coup, but because there are no doctors left in Equatorial Guinea: they are either dead or in exile.[1] Whatever treatment the Spanish doctor recommended seems to have failed, and Macías has persevered with his marijuana habit and a strong herbal hallucinogenic drink called iboga. That has made him even less stable. Few can forget how he ordered the hanging, on Christmas Eve 1975, of 150 'opponents' in the national football stadium and how the spectacle was played out to music. *Those were the days, my friend*, as the nooses were placed around their necks: *we thought they'd never end, we'd sing and dance forever and a day…*

Most of Equatorial Guinea's territory lies many miles away on the mainland. It is a small square of rainforests and slow rivers called Rio Muni, located on the West African coast just above the equator. You have to cross the Bight of Bonny to get there, but there are no boats because Macías has had them confiscated or destroyed to stop people fleeing. Along his land border with Cameroon and Gabon his men have dug camouflaged ditches and lined them with timber spikes. Yet, despite such efforts, around a third of the population has managed to escape.

Tonight Macías is close to the border with Gabon, in his ancestral village of Mongomo where he has built himself a palace compound. There is a bunker to hide in if the plotters come, and a military camp that is home to his personal guard. There is even a small prison. Macías is alone, as usual, wandering around his compound, chattering, and crying out the names of his victims. Nearby is a collection of human skulls that he worships in the hope of accumulating more power. It is a tradition in the Fang tribe to which he belongs, but it has done little to calm his paranoia. Recently his servants have witnessed him ordering a table to be laid for eight guests and then sitting alone and keeping up a conversation with the dead. President Macías, 'The Unique Miracle', is dangerously, mentally ill. Hidden nearby are the contents of the National Treasury. Some say he has more than a hundred million dollars in foreign currency.[2]

Back in the island capital, Commandant Obiang is awake and tense. If tomorrow morning's plan goes wrong, he will be killed. So, too, will all those who have attended his covert meetings, mainly cousins and nephews of the president. Being a relative will offer no protection. Neither will the backing of Spain, Equatorial Guinea's former colonial master.

Above the banks of the Rio Campo an agile line of women make their way through dripping ferns, along a narrow track and down to a mud shelf. They enter the brown water easily with their woven baskets. The riverweed mimics the currents of the water, ribbons of lime and gold leaning towards the thunder of the falls. The women scoop the weed up and lay it in the bush to dry. If they catch a frog in these waters they will cook that later too.

On the hillsides of Kogo, pastel-coloured shacks spill down to the beach. From inside the abandoned schoolroom you can hear the surf pounding against the shoreline. A broken picture of Macías hangs on a bare wall. A viper sleeps in the dried grass that has pushed through the floor.

In Malabo a man cradles a handful of cigarettes as he walks across the empty tarmac of Independence Avenue. He used to sell fruit: cherry-red mangos, plantains, pineapples, rows of produce decorated with stems of ginger and purple orchids. Now he lays out single cigarettes on the side of the road alongside a rare box of matches and hopes today might bring a customer.

Raimundo had never understood how senior his father was in the regime. In fairness, he had never known there *was* a regime, not in those early days when the bootprints of the Spanish colonialists were still fresh on the muddy roads and the whitewashed verandas of the capital.

Spain had controlled the territory since 1778. It was a back-water of colonial endeavour, a sparsely populated, sodden jungle, whose people were riven by sleeping sickness, smallpox and alcohol addiction. Spanish Guinea was used as a vast plantation, with slave labour shipped in from neighbouring countries to work on the cocoa and coffee farms. The colony's unusual feature was that it was split into two distinct and separate geographical regions. The main island, Bioko, which the Europeans called Fernando Po, lay in the azure waters of the Gulf of Guinea, just south of Nigeria and west of Cameroon. It was there that the country's capital, Malabo, would be located. The mainland territory of Rio Muni was a pocket of mosquito-ravaged rainforest tucked between southern Cameroon and Gabon, and separated from Bioko by 240 kilometres of sea.

Disease regularly decimated the population to such an extent that massive supplies of forced labour were shipped in from Liberia and Nigeria right up until the 1950s. The dominant Fang tribe on the mainland regularly rose up against the Spanish, and were only pacified in 1929. In short it was a hostile, ungovernable, steam-house, but it was Spain's only colony in sub-Saharan Africa, and it was of symbolic and strategic importance as well as a provider of cheap coffee, cocoa and timber.

The oil was yet to come. As Africa's independence movements grew in strength, Madrid tried desperately to hang on to Spanish Guinea. With an eye on Shell-BP's oil discoveries just up the coast in Nigeria, the Spanish began excitedly auctioning exploration rights, attracting Mobil and Spanish Gulf Oil. It became a race against the clock. By independence in 1968, with the territory renamed the Republic of Equatorial Guinea, still no oil had been found.

In fact, Equatorial Guinea was sitting on one of the largest oil-fields in Africa, with more than a billion barrels hidden beneath the sea around Bioko island. But all that would come later.

For now, Raimundo's father was telling him about his role during the struggle for independence. As he listened, Raimundo was even more proud that he had been christened with the same name. He and his father were both called Raimundo. 'You are me,' his father would whisper, and Raimundo Jnr hoped one day he would be.

Raimundo Snr was a bullet of a man, compact in stature with a voice that ricocheted effortlessly around the largest room. It was a voice the entire country could tune into once a week during the late 1960s, when he hosted the radio show that had made him famous. The crowds in the Santa Isabel market and the Plaza de San Fernando would have transistor radios pressed to their ears. His broadcasts had become legendary, particularly since his arrest by the colonial administration for stirring up nationalist passions. The Guardia Civil had pinned him to the floor of a sailing boat, blindfolded, with his hands bound. He was so disorientated he didn't know whether they were still in the harbour or far out at sea. 'We could throw you overboard and no one would know!' the Spanish had shouted into his ear. But Raimundo Snr had connections. He was always back behind his microphone before too long.

It was no surprise that when the Spanish finally agreed to surrender Equatorial Guinea, Raimundo Snr backed the most outspoken nationalist candidate to be president. He knew little about Macías in those days, other than that the man's speeches seemed as passionate as his own. He was unaware of Macías's incoherent eulogy of the Nazis in a speech he made at a conference on independence that was held in Madrid. 'I consider Hitler to be the saviour of Africa,' Macías had told puzzled delegates. 'Hitler's intention was to end colonialism throughout the world.' Even when Macías was being told to sit down, he had continued: 'Although it is said that he persecuted the Jews, what he wanted was to combat colonialism but he got confused and then he wanted to command all the peoples of Europe.'[3]

Macías had been a lowly clerk during Spanish rule, but they had misinterpreted his primitive scheming as a talent for leadership. For a time they had used him as a court interpreter. Macías would take bribes to twist his translations and either incriminate or absolve the defendants according to who was paying him, but with so many people hanging on his words, the Spanish thought he must be a man of influence, and a series of darkly comical promotions followed. He climbed from being assistant interpreter, to mayor, to minister of public works and then deputy president of the Governing Council in the space of a year. Even Macías must have been baffled, but the Spanish viewed him as someone they could do business with and manipulate.

As the time approached for Spain's withdrawal from the territory in 1968, Macías was travelling rural villages on the campaign trail for the presidential elections, with his wedge-shaped haircut, skinny suits and narrow tie, barking out jumbled words, swapping languages and subjects mid-sentence, offering everybody whatever they wanted to hear. In fact his speeches and campaign literature were written by a Spanish lawyer, but Macías was easily distracted from the script. He was already sinking into madness, but his behaviour could easily be misinterpreted as fearless, or wildly charming, and his chaotic public appearances as thrilling, visionary theatre. While his rivals picked their way cautiously over the issue of future collaboration with Spain, Macías cut to the chase in front of cheering crowds. 'Do you want that?' he would shout, pointing at a house owned by a European, and the people would shout, 'Yes,' and Macías would respond, 'If you vote for me, I will give it to you.'[4]

On 12 October 1968, after a closely contested election, Macías became the first president of the Republic of Equatorial Guinea. Raimundo, the radio announcer, won a seat on the country's first national assembly.

Emilio Fumu was a man who rejoiced in order and routine and cared little who was running the country, so long as his wife and eight children had stomachs full of food and heads full of books. Each evening he would rush home from his job at the Department of Education as if he were tethered by elastic. He sat on his bed, removed his neat leather shoes, placed them beside each other on the tiled floor, peeled off his socks, flexed his long toes, and then, when he was barefoot, the children knew it was time to play.

Emilio's work in the civil service had begun during the Spanish occupation, and when Macías became president he assumed his life would shift seamlessly into the new era, that 'intellectuals' would always be needed to run government departments. He certainly didn't believe there was anything to fear. Perhaps independence had come a little too soon, but Emilio was ready to work with the new administration and make the republic a success. Within months of independence, he had seen Macías on television shouting about Spanish meddling and alleged plots to overthrow him and Emilio had found his tone disconcerting. He felt even more uneasy when nationalist youths pulled a Spanish flag from the embassy in Malabo and set it on fire. When a Spaniard was killed in the street he prayed that was the end of it. But the hostilities worsened. The popular politician, Bonifacio Ondo Edu, who had been runner-up to Macías in the presidential election and was the former prime minister, fled across the border to Gabon.

In March 1969 Macías had his own foreign minister arrested
and killed. Emilio wasn't sure what had happened, but there was
talk of an attempted coup and rumours that Macías had delivered
the beating himself before throwing his minister out of a window.
Shortly afterwards Edu was captured while on the run in Gabon,
and returned to Equatorial Guinea, where he was executed. More
killings of senior officials followed. There were chilling rumours
emerging from Black Beach prison of deaths caused by immersion in
barrels of water and eyes gouged from heads.

Just five months after Macías became president, Spanish citizens
were being airlifted to safety. Spain's leader, Francisco Franco, judged
it too dangerous to let them remain. The British ambassador called
the situation in the capital 'virtual anarchy'.

It was becoming increasingly difficult for Emilio to maintain the
spirit of fatherly calm that once accompanied him into the apartment
each evening. There were thousands like him who had once worked
for the colonial regime, but who were now under suspicion. Macías
had offered a promotion to anyone who informed on a Spanish
spy. Suddenly even sharing a glass of beer with a friend was a risk.
Conversations could easily be misinterpreted, and members of the
new militia weren't in the habit of checking evidence. The militia
was called *Juventud en marha con Macías*, 'Youth Marching with
Macías', or JMM, and its members, many of whom were recruited
by Macías's nephew, Obiang, quickly became gangs of marauding,
power-drunk thugs. Anything that could connect a suspect to Spain
was all they needed: a book, a newspaper, a misjudged comment.
When they searched Emilio's house, they found Serrano ham and
Spanish olives. His wife often cooked using Spanish produce. It hadn't
occurred to her to hide it. What more evidence could the JMM need?
There was no time for Emilio to kiss his wife goodbye. They handcuffed him, pushed him in a car, and took him to Black Beach.

The Spanish villa with its tin roof and white plaster walls was the
most impressive residence on the eastern side of Malabo. Raimundo

Jnr shared it with his twelve siblings, five members of staff, and three of his father's wives – the other two residing in a smaller house nearby. Each evening his father would be driven home from the national assembly in his Land Rover, the cook would serve them spicy fish soup, or *succotash* made from giant beans and smashed tomatoes, and sometimes they might go for a drive to his father's cocoa farms. He was the leading authority on the crop and, in those days, it was still the country's biggest export, and his father's greatest passion.

Raimundo Jnr spent his days playing football on a circle of tropical grass in front of the villa. When the raindrops began to pop on the metal roofs he would hurry to the shelter of the cinema to watch Mexican cowboys and Spanish-speaking vampires. But even at seven years old he had begun to notice how strangers treated him differently. Raimundo didn't have to queue at the cinema like the other boys; a man would usher him straight into the auditorium. He soon started collecting friends from around the neighbourhood and taking them in for free too. And because Raimundo's father never spoke of his work or what was happening in the country, his universe was the circle of tropical grass, the cinema and the villa. Equatorial Guinea seemed a place of privilege and plenty. Fear and death touched him only through the flickering men with Mexican moustaches sneering from the screen of the San Fernando cinema. But his father was having to work hard to keep the darkness out.

Opposite their villa was the Iglesia de San Fernando, a twin-towered colonial church with bone-white plaster walls, ribbed ceilings and polished pews. The family would attend each Sunday, and there beside the Blessed Virgin Mary appeared a portrait of a narrow-shouldered man with a blank stare. Beneath the picture was written, 'God created Equatorial Guinea thanks to Macías.' Raimundo Jnr was puzzled. He had seen similar portraits in his school. At the start of each service the priest would announce, 'We must thank Macías, the tireless and sole miracle of Equatorial Guinea.' Then, one Sunday morning the front doors of Iglesia de San Fernando were padlocked. Raimundo's father seemed unperturbed. He led them through a side door, down some stone steps and into the vault beneath the altar. The priest was there, and a thin congregation with faces lit by kerosene lamps. Christianity was now outlawed; covert worshipping had begun.

It was around this time that Raimundo observed his father meeting the man with pinned-moth eyebrows. The man always wore military fatigues and a soft peaked cap. He would park outside their villa and his father would stride out to meet him. Even though the conversation would sometimes be lengthy, the man was never invited into the house. One day, his father explained that this man had been present at Raimundo's christening, and that his name was Obiang, nephew of the president, and a distant relative of Raimundo's family too.

In his memory the rest of that period is a series of fragments. The damp sea air spilling into their garden as the wind changed direction each afternoon. The Nigerian private tutor who visited their home when the school shut down. His mother's crystal earrings that used to shake when she laughed, but hung lifelessly for those final months. His father's whispered conversations about the 'Lion in the tree', which Raimundo Jnr assumed was an animal in the mainland forests, but turned out to be a nickname for Obiang – 'sitting up there slyly looking for flesh to eat'.

Emilio had a son of similar age to Raimundo who he also tried to protect from knowledge of the new regime, but young Felipe had been there on the night of his father's arrest for the ham and olives, and would never forget what he saw. The hammering on the door, his mother's polite but apprehensive voice, 'What's happening?', the confident strangers filling the front room, his father's failed attempt to kiss his mother goodbye, the police car filled with militiamen. Felipe, the sixth of eight children, 'Little Fey', had known there was something wrong before the others. He had sat at his father's feet a few weeks before, watching him remove his shoes and socks as usual and waiting for his father to swing him onto his back like a strutting ostrich. But his father had sat shoeless and hunched so tightly that his back looked as hard as a turtle's shell. When he unfolded himself, he stretched his legs out on the bed and shut his eyes, and Little Fey could see that his cheeks were wet with tears. The militia had already been closing in on him, and his father had known it. If it hadn't been the ham and olives it would have been something else; birth certificates or crucifixes that could link a household to the banned Christian faith, textbooks or novels from the colonial era, even children's schoolwork that could be examined for evidence of disloyalty. Allegations of coup attempts and conspiracies were so plentiful that fifty or sixty people a day were being executed.[5]

Emilio was seized in 1972 when Little Fey was just five years old. Since all the country's judges had either disappeared or were in jail, his court hearing would be in front of a group from 'Youth Marching with Macías'. No legal training was required for these judges, just unquestioning loyalty to the regime. By this time, Macías had declared himself President-for-Life and Commander-in-Chief of the army. He was so indignant about his own lack of schooling that he took the title Grand Master of Education too. The Department of Education, where Emilio had worked, was viewed by the regime with particular suspicion. The use of the word 'intellectual' was banned. At least one director of education was beaten to death with rifle butts in Bata prison. In the circumstances, Emilio was, perhaps, fortunate to receive just five years in Black Beach prison for his ham and Spanish olives.

Felipe's mother, Jami, tried to move their lives along in the most spirited way she could, adamant that her husband would be released one day, and that all would be well again. Little Fey was too young to know that the military governor of the island took a keen interest in events at Black Beach and had a terrifying reputation: Obiang, the president's nephew, already composing his lists of those who needed to be neutralized.

Some months later Little Fey was being driven through Malabo in the back of the family car. They were near a school, no more than three kilometres from their apartment, when he spotted a stranger who caught his attention. The man was being guarded by soldiers and was obscured by uniforms and rifles and bobbing heads. He only caught a glimpse: shaved scalps, slack muscles, beaded skin, a whole line of them, men with brooms and spades pushing rubble and litter into roadside heaps. Felipe shouted something: 'Look!' or 'Stop!' or 'There!' he cannot remember. Perhaps he just cried. One of the prisoners was his father, he was certain, but the car didn't stop. It couldn't stop. No one was allowed to approach prison gangs in the street.

It was when Jami was cooking bean stew one evening, clattering around the kitchen with her metal dishes, spilling bags of tomatoes and sachets of oregano, stirring with one hand, jousting the children with the other, that the militia appeared at their apartment door. 'You must leave,' said the youth nonchalantly, as though he was commenting on how good the food smelled. 'These homes are for civil servants. You no longer have a civil servant in the family.' Jami nodded and saw him out. There was no time to collect books and furniture, clothes and shoes, they just took all they could pack in a suitcase and boarded a boat for Rio Muni, where they found a house in Bata, the biggest town on the mainland. Shortly after, their father was transferred to the town's prison. It meant Jami could visit and take him food. She gave him a sun hat too, for the gang work, but the authorities confiscated it. Working unprotected in the sun was part of the punishment.

The family had hardly settled in Bata before they were instructed to move again. Macías had announced that families of so-called collaborators and intellectuals were banned from living in towns and urban centres. They must relocate to where they could be more easily monitored. Jami and her family were allocated to a remote cocoa village in the north of the country, close to the sea and the border with Cameroon. The militias at the checkpoints forbade them from travelling anywhere outside. They were marooned: eight children and their mother living in a wooden shack in the forest. And it continued that way for several months, until the day of the strange meeting.

Jami saw it first, a bus rocking along the rutted track near their home. Out of it climbed a unit of soldiers clutching rifles. They stood near to an untidy slope where the creak of falling timber could be heard way up in the forest, and formed a corridor for the prisoners. She saw him immediately: her husband, Emilio, trying to appear tidy in the clothes she had given him during her last prison visit. Jami wanted to run over and touch him, take his hand and lead him to her new home, to gather up their children and walk with them across the border into Cameroon. Instead she watched from a distance as the prisoners were marched up the hillside.

There was a chief alongside them shouting instructions. Jami wandered over, smiling warmly and bowing to his rank. Could Prisoner Emilio visit his family at home today for lunch? she asked.

She and the children collected fruit and eggs and bought palm wine from a neighbour. They brushed the clay floor, found some plastic chairs, carefully cut the cheese and the bread into generous portions, and started a fire for the chicken stew. Emilio arrived in the mid-afternoon, damp and itching with wood chippings. He walked over to embrace her and as she rested her chin on his bare shoulder she saw that several other men had followed him along the track. Lunch would be shared with the chief and fifteen soldiers.

'Señora, the cheese is delicious', 'Señora, the wine too,' 'Señora, you prepare food so well.' They made jokes and the children played, and it was as if Emilio could raise himself from the table at any time, thank his new friends for coming and tell them he really needed to sleep now, to sit on his bed, remove each of shoes in turn, peel off his socks, stretch his long toes, and sleep. But instead, when the food was finished, he was abruptly escorted back to the prison bus, and driven away.

It was June 1974 when Equatorial Guinea radio announced that 118 inmates had been caught plotting a coup from inside the walls of Bata prison. Some of them were killed that same night with wooden clubs – the favourite method of execution at the time – while others are said to have committed suicide by taking poison smuggled in by a doctor. Some 27 of them appeared in a makeshift military tribunal at a cinema in Bata where the prosecution was carried out by the militia. The prisoners' own defence team asked for the death penalty.[6] Emilio was killed in the first tranche, bludgeoned to death with a wooden club.

★

Raimundo Snr waited nervously in his Land Rover near the village of Batoikopo, not far from the capital, in the summer of 1974. As an assembly member and civilian governor of the island, he had heard rumours about what was to happen to the village and had spent the morning considering his options. If one man was suspected of dissent there, all would suffer. Raimundo Snr knew he had to tread carefully. His plan could be interpreted as disloyalty to the regime, collaborating with the enemy, even. He could argue that he outranked Macías's nephew, Obiang, the island's military governor but it was not something he wanted to put to the test. Obiang had just turned thirty-two and was already viewed as Macías's second in command.

When the military convoy rounded the corner, Raimundo steered his Land Rover into the centre of the road and blocked it. 'As civilian governor,' he shouted, 'I request that you go no further!' The men already had their orders. Barrels of petrol were stacked in the back. The houses of Batoikopo were largely wood with grass roofs and wouldn't take long to torch. 'Turn around!' shouted Raimundo. 'Return to Malabo!' The unit's commander moved his men closer to the Land Rover.

The road they were on was a jungle track near the sea. Huge, drizzly clouds were already blowing in. The afternoon smelt of thunder.

Raimundo leaned against his vehicle and waited. The commander radioed his base. He needed to know whose orders prevailed.

Within an hour, a suited man came stumbling down the side of the convoy, surrounded by bodyguards. Raimundo knew what he had to do. He fell to one knee and bowed his head. The appearance of Macías himself was something he had not anticipated.

Raimundo's options had been narrowing for some time. If he tried to resign, it would be interpreted as disloyalty; if he fled with his family and was caught, they would kill him; if he openly questioned Macías from within the regime, the same fate awaited.

'Raimundo Ela Nve!' shouted Macías, each syllable in a separate breathy bark. 'What is happening here?'

Raimundo remained on the ground. 'Excelencia,' he spoke softly, 'in this village there are only women, children and the elderly.'

The soldiers stepped down from their vehicles and stood curiously, in a row behind the president.

'The young people have already escaped,' Raimundo continued. 'I beg you to spare this village.'

Macías was panting. His experience of insubordination was extremely limited. The man on the ground in front of him was not only a colleague but also a relative, and yet here he was defending a village of plotters who were from the minority Bubi clan.

Raimundo waited. The soldiers waited.

'I respect you,' shouted Macías suddenly, 'but… you must never do this again!' The president then turned to the convoy and began waving the vehicles back towards town.

Raimundo Ela Nve climbed into his Land Rover and returned to his Spanish villa. He ate supper with his family and said nothing about the day's events. When the people of Batoikopo heard about the circumstances in which their lives had been spared, they changed the name of the village to incorporate Raimundo's name. It became 'Batoikopo Ela Nve', an honour Raimundo fervently hoped that Macías and Obiang would hear nothing about.

But his failure to comply enthusiastically with the regime was already arousing suspicions elsewhere. Obiang and Raimundo were related and had known each other since their youth, but they had never been close, always co-existing rather than collaborating. Obiang didn't appreciate Raimundo's refusal to assist with neutralizing opponents and his apparent lack of respect for the militias. Raimundo was something of a loner; no one knew what was going on inside his head. Now, with dissent silenced, his quiet scepticism looked very much like dissatisfaction – defiance, even. Obiang and a group of his colleagues concluded that Raimundo must be organizing a coup. In the spring of 1979 they informed Macías in his jungle palace, and that is why Raimundo's name was placed on the regime's death list.

It wasn't long before Raimundo's family heard that a militia was preparing to take his life.

There was little time to waste. One of Raimundo's wives set off for the mainland, heading for Mongomo and the presidential compound. She was related to Macías through marriage, her uncle being married to one of Macías's nieces, and so she was confident of securing a meeting. She told Macías that rumours of a Raimundo-led plot were untrue. 'Obiang and the others are making a storm,' she said. 'Raimundo does not want your job. He wants a quiet life.'

Macías took some time to consider. He needed to choose between the word of Obiang, his nephew, and that of Raimundo, his loyal, though detached, civilian governor. Macías had known Raimundo since they campaigned for independence together and had never seen him scheme or push for promotion. He seemed a straight-forward man. He was opinionated on occasions but openly, to Macías's face.

Remarkably, even in his deteriorating mental state, it seems Macías was persuaded. To smooth things over with Obiang it was agreed Raimundo would be cut loose from power, and given a job where he couldn't cause trouble – back among his beloved cocoa bushes, as a specialist at the Ministry of Agriculture.

After the execution of Emilio in Bata prison, Jami sat on a small stool and remained there even when the rain came. 'Let it happen,' she whispered. The children were unsure what she meant. 'Let them do what they want,' she said. There had been such wailing since the announcement of Emilio's death that silence and sadness were all they could wish for. The children would present her with peeled mangos or plump tomatoes; they would pull her fingers and try to hug some life into her. 'I don't care anymore,' she would say. When she finally rose, she told them they were going for a walk.

They set off in the early morning, sliding their shadows before them, eight children and their mother on a rose-pink jungle path, heading quietly north. The Rio Campo lay ahead, warm and wide, patrolled by crocodiles and mantraps and military observation points, but beyond was Cameroon and the rest of Africa.

Before they had even left the outskirts of the village, however, the local tribal chief spotted them and blocked their way. He was a

Macías supporter, eager to claim his reward for uncovering criminal activity. Two of Little Fey's older brothers made a run for it, leaping into the jungle and then the river. They made it to Cameroon and freedom, but Little Fey and the others were too small and gathered nervously around their mother to wait for the soldiers. They were transported to Bata prison, the scene of their father's execution, and later transferred to Malabo, and Black Beach.

Little Fey is in his forties now, and sitting opposite me sketching a diagram. We are seated in a quiet bar in a European capital, he doesn't want me to say which. He draws an oblong shape. 'Entrance' he writes, and then 'Office'. He would rather not be here. 'These are the two wings,' he says, drawing two lines along the sides of the oblong 'Men's and women's. I was in the women's; I was too young to be in the men's.' He draws more quickly now, small squares in rows between the word 'Office' and 'Women', lots of them tightly squashed together. 'Cells,' he says, 'but so small they couldn't lie down, with no light, for punishment'. He draws more of them. 'And then here, next to the cells, this room is where they went to die.'

Little Fey was allowed to walk around in the courtyard during the day. When night fell, the soldiers would encourage the prisoners to sing and dance. 'Sing more loudly!' they would shout, and Little Fey didn't understand why.

'This is where Obiang stood,' he makes a dot at the entrance. 'Always when he came, something had to happen. And he came often.' The map of the jail is almost complete, but he keeps retracing the squashed cells and prodding the place Obiang would stand. 'The soldiers would shout, "Get the children out of the way! Put them in the wings: the commander is coming!" because they knew Obiang didn't like children to see what was happening. And he would look okay during the day, a bit polite even, but then he would return at night and he was different.'

Obiang often involved himself in the interrogations and executions at Black Beach. They would almost always take place at night, sometimes in the room next to the office, sometimes in the small cells. The dancing and singing was intended to mask the screaming, but Little

Fey could still hear it through the walls of the women's block. The soldiers were at work with their wooden clubs.

Sometimes, for sport, the soldiers would invite their wives and children to watch as they forced prisoners to dance around a fire. The spectacle would continue for hours with the prisoners forced to chant:

> Macías is a serious man,
> The population adores him.
> Let us enjoy ourselves in independence.
> Work and remain quiet,
> And the Lord of Guinea will take care
> Of you for a long time.[7]

As they tired, the prisoners would begin to stumble and fall, and the soldiers would reach for an iron bar that had been heated in the burning embers, and strike them. Every time one fell, the same would happen, until they were staggering around delirious with fatigue, struggling to remain on their feet while the soldiers jeered and taunted them with the red-hot iron bar.

The next day prisoners would stand around the courtyard in huddles and Little Fey would hear them whisper, 'Oyono isn't here anymore,' or 'Ochaga is gone,' and they would wonder when Obiang would return because, whenever he did, the killing would start again. That was the pattern. His Uncle Macías was out of the picture, and it was Obiang who was deciding who to liquidate and when.

'One day a soldier came to me and beckoned me into the small cells and I followed him,' says Little Fey. 'It was very dark,' he says, 'I remember the only light was through some small holes in the top of the walls.' He explains that the men were usually naked and their cells soiled with excrement and alive with insects. Little Fey was led between the rooms and through an open door into a dark space. 'And the man, he was curled up and he had...' he fumbles around at the back of his head, 'wide gashes here, and here... openings', and he points to his neck and shoulders.

Little Fey was instructed to help drag the corpse across the court-yard, through the animal pen, and out of a back door onto the beach. It happened on three occasions. He was eight years old.

On the morning of 3 August 1979, after eleven years of Macías's rule, Obiang launched a simple and bloodless coup against his uncle. His mind had been focused by the fact Macías had begun executing members of his own family, including Obiang's brother. The coup met with no resistance. His collaborators were mostly cousins who had attended Spain's elite military academy together in Zaragoza during the colonial period, and between them they now controlled Equatorial Guinea's entire armed forces. Their Uncle Macías was, of course, indisposed at the other end of the county in his isolated palace complex in the Rio Muni mainland, nursing his perpetual fears of a coup.

When he discovered what was happening he fled into the jungle.

Within forty-eight hours Malabo Radio announced, 'A grim page of history has been turned.' But wherever the word 'grim' had been written in the country's history, Obiang's name was close by. This was hardly a coup, more a familial transfer of power. In order for the illusion of a coup to persist, though, Macías would need to be put on trial.

Obiang's soldier's found him sitting beneath a tree, chewing on a piece of sugarcane in Rio Muni. Nearby, in his car, were several suitcases full of money. It is said he had burned the rest of the country's cash reserves, about 100 million dollars, before abandoning his compound and making a run for the border, as so many of his subjects had done before him. It must have been a bewildering sight for the old lady who stumbled upon him. Apparently Macías was propped against the tree, exhausted, probably delirious, and alone. His guards had either been caught or had melted away.

Crowds gathered outside the low, whitewashed building of the Marfil cinema in Malabo, where Macías's court case was to be held. People milled in the road and hung over the balconies of nearby apartments. There were no celebrations, no screams for retribution; people were just drifting and bumping as if they were emerging from a coma. Some had transistor radios, others stared up at the speakers that would relay proceedings to the thousands waiting in the sunshine. In the main auditorium, beneath where the cinema screen used to be, was a stage where a few wooden desks and chairs were arranged. Military officers strutted, and men in lawyerly black cloaks checked paperwork. In the cinema's sloping auditorium, row after row of expectant faces waited. It was a skilful piece of theatre, organized by Obiang. He had invited officials and journalists from around the world to bear witness to his military junta's eagerness to bring those responsible to justice. And, to add to the event's credibility, Macías wouldn't be the only one on trial; there would be ten others, supposedly the president's most loyal officials. To the foreign observers it might have seemed like a significant slice of the regime was being cut away. But their titles made it clear what was going on: 'soldier', 'chief bodyguard to Macías', 'prison guard', another 'soldier'. They were bit-part actors, helping to fill the stage. Obiang had made himself head of the Supreme Military Council after the coup, but most of the indigenous spectators knew it should have been him standing beside Macías.

A side door was opened. Some of the European journalists had their hands to their mouths. Macías was led in wearing an orange polo shirt and tan cotton trousers. All eyes followed him across the auditorium to a metal-framed chair where he was lowered into place by a doctor and a soldier. He stared back at the audience, self-conscious but seemingly unafraid. The charges were genocide, mass murder, embezzlement of public funds, torture of political prisoners, and burning entire villages as punishment for subversion. Many people believed Macías's calmness meant he had struck a deal with Obiang to keep quiet about the roles of his closest lieutenants in return for his life.

From the original triumphant team of personnel who had won independence eleven years before, few had survived. Two-thirds of the country's first national assembly had either died violently or disappeared. Of the twelve ministers from his first cabinet, only two were left alive.

Unlike Pol Pot in Cambodia, or Hitler's death camps, the regime had not kept meticulous records of the slaughter. Instead, a sample was taken consisting of 474 names, and the crowds stood patiently outside waiting to hear mention of a relative or friend. The *Lista de Asesinados* included the names of officials, ministers, teachers, intellectuals, Spanish sympathizers, coup-plotters, ambassadors, traitors, and Raimundo Ela Nve. The old radio announcer with a gift for poetic polemic, one of the fathers of independence and a member of the country's first national assembly, was announced as one of the dead. After his name was read out, a compact man rose from his seat in the auditorium and interjected in a voice that boomed unexpectedly around the room.

'No, I am here!' said the voice.

Heads turned. 'I am Raimundo Ela Nve.'

Raimundo Ela Nve had managed to survive, thanks to his wife's meeting with Macías just four months before the coup. He had withdrawn from public life, quietly looking after his cocoa plantations, and his absence had been assumed to indicate his death.

For the charges of genocide to stick, the tribunal would need to find Macías had systematically eliminated a particular ethnic, linguistic or cultural group. That couldn't be proven in law and, besides, Equatorial Guinea hadn't ratified the United Nations convention on genocide during Macías's rule. The offence of mass murder, on the other hand, was abundantly established, with audience members spontaneously giving evidence from the auditorium, and some engaging in exchanges with Macías himself.

On the charges of embezzlement, Macías claimed the nation's reserves were transferred to his palace because he was afraid there might have been a bank robbery if they were left in Malabo. The $4 million in his car, he explained was the profits from his own coffee plantations.[8] The court didn't believe him.

After his conviction on 29 September 1979, Macías was taken from the Marfil cinema to Black Beach prison. Apparently he swore his ghost would return to avenge those who condemned him, and so soldiers from Equatorial Guinea refused to be involved in his execution. It was left instead to an elite hired unit of Moroccan troops to form a firing squad. Within six hours of sentence being passed, Macías, 'The Unique Miracle', was dead.

Obiang's conjuring trick had worked. Spain renewed its diplomatic ties with Equatorial Guinea, as did several other countries. Tens of millions of dollars in international aid poured in from Madrid and Paris, much of which vanished into the bank accounts of the new regime's officials. But such was the excitement about ridding Africa of yet another tyrant that few seemed to care. Idi Amin of Uganda had been toppled just months before, and the self-styled 'emperor' of Central Africa, Jean-Bédel Bokassa, had fled into exile during Macías's trial. It seemed as if a new spirit of reform was sweeping the region and Obiang was, incongruously, part of it. It is true, he had released all political prisoners the moment he had seized power, but a look over the walls into his Presidential Palace told a different story.

Obiang declared himself not just president but chairman of the Supreme Military Council, minister of defence, minister of economy and finance, and minister of information and tourism. He awarded six senior members of 'Youth Marching with Macías' ministerial positions, and gave a military governorship to the organization's former boss. The vice-presidency went to one of Macías's nephews, and the rest of government was divided among family and fellow clan members – Fangs from Mongomo like Obiang and Macías. It meant the new power structure was largely indistinguishable from the old, and that the dominance of their ancestral clan could continue.

The international community may well have been taken in, but the vast exile community scattered through Spain, Cameroon and Gabon, were not. Few returned, fearing punishment for having abandoned the country during the rule of Macías. One of those who did was climbing down the steps of his plane in Malabo airport when an official marched over and punched him in the face.

The pattern of coup attempts continued during Obiang's rule just as it had under his uncle: some genuine, others fictitious, dreamed up by Obiang as a pretext for murdering opponents. They became almost annual events. Fewer alleged conspirators were killed than before, but then Obiang was still trying to court foreign governments and didn't want to attract the kind of attention that might lead to an investigation into his past. He was desperate for more foreign aid and investment, and for a while both Spain and France competed for his friendship, hoping to prevent the Soviet Union from gaining a strategic foothold, and expecting to be rewarded with cheap trade deals for cocoa, coffee and timber.

His uncle had imposed control through terror, not patronage. Macías's corruption, although enthusiastically pursued, was hindered because of the very limited pickings available in each sector of his paralysed economy. Obiang's presidential journey had begun with similarly thin options, but his fortunes were about to be transformed.

Throughout the 1960s, Nigerian waters around the Niger Delta were choked with exploration ships and geologists and, by the 1970s, offshore rigs were being constructed out in the Gulf of Guinea in more than a thousand feet of water. One hundred kilometres south of the Nigerian coastline, the sea floor rises to form a volcanic peak. This is Bioko, the main island of Equatorial Guinea. The country shares its offshore geology with Nigeria. But whereas the Nigerians were busily drilling into the seabed and discovering reserves that made it the biggest oil producer in Africa, the waters of Equatorial Guinea were empty. In his drive against modernity and foreign meddling, Macías had blocked oil exploration. Geologists had long suspected the presence of oil but, during the oil boom of the 1970s, Equatorial Guinea was shut for business.

Now, Obiang began to reopen the country. The eagerness of Paris and Madrid to offer aid at the start of the new regime paid dividends. First, Obiang invited in the Spanish state oil company, Hispanoil, in a joint venture with his own government. The French companies ELF and Total followed close behind. The Americans were interested enough to reopen their embassy in Malabo, from where they could watch developments more closely and decide whether to start bidding for concessions. Oil exploration in Equatorial Guinea was going to be a slow and expensive business. All drilling would need to be offshore beneath thousands of metres of water.

In the early 1990s came the first promising signs: gas and condensate were discovered in the Alba field just north of Malabo. Then, while exploring a deep-water geological structure close to Nigerian territorial waters in 1995, Mobil struck oil. Suddenly Equatorial Guinea was the most desirable new frontier in Africa. Marathon, Chevron, Australia's Roc Oil, London-based Ophir, South Africa's PetroSA and many more poured in.

From a slow start, the microstate of Equatorial Guinea began rising quickly through the oil-producing ranks. Six thousand barrels a day, 100,000 a day, and within a decade, almost 400,000 a day. It overtook South Africa and Congo. The rate of growth was spectacular. From being a net importer of oil at the start of Obiang's regime, it was now exporting across the world. Soon it was the third-biggest oil producer in Africa, behind only the giants of Angola and Nigeria, and economists were having to recalibrate their charts. While Nigeria's oil profits were larger, they were spread across a population of 180 million people. Equatorial Guinea, on the other hand, had one of the smallest populations on the continent – fewer than a million people. Discoveries of this magnitude were enough to make it Africa's Kuwait.

In September 1991, before the oil boom had begun, US Ambassador John Bennett was staring out of the window of an Iberia Airlines flight as it dipped low over the surf off Bioko Island, skimmed the steaming canopy of rainforest and touched down on the narrow landing strip of Malabo International Airport. 'Welcome to Fantasy Island,' said a fellow passenger as the plane taxied towards the tiny airport building. Bennett had to concede that it was the most spectacular approach he had seen in more than twenty years of embassy-hopping for the US State Department, but he also knew the true nature of President

Obiang's regime. He had done his homework, and if Washington thought its new ambassador would simply play cocktail host and trade negotiator, it didn't know John Bennett.

His home was to be a former government minister's house, modest in size but with lush gardens, a terrace and a pool, standing beside the embassy itself, which was equally small, but adequate for the five members of staff. The only other expats in town were half a dozen ambassadors, thirty or so Peace Corps volunteers, a handful of missionaries, and a small team of oilmen from the only oil company in Malabo at the time: the US company Walter International Inc. Bennett's predecessor had encouraged Walter to open an office in the capital and Obiang had supported the move. If there was oil beneath the seas of Equatorial Guinea, it would require foreign millions to find it.

Ambassador Bennett settled into his new post, jogging around town while locals shaded themselves indoors, driving himself to functions in the embassy's Oldsmobile, attending church services on Sunday mornings, and gradually becoming familiar with Obiang's secret service agents, who followed him wherever he went. Sometimes he would rise and leave his residence at a god-forsaken hour just so they would have to do the same. But it didn't require secret police-men to reveal Ambassador Bennett's reservations about his new host.

Whenever John Bennett had the opportunity to make a speech, he would seize it: not for reasons of vanity, but because it presented a platform to question Obiang's record on human rights. A subversive US ambassador was not something the regime had experienced before. There had been no US ambassador in Malabo during Macías's time; only the embassies of Libya, Nigeria and China had remained open through the terror. The role of US ambassador was carried out from next door in Cameroon. Washington had reopened its Malabo embassy immediately after Macías's execution. Bennett was the fourth to take the role in the Obiang era, and the first to express criticism of the regime. He didn't just give speeches to private audiences in the embassy; he xeroxed them many times over and had his staff distribute them on the street outside. In them he called for 'free, fair and competitive elections... independent judiciaries... a free press'. Any local who had tried to do the same would have been locked up in Black Beach prison. But Bennett represented Obiang's main source of finance at the time – US foreign aid – and his best hope of finding oil. It meant the man from Washington had to be dealt with cautiously.

Ambassador Bennett's meetings with President Obiang took place about once a month. The man who had once overseen skulls being smashed in a squalid room at Black Beach was now suited, restrained and considerate. He would offer wine or cold drinks and listen attentively to his guests. He sipped wine himself but never overindulged. He was controlled, cautious, never loud, never rancorous: a man who had played regime politics when a single misplaced word could lead to a bullet in the head, and who had emerged as last man standing. If he needed to control the US ambassador, he would find a way that was untraceable to him, a way that wouldn't scare the oil companies starting to take an interest in the country.

It was around this time that Bennett bumped into an employee of Walter International who had a problem. 'The president's son,' said the man. 'We don't mind paying his school fees, but he has racked up an extra $50,000 dollars of expenses in his first year of study.' Bennett was puzzled. The oilman went on to explain that President Obiang had wanted his son, Teodoro, to be educated in America. Walter International had agreed to arrange this and pay his fees, but instead of concentrating on his English lessons in southern California, Teodoro had discovered sports cars and girls, and the company was footing the bill. What amazed Bennett was that the oilman didn't think the arrangement unusual, just that Teodoro had pushed it a little too far. But then, Walter International was a small company, experienced at punching holes in the earth, inexperienced at doing deals with African dictators. When the oil rush began, the big players, along with a US bank, lawyers and real estate companies, would pay court to Obiang and his family on a scale the oil industry had seldom witnessed.

In early 1993 John Bennett was awoken at 2 a.m. in his residence by a phone call. It was a colleague from the embassy. A letter had just been delivered and he wanted Bennett to read it, urgently.

The two men met downstairs in Bennett's house and studied the contents. The letter was typewritten and about a page in length. It described the recent death of the French ambassador in Mobutu's Zaire, a man shot in the head by a stray bullet. Wouldn't it be a good thing, the writer suggested, if a similar bullet were to find its way into the head of the US ambassador in Equatorial Guinea? Bennett and his colleague ruminated on the urgency of the threat. Then Bennett returned to bed, told his wife not to worry, and went to sleep.

Washington was uneasy. It arranged for a State Department official to fly into the country to assess the seriousness of the situation. A meeting was hurriedly arranged with Obiang and one of his confidants for the Sunday evening. Obiang appeared in his office, glutinous with courtesy. 'Mr Ambassador,' he began, placing his hands together as if in sincere prayer, 'I have been told someone threatened your life.' Bennett paused. He knew who had written the letter. He knew Obiang knew. And he knew that Obiang's 'smooth as hell' assistant knew, because it was he who had written it.

The regime wanted Ambassador Bennett out. Not only was he making embarrassing proclamations about human rights, he was spreading the message to oil companies as well. They would often call Bennett from Europe or America for a country-briefing before deciding the best method of securing a drilling concession. Bennett would tell them all they needed to know and then mail them one of his human rights reports. One Texas oil boss was so cross he began yelling at Bennett to stop 'bad-mouthing' President Obiang; it was, he said, entirely inappropriate. Other petroleum executives, Bennett believes, complained to his bosses in Washington, saying that he was running the country down over human rights just as they needed to get closer to its government.

Ambassador Bennett was withdrawn from the embassy for a short while, but he returned to see out his tour of duty, finally leaving Malabo in the summer of 1994. Before he went, he decided to deliver his most combative speech yet, the text of which was photocopied and distributed as usual. 'Sadly,' he told those gathered at his Malabo residence, 'I do not believe that any balanced observer could conclude that the rule of law exists today in Equatorial Guinea.' His audience included the secretary general of the Ministry of Foreign Affairs as well as Obiang's own representative, but John Bennett did not hold back. 'In my three years, I have not seen one case where political violence has come from any quarter other than agents of the government.' He looked around the room and knew that if he didn't do it now, he never would. 'The same names keep coming forward as alleged violators of human rights,' said Bennett, 'through physical mistreatment, intimidation, or monetary sanctions... it may seem impolite – not to say undiplomatic – to mention such names in public...'

He then went on to do just that: names, ranks and titles, among them military officers and even a police commissioner.[9] But state-sponsored killing and torture were not going to trouble the energy companies eagerly queuing for a taste of Obiang's oil.

It must have been a strange sight: a smart bank official hauling heavy suitcases across Washington DC in the spring of 2002, across Massachusetts Avenue at Dupont Circle, and through the impressive neoclassical façade of Riggs Bank, the bank of US presidents and foreign embassies for more than a century. Each case weighed the equivalent of a small child and the man struggling with them was the manager of the bank's African and Caribbean division, Simon Kareri. On arrival, the contents were removed and the loose notes placed into high-speed counting machines. The rest stayed wrapped in plastic bundles. The total came to $3 million, but it raised little suspicion among the staff at Riggs Bank. They had already seen suitcases full of cash – $11.5 million in banknotes – from the same source: the embassy of Equatorial Guinea. It had been handed to the bank by high-ranking officials, sometimes by the ambassador, and even by President Obiang himself.[10] For Riggs, the cash amounts must have seemed unremarkable in comparison with money sloshing around in other accounts controlled by President Obiang and his family. Between 1995 and 2003 Obiang's regime had become the bank's largest customer, holding more than sixty accounts with total balances and loans of around $700 million.

Meanwhile the people of Equatorial Guinea had seen little improvement in their living standards since the oil boom. Average life expectancy in 2007 was fifty-two years. More than a third of the population were dying before they reached forty. Almost twenty per cent of toddlers were either moderately or severely malnourished. More than three-quarters of the population were living beneath the poverty line, with levels of severe poverty similar to those found in Haiti. And it was American companies that were, and still are, responsible for producing most of Equatorial Guinea's oil.

On Pennsylvania Avenue, Riggs Bank had taken to wining and dining President Obiang during his visits to Washington. Of those sixty accounts it held on behalf of the government of Equatorial Guinea, the main one was the 'oil account', where energy companies would deposit their royalty payments for the regime. Its signatories were President Obiang, one of his sons, and a nephew who was the secretary of state for treasury and budget. Withdrawals could only be made with two signatures, one of which had to be Obiang's. Another account, which at times contained more than $500 million, needed only one signature – again that of President Obiang. The other five dozen or so accounts were held by family members and officials (usually one and the same) and by two entertainment companies based in California and owned by Obiang's playboy son, Teodoro.

Riggs Bank helped the Obiang family establish offshore shell corporations for the president and his sons. It also facilitated wire transfers totalling more than $35 million from Obiang's 'oil account' to two companies with accounts in tax havens. Obiang had found a bank right at the heart of the American establishment willing to handle his corrupt finances without asking difficult questions, a bank which must have suspected money laundering and misappropriation of funds but didn't seem to care. In May 2001, top officials from Riggs Bank wrote to Obiang thanking him 'for the opportunity you granted to us in hosting a luncheon in your honour here at Riggs Bank'. The letter went on to say that Riggs had 'formed a committee of the most senior officers of Riggs Bank that will meet regularly to discuss our relationship with Equatorial Guinea and how best we can serve you'. At one point a Riggs Bank board member invited Obiang to visit the Ronald Reagan Library in California. In turn, the bank's chairman, president and six other senior Riggs officials enjoyed a week-long business trip on the tropical beaches of Malabo.

We know all this because a US Senate committee reported into Riggs Bank and its non-compliance with money-laundering laws in 2004. Some of the bank's executives were hauled in front of senators for what became a grimly comical set of exchanges. When the bank's president, Lawrence Hebert, apologized for not 'fully meeting the expectations of our regulators', and blamed the bank's computer system for failing to flag suspicious activity with Equatorial Guinea, an astonished senator shot back, 'You don't need a computer system to realize suspicious activity when you've got 60 pounds of cash being walked through the door in a suitcase.'[11]

The US Senate committee also examined the role of oil companies in Equatorial Guinea. It turned out that Walter International wasn't the only one paying for the education of Obiang's family and that of the regime's elite. As the oil boom took hold, six other major energy companies did the same. More unorthodox still were large payments made directly to regime members and their families, often for land and the provision of 'security' – a euphemism for gangs of thugs. One major energy company, Triton, leased property for its business in Equatorial Guinea from a fourteen-year-old schoolboy who happened to be a relative of the president, and who, along with his mother, received almost half a million dollars.

Ambassador John Bennett was in Washington at the time of the Senate hearings and decided to spend a day observing. It was a decade after his departure from Equatorial Guinea, but his early suspicions about the behaviour of oil companies were confirmed. 'I wasn't surprised,' he says today at his home in Virginia. 'These oil guys, they are looking for a cut in everything. It is in their DNA. They can rationalize any behaviour in the world.'

One of the names that cropped up repeatedly in the final committee report was that of Obiang's son, Teodoro, the original Big Oil-funded student who enjoyed California so much he decided to buy a home there for $7.5 million, with the help of a Riggs Bank loan. This was just temporary accommodation until he could find a more suitable place to stay. Teodoro became the forestry minister in his father's regime in 2003, and owned a company with exclusive rights to export the country's timber. He was also about to become Equatorial Guinea's vice-president. For a job of such importance he would need to live somewhere more suitable: among the Hollywood elite on a hillside above LA.

Near to the homes of Brad Pitt, Halle Berry and Paris Hilton is a peaceful plateau where the grass is lime velvet and the trees are bathed in sea air and sprinklers. There is a villa up there in Malibu, above the Pacific Coast Highway, with a golf course, turquoise pools, and tennis courts overlooking the exclusive Surfrider Beach. It is a vast property, a whitewashed Spanish-style house with the look of an exclusive country club. This is the home that Teodoro bought for himself in 2006 for $35 million – the most expensive sale the real estate company had ever handled. Teodoro's official salary at the time, as forestry minster, was approximately $5,000 a month.

Until late summer of 2011 there was a regular procession of supercars making their way through the property gates. They were part of Teodoro's collection: an Aston Martin, five Bentleys, two Bugattis, seven Ferraris, a Lamborghini, four Rolls-Royces, five Harley Davidson motorcycles – twenty six vehicles in all, valued at around $12 million. He kept some of his fleet at his property in Paris, Number 42 Avenue Foch, which is said to have been worth $180 million and housed two gyms, a Turkish bath, and a movie theatre. It was decorated with around $50 million of jewel-encrusted fittings. He also owned two luxury homes in Cape Town and a property in Brazil. Nevertheless, Malibu seems to have been Teodoro's favourite spot.

Nearby, at a local Californian airfield, stood his $38 million

Gulfstream G-V jet airplane. Teodoro had purchased it with funds transferred from Equatorial Guinea, through an escrow account in London, into bank accounts in the US. His resourcefulness in slipping vast sums of suspicious money into America had been aided by many eager lawyers, bankers and real estate agents.

One Californian attorney, Michael Berger, helped Teodoro buy the Malibu mansion and also assisted him with the creation of shell companies and with concealing his activities from various regulatory authorities. Berger was well aware of the suspicions surrounding Teodoro's wealth because he collected press cuttings about his client. Nevertheless, he received many hundreds of thousands of dollars for his services over four years and became Teodoro's 'loyal friend'. 'Thank you very much for inviting me to your party and for being so nice to me at the party,' wrote Berger to Teodoro after his 2007 'Summer Bash' in Southern California. And he continued:

> I appreciate the super VIP treatment that you gave me. I appreciate you telling your friends that I am your attorney. I am proud to work for you... The food was great, the drinks were better than great, the house, the view, the DJ, the white tiger were all SO COOL! Best of all were the people that I met there because of you.[12]

But while Teodoro, the forestry minister, was partying with his white tiger in California, the UN was preparing for a visit to his homeland to investigate systematic torture and arbitrary imprisonment. The investigation happened in November 2008, and confirmed what exiles had been alleging for years while being shouted down or ignored by oil executives, banks and oil-thirsty governments. The researchers found evidence of regular torture by police, including severe beatings and electroshocks. Black Beach prison had been renovated since the days Little Fey was forced to drag broken corpses across the courtyard, but still the researchers heard about torture during interrogation and found torture devices in the front office, including iron bars, a car battery and a thick black cable. The UN Special Rapporteur was so concerned that the country's oil reserves were blinding the world to the true nature of Obiang's regime that he urged oil companies and governments to question their own behaviour and ensure they were not complicit in the regime's vicious repression. Maybe he had in mind Secretary of State Condoleezza Rice, who had posed for pictures with Obiang in Washington in 2006 and called him a 'good friend to the US'.

Back in California, Teodoro would have been aware by 2009 that trouble was looming. International law enforcement agencies were focusing their attention on some of Teodoro's assets and how he might have acquired them. There was a police investigation in France, civil actions in South Africa and Spain, and a criminal investigation in the US. Prosecutors suspected that most, if not all, of Teodoro's assets were derived from extortion, bribery or the misappropriation of funds. But instead of hiding away in one of his many properties, Teodoro indulged in ever more outrageous spending sprees.

In September 2011 Teodoro was out of town when there was frantic activity around his Malibu residence. One of his assistants had flown into LA International Airport from Paris, as instructed by Teodoro, and made his way to the mansion. Emanuel Asamoah had some important work to do and needed to be discreet. A delivery had been made that week and he needed to take charge of it: a collection of Michael Jackson memorabilia now hidden in the garage. Teodoro had become an obsessive fan, spending millions of dollars to create one of the most impressive Jackson collections in the world – he had the singer's 'Bad Tour' white crystal glove, a signed 'Thriller' jacket, a set of 'Neverland Ranch Life-Size Statues' and much more besides. Asamoah moved some of it from the garage into the main house. Later a security guard noted in his Daily Activity Report that five pieces of luggage full of Michael Jackson souvenirs had been taken from the property and that Asamoah, along with another assistant, was on his way back to LA International Airport. Asamoah boarded a Delta Airlines flight to Paris with his boss's prized possessions and, it seems, delivered them to the Paris property.

Ordinarily, the global movement of Michael Jackson memorabilia, even a million dollars' worth of it, wouldn't trouble law enforcement agencies, but this was a potential criminal offence. The US authorities had finally decided that Teodoro's assets in the US were purchased with corrupt money and had signalled to him that they were going to seize some of his property. But Teodoro had other plans. After smuggling his Jackson collection to Europe, he tried to sell the Malibu house.

That attempt failed. Instead, in 2014, the US Department of Justice announced that, 'through relentless embezzlement and extortion' Teodoro (who was by then vice-president of Equatorial Guinea) had 'shamelessly looted his government and shaken down business... to support his lavish lifestyle while many of his fellow citizens lived in extreme poverty'.[13] In return the authorities forced him to relinquish assets worth an estimated $30 million and warned him that if he ever flew his Gulfstream into California again they would seize that too. But, with the oil still flowing back home, $30 million was small change.

President Obiang is now in his seventies and has been in power longer than any other African dictator alive today – thirty-eight years – a year longer than Robert Mugabe who hosted Obiang at his daughter's wedding in Harare in March 2014. The pinned-moth eyebrows have greyed a little but he is still the same man whose decisions led straight to the execution room at Black Beach prison, who oversaw torture and killing, and who was viewed as 'Number Two' in a regime of almost unparalleled barbarity.

During that period, the Soviet Bloc and the West ignored the pleas of refugees and political exiles who managed to escape the terror of his uncle Macías. They were more interested in lucrative concessions for rare tropical hardwoods such as ebony and mahogany, and the offer of cheap coffee and cocoa. The United States was keen to explore the territory for tin, copper and uranium, and tried to keep Macías sweet so they could acquire sole rights. The Soviets were interested in fishing deals. African neighbours often had complex tribal links to Macías that discouraged any interference. Several of the most notorious African despots of the era signed treaties of friendship with Equatorial Guinea – including the self-styled 'emperor' of the Central African Republic, Jean Bedel Bokassa, and Idi Amin in Uganda. There were political and strategic considerations too; in the mid-1970s the Soviet Union used Bioko as a transfer point for weapons and troops bound for the war in Angola. China provided arms, and sent officials to train the paramilitaries of JMM – 'Youth Marching with Macías'. Colonel Gaddafi viewed Macías as a maverick who had escaped the yoke of imperialism, and sent him a $1 million gift. All this meant that there was little international pressure on Macías to reform, and that the world was never properly informed about what was happening in Equatorial Guinea.

Writing about the regime in 1989, historian Randall Fegley said:

> Only a handful of scholars tried to alert the world to the terror which had overtaken the tiny, young nation. Many parties were involved in a cover-up which allowed Macías to continue his brutal rule unfettered... the Soviet Bloc, the People's Republic of China, France, the United States of America and a host of European and African states. The cover-up was a series of small efforts on the part of each group concerned. However, had it existed, a grand conspiracy among all would not have been any more destructive than the net effect of these piecemeal attempts to conceal the truth.

Those words were written before Equatorial Guinea discovered oil. The scramble that happened during the 1990s, involving the energy industry and its international backers in government, continues the cover-up on behalf of Obiang. In 2014, he stood in the White House alongside President Obama and the First Lady, all of them smiling for the cameras, affirming their common interest in Equatorial Guinea's oil. The next US visit by the leader of Equatorial Guinea may not involve Obiang at all, but his successor. He has already anointed the man that will take over: his son, Teodoro.

Riggs Bank was fined $25 million in 2004 for violations of anti-money laundering laws in relation to both the embassy of Equatorial

Guinea and that of Saudi Arabia. Similar fines and damages had to be paid in 2005 as a result of the bank's arrangements with the Chilean dictator Augusto Pinochet. The judge in that case referred to Riggs Bank as 'a greedy corporate henchman of dictators and their corrupt regimes'. In May 2005 Riggs was taken over by another company and closed its doors for the last time.

PART THREE
Chocolate

CHAPTER SEVEN

Before the Dictators

SÃO TOMÉ AND PRÍNCIPE

*If this is not slavery, I know of no word in the
English language which correctly characterizes it.*

JOSEPH BURTT, AGENT OF
THE CADBURY FAMILY, 1907

DRIVING WEST ALONG the coast from the Ghanaian capital, Accra, the road is a sleek python of tarmac, fringed by fields of tall grass that bend with the rush of the timber lorries and buses. It's the route the slave traders used to take, riding on their ox-carts, while the captives marched in front, manacled with neck braces. They walked for weeks to reach here, from modern-day Burkina Faso, Niger and Nigeria, through rainforests and savannah, to the transportation hub of what was then called Gold Coast. There is still a giant hollowed-out tree, a natural wood dungeon, into which the slaves were forced while the traders slept.

There is no other road like this in Africa. Every few miles, there is another reminder of the trade that first attracted Europeans to these shores in the fifteenth century and which lasted 400 years. First, Cape Coast Castle, a stained, crenellated fortress rising from the palms, its gates facing the Atlantic Ocean. Above its dungeons, where thousands waited in the darkness, is a small stone church where Europeans would sing and pray as the slaves were herded onto waiting boats. Then Elmina Castle, its contours blurred by the crashing surf. Others are just ruins now, lumps of stone falling into the surf; some have been preserved to remind us of the history many would rather forget. Thirty more lie between here and Côte d'Ivoire: Portuguese, Danish, Swedish, Dutch, British, they were all busy on this coastline, rarely venturing inland, preferring to wait for their human wares in the comfort of fortified buildings. Most of these places were built to take possession of gold, but gradually turned to the more lucrative trade in people.

I reached the former slave post of Axim in the late afternoon. It is a row of empty tourist huts now, clinging to a rocky slope. To the east is a wild and empty beach where breakers sluice right up to the palms. To the west lies a hissing shoreline of chiselled rocks and mangrove forests. And one of the richest cocoa-growing regions on earth is north of here.

A journalist called Henry Nevinson passed this coastline in a steamer in December 1904. His trip was billed as an 'adventurous journey' in the spirit of the great explorers, for the American magazine *Harper's*, but his true purpose had to remain secret. He observed the same European forts from the deck of his ship, 'The white man's settlements with their ancient names so full of tragic and miserable history, Axim, Sekundi, Cape Coast Castle...' he wrote in his diary. 'The further down the coast you go, the more melancholy is the scene.'

Nevinson was bound for two tiny islands further south, a pair of commas off the coast of West Africa, both owned by the Portuguese. São Tomé and Príncipe were the kind of distant, palm-fringed lands that had inspired Robert Louis Stevenson's *Treasure Island* twenty years before. Their surface area was smaller than that of Greater London, but they had recently acquired a central role in the insatiable global appetite for chocolate.

Cocoa isn't an easy crop to grow. It requires the kind of steamy, hot climate that can be found only a couple of degrees either side of the equator. When Europeans first arrived in Africa, there was none. It wasn't native to these shores but to the rainforests of South America, where it was considered the most refined of fruits, its consumption restricted to chiefs and aristocrats. Their servants dried and crushed the beans to make a paste which they mixed into a frothy drink. It was believed to possess rare, health-giving properties, and the ancient Mayans assumed it must have come from heaven, as a gift to their leaders from god.

The melon-shaped fruit had never been seen beyond the Americas, but as the slave ships from Portuguese West Africa sailed to the New World to deposit their captives, and then returned to Europe on the final leg of the trade triangle loaded with cotton, cocoa and sugar, they also began throwing in the occasional crate of cocoa pods as a curiosity from South America. The fruits were ferried to the tables of Europe's elite, to show off over dinner as a symbol of refinement and of territories conquered on the other side of the globe. Spanish monarchs mixed cocoa with vanilla, cinnamon, cloves, sugar and milk to create a thick, gluey broth, and soon its appeal spread. In the salons and bars of Enlightenment Europe, cocoa was sold as a mental stimulant and aphrodisiac. Apothecaries began selling it in tall glass jars alongside tobacco. Few were concerned that it was produced by slave labour in the tropics, and demand kept growing.

The practical problem with cocoa had always been its fatty by-product: cocoa butter. It had been much valued by the Mayans for its energy-giving properties, allowing them to march through the jungle for days on end, but its bitter taste did not appeal to the European palate. In the early nineteenth century, cocoa companies attempted to boil, grind and skim the butter away, but it required a lot of effort and the final chocolate drink was still fifty per cent fat. Cocoa began to fall out of favour, overtaken by more convenient stimulants like coffee and tea. But, in Amsterdam, in 1828, a visionary inventor, Coenraad Van Houten, devised a piece of equipment that was to revolutionize the industry. The Dutchman constructed a cocoa-pressing machine with fluid-driven pistons that used six thousand pounds of pressure to squeeze the grease from the beans. It produced hard cakes of cocoa, which he then ground into a fine powder, to be mixed with milk or water. The new, purer and healthier product was soon a favourite across Europe, sold in glass jars with the label 'Van Houten's Dutch Cocoa'. The next step would transform the humble bean into the world's favourite treat, and it happened in the back of a small shop on Union Street in Bristol.

Dr Joseph Fry opened his chocolate company in the mid-1700s, marketing the powder for medicinal purposes, but it was his grandson, Joseph Storrs-Fry, who achieved the historic breakthrough. Combining Van Houten's pressing machine with the Watt steam engine, he began mass-producing cocoa cakes and experimenting with the mix of butter and flavourings to produce something they could mould into shapes. By 1847, Fry had the balance of sugar, clarified butter and cocoa solids just right, and began selling his confection in easy-to-handle nuggets: the world's first chocolate bars.

By the time Henry Nevinson undertook his journey to São Tomé, Fry was manufacturing multiple lines of chocolate snacks, including the first Easter eggs. Cadbury was using the same techniques to produce milk chocolate bars, sold in its distinctive purple wrappers. Rowntree had diversified from fruit pastilles into chocolate blocks, and in America, Milton Hershey had moved away from caramel to concentrate on chocolate candies.

Demand for cocoa soared. It mirrored the sudden and destructive demand for rubber that had happened in Congo after the invention of the inflatable tyre and, just like rubber, cocoa couldn't be farmed in straight orchard-style lines, it grew wild. The companies needed a vast army of pickers who were cheap, compliant, and living close to the equator. Slavery had been abolished. That option was gone. So, too, had Europe's governance of South America. But Africa, on the other hand, seemed like the perfect solution.

It began as a small agricultural experiment in the 1860s. Someone – no one's sure who – sailed a few cocoa seeds to the islands of São Tomé and Príncipe, just to see if they would take to the climate. Success was swift. The plants quickly spread. By 1870, cultivation was being taken more seriously, and the islands' Portuguese administrators realized there was money to be made.

Henry Nevinson first caught site of São Tomé and Príncipe through an ocean fog. 'The valleys at their base were shrouded in the pale and drizzling mists which hang about them almost continuously,' he wrote. 'Here and there a rounded hill, indigo with forest... the whole place smoked and steamed like a gigantic hothouse.'[1] Cocoa had only been cultivated seriously on the islands for thirty years, but had swept across the landscape at the expense of almost all other crops. The small, bushy trees had taken root easily, growing in ideal conditions beneath the cover of rainforest. The Portuguese had never been much interested before in the two little islands, with their modest crop of bananas and breadfruit, but now they were sitting on an agricultural gold mine. With little effort, other than organizing cheap labour, they quickly pushed production from a few hundred sackfuls a year to several thousand. Major chocolate companies from America and Europe began sourcing from the islands, notably Cadbury, Rowntree and J.S. Fry and Sons. São Tomé and Príncipe steadily eased their way up the world rankings, overtaking the powerhouses of Brazil and Mexico, until, when Henry Nevinson arrived in 1905, they were the biggest cocoa producers in the world.

Nevinson was not only a journalist, but a radical and a social reformer who marched with the suffragettes and railed against Victorian conservatism. At Oxford he was inspired by the accounts of Henry Morton Stanley and his adventures in Congo, and when he graduated, he found his own way of reaching distant and exotic lands: as a war correspondent, reporting alongside Winston Churchill, Arthur Conan-Doyle and Rudyard Kipling. In southern Africa, while covering the Second Boer War, Nevinson acquired a taste for investigating how Europe misused its colonial power. He was there at the time Cecil Rhodes was making his fortune in the diamond mines of Kimberley and the gold fields of Witwatersrand, and came away with the conclusion that Britain's real objectives were 'to paint the country red on the map, and to exploit the gold'.

Once back in London, he found further inspiration to support his convictions. The unmasking of Belgium's King Leopold, whose Congo Free State had caused the death of 10 million people, many as a result of forced labour on his rubber plantations, had helped alert Europe to conditions being endured at the sharp end of the West's capricious demands. Nevinson was in search of a story to match. We can picture him, sitting in his Hampstead home, poring over copies of the Anti-Slavery Society newsletter. There were accounts from missionaries who described shipments of young men and women to São Tomé and Príncipe being unloaded in a fashion that sounded very much like slavery. He would, no doubt, have compared them with reports from Leopold's Congo that dominated the newsletter's front page. While journalists and campaigners were preoccupied by Leopold, few seemed interested in Portugal and chocolate. If anything, it was the confectionary companies themselves who scented a problem. Cadbury,

Rowntree and Fry were run by Quaker families who spent much time campaigning against slavery, and subscribed to the newsletters where reports of slavery were appearing. It was they who approached the British government to ask for advice as to whether the reports were correct. But concrete information was hard to come by. São Tomé and Príncipe were just too remote and impenetrable.

Britain's nearest contact was its consul on the mainland, in Luanda, the capital of Portuguese Angola. It was no secret that the cocoa workers were recruited from there, but the details were fuzzy. Some sources said they were driven from the interior in chain gangs, and loaded onto ships for the islands. The British consul hadn't actually visited the plantations, but was able to tell his colleagues in London's Foreign Office not to worry, that the workers were 'well treated and cared for'.[2] He advised them to let the matter go. Without cocoa and the services of mainland labour, he warned, the islands would be in 'absolute ruin'.

The Portuguese were dismissive too. These were the fevered stories of Europeans unused to the jungle climate, they said; there was nothing untoward happening in São Tomé and Príncipe.

That was a relief to the British government. Portugal was a key ally, and London didn't want to become embroiled in a diplomatic row. With the islands beyond the reach of proper inquiry, they would just have to take Lisbon's word.

And so it was that, in 1904, Henry Nevinson found himself in the Southern Atlantic Ocean.

A hundred years later I was in a Land Cruiser driving through Ghana's western region towards the cocoa fields that occupy thousands of square miles along the border with Côte d'Ivoire. As we turned off the main road, the tarmac was replaced by sticky orange clay and grit that clattered beneath the wheel arches. The rainy season had just ended and the lorries that came this way had gouged out trenches too deep for clearance, and so we drove at a 45-degree angle, two wheels on the ridge in the middle.

After an hour creeping through the forest, there was movement on the road ahead. A line of young men poured from the undergrowth, and walked in single file down the side of the track. They were dressed in stained shorts and vests, each with a machete slung over a shoulder: cocoa workers on their way home from the fields. Several looked as young as ten. I was there for a BBC investigation, and we settled ourselves into lodgings at a small town called Enchi, in the heart of the cocoa-growing region. Every morning, we would set off into different parts of the remote forests, sometimes on foot, to find out how the West's chocolate was being made.

You can tell when you are approaching a cocoa village; the smell of sweet cherry liquor and smoked leaves hangs in the air, and the trees are no longer green. Everything is encrusted with a fine orange dust. The only vehicles on these tracks were the lorries that arrived to pick up sacks of cocoa beans, churning up the soft clay so that everything appeared through a blinking, orange haze. Our wipers were on but there was no water for them, so we peered through two fan-shaped holes. Even the grass had that yellow-red patina.

Finding the farms was not as straightforward as it seemed. We crawled through one of the tunnels in the undergrowth we had seen the workers use. On the other side was a shaded path leading up through the forest, cool but steamy, and eerily silent but for the distant whoops of monkeys. About a kilometre in, a man with two children came into view, wandering from tree to tree, peering upwards. Occasionally he would push the smaller of the two lads into the branches, and stand beneath with an open sack, as the boy lopped off ripe cocoa pods that came crashing through the leaves. You wouldn't know it, but this was a farm.

Cocoa 'farms' are not farms in any conventional sense. The trees aren't arranged in neat lines. There is no fencing to demarcate ownership. It is just wild jungle with cocoa trees positioned randomly among the rest. British colonialists did try to impose some order, planting them in rows like corn, but that didn't produce fruit. The trees can't be tamed. Cocoa grows best in its natural habitat, crowded by other trees in the shade of the jungle floor. That's why it is so labour-intensive to harvest.

Inside the pod, the beans sit in grinning rows, cream-coloured and covered in clear, sticky, pulp. The farmer offered me some on the end of his machete. They taste like lychee with a squirt of lemon, but there is a long process before they can be transformed into chocolate.

Back in the village, dozens of boys sat around a pile of pods, smashing them open with machetes and scraping out the pulp. They wrapped it in plantain leaves and left it to ferment in the sun. This is the magical part, the alchemy that can't be replicated in a factory. It requires tropical heat, the slow chemical reaction of the plantain with the juices of cocoa, the gradual release of sugars and acids. After a week, the beans are starting to smell of chocolate. They are scooped up in handfuls and spread over trestle tables and plastic sheets to dry in the sun. Young boys scurry around, turning them throughout the day. Only then can they be poured into sacks and left by the side of the road for collection.

It has been like this since cocoa was first introduced to Africa. All attempts at mechanization have failed. Exactly the same techniques were used when Henry Nevinson came this way more than a century ago.

Nevinson opted to start his enquiries on the mainland, where he knew the labourers for São Tomé and Príncipe were recruited. After passing the mouth of the Congo River he continued southwards and was soon steaming along the coast of Portuguese Angola, where he docked in a deep and quiet inlet called Lobito Bay. Looking out across the unpopulated grasslands, he mused that one day he expected it to become a thriving city, a port with European cargo ships waiting to take collection of West Africa's resources. Engineers had already been there, sizing up the area for the Scottish explorer and entrepreneur Sir Robert Williams, who was a long-term business partner of Cecil Rhodes. Williams had discovered vast deposits of copper in the Katanga region of Congo, and planned a groundbreaking 1,400-mile railway line to transport it to the Angolan coast.

Nevinson disembarked and made his way to the start of the old slave routes, which he saw running in white lines far over the hills. He hired an ox and a cart and set off for the interior, travelling at three miles an hour through the eucalyptus trees on a journey that would take several weeks. It gave him time to contemplate one of the great difficulties of his quest.

He had enough experience of Africa to know that what Europeans would describe as 'slave labour' might be seen in Angola as traditional tribal practice, and that the two were tangled together like a hook in a ball of fishing line. Tribal chiefs would often exercise despotic powers over their people, making them surrender crops, money, and even wives and daughters, in return for wisdom and protection. When the Europeans came, it was the chief's prerogative to hire out some of his fittest youths to work the cargo boats that sailed up and down the coast. The youths would happily volunteer, paddling out in canoes and clamouring to be taken on board. The chief's only condition was that they received a shilling a day, were fed and looked after, and that they were brought home within a year. Everyone benefited. It was an early form of labour exchange. No one was doing anything against their will, and when the labourers were delivered home they would divide their earnings with the chief.

The next step was where the moral fog began to descend. What if the same chief decided the youths could be handed over permanently, for a fee? What if the youths didn't want to leave their village, but the chief nonetheless insisted? That is what Nevinson had observed when he was covering the Boer War – the British buying up labour from chiefs to work in the gold mines. He prepared himself for an investigatory journey where the distinctions between what was acceptable and what was not would be narrow.

Nevinson arrived in the highland forests of Bihé, deep inside Angola, and waited. This was where convoys of labourers were led through on their journey to the coast, before being shipped off to the cocoa farms on the islands. What Nevinson soon realized was that Portuguese officials didn't venture this far inland. They left recruitment to agents and middlemen who would mysteriously acquire work gangs with no explanation. These agents were hard-bitten young men, mostly Europeans, who would trek deep into the bush carrying trading goods: rifles, ammunition, rum and bales of Manchester cotton. The chiefs of these remote tribes, desperate to protect themselves against rivals, as well as to acquire a few European treats, would offer their strongest youths in return. The ancient practice of slave-raiding had re-emerged, with tribes kidnapping each others' fittest men, uncles selling nephews, and parents selling children, in a trade driven entirely by the need for cheap labour.

Witnesses told Nevinson they had seen men in neck irons being led through town just a few weeks before, followed by white men with whips. The journey to the port was 300 miles, through jungle and then parched savannah known as 'Hungry Country'. The challenge for the agents was to pass through without losing too much of their newly acquired property. One group of 900 captives had recently become so ill and exhausted that the agent arrived at the coast with just 300 survivors.

Pulled along on his ox-cart, sometimes semi-conscious through heat and illness, Nevinson's attention was caught by several wooden shapes hanging in the bushes by the side of the track. He inspected them and saw they were pieces of timber through which a hole had been cut, just large enough for two hands or two feet. Some had wooden pins driven through the holes. These were slave shackles, he realized, used for securing the limbs of recruits to stop them running away at night. The forest was thick with them.

Further along, the path was 'strewn with dead men's bones'. Femurs stuck from the earth, skulls lay in the undergrowth, all of them relatively fresh. They were the remains of labourers who had been unable to keep up with the march and had been murdered or left to die. One man's corpse was only a few days old. 'When I tried to raise the head,' wrote Nevinson, 'the thick, woolly, hair came off in my hand like a woven pad leaving the skull bare and revealing the deep gash made by the axe at the base of the skull...' Later, as the routes converged, he came across processions of men and women, led by agents dressed in white jackets and carrying rifles. The labourers had all been purchased by a European company engaged in cocoa production on the islands. But it was in the bustling port of Benguela that Nevinson found the centrepiece of the Portuguese operation.

The town began to stir in the cooling afternoon breeze. In the old Portuguese courtyards, agents shouted at their labourers to stand and prepare to march. A ripple of excitement passed through the stagnant town. At a long, low building known as the Tribunal, windows and doors were thrown open and a Portuguese state lawyer took his seat at the head of the chamber. He checked the documents, made amendments, and then signalled to the room that he was ready. Into his presence were herded a group of half-naked natives. With little more than a glance, the lawyer called out the question. 'Will you go willingly as labourers to São Tomé?'

There was no answer given, and none expected.

Legal papers were passed between officials. Agents shook hands with the Portuguese staff, and collected their money. The natives were assigned numbers and given identification discs to be hung around their necks. They were then designated 'contract labourers' who had just agreed to work for five years on São Tomé and Príncipe. Nevinson watched from among the crowd of agents, eagerly shouting for their group to be paraded. The next were all women, and the process began again. At the conclusion of each round, recruits were led onto the pier and loaded straight onto steamers. 'Bemused with a parting dole of rum,' wrote Nevinson, 'bedecked in brilliantly striped jerseys, grotesque caps and flashy loin cloths to give them a moment's pleasure, the unhappy throng were escorted to their doom.' Now formally recruited, the labourers were called *serviçeas*. 'The climax of the farce has now been reached,' continued Nevinson.

> The deed of pitiless hypocrisy has been consummated. The require-
> ments of legalized slavery have been satisfied. They went into Tribunal
> as slaves, they have come out as contract labourers. No one in heaven
> or on earth can see the smallest difference. But by the change of name

Portugal stifles the enfeebled protests of nations like the English, and by the excuse of law she smooths her conscience and whitens over one of the blackest crimes which even Africa can show.

In Ghana, we reached a remote, rundown village of clay and thatch homes deep in the rainforest. Cocoa beans were drying in the sun on trestle tables. Women pounded plantain in giant stone mortars. But the villagers were unexpectedly timid, and when they saw us approach, they scattered. Doors were firmly shut, men ran into the bush, metal pans were left bubbling on fires. Only a few scruffy goats remained. We wandered around the perimeter to see if we could beckon anyone back, and found a group of young boys sitting on a log. It's no secret that most cocoa villages use children to help on the farms. Child labour within the family is an accepted practice, just as in Europe and America children might help with the harvest in the holidays or in their parent's shop, so long as they attend school and are not mistreated. The hours, conditions and intensity of work are a continent apart, but the principle remains the same. But what has afflicted the cocoa industry for decades has been rumours of a trade in children; kidnapped boys and girls, smuggled across borders to be sold into labour gangs against their will, and locked away at night to make sure they don't escape.

On these distant farms, it is easy to conceal such a trade. Few officials ever pass through, just cocoa-buyers arriving to collect their consignments. The villages supply some of the biggest names in chocolate, but Western companies have managed to place a partition between themselves and their labour force. They say it is the government's responsibility, and that they are simply purchasing the product. Occasionally they do send representatives, but there are 3 million cocoa farmers in Ghana to check, all looking to cut their margins by employing the cheapest labour. Farmers are canny too; they know to hide slave children as soon as strangers approach.

The boys on the log were bemused. 'We all work in cocoa,' one of them said, 'but we all go to school as well.' They waved light-heartedly at the men hiding in the trees. 'But there are some other children in the village,' one of them volunteered, scraping the dried pulp from his blade. 'They are different from us... we don't play with them... they don't go to school... they don't come from Ghana. They are here to work.'

We were presented with a tired, undernourished twelve-year-old, who the boys sat down like a stiff doll in between themselves and tried to encourage to speak. He didn't understand, and sat anxiously staring at his bare feet. They tried a little English and a couple of tribal tongues, and when they finally coaxed a word from him, it was in French. Francophone countries lie to the north and west.

His name was Fatau, dressed in tatty shorts and an oversized Chelsea shirt, disorientated and scared. He communicated through an older boy, whispering responses through cupped hands. We were led to understand he had been in the village a year. But his family background was sketchy. They said he came from a border town far away in the savannah of neighbouring Burkina Faso. His mother and father were dead. Fatau was an orphan. A kind man had found him and brought him to Ghana to find a new home.

Who was this man? They nudged each other and laughed. One of them ran off to find him.

Pappa Gyan was short and solid, with a shaven head. As the other adults began drifting back into the village, dressed in tired and dirty clothes, he wandered among them in a spotless blue vest and white trousers. Pappa Gyan had been away for a while, and went around shaking hands and gathering the others into huddles. 'Me?' he laughed in a vapour of palm wine. 'No, no, I have no idea how Fatau came to work here.' The only person who could help, he said, was Fatau's master, a man called Kweku.

He lived on the outskirts of the village, his home set in the shade of the forest. There were children and chickens running around his feet, and a plump and harried wife trying to organize vegetables for the pot. Kweku twitched like a squirrel. He explained that he was a good friend of Fatau's father, who lived nearby and who had loaned out his son to be used in the cocoa fields.

'So, do you know his mum as well?' I asked.

'Oh yes,' he nodded eagerly, 'both are just here,' and he motioned vaguely in the direction of the bush.

As we left for the day, I was shown where Fatau slept. It was a dark stone hut with grass sleeping mats and a pail of water. It looked more like a kiln than a home. They said Fatau stayed there along with eleven other boys 'from another country'. Attached to the wooden door was a padlock.

'To keep them safe,' said one of the villagers as we headed back to the road.

The southern Atlantic Ocean sparkled turquoise, its cream-topped breakers dancing all the way to the horizon. There was a storm out there, and the wind whipped against the steamer that was carrying the *serviçeas* to São Tomé and Príncipe. It was June 1905 and Henry Nevinson was on board. Before they struck off across 800 miles of heavy seas, there was another batch of labourers to pick up from the port of Novo Redondo.

The new arrivals were prodded and pulled up the boarding ladder as the steamer pitched and rolled. Nevinson watched from among the European passengers standing outside their cabins on the higher decks. When it was the turn of a young mother, the loading party became impatient. She had her baby tied to her back, and was struggling to clamber up the ladder. Each time she tried, she misjudged the rhythm of the waves, and was slammed against the side of the boat. The officials slapped her and pushed her back on. The Europeans hung over the railings to get a better look, and eventually saw her clamber on board and fall flat against some sloping stairs, which she then ascended on all fours. When she reached the top she was bruised and bleeding, soaked with water, and most of her clothes were hanging from her in strips.

'I have heard many terrible sounds,' wrote Nevinson, 'but never anything so hellish as the outbursts of laughter with which the ladies and gentlemen of the first class watched that slave woman's struggle up to the deck.'

The following morning, the storm had cleared, and the steamer prepared to raise anchor. The contract workers had been locked in the hold overnight, and were now out on the lower deck where they lay bewildered among the mules, sheep and monkeys. One of their number must have had an inkling of what faced him on the cocoa plantations, and had managed to make his way undetected to the bow, from where he fancied his chances of escape. The beach wasn't far away, and on a clear day like that, it seemed he had every chance of making it. The man leapt into the water and began to swim. A shout went up. Officials ran around releasing pulleys and ropes, and a wooden life boat was launched to give chase. These were shark-infested waters, the Europeans reminded each other. It was barely ten minutes before the crew had made up the distance. They leaned over the side and began to batter their quarry with oars and sticks. Once they had dragged him on board, they threw a sail over his bleeding and naked body so as not to embarrass the ladies. Then a doctor and government agent took him to the hold and chained him to a post to prevent any further trouble.

'Flog him! Flog him!' cheered the Europeans. 'A good flogging!'

Four years before these events, in the spring of 1901, William Cadbury had been sitting in his study overlooking the manicured lawns of Bournville near Birmingham, when he received a letter concerning a business proposition on São Tomé. William was the future of the chocolate dynasty, still not yet forty, and seen as the creative brains that would take the brand into the twentieth century. The family were already rewriting the rule book on industrial Britain, relocating their workforce from the squalid and polluted inner city to the fields south of Birmingham, where they had built a model village for employees to live: cottages with gardens and modern interiors, lakes around which the workforce could take bracing country walks. The construction of Bournville had grabbed world headlines, and confirmed the Cadbury family as progressive, even visionary in their approach to labour relations. They had built lecture rooms, gymnasia and a swimming pool, all to encourage peace of mind, good health, and a more positive attitude towards work. At the turn of the century their competitors at Rowntree and Fry were watching every move, wondering what workplace revolution this great philanthropic family was going to unveil next.

William Cadbury turned the letter over in his hand. It was perplexing that anyone could think his company might be interested in the offer he'd been made. It concerned a plantation, or *roça*, on the western side of São Tomé, called Trás-os-Montes. Land prices had been soaring over recent years, and the Cadbury company already had extensive interests there, sourcing, as it did, half of its cocoa from the island. It was the particulars that made William Cadbury uneasy. Among the *roça*'s interests was listed a workforce of 200 black labourers worth £3,555. The letter explained that the *serviçeas* had been obtained 'through contract with the African chiefs in Angola'. It went on to explain that they were fed primarily bananas, and clothed at minimal cost, and that 'their treatment, when ill, is of slight importance'.[3]

The Cadbury family had been following events in the tropics closely. As committed members of the Anti-Slavery Society, they would have received the same newsletters as Henry Nevinson. Like him, they couldn't have been sure about what they were reading. The allegations of slavery were often based on hearsay, and seemed to contain little concrete evidence. Certainly Cadbury wasn't persuaded to undertake an expensive relocation of the company's cocoa sourcing, but that letter began to focus his mind.

In the following weeks, a board meeting was called in the Bournville offices, and the new evidence discussed. 'This seems to confirm,' the members concluded, 'other indirect reports that slavery, either total or partial, exists on these cocoa estates.' Imminent action seemed likely. But William Cadbury wanted to be certain. He took a boat to the Portuguese capital, Lisbon, for a fact-finding mission in the spring of 1903, during which he was introduced to various government officials. They, too, had seen the reports of slavery, and explained that they had now established a minimum wage on the islands, and were in the process of helping workers return to their families on the mainland when their five-year contracts were up. Cadbury must have been relieved to hear an alternative narrative, after all the dark talk in London. Before he left, he was introduced to one of the biggest plantation owners on São Tomé, an absentee landlord who employed several thousand workers there. Francisco Mantero was building a palace in Lisbon at the time. Its centrepiece was a lake onto which he had built models of São Tomé and Príncipe, to remind him of the source of his fortune. Mantero told Cadbury not to worry. He shared his concern for the rights of workers, but any problems on the islands were 'caused by wasteful and dissolute natives'.

The Lisbon trip gave Cadbury only brief respite. On returning to Bournville he was beginning to foresee a potential public relations calamity. Up until then, reports of slavery could be dismissed as speculation, but if proof were to come out of São Tomé from the pen of Henry Nevinson, then the chocolate company might easily be subjected to a consumer boycott, as would Fry and Rowntree. Cadbury came up with a plan. What if they recruited their own agent, and sent him to the islands to settle the issue once and for all? The other chocolate companies agreed. The difficulty was finding a suitable candidate. Anyone from the Anti-Slavery Society might be considered too partial, as would a chocolate company insider. They needed someone independent, preferably an adventurer who could survive the tropics and work undercover on the islands. And they needed to act quickly, to beat Nevinson and help remedy anything undesirable before he splashed it all over the newspapers.

It was then that Joseph Burtt hove into view. Burtt was a lean, well-groomed forty-one-year-old with a head full of dreams and theories, whose principal qualification for the job seemed to be that he had established a commune in Gloucestershire in the late 1890s where he had lived in 'poverty and joy' for a year. William Cadbury had first made his acquaintance some years before, and referred to him as a Quaker and 'an intimate friend who was welcome in any company for his good humour and charming personality'. That was it, then. The young man who had never set foot in Africa was awarded the position. Time was of the essence. He needed to leave almost immediately if he were to beat Nevinson to the islands.

But there was one issue to attend to first. To ensure Burtt was adequately prepared, Cadbury decided that he should learn Portuguese. There was little opportunity to do so in London and so he was dispatched to Lisbon. At the end of his studies, instead of sailing directly from Portugal to West Africa, Burtt decided to return to Britain to visit his sick mother. It was all maddeningly slow. Burtt finally set sail from England in the summer of 1905, four years after the first credible reports of slavery had surfaced.

On 17 June that same year, Nevinson's steamer was already approaching São Tomé. When the island finally emerged from beneath the rain clouds of the southern Atlantic, it appeared as an enchanted place. From the top deck he could observe high peaks and rounded indigo hills shrouded in pale and drizzling mists. There were deep valleys filled with tropical forests where the cocoa plantations lay, and as they sailed closer he could even make out the huts and outbuildings that would soon become home to the 250 *serviçeas* they were delivering to the island. As Nevinson and the other Europeans on board waited for carriages to take them inland, he watched the labourers being dragged from the steamer by their arms and loin-cloths, and dumped like bales of goods onto the pier.

Nevinson soon inveigled his way into São Tomé society, accepting invitations to lunches where Portuguese plantation owners regaled him with gleeful accounts of how they rounded up *serviçeas* who tried to escape. They would sometimes call a hunt, he was told, with guns and horses as though they were looking for foxes in the British countryside. One planter described how he had come across a recently abandoned forest camp, in an area thick with escapees. As they inspected the huts and the remnants of cooking, they saw an elderly man hiding in the bush.

'Where are the others?' the Europeans demanded. The elderly *serviça* refused to respond. The cross-examination continued for a while, with the man becoming increasingly tired and desperate. At some point, during a long silence, he lifted a hand and pointed into the trees above him. The whole camp of escapees was perched up there, hanging above the search party's heads 'like bats'.

'It was not long, I can tell you,' said the planter, 'before we brought them crashing down through the leaves to the ground. My word, we had grand sport that day!' By this time, Nevinson had long-since dispensed with the term *serviças*, and was simply referring to them as slaves.

Their whipping and beating seemed to be of little concern to the good people of the islands, to the doctors, businessmen, engineers and agriculturalists Nevinson ate and drank alongside. They treated the place as if it were a correctional facility whose inmates needed a firm hand. The death rate among the slaves was fourteen per cent a year. When Nevinson asked a Portuguese doctor for an explanation, he casually replied that it was anaemia, brought on by unhappiness. But the islands' cocoa output continued to rise, doubling over a five-year period, and sending land prices even higher. Plantations that once changed hands for a pittance could command tens of thousands of pounds. Old coffee plantations were abandoned, cleared out, and sold as forest capable of growing cocoa. The plantation houses occupied by moneyed Europeans could rival those anywhere in the colonies: grand whitewashed piles with verandas, sweeping staircases and pink-tiled roofs. They would hold dinner parties where guests could indulge in Portuguese beef from cattle reared on the islands, and consume Europe's finest wines. Land was bought and sold in the manner of a gold rush, investors in London, Madrid and Lisbon buying it blind, and selling it on for near-immediate profit. One estate was reputedly worth a million pounds. Today, that would be the equivalent of £100 million.

Among the stories of glittering fortunes, none matched the rags-to-riches tale of one José Constantino Dias. He arrived on the islands in the early days with next to nothing and bought a modest plot. His cocoa grew strong, he purchased more rainforest, and imported workers from Angola. After some canny trading and a fair bit of luck, Dias became the biggest landowner on the islands. He was pro-ducing twelve per cent of the entire cocoa crop, for which he relied on a workforce of 4,000 slaves. He built hundreds of kilometres of light railway to connect his plantations and transport the beans to processing plants. Such was Dias's determination to control every aspect of production, he even purchased a fleet of coastal steamers.[4]

Back home in Lisbon, his fortune gave him entry to the elite of Lisbon society. He became close friends with the king, and bought a grand palace decorated with frescoed ceilings and stained-glass windows, and filled with the usual trappings of the super-rich. Dias's cocoa growing had made him the wealthiest man in the Portuguese empire.

Today his palace has been converted into a sumptuous hotel, which counts Madonna and Bill Clinton among its regular guests. 'It is all thanks to José Dias,' says the handbook distributed to visitors, 'an entrepreneur who made a fortune producing cocoa to feed Europe's insatiable appetite for chocolate.'

Nevinson decided to depart São Tomé on 30 June 1905. But, just as he was concluding his inquiries, he received unexpected news. Cadbury's agent, Joseph Burtt, had just arrived on the island. The two men arranged to meet, and took a walk to a local fishing village. They spoke amiably, and even agreed to visit a plantation together. Nevinson seems to have taken on the role of guide, and enjoyed hinting at dark discoveries in the manner of an old campaigner to the new recruit. He returned to his lodgings that night with a mixture of bewilderment and pity, and scribbled down his account of the meeting. Burtt, he said, was the youngest forty-three-year-old he had ever met.

> Thinks the plantations greatly increase human happiness & so on. All very crude & youthful stuff, full of contradictions & very astonishing. I warned him of Benguela & then was rather sorry, for he is full of fears. Which he bravely admits.[5]

In New York, the presses were turning. Nevinson was back in London and had begun filing a series of articles for the influential *Harper's* magazine. It was already the publication of choice for Mark Twain and the writer and social commentator Jack London, and was bound to be greeted with concerned attention across America and Europe. 'Islands of doom' roared the headline. Cadbury was anticipating a fair degree of flak. So, too, was the British Foreign Office, which was already facing accusations of inaction and complicity with the Portuguese. William Cadbury responded first, dismissing Nevinson's reports as 'embellished'. He would await evidence from his own, independent agent, he said, rather than making a hasty decision. The British government was equally unmoved. It half-heartedly sent its own investigator to the islands, the consul from Angola, Arthur Nightingale, who complained about the 'rough mountainous paths, the scorching tropical sun, drenched tornadoes, and badly prepared food'. His visit overlapped with that of Burtt, who now found himself the old campaigner, passing on the baton to the latest newcomer. Nightingale's report was expected to be pro-business and stoutly defensive of Britain's ally, and it was. But it also dropped a bombshell.

Despite giving the Portuguese planters the benefit of the doubt, he informed his bosses that there was 'a black spot, and it is a big black spot... the non-repatriation of the Angolan labour'. Like Nevinson, he had concluded that the cocoa workers had no prospect of leaving the islands, that they were captives, working and dying without the option of returning home. Nightingale described it as 'one great evil' and insisted pressure should be exerted on Portugal to put an end to it.

The Foreign Office was going to do no such thing. They greeted Nightingale's report with weary annoyance, wrapped it in as much red tape as they could muster, and sent it on a slow boat through the fathomless waterways of Whitehall.

William Cadbury settled down to await the return of his own agent. It would be another eighteen months before Joseph Burtt arrived back in England.

★

From the cocoa forests of Ghana, in 2009, we followed the child-smuggling route that had taken Fatau from his family, and traced it back to its source. Zabre was a lively border town in Burkina Faso, crackling with motorbikes and mule traps, and situated in the middle of a parched plane. Great tufts of straw tumbled across its mud roads. We were only 150 miles from the cocoa belt, but no cocoa trees could survive here. The vegetable sellers had a few dusty items, brought in from bigger cities, but there hadn't been rain for months.

A man we'd met who knew about the trade had gathered together a group of women who had all lost a child to slavery. They arrived by donkey and on foot from far out in the savannah, and sat in the shade of acacia trees, head-wraps tied like giant and colourful butterflies.

'My son is twelve years old,' said one, lowering her eyes. 'I haven't seen him for six years.' She was a tall, proud woman, but crumpled at the recollection. Beside her was a younger woman who moved her hands as if she were picking words from a tree. 'Sometimes just thinking about him makes me cry,' she said. She had woken up one morning, and he had gone. Not a sound, not a warning. 'What can I do?' she asked. 'I am just praying to God to keep him in good health and give him enough to eat.'

All were familiar with the smuggling route, and knew some of the Zabre traders who used it. Fragments of information sometimes reached them from the farms in Ghana. 'He is working in cocoa,' says one. 'I heard that my son is suffering,' said another. Some knew the villages where their children were kept, and even the identities of those who had sold them. And then something unexpected began to emerge.

'To be honest, I wasn't happy for him to go there,' says the first woman, 'but we are suffering. That is why his father arranged with the traffickers to take him.'

I glanced at the translator to make sure I had heard correctly.

'Your husband sold your son?'

She screwed her face and looked away. 'We have nothing,' she said. 'What else can we do?'

Another woman smiled sorrowfully. 'I wasn't happy,' she said, 'but what else is there? He might be able to raise some money to help care for his brothers.'

Husbands, brother-in-laws, uncles, all had been complicit in the kidnaps. The women had known nothing until after the disappearances. They had resigned themselves to it as if it were a sandstorm or a failure of the crops: a miserable inevitability of their fragile lives. One of them added up how much her family had received in recompense. It amounted to the occasional payment of £2.50, whenever the smuggler had money to spare.

It was the spring of 1907 when Joseph Burtt quietly slipped into an English harbour, carrying notes and recommendations from eighteen months in West Africa, and took the train north to meet William Cadbury. A draft report was hurried off to the Foreign Office and to Rowntree and Fry. They would have read it with mounting incredulity. Burtt's early impressions of the island had not survived sustained exposure to the reality of the cocoa plantations. His findings were even more damning than those of Nevinson.

Burtt shuttled between a series of private meetings, attended by friends of the Cadbury family, giving impassioned speeches about the 'cruel and villainous' practices he'd observed. It was, he told them, 'beyond all doubt' that the islands' cocoa was produced in 'conditions of practical slavery'. Burtt argued that the newspapers should be briefed straight away and a boycott launched. The chocolate companies were very much opposed to the idea. Burtt had only just returned home, they said, and was in need of rest. His findings must be dealt with in a calm and dispassionate manner. If his report was circulated publicly, then the reputation of Cadbury and the others would be in tatters. Far more effective, they argued, would be to use Burtt's report as leverage against the Portuguese, insisting that they made wholesale changes on the islands or face a boycott. The British government agreed.

The summer of that year was spent correcting and editing Burtt's report, as a growing body of journalists circled, eager to know what was in it. Some humanitarian societies were kept abreast of the findings, on condition that they kept silent until it was published. In the meantime, it was discreetly translated into Portuguese and copies sent to the government in Lisbon. Further copies were forwarded to Portuguese planters with interests in São Tomé. They responded by angrily questioning Burtt's abilities, and contending that they 'had the right to transfer labour from colony to colony at will without foreign interference'.

A meeting was organized between Cadbury and the planters for 28 November 1907 in Lisbon. It promised to be an awkward encounter. The great Liberal philanthropist and millionaire was viewed by the Portuguese as representing the British government, which at the time was using forced labour in its gold mines in Transvaal. Now he was threatening some of Portugal's most powerful men that if they didn't reform their business, he and the other British manufacturers would pull out of São Tomé and Príncipe. It looked like hypocrisy.

The meeting continued for eight hours. The cocoa barons had copies of Burtt's report in front of them. Glancing down, they would have seen their businesses portrayed as cruelly exploitative operations that used beatings and inadequate rations to control their captive labour force. They would have read Burtt's allegation that thousands of natives were seized against their will each year from villages in Angola, and taken across the sea to work on 'unhealthy islands from which they would never return'. The final line proved the most difficult to swallow, 'If this is not slavery,' wrote Burtt, 'I know of no word in the English language which correctly characterizes it.'

Ever the polished diplomat, when Cadbury addressed the planters, he wrapped the report in a feather blanket of tributes to their 'courageous' and 'energetic' industry which had raised São Tomé to 'a colony of the foremost rank', worthy of the 'greatest colonizing powers of the earth'. It seemed to do the job. The Portuguese agreed to make concessions, chiefly around the issue of repatriation. It was agreed that labourers would be allowed to leave the island once their contracts were up. But there was no commitment on how long this would take.

The British government, meanwhile, was coming under increasing pressure to release Burtt's report. Cadbury's agent had been back in the UK for seven months. If he'd found nothing of great concern, why the silence? What about Arthur Nightingale's report? Why had that vanished into the backwaters of Whitehall? It was starting to look like a whitewash. And there was more. The British government announced another investigation, by a different consul in Angola. It would be carried out with the permission and co-operation of the cocoa barons on the islands.

One newspaper, the *London Standard*, had heard enough. On 26 September 1908, its editor decided to take on William Cadbury and accuse him of being part of an historic cover-up of slave labour.

There were no roads, just rose-pink savannah and weathered mud-shacks. It was 2009 in Burkina Faso, and the only chance of finding Fatau's mother was to broadcast an appeal on Zabre's radio station. In a region with no internet, no post and almost no cellphones, it was the only hope. Once an hour, every day, we ran a message. Shepherds would have heard it on the transistors they keep in their goatskin sacks; so, too, would passengers on remote desert buses, and women hiding from the heat in their cramped clay huts. It wasn't Fatau's kidnap that intrigued them so much as why his disappearance was any different from the many thousands that happened ever year. And of course, it wasn't. Our choice of exploring Fatau's village that day had been random. We could have picked any other along that pathway and found another group of child-slaves. There was no shortage.

In Zabre, a slight, skeletal woman walked into the radio station one morning. She had travelled across Burkina Faso by bus from a remote collection of mud dwellings deep in the bush. Around her tiny frame was drawn a snow-white wrap, and a cotton shawl protected her head from the sunshine. She explained that a friend had heard our radio appeal, and that she had come straight away. Her name was Zenabo and she was Fatau's mother.

Zenabo explained that she had last seen her boy a year ago. She had wanted him to attend school and, with none available nearby, she had taken him to stay with an uncle who lived closer to town. The man had promised to look after Fatau, and make sure he attended lessons every day. But when she returned to pick him up at the end of term, Fatau had vanished.

'He is a wicked man,' she said. 'He must have sold him to the traders.' She had no idea where Fatau had been taken, or indeed, whether he was still alive. I passed her a photograph of him, sitting among the cocoa bushes in Ghana. Of course, thousands of other women in Zenabo's position live in uncertainty for many years. Sometimes slave-children escape and make it home, but often they remain in the dense cocoa forests until they are old enough to put up a fight. Others are so young when they are traded, their memory of home eventually fades, and they end up staying; marrying and having children. In Zenabo's case, we did manage to reunite her with her son, but it was expensive and time-consuming, a result engineered for the television documentary we were making. Everyone wants a happy ending: Zenabo tearfully hugging Fatau on a Ghanaian beach, backlit by a flame-red sunset. And that's what we delivered. But it was a sugar-coated confection. Away from the television cameras, that simply doesn't happen. The arrest, and later imprisonment of Fatau's kidnappers, was the first ever by Ghanaian police, and was prompted entirely by our presence. The trade is normally tolerated as an inevitable consequence of poverty coupled with a global demand for a commodity whose production is reliant on cheap labour. Just as Henry Nevinson observed youths being sold to Portuguese traders in Angola a century ago, a child is still, today, the final saleable asset for many in Burkina Faso.

On the morning of 26 September 1908 the *London Standard* was flying off the stands as commuters emerged from Oxford Circus Tube station that morning. The Cadbury family had tried to keep a lid on Burtt's report for eighteen months. A couple of papers had tip-toed close to denouncing the chocolate dynasty for a cover up, but had backed down after legal threats. George Cadbury, William's uncle, had taken over one of the country's biggest newspapers, the *Daily News*, in 1901, to ensure that his Liberal view was heard on a whole range of issues, including conditions in Portuguese West Africa. They weren't going to allow any journalist to damage what was fast becoming a global chocolate brand. But they could exercise no control over the *Standard*, and that day it featured a rip-roaring editorial:

> The white hands of the Bournville chocolate makers are helped by other unseen hands some thousands of miles away, black and brown hands, toiling in plantations, or hauling loads through swamp and forest.

As William Cadbury read the paper over breakfast that morning, it wasn't the description of slave labour that infuriated him most, but the allegation that he was doing nothing to stop it, that the absence of any meaningful response from his company signalled collusion. To Cadbury's intense irritation, the editorial quoted Nevinson's work, holding it up as the damning evidence to which Cadbury had failed to respond:

> No Englishman can read it without a certain sense of shame; for it shows that the negro slavery... still flourishes in its wickedness and its cruelty in those Portuguese colonies... it is that monstrous trade in human flesh and blood against which the Quaker and radical ancestors of Mr Cadbury thundered in the better days of England.

Cadbury had announced the previous week that he was going to visit São Tomé himself, to see if the Portuguese had implemented reforms since their meeting in Lisbon. But the *Standard*, using all the mocking courtesy of the time, expressed their 'respectful surprise that Mr Cadbury's voyage of discovery had been deferred for so long'. It had been three years since Nevinson's return and, the paper suggested, Cadbury had responded with 'strange tranquillity' to all the horror he had seen.

The message was plain. Cadbury was a hypocrite and a phoney. His moral concerns over labour were restricted to his little settlement in Bournville, and he cared nothing for the natives whose 'grimed African hands' provided him with cheap cocoa.

A scandalized William Cadbury decided to sue the *Standard*.

Crowds gathered excitedly outside the red terracotta law courts on Birmingham's Corporation Street. Reporters swapped notes beneath the golden chandeliers of the Grand Hall, and pointed out the wives and daughters of the Cadbury clan as they swept in wearing high lace collars and wide-brimmed hats. Mingling with his admiring colleagues was Henry Nevinson, whose writing would provide much of the evidence, and Joseph Burtt.

They filed into the courtroom just after 10 a.m. on Monday 29 November 1909, the great and the good scrambling for seats in the public gallery. It was already billed as the trial of the century, with the expected appearance of the Liberal foreign secretary, Edward Grey, and Britain's most well-known industrialist, William Cadbury, facing several uneasy days on the witness stand. The other big draw was the presence of the two most celebrated silks of the era.

Representing Cadbury was Liberal MP Rufus Isaacs QC, a roguish extravert, who could 'pass at will from thunder-tones to a not less menacing calm, from a cynical drawl to a deadly hiss'. For the *Standard* was Edward Carson QC, a brilliant, theatrical Irishman who was a master of cross-examination and claimed he had 'once burst into tears as a result of his own eloquence'.[6] He had also once destroyed Oscar Wilde in court, dragging his gay sex life into the public gaze (and shortly after the Cadbury trial he would become the great orator of Ulster's resistance to Home Rule). Carson, too, was a member of Parliament, for the Conservative Party. The personal battles were numerous and absorbing. Among the *Standard*'s lawyers, passing notes and whispering advice throughout, was Henry Nevinson.

In the months before the hearing, William Cadbury had finally undertaken his visit to São Tomé. He was not disputing there was slave labour there; he was defending his company's reputation from the allegation that for eight years he had been insincere about his desire for change. He and the other British manufacturers had stopped importing cocoa from the islands the moment he returned home in March 1909. But why not sooner? Had he not trusted the accounts of his own agent? Perhaps his belated withdrawal was an attempt to sway the Birmingham jury?

Cadbury's tactic would be to place all blame at the government's door, because it was they who had told him not to publicize Burtt's report and to give diplomacy a chance. During the opening two days, Cadbury was led, comfortably, through his evidence by Rufus Isaacs. But then came the aggressive and relentless scrutiny of Edward Carson.

Carson wanted to take him on a journey through the plantations of São Tomé, to allow the jury to drink in every dreadful detail.

'Would you say that it was slavery of an atrocious character?' asked Carson.[7]

Cadbury knew he had to agree, anything else might sound like a partial endorsement. 'Generally speaking, as far as the collecting of labour in Angola goes, that is true,' he responded.

Carson pushed harder. 'The cocoa you were buying was procured by atrocious methods of slavery?'

'Yes,' said Cadbury, trying not to appear impatient.

'Have you formed any estimate of the number of slaves who lost their lives in preparing your cocoa during those eight years?'

'No, no,' responded Cadbury, visibly wincing.

The allegation that kept resurfacing was that Cadbury refused to relocate from São Tomé because of the cost to his business. That he had now done so was of little help. His own chief buyer told the court that world cocoa production had increased dramatically during the previous twelve months, making it easier to find more affordable sources.

Carson surprised everyone by calling no witnesses for the *Standard*, unwilling to subject them to Isaacs's cross-examination. Nothing mattered other than the jury's view of William Cadbury, and whether Carson had done enough to undermine his credibility.

On Saturday 4 December, the sixth day of trial, Carson rose to deliver his closing speech. 'Slavery!' he announced. 'Have you ever heard at any time of the world's history (and that is a broad statement) of worse conditions more revolting, more cruel, more tyrannous and more horrible than what has been deposed to as regards the slavery in São Tomé? Men recruited in Angola, women recruited in Angola, children recruited in Angola, torn away against their will from their homes in the interior, marched like droves of beasts through the Hungry Country, and when they are unable to walk along for a thousand miles to the coast, shot down like useless dogs or useless animals and the others brought down to be labelled like cattle and brought over to São Tomé and Príncipe, never again to return to their homes.'

It was, contended Carson, the journalists' job to reveal the heinous nature of slavery that had been tolerated by the Cadbury company. Why, during the eight years they had known about conditions on the island, had they continued to purchase £1.3 million of cocoa beans? The company had been painfully slow in tackling the issue because it was only concerned about its bottom line, he argued. The *Standard* was performing the crucial job of pointing out the company's hypocrisy. Cadbury, said Carson, was no ordinary family. They presented themselves as humanitarians, and so their case was not comparable to that of 'an ordinary individual, attacked by a newspaper, brought into prominence by a newspaper over questions of this kind'. After a speech lasting two hours and thirty-five minutes, it was the turn of Rufus Isaacs.

Isaacs made his closing speech before a packed and expectant court room. It was Cadbury, he said, who had pressed relentlessly for change, spending a quarter of his working hours trying to change the attitudes of the Portuguese. He had wanted to release Burtt's report to the planters earlier, but the British government had insisted on slowing everything down in the interest of diplomacy. His client, said Isaacs, had 'suffered the greatest injury', and the jury should rectify it by imposing significant damages against the *Standard*. When Isaacs finished after five hours on his feet, he sat down to a burst of applause from the public gallery.

By the seventh day, the proceedings were over. The jury were sent out to deliberate, the reporters gathered in huddles, and the cavernous hallways echoed with noisy speculation. After just fifty-five minutes, a shout went up from the clerk of the court. The jury was ready. A verdict had been reached. The crowds hurried back in.

If Cadbury were to lose, it would seriously undermine his brand, cut his profits, and allow his competitors to take at least some of the market. For the *Standard*, all that was seriously at stake was money. It was for the jury to decide the level of damages, and they assumed the proprietor of the *Standard*, Sir Arthur Pearson, who also owned the *Daily Express*, had reserves to draw upon.

The jury filed back in just after 6 p.m. The foreman rose, and announced that they had found in favour of Cadbury Bros. As for the damages awarded against the *Standard* newspaper, they were set at 'one farthing', a quarter of a penny. It was known as 'contemptuous damages', a token amount set by the jury when the case had been technically won, but the libel was deemed utterly trivial.

William Cadbury's voyage to West Africa hadn't been simply to inspect the cocoa plantations of São Tomé and Príncipe. On his way back, he had dropped anchor at the British territory of Gold Coast, where he and Burtt trekked inland to scout conditions for a new cocoa plantation. Cadbury had sent out an advance party of agriculturalists the previous year to test the soils and climate, and now they had the results. The area they had studied was in the western region of what is now Ghana, close to where we discovered Fatau being used as slave labour a century later, and it had proved ideal. Cadbury bought fifteen acres.

From that small base, cocoa production was to increase steadily, soon overtaking São Tomé and Príncipe. By the time Ghana became independent in 1957, it was the biggest cocoa producer in the world. Together with its neighbour, Côte d'Ivoire, it quickly became dangerously dependent on the crop originally imported from South America. Ghana's first post-independence leader, Kwame Nkrumah,

ploughed all his cocoa profits into a programme of mass industriali-
zation. When prices slumped, he found he had overstretched himself.
The ensuing economic crisis helped bring about his demise. But it
was in Côte d'Ivoire that a cocoa farmer rose to become a dictator. Others had expropriated diamonds, gold and oil, but for Felix
Houphuet-Boigny it was the humble cocoa tree that he would use to
keep himself in power, and make himself fabulously rich.

CHAPTER EIGHT
Côte d'Ivoire

CÔTE D'IVOIRE

*My accounting book, I held it and I placed it at
the foot of the eternal. He alone knows what I
got and what I gave.*

FELIX HOUPHOUET-BOIGNY,
FORMER PRESIDENT OF CÔTE D'IVOIRE

ALL THIS USED to be mango farms and savannah until the big church
came, mango farms on the edge of a smoky village that looked just
like all the other villages in the tropical heart of Côte d'Ivoire. Women
pounded yams or fried bananas with chilli oil. Men and children
clambered among the trees, lopping off ripe cocoa pods and piling them
into wicker baskets. Families rose with the sun and slept with the dying
of the fire, and everywhere was infused with the smell of chocolate.

In the village of Yamoussoukro lived a Baoulé chief who owned
enough cocoa-growing land to run his own plantations. The chief
had a son who he named Felix, a cheerful and industrious child who
dreamed of becoming a doctor, and who, with his parents' wealth
and his own academic ability, stood every chance of succeeding. But
it is the church, the one that appeared in 1989 like a grotesque slab
of Renaissance Rome crashing into the African bush, that tells us
more about the man Felix would one day become.

Into Yamoussoukro came architects, builders, stonemasons and
marble-cutters. Heavy machinery squeezed along the narrow jungle
roads. Smoke and dust mushroomed into the sky, and the bemused
farmers stood and watched as the new church began to take shape.

The building was thirty-five storeys high with room inside for four
football pitches and enough space in its gardens to land a Boeing
747. Its main dome was modelled on that of St Peter's Basilica in
Vatican City.

The walkways are crumbling a little now, weeds poking through
the stone, beggars sleeping against Corinthian columns, but once
inside, you are transported to a cool Renaissance interior where light
streams through the towering stained-glass windows in a confetti
of lilac and blue. The scrape of chair-legs echoes around the marble

columns and gilded arches as the congregation take their seats. There is enough room for 16,000 worshippers, though rarely more than a hundred attend. As they pray, they are lit by the building's spectacular centrepiece. It is a stained-glass window larger and more exquisite than all the rest, a rendition of Christ entering Jerusalem. Kneeling at His feet among the apostles, hands raised above his head in prayer and touching Christ's robes, is the former president of the country.

It was the late 1920s and Felix Houphouet was dressed in white cotton trousers and a starched Parisian shirt, riding a bicycle through Abidjan. He was wearing a necktie too, just like the French administrators, neatly knotted and tucked into his cream buttoned blazer. It was a fiercely hot day but Houphouet was in high spirits. He had recently graduated from medical school, not as a full doctor – that wasn't possible for a native living under French rule – but an African one. It was a shade short of the real thing, but a rare achievement nonetheless.

Houphouet pedalled along the wide clay streets of Abidjan, past the pink-faced Europeans in their pith helmets, and the new art deco buildings with Renault motorcars parked outside their gates. Some viewed their presence as a foreign occupation, but Houphouet saw it as the arrival of order and investment. He was a fortunate beneficiary of colonialism, a young doctor in a young town, embarking on a promising career.

His route took him through the port, where shirtless men hauled sacks of cocoa and coffee onto European steamers. Côte d'Ivoire was fast becoming the jewel of French West Africa, and Abidjan, set on a palm-fringed lagoon overlooking the Atlantic, was set to become its capital. The town was bustling with French bureaucrats. Exports were booming. Paris was a guaranteed customer, and French francs were rolling into Abidjan.

While the masses were confined to a lifetime in agricultural labour, the French saw merit in allowing a small elite of Ivoirians to lead relatively privileged lives. Felix Houphouet's family had been permitted to keep their cocoa plantations, and their hereditary status as chieftains. Houphouet himself had been sent to the most prestigious boarding school in the region. It was all part of the delicate balancing act: keeping the intellectuals and tribal leaders compliant, without allowing them so much freedom they might start questioning the colonial order.

The French recognized Houphouet's academic potential early on, and gave him a place at the renowned William Ponty College in Senegal, an academic hothouse offering lessons in Romantic poetry, ancient Greek, music and art, all conducted in refined Parisian French. Its intake was limited to a few dozen students each year, handpicked from the children of landowners and chieftains living in the French possessions of West Africa. Its purpose was to provide clever assistants for the French administrators, binding them seamlessly into the system, as a bridge into the indigenous communities. But Ponty was too good at its job. Its list of graduates reads like an A to Z of the nationalist leaders who would later challenge French rule: Hamani Diori, first president of the Republic of Niger; Modibo Keita, firebrand anti-colonist and first president of Mali; Mamadou Dia, first prime minister of Senegal; Maurice Yameogo, first president of the Republic of Upper Volta. Felix Houphouet had joined exalted company.

The meeting he was on his way to, riding his bike through Abidjan that day, was at the main hospital. He had decided to organize an *amicale* for his fellow African medics, a trade union to protect their labour rights from the French. It was low-level stuff, nothing like the kind of resistance organized by his fellow alumni from Ponty. This was an organization devoted to mundane issues like hours and working conditions. But in the eyes of the French, it amounted to political activity which had to be stopped before it escalated. Houphouet was suddenly moved on, to a lesser hospital in a small provincial town.

Instead of enjoying the privileged circles of Abidjan intellectual society, Houphouet found himself shuttling between small, unsanitary bush-villages in the far west of the country, close to the Liberian border. He moved again, to a similar job in the cocoa forests of the west, becoming a peripatetic doctor, and encountering people from many of the sixty different Ivorian ethnic groups. They had met no one like him before. He taught villagers how to discard their excrement in sanitary boxes, and the importance of keeping drinking water separate from raw sewage. They became healthier when Houphouet was around, and the local chiefs came to know and respect him.

It was during this nomadic phase that he met a young woman with royal heritage and a bloodline that crossed ethnic lines, a useful social tool in such a diverse country. Her name was Kady Racine Sow, whose mother was a princess in the powerful Agni tribe, and father a Muslim from a prominent and wealthy Senegalese family. Houphouet and she were married in 1929 at her ancestral home-town of Abengourou, set among the cocoa forests close to the border with British Gold Coast. He settled down there, raised a family, and showed little interest in politics.

But as Houphouet worked more closely with the agricultural labourers of the cocoa farms, he began to see disturbing signs of French oppression.

As a result of the Cadbury trial two decades earlier, most leading chocolate manufacturers had moved their production away from São Tomé to avoid further allegations of slave labour. They had chosen to relocate in British Gold Coast, just a few miles from the border town where Houphouet was based. He was in an ideal position to observe the effect the cocoa industry was having. The streets of Abengourou were busy with Ivoirian cocoa workers night and day, gathering in groups to smuggle themselves across the border. Tens of thousands were leaving their homeland. When Houphouet enquired why, he uncovered a system of French labour he had previously been unaware of.

The cocoa workers passing through Abengourou were members of work gangs that had been formed by rounding up and kidnapping young men from their villages. The French had seen it as an exercise in filling vital agricultural jobs, but had ended up herding unwilling young men onto buses, and transporting them to cocoa farms in the tropical forests. Once there, they were held in camps and fed just enough to keep them labouring in harsh conditions for twelve hours a day. They were paid nothing; all they received in return was food and shelter. The men were not allowed to leave. Nevertheless, many had managed to escape the camps at night and join the exodus to Gold Coast.

It was a form of slavery, and the French didn't even bother denying it. When confronted by other European powers, they responded dismissively: 'The regime of forced labour is an established fact,' reported the French newspapers. Many politicians had no intention of stopping it. The benefits of cheap cocoa and coffee in Paris were one of the perks of running an empire in Africa. Instead, they promised to 'reduce its drawbacks as much as possible and to give it an educational role'.[1]

It should have been enough to stir the embryonic nationalists into action and mobilize Ivoirians into a coherent protest group. But there was no tradition of organized resistance. Before the Second World War most potential agitators – no more than a handful of intellectuals – believed in the supremacy of Western civilization, and drew the battle lines along narrow and often selfish lines. They sought a greater role for themselves in political decision-making rather than the overthrow of colonialism. To many of them, much of Africa's heritage was primitive, and needed to be replaced with a modern, Western way of life. It was an attitude encouraged by the French, protecting them as it did from any organized dissent. The French rewarded loyal aspirants with *évolué* status, as the Belgians had done with Patrice Lumumba in Congo. In the strictly hierarchical French structure, *évolué* could never reach the same heights as a French colonial, but the privilege offered entry to administrative positions in government offices. One step beneath *évolué* was another title that could be earned, that of *citizen*. Usually French Africans were considered subjects, because the French thought them unsuitable to share citizenship with the authentic, indigenous French. But between the wars, those with appropriate qualifications – in practice just a handful of already-privileged individuals – could be elevated to the status. By 1921, Côte d'Ivoire had just 308 citizens, and by 1936 there were only 2,000 in the entire federation of French West Africa.

Houphouet was *évolué* and would have lived off the fruits of forced labour just as the French had. At first, he was hesitant to protest about how his countrymen were being exploited. He did pen a scathing article in an Ivoirian socialist newspaper in December 1932, which he boldly entitled 'They have stolen too much from us', but he was afraid of falling foul of the French administrators, and published under a nom de plume. When change came, it was not from inside Côte d'Ivoire at all, but from the capital of the empire itself.

In Paris, left-wing intellectuals had become enraged by news of forced labour in the colonies, and were more passionate about African empowerment than many Ivoirians themselves. Paris was hot-wired to events in its colonies in a way that London, Lisbon and Brussels were not. The political direction chosen by voters in France would quickly feed through to their two African federations: French Equatorial Africa, which comprised Gabon, French Congo, Chad, French Cameroon and Ubangi-Shari (now Central African Republic); and French West Africa, a larger group of territories that included Côte d'Ivoire, Upper Volta (now Burkina Faso), Senegal, French Guinea, French Sudan (now Mali), Mauritania and Niger. In May 1936 the left-wing 'Popular Front' swept to power in Paris. It was a tripartite alliance dominated by the increasingly popular French Communist Party (PCF), and soon its progressive principles worked their way through to both African federations. It was as if a button had been pressed in the Champs Élysées, and the lights had come on in Abidjan.

Colonial appointments had always been distributed among French political parties according to the balance of power within a government coalition. Now, reformist French officials flew in to replace the old. The Côte d'Ivoire novelist Bernard Dadié, a graduate of William Ponty College, described the impact of the Popular Front on the country:

Relationships between Europeans and Africans seemed to become more cordial, more human. Europeans and Africans stood side by side in all public gatherings, on May 1st at the Governor's Ball, etc.

Where, previously, ethnic identities had been buried, and Ivoirians forced to assimilate themselves into French culture, now they were encouraged to go out and rediscover their tribal roots. There was an explosion of interest in heritage and African culture. The Ivoirian intellectuals who had been scattered around the country now saw a chance to set up interest groups in major towns, quickly merging them with others to form large regional societies. Some had thousands of supporters, and their leaders became influential figures with whom the French administrators would need to consult. Trade unions sprang up, rapidly covering every conceivable type of employment. People joined several societies simultaneously: ethnic, leisure, regional, city and trade.

Houphouet's people, the Baoulé, formed one of the largest and most powerful groups: the Union Fraternelle des Originaires de Côte d'Ivoire, the Fraternal Union of Native Ivoirians. Competition for its leadership was strong, representing, as it did, a block vote of tens of thousands of people.

But it was a society of cocoa farmers that promised to dominate the charge for power, influence and prestige. Whoever led such a group would cut across all ethnicities, attracting support from hundreds of thousands involved in Côte d'Ivoire's most important export. But there were squabbles among the chiefs about who should be in charge, and in the end the French stepped in and ran the cocoa union themselves.

In the dry season of 1939, Felix Houphouet was summoned to his ancestral home. His older brother had died, and he was to inherit the chieftainship, together with the family's cocoa plantations. There he stood in his blazer and tie, hanky neatly folded in his breast pocket, tailored French waistcoat buttoned over his fine cotton shirt, about to embark on his new role as *chef de canton*, the chief of thirty-six villages. He was thirty-four years old, with four children and a quietly devoted wife. The future on offer was the peaceful, plentiful, family life of a plantation owner in the fertile Ivoirian tropics. But Houphouet saw there was something missing. The chieftainship was no longer a symbol of power and status. Fifty years of colonialism had reduced it to little more than an administrative role, helping the French collect taxes and recruit labour. He felt deprived, cheated of his inheritance. It was hardly oppression in the way his countrymen were experiencing, but it stirred a desire to wrest back from the French some degree of political control.

Before he could begin to apply himself to finding a role in one of the new societies, events in French Africa were overtaken by those 3,000 miles away in Europe: the outbreak of the Second World War.

On 22 June 1940, ten months after the war began, France was defeated and partitioned under the terms of the armistice at Compiegne. German forces occupied the north and west, including Paris. Italy took control of a small zone in the southeast, and the French retained just the south, the nominally Free Zone, headed by Marshal Philippe Pétain from his new capital, Vichy. The question now arose: who would control France's many colonies around the world?

At the start, the job fell to the Vichy regime, and Pétain, a Nazi collaborator. The swing to the right in Vichy France was projected in enlarged form on Africa. Vichy colonial officials reinforced systems of near-slavery in its colonies that the Popular Front had been dismantling. Africans were now compelled to produce quotas of commodities like cocoa and coffee. They were forcibly removed from jobs in indigenously run plantations, and transported to European-owned farms instead. Houphouet struggled to find the labour necessary to keep his plantations afloat. More significantly, he and other members of the African elite had their privileges removed. They were no longer *évolué* or even citizens, but liable to be conscripted as common African subjects, working in labour gangs themselves.

All this had the effect of forcing the African elite to identify with the masses. The hierarchical system of which they had been part had gone, and so, too, had their respect for their colonizers. The French were no longer invincible.

At the same time, General Charles de Gaulle escaped to London and set up his Free France government-in-exile, to fight alongside the Allies. De Gaulle began expanding his army, the Free French Forces (FFF), and French West Africa became a major recruiting ground. The colonies were forced to choose sides, either fighting for Vichy France or for de Gaulle. On several occasions the two armies fought each other, African against African, proxy armies risking their lives for reasons that few of them could have understood. De Gaulle's FFF took Gabon in the Battle of Libreville in November 1940, with the general personally overseeing the attack from French Cameroon and later travelling north to Chad, from where he hoped to launch attacks against the Italians occupying Libya. By the end of 1940, Free France had seized control of all French Equatorial Africa, and two years later it had French West Africa too, including Côte d'Ivoire. Once again, the spirit of liberal reform returned to the country, and Felix Houphouet seized the moment.

Along with seven other Ivoirian landowners he created an independent agricultural union. It was to be called the *Syndicat Agricole Africain*, the SAA, and it appealed for members across the country. The French reformist administrators thought the SAA so important that the new French governor himself sponsored the idea, and helped to launch it.

Tens of thousands flocked to join. Previously voiceless young men and women sensed the possibility of an end to forced labour. It was Houphouet's good fortune that the agricultural lands of Côte d'Ivoire were concentrated around his home region, where the Baoulé people dominated. They became the dominant ethnicity among members of the SAA. As the only Baoulé on the list of candidates to be the union's leader, it couldn't have been a simpler exercise. Houphouet was a shoo-in.

In just two years, the SAA became the largest mass movement in Côte d'Ivoire. Houphouet was savouring the public adulation and his proximity to political power. By now, a series of land deals had made him the wealthiest indigenous cocoa grower in the country. His profile grew quickly, as he visited supporters and delivered speeches all over Côte d'Ivoire. His members' list became so extensive that the French asked to use it as the basis for the country's electoral register. The SAA had branches in every village, members in every farm. Felix Houphouet became the most well-known Ivoirian in the land. This newly created trade union with its novice leader was the embryonic stage of Côte d'Ivoire's single-party authoritarian state.

THE FRENCH COLONY OF MIDDLE CONGO

JANUARY 1944

There were people climbing trees, white-shirted men holding on as if they had been blown there by the warm equatorial winds. Others were leaning from windows or crowding on the grass slopes outside Brazzaville's legislature, wheeling and waving as the troops marched by. French soldiers led the way in their pith helmets and khaki uniforms, Africans followed behind wearing traditional kufi hats, bayonets pointing proudly to the sky.

Charles de Gaulle had arrived for an historic conference. He saluted his troops, shook hands with rows of dignitaries and strolled confidently into the chamber. The leaders of Free France were indebted to the men and women from the colonies who had helped fight for liberation, and they had pledged a new deal for their possessions in Africa. The Brazzaville Conference was to start the process of limited self-governance. In each colony, there would be elections, with French and African citizens allowed to vote, but initially, only a small number of African subjects. It was no accident that the conference was opened with the firing of a gun.

The colonies would still be very much under French control, but Africans would have some say in their own affairs. Most significantly, Brazzaville agreed that each colony would elect a representative to serve as a delegate in the legislature in Paris. It was something the British and Belgians had never considered, and effectively made French colonies satellite constituencies. Houphouet knew exactly what he needed to do.

His first target was Abidjan city council. No one could run alone; they needed to submit a slate of candidates like a political party, consisting of nine citizens and nine subjects. Most of Houphouet's rivals chose a mixture of Europeans and Ivoirians for their list. Others selected members of a single ethnic group. Houphouet decided that both approaches were doomed to failure. Instead, he called for whites to be banned from the election altogether, and submitted a list of candidates from several different ethnic backgrounds, a broad coalition of Côte d'Ivoire tribes and foreign Africans.

The Europeans withdrew in protest. Houphouet's Ivoirian rivals realized that, by narrowly appealing to just a single ethnicity, they had miscalculated the public mood. Most of them withdrew too. It left Houphouet's *Bloc Africain* almost alone in the field, and his party won with a landslide. But the real prize was up for grabs two months later, a seat in the National Constituent Assembly, the parliament in Paris that would draft the constitution for the new Fourth Republic.

France was in a state of post-war turmoil. One hundred and fifty thousand people had been detained on suspicion of collaborating with the Germans. Women who had taken German soldiers as lovers were shaved and paraded through the streets in front of jeering crowds. Some were set upon by lynch mobs. There was bitter debate about how to deal with the captured leaders of the Vichy government and the thousands of paid officials who had worked under German occupation: policemen, teachers, civil servants. De Gaulle, by now the embodiment of France, was responsible for imposing a centralized, unified state.

He headed a provisional government (GPRF), comprising an uneasy tripartite alliance between the French Communist Party (PCF), the French Section of the Workers International (SFIO) and the centre-right Popular Republic Movement (MRP), which was loyal to de Gaulle. But it was the PCF that had been steadily increasing in popularity and influence. During the war, communists had dominated the Resistance movement, organizing guerrilla groups and carrying out many daring political assassinations. Buoyed by its prominent role, the PCF had enjoyed a surge in membership, rising to more than a million in 1945. Initially, many of its supporters wanted to launch a revolution in France as soon as the Germans were defeated, but PCF leaders, on instruction from Stalin, chose to be part of the provisional government instead. De Gaulle was suspicious of them from the start and gave them only a very limited role. This was going to be an extremely bumpy ride.

It was de Gaulle's job to transform the provisional government into one that was democratically elected. The elections of October 1945 would take place across the whole of the French empire, including French territories in Africa. In Côte d'Ivoire, Houphouet was busily preparing.

It was now that his earlier legwork in the SAA came into play. The agricultural union provided him with a ready-built electoral machine that reached into every household in the country. Agents of the SAA were effectively his campaigners, visiting remote villages with loudhailers and proclaiming Houphouet the candidate of unity. His entire adult life had been spent, inadvertently, acquiring connections for this very moment. His medical work in the bush had brought him influential supporters among the chiefs. He had the powerful Baoulé already won over. Then there were his wife's people in the east and his Muslim father-in-law's clan scattered throughout the country. Houphouet was almost miraculously well placed.

His chief rival, Tenga Ouedraogo, was from the north of the colony, Upper Volta, a region that had little in common with the south, and would eventually become an entirely separate country, Burkina Faso. That had the effect of unifying southerners behind Houphouet, rather than running the risk of being led by a man from a distant and unfamiliar place. There are photographs of Houphouet from the time, beaming and waving from the rooftops of various buildings, hundreds of shining faces staring up at this diminutive, articulate African, from their tin-roofed shacks. They had never seen anyone like him: an African in a white man's suit, educated, eloquent, overflowing with confidence, and asking to be their voice among the white faces of the Paris legislature.

Nevertheless, the result was extremely close, the only vote in Houphouet's life that was still in the balance until the moment the polls closed. After he failed to achieve fifty per cent in the first round, a second ballot was required. On 4 November 1945 came the announcement that Houphouet had won, with 50.7 per cent.

During the wild celebrations that followed, he decided to take a new name. 'Felix Houphouet' was not resonant enough. He needed something a little more flamboyant, more in keeping with his remarkable success. So he added 'Boigny', a word that, in his native language, means 'battering ram'. Felix Houphouet-Boigny set off for Paris in November 1945, a moneyed but unworldly Ivoirian, plunged into a freshly liberated city. Edith Piaf was performing on the Champs Élysées, there was jazz, experimental theatre, and now Houphouet-Boigny was taking his seat among the men of empire. He was also entering a world of political instability, an assembly bandaged together by the need for unity, through which old wounds would soon start bleeding.

Victory in those elections had gone to the communists, with the PCF winning 26.1 per cent of the vote. They would rule in a tripartite alliance, together with the socialists and the MRP, all of whom agreed on de Gaulle as head of state. But the general's distrust of the communists manifested itself again. He refused to give them any important government ministries, saying that he couldn't work with politicians who were ultimately being run by Moscow. The alliance managed to stagger on for a further three months, but then de Gaulle dropped his bombshell. He resigned on 20 January 1946. France was plunged into a constitutional crisis.

This was Felix Houphoeut-Boigny's introduction to the politics of the metropole. But he wasn't going to be put off his stride. He had come to Paris with one purpose above all others. It was to become the stuff of folklore in Côte d'Ivoire. People still sing songs about it today.

While the French were effectively leaderless, and assembly members were trying desperately to draft a constitution, Houphouet-Boigny tabled a bill to abolish the use of forced labour in the colonies. It was supported by the communists and by the other African delegates, and in the febrile circumstances of the time neither a debate nor a vote was required. Instead it was rubber-stamped as a decree, and the 'Houphouet-Boigny Law' was passed.

The ecstatic celebrations that followed were not confined to Côte d'Ivoire. Forced labour had become a brutal fixture in other French territories too – in the rubber plantations of French Guinea, and the salt mines of Senegal – and now it was over, thanks to Felix the Battering Ram. He had eliminated the hated symbol of colonial rule, and, in doing so, created a legend around himself overnight. Other decrees granted at the same time brought about the abolition of the *indigénat*, the harsh system of arbitrary justice in the colonies, and also opened the way for the establishment of African political parties. But it was the Houphouet-Boigny Law of 3 April 1946 that earned the Ivoirian leader the gratitude that would sustain him in power over the next five decades. For many years, people in Côte d'Ivoire believed that if Houphouet-Boigny wasn't returned to office, then the system of forced labour would return.

'When politics began,' explained one of his colleagues years later, 'Houphouet said he would do everything to eliminate this barbarous practice. We didn't know whether he could do it but he kept his word. Since then, I have followed him blindly and I shall continue to do so as long as he remains faithful to this principle.'[2] That was fifteen years after Houphouet's law was passed.

In Paris, the political turmoil continued. A first draft constitution was defeated in a national referendum. New elections were required, just seven months after the first, and Felix Houphouet-Boigny triumphed on a scale normally associated with absurd dictatorial fixing. On this occasion it appeared to be more or less genuine. Under the banner of his newly formed political party, Parti démocratique de la Côte d'Ivoire (PDCI), the man who had ended slavery managed to unite the whole country behind him, taking ninety-eight per cent of the vote. The fixing would come later.

A French constitution was finally agreed in October 1946, transforming the French empire into the more inclusive French Union. But immediately, Houphouet-Boigny and his fellow African delegates became concerned that a powerful lobby of French businessmen, the Marchés Coloniaux – a group of French merchants and landowners – were trying to arrest any further meaningful reform.

Houphouet-Boigny could see that African delegates were still the poor relation, marginalized in the assembly, their voices hardly heard. He organized a conference in Bamako, French Sudan, to discuss how best to unify the myriad nationalist parties across French Africa. The aim was not to achieve independence – the majority didn't feel they were ready for that – but to insist that their people received equal rights. The conference agreed on the creation of a huge anti-colonial, pan-African political movement that stretched across all French African possessions. Called the Rassemblement Démocratique Africain, the RDA, it became an umbrella organization, its members retaining their old political parties but operating under one name for the purpose of creating a unified block in the French assembly. This was an alarming move in the eyes of some French politicians, who saw the RDA as a dangerous nationalist group that might turn militant. At the helm was Felix Houphouet-Boigny. With the constitution now in place, there was one further set of elections, in November 1946, for seats in the first parliament of the Fourth Republic. Houphouet-Boigny stood under the RDA banner, and the party secured ten seats, enough to be taken seriously as a potential coalition partner in the heavily fragmented French chamber.

Nothing could be achieved in French politics without becoming part of an alliance. Positions on committees were awarded according to the size of each political group, and Houphouet-Boigny aligned his RDA with the only party prepared to support him, the French Communist Party. He could hardly have been more out of place. Here he was, a landowning capitalist and one of the wealthiest politicians in the chamber, sitting with representatives loyal to Stalin's Cominform and the idea of proletarian dictatorship.

Houphouet-Boigny's ambitions were now pinned on his ability to keep his head above water in the turbulent political currents. In May 1947, the tripartite alliance that had survived since the days of the provisional government finally collapsed. With the influence of the communists on the wane, the RDA needed new allies.

Freed from a marriage of convenience with the communists, Houphouet-Boigny was in his element, circulating among members of the assembly, schmoozing potential partners in the smartest Parisian restaurants and bars. He made a name for himself as a gifted deal-maker who could tease compromise from even then most obdurate of opponents. And then, in 1956, came the breakthrough.

As parties coalesced into workable blocks, Houphouet-Boigny forged an alliance with the small Democratic and Socialist Union of the Resistance (UDSR), a party with the same number of seats as his own, and led by the young François Mitterrand. The UDSR had, in turn, manoeuvred itself into partnership with the centre-left coalition of the Republican Front (RF), and the RF was the party of government. One month after the elections, in February 1956, Houphouet-Boigny was rewarded for his support by being made a government minister.

It was an astonishing achievement. Across the Atlantic in the United States, segregation was still very much in place, overtly in the South and more insidiously elsewhere. In Montgomery, Alabama, civil rights activist Rosa Parks had just been arrested for refusing to give up her bus seat to a white passenger, and here was Houphouet-Boigny helping to run a white colonial government. It was the highest office any African had achieved in France and he was still on the rise. He became minister of health, and a member of the French cabinet.

In neighbouring Gold Coast the British were watching with bewilderment. The nationalist leaders fighting for independence there had been treated as seditious criminals. Several had been in and out of jail for years. One was, of course, Kwame Nkrumah, who became the first prime minister of newly independent Ghana in March 1957, the year after Houphouet-Boigny had become a minister in Côte d'Ivoire. Nkrumah soon became something of a nationalist prophet, with a generation of leaders beating a path to his door, Robert Mugabe and Patrice Lumumba among them. But Houphouet-Boigny regarded him as a hot-headed Marxist who had achieved independence at breakneck speed.

Nkrumah decided to drop in on Houphouet-Boigny, on his first foreign trip as Ghanaian leader. We can imagine the two men, translators and advisors in tow, meeting in the Ivoirian's hardwood study. Houphouet-Boigny, immaculate as ever, moderate in tone, always looking for agreement. Nkrumah, irascible, fiercely intelligent, never conceding an inch. Nkrumah believed political change was the priority – in Africa's case, decolonization – and that economic prosperity would follow. Houphouet-Boigny argued that decolonization was unnecessary for now, that there were benefits to be had from French rule. He insisted a country should build its economy before going it alone.

The two men discussed the issues at length, and then rose from their chairs and agreed on a wager. Each bet that their country would be better off in ten years' time than the other. 'Let us undertake this experiment in absolute respect for the experiment of his neighbour,' announced Houphouet-Boigny, 'and in ten years' time we shall compare the results.'[3] The pair shook hands, and parted.

Houphouet-Boigny immersed himself in the Parisian high life. He was photographed beside his friend, the justice minister François Mitterrand, white silk scarf knotted flamboyantly, trilby in hand, footmen helping him with his heavy coat. There were cocktail parties, lavish meals, visits to the theatre. He purchased properties around the capital, and spent more time in France than at home. But the winds of change sweeping across British territories had also reached those of the French. Many were no longer content living under colonial rule, albeit with democratic tweaks. Only self-government would do – a complete break with Paris. When change came, it was through France's most bloody colonial conflict.

By 1958 the French grip on its most promising source of oil – Algeria – was weakening, at the hands of the nationalist guerrillas of the FLN, the Front de Libération Nationale. Twenty-five thousand French soldiers had been killed. The death toll among Algerians was 900,000. International pressure to find a peaceful solution was intensifying, and the global consensus was that Paris must grant immediate independence. But France's national assembly was in no state to make any decision, even with world leaders breathing down its neck. Without de Gaulle the whole chamber had become a political marketplace of fast deals and fleeting alliances that had left the country paralysed by indecision. Watching from Algiers, exhausted, short of supplies, and on the brink of defeat, French army commanders decided to take matters into their own hands.

On the night of 13 May 1958, a group of officers led by General Jacques Massu seized control of Algiers from their own French civilian governors, and announced that they were taking over the country until General de Gaulle came out of retirement to reclaim his presidency. If it didn't happen, Massu warned, then he and his co-conspirators would employ 'Operation Resurrection', a military takeover of Paris. There was outrage in the metropole, and among the communists in particular. But the majority of French politicians saw no alternative.

By the end of the month, de Gaulle was back in control, and announced there was to be an important referendum on 28 September 1958. All French colonies in *Afrique Noire* – sub-Saharan Africa – would vote to decide on their future relationship with France. They could remain a partner under a watered-down French Community, a little like the British Commonwealth, or they could choose to break all ties and become independent. Houphouet-Boigny rushed back home to make sure his electorate didn't embarrass him. There was only one choice and that was a 'Oui' vote. He wanted to stay as close to France as possible, and in order to ensure it happened, his authoritarian tendencies were about to surface for the first time.

Driven in an open-top car, through the humid streets of Abidjan, he arrived at a sports stadium to address a crowd of 40,000 people. Anyone planning to vote the wrong way in the referendum, he told them with great sweeping gestures, would be given twenty-four hours to leave the country. If they remained, they would be jailed. There were, he announced, plenty of examples in history where civilized countries had needed to do the same. America had rightly purged its communist troublemakers in the early 1950s. Russia had needed to silence its bourgeoisie.[4]

The vote never really looked in doubt, but the scale of the victory pointed to heavy rigging and intimidation. The 'Oui' vote was carried by 99.9 per cent. Out of an electorate of 1 million, only 225 people had voted against Houphouet-Boigny.

But world opinion was shifting irreversibly against colonialism. Eighteen months after the referendum, with the French all but defeated in Algeria, and European powers gradually handing back their possessions across Africa, the momentum had moved decisively towards decolonization. The sun was setting on French Africa, whether Houphouet-Boigny liked it or not. De Gaulle travelled around his colonies in 1960, lowering the tricolour and renouncing French sovereignty. If it were any consolation to Houphouet-Boigny, he was in a strong position to win the planned presidential election and become the first leader of the newly independent Republic of Côte d'Ivoire. He didn't want to take any chances, though, and insisted he must stand unopposed.

A few weeks later, the presidency secured, he gave French reporters a tour of his plantations and the swamps where he fed crocodiles around his vast acreage of land, and reminded them that he wanted to be regarded as a man of the people. 'Posterity is not consecrating me as the first president of Côte d'Ivoire,' he told them with a smile, 'it is consecrating me as the first peasant of Côte d'Ivoire.'[5]

All the villages had brass bands. That's what struck them, that these remote communities in Côte d'Ivoire had bands, marching bands like British mining towns, with polished instruments and crisp white shirts and proud musicians puffing their cheeks. Even the smallest village had its own, to parade at Easter and Whitsun and whenever else they got the chance. No matter how poor they were, they would save and invest in an instrument. Judith and Philip Chapman had recently arrived from Britain, along with a wave of French expats, and were welcomed by musicians and dancers at their modest rural home in Agboville, a town so isolated that a letter from England took six weeks to reach them.

At independence, most former African colonies saw an exodus of Europeans, but not Côte d'Ivoire. Not only did Houphouet-Boigny encourage French government officials to stay, thousands of new-comers flocked to France's most successful former possession, lured by Houphouet-Boigny's low taxes and business incentives. He wanted to maintain his ties with Europe wherever he could. The Chapmans saw their role as bringing enlightenment. They were Methodist missionaries.

Philip Chapman was a minister: tall, bespectacled, with an unexpected streak of mischief. As he settled into their modest new home, he was relieved to discover that some of the tankers that delivered water to outlying communities sometimes delivered wine too. On his way to a service, he would hear the haunting sound of band practice drifting through the forest, but the music was sometimes drowned out by the scream of chainsaws. In those early days, the French timber industry was hard at work bulldozing kilometre-long tracts of woodland. Houphouet-Boigny's new administration quickly saw a business opportunity. No contract would be granted without passing through government officials first, and signatures cost money. In Congo and Zimbabwe the Ministry of Mines was the most sought-after department in government, because of the opportunities it presented in diamonds. In Côte d'Ivoire, the Ministry of Water and Forests was a favourite, with its officials overseeing timber production. But it sill didn't compare with the Ministry of Agriculture, the department that controlled the cocoa industry.

Philip Chapman's church services were held in a simple hut with benches and gas lanterns, after which he would sit with a bowl of goat stew and breathe in the aroma of cocoa drying in the sun. 'The smell of riches,' the farmers would say, and for the first five years of independence it was just that. Côte d'Ivoire's economy grew faster than any in tropical Africa: a remarkable 11.5 per cent a year. The growth rate was outstripping many in Europe. For a country without oil or diamonds, it was unheard of. The boom was down to a combination of good harvests, and well-organized farming, and was also reliant on strong world markets for cocoa and coffee. It was the start of what would become known as the 'Ivoirian Miracle'. But there was hardly a moment for Houphouet-Boigny to enjoy it.

A pattern was establishing itself in post-independence Africa, and it involved violent upheaval and coups. In Congo, Patrice Lumumba had been abducted and murdered. In Togo the new prime minister had been assassinated. And now, in February 1966, his socialist neighbour in Ghana, Kwame Nkrumah, had been overthrown while he was abroad. It was hardly the way Houphouet-Boigny wanted to win his wager, but he allowed himself a moment of wry satisfaction, no doubt. The Ghanaian president never returned home, and chose to live in exile in Guinea Conakry, where he became so paranoid about assassination that he fled to Romania to live out his final days.

Now Houphouet-Boigny was worried there might be some in his own party who wanted rid of him. There seemed to be evidence stretching back before independence, when some communist-inspired members of his PDCI saw him as the imperialist's chief lackey on the continent, an Ivoirian who had morphed into a Frenchman and was preventing the formation of a true nationalist movement. In 1959 Houphouet-Boigny had been at his family home in Yamoussoukro, enjoying the refined calm of his plantation house, when a terrified gardener entered holding the body of a dead black cat. He had discovered it buried in a shallow grave somewhere in the grounds with something sinister attached to its body. Around the animal's head was tied a picture of Houphouet-Boigny, a cat in a human mask. It could only indicate one thing: an attempt to kill him using black magic.

Houphouet-Boigny spent some time making a meal of the whole episode, calling it the *complot du chat noir*, the plot of the black cat, and seeming to relish being at the centre of a sinister mystery. Then he changed tack and his mood darkened. He had found the culprit, he announced. It was his second-in-command in the PDCI, John-Baptiste Mockey, the party's secretary general. Mockey stood in for Houphouet-Boigny when he was away, and now he was an assassin? The population pictured him lingering around the leader's house with a dead animal, a spade and a box of magic potions. But the truth was less arcane.

Mockey was the most popular politician in the party: smart, charismatic and urbane. Houphouet-Boigny had been terrified he would mobilize his supporters on the communist wing of the movement and usurp him. The cat had provided a convenient excuse. As if to confirm as much, Mockey wasn't put on trial, but banished to Israel to become ambassador. Three years later, he was invited back to Abidjan to head the Special Security Court, the body established specifically to put suspected coup-plotters on trial. The whole black cat business was apparently forgotten.

The possibility of a plot became a little more credible in April 1963.

Without warning, Houphouet-Boigny rounded up 200 alleged conspirators as they arrived in Yamoussoukro for a PDCI conference. Many of them were senior figures in the party: cabinet ministers, youth-wing officials, and some of his own personal aides. They represented a sizeable portion of the party hierarchy. The defendants were taken to the president's compound and held incommunicado while an investigation was carried out. Eighty-six of them ended up being put on trial in front of a Special Security Court that was set up behind closed doors in Yamoussoukro. The plot had apparently been uncovered six months before, and was ideological in nature. It was said that the communist-inspired youth wing of the party had been planning to have Houphouet-Boigny arrested so that the PDCI could follow a Marxist–Leninist path.

The problem was that these stark political differences within the only legal party in the country, the PDCI, were never going to go away. It was all part of a healthy democratic debate, but this wasn't a healthy democracy. Forty-four of the defendants were sentenced to hard labour for periods ranging from five to twenty years, seven to hard labour for life, and thirteen received the death penalty.

Four months later, in August 1963, there was another wave of arrests, relating to the same supposed plot. This time, Houphouet-Boigny alleged that the conspirators had been receiving outside help from the Ghanaian ambassador working on behalf of his Marxist president, Kwame Nkrumah. The suspects included six cabinet ministers and five founders of the PDCI who had also been serving on the security courts. Now they were hauled in front of their own former court officials as defendants. To add to the surreal nature of proceedings, the head of the court was John-Baptiste Mockey, fresh back from Israel. Nineteen jail sentences were handed down, and six death sentences.

In the end, none of the death sentences from either trial were carried out, making Houphouet-Boigny appear a magnanimous and forgiving leader. Many of the jail terms were commuted, and several of the defendants, old party militants who had been close to Houphouet-Boigny since the start of his career, were absolved on condition they make public confessions and apologize. It was an offer they all hastily accepted. Except for one. Ernest Boka wasn't in any position to accept anything. He had died under mysterious circumstances in a cell in Houphouet-Boigny's compound.

Boka was a well-known lawyer and former government minister who had been appointed president of Côte d'Ivoire's Supreme Court by Houphouet-Boigny at the age of just thirty-five, but had resigned the year prior to his detention. He was suspected of having communist sympathies, and had been picked up during one of several sweeps connected to the alleged conspiracy, after which he had been kept in a cell in Yamoussoukro like the others. In April 1964, with the trials over and still no mention of Boka, it was announced that he had been found hanging from the ceiling of his cell.

Rumours quickly spread that Boka's death was not suicide, but that he had been assassinated or died of ill-treatment. Houphouet-Boigny decided a swift rebuttal was required. He called together foreign diplomats, religious figures and businessmen, and announced that Boka had killed himself, despite the fact that his body showed clear signs of torture. He devoted the major part of his address to reading out a bizarre Soviet-style confession allegedly written by Boka before his death, in which he admitted being sympathetic to the French Communist Party, and using his influence to place communists in top government posts, so that he himself could become president. The event seemed, to many, like a desperate attempt at a cover-up, especially when Houphouet-Boigny said that Boka had confessed to trying to use black magic to assassinate him.

Boka was sorry, declared the president, still reading from the confession, and had realized his terrible mistake. He asked for his family's forgiveness and wished to be executed. The president then displayed two suitcases, allegedly seized from members of Boka's family. Inside one was a rack of magic potions, in the other a collection of tiny coffins containing Houphouet-Boigny's corpse in effigy.[6]

Philip Chapman settled into village life constructing small breeze-block churches around the bush, while Judith taught in local schools. They soon encountered evidence of how all-pervasive Houphouet-Boigny's PDCI machine had become. Everywhere they turned, in the local store, down at the cocoa-weighing station, at the livestock market, PDCI representatives were hanging around. They portrayed themselves as concerned neighbours, eager to hear the most trivial problems. But the information they collected travelled one way: up. Everyone in the country was being monitored.

The largely compliant electorate seemed unconcerned. They called Houphouet-Boigny 'Le Vieux', the wise one, and expected to consult him on a whole range of inconsequential family matters. 'We are just off to see Le Vieux!' people would shout, nonchalantly, as they cycled by. 'Problems with the inheritance', or 'A disagreement over land'. The Chapmans thought them innocently optimistic, but, time and again, they would return with breathless stories about Le Vieux's hospitality and how he had offered such kind and wise advice.

The Chapmans had a friend, a local Methodist minister called Pasteur Jean Nanga. Jean was a humble man from a low-status family, a man who recoiled from argument or conflict, but whose son had different ideas. He was young, bright and restless, and when he won a place at medical school he became involved in student politics. It was normal teenage behaviour, nothing to threaten Le Vieux and his team, just marches and demonstrations. Jean Nanga was worried, though. He had brought up his son properly and didn't want any trouble. When the PDCI network of officials came to hear about the young man's activism, and Le Vieux summoned him in for 'a chat'. He had no choice but to attend.

Then there was silence. Jean Nanga waited for news.

In those early years as president, Houphouet-Boigny, ever the cocoa farmer, was rubbing his hands at the prospect of retuning the country's economy so that it became entirely self-reliant. The fertile earth could make Côte d'Ivoire a peaceful and relatively prosperous land. The production of cocoa, coffee and pineapples was not dependent on securing foreign investment like the oil in Libya and Nigeria, but neither could he take his resources for granted, like Congo and South Africa, with their limitless supplies of inanimate diamonds. Agriculture required loving attention, efficient organization of labour, and the luck of the gods when it came to harvests. The president offered relocation packages to tempt people away from the barren savannah regions into the fertile central forests. He invited people from neighbouring countries too. 'Come and resettle,' was the message, 'and be part of an agricultural revolution.' He gave farmers generous deals to acquire their own land, and educated them in the most advanced agricultural techniques. Soon the majority of the population were involved in his Ivoirian Miracle. In the first decade and a half of independence, coffee production increased by 200 per cent, cocoa production by 600, and pineapples by a staggering 4,000. Economists in Britain and America were scratching their heads. It seemed that Houphouet-Boigny had managed to buck the trend of post-colonial economic decay that was afflicting much of Africa. But then he over-reached.

In the late 1960s Houphouet-Boigny began to borrow money to fund an ambitious construction programme. There was to be a world-class port at San Pedro to export cocoa and coffee. A hydro-electric damn, one of the most expensive in Africa, was planned for the Bandama River, which would create a lake three times the size of Lake Geneva. Public buildings were to be constructed in all major cities, and tarmac roads built through remote districts, connecting towns and villages that had previously only been accessible by jungle tracks. It was a modernization plan worthy of a 'battering ram' president, and its centrepiece was to be a church in his own ancestral village.

In the 1950s Yamoussoukro had been a nondescript farming community north of Abidjan, one of many hundred tucked away in the bush, quietly producing its weekly sacks of cocoa. In his youth, Houphouet-Boigny had viewed it as a bucolic retreat, but his Parisian years had changed him. How could he invite international statesman to his country and have them see there wasn't even a road named after him, or a public building with a proud bust of Houphouet-Boigny?

The monumentalizing of a leader's birthplace had become a fashion among post-colonial strongmen. Hastings Banda of Malawi was one of the first, shifting his entire capital city with all its administrative apparatus to his ancestral fishing town of Lilongwe. Mobutu opted to keep his capital where it was, but to erect his 'Versailles of the jungle', with its immensely long runway in Gbadolite.

Houphouet-Boigny was dining with Tunisia's President Habib Bourguiba when he hit upon the idea. Bourguiba was transforming his ancestral fishing village into a thriving tourist city. Weren't all self-respecting new African leaders doing the same? He recommended a good architect, and Houphouet-Boigny went away dreaming of building an exciting, modern village capital in Yamoussoukro.

He would have six-lane American-style freeways leading out of the bush to a giant artificially flooded lake to mimic the lagoons of Abidjan. The scrubland would be turned into golf courses, the trees cleared for resort hotels, and at the heart of it all would be an architectural eulogy to God and himself: a basilica in the bush. It would be expensive, but he was in the midst of the Ivoirian Miracle. The country's credit rating had never been higher, and Houphouet-Boigny borrowed enormous sums to begin the building. It all rested on the world's precarious commodity markets, and sustaining the prices of cocoa and coffee.

In the 1970s Côte d'Ivoire overtook Ghana as the world's largest producer of cocoa. French investors clamoured for a piece of Ivoirian real estate. International businessmen struck deals in the foyers of Abidjan's newly built hotels. For the small, land-owning elite around Houphouet-Boigny these were immensely prosperous times. Enough money was rolling in for the purchase of second homes on the French Riviera. The president's wealthy friends would cruise around the capital's well-maintained tarmac streets in brand-new Citroën and Mercedes cars. Houphouet-Boigny became the country's biggest exporter of cocoa, and quickly expanded his business into pineapples and avocados. He could see no conflict of interest with his role as president, and took to announcing publicly just how rich he had become. His money, he said, accounted for a quarter of all deposits in Abidjan's main bank. He had more in tax havens abroad. 'Is there any serious man in the world who does not place a portion of his assets in Switzerland?' he smilingly asked during one interview.[7] These were the glory days. Houphouet-Boigny travelled Europe collecting trophy homes, several in France, one in Geneva, and a castle in Italy close to the summer residence of the pope.

The president spent much of his time in Paris. Gone were the dark days of paranoia about coups. Now he could hardly be coaxed back into the country unless it was for business. During the 1970s he lived for months at a time in his property at 11 Rue Masseran, a palace built for a Spanish prince, into which he crammed Louis XVI furniture and Russian imperial porcelain. While his aides kept an eye on world events from their sticky offices in Abidjan, the president wandered through his aromatic gardens in the 7th arrondissement or dined with Valéry Giscard d'Estaing and Jacques Chirac. He became the French government's political agent in West Africa, relied upon to push their cause on the international stage. Instead of them backing his political campaigns, he was backing theirs, supporting his best French friends with funds to help them stay in power.

From his home in Paris his reach extended into every meeting in every public building in Abidjan. That included the twenty-five-storey slab of corporate secrecy that was the headquarters of the powerful Cocoa and Coffee Marketing Board. It was responsible for ninety per cent of Côte d'Ivoire's exports during the 1970s and was a place over which Houphouet-Boigny exercised complete control. Around him he spun a whirligig of black-market deals and untraceable middlemen, of informal contracts and hidden surpluses that no one could easily disentangle.

Importantly, Houphouet-Boigny also controlled the surplus crop, the cocoa put aside for a rainy day. It was supposed to act as a buffer against harvest failures or unexpected changes in the markets. But if anyone bothered scrutinizing the warehouses where it was supposed to be kept, they would have found scandalous scenes. The president bought and sold the surplus as he saw fit, rewarding his cronies with favourable deals, and dishing it out to his friends in Paris as gifts. A French investigation later found that he kept at least ten per cent of the country's cocoa revenues in his personal bank accounts.[8] His cronies hid the scale of his theft by creating bogus accounts and log books, a ploy so successful that even today in Côte d'Ivoire many still believe he did no wrong.

Philip and Judith Chapman finally received news of what had happened to Pasteur Nanga's son at a church service one Sunday morning. As instructed, he had gone to visit Le Vieux, and been given a dressing down about his potentially subversive activities. He was, the president told him, in need of re-educating. Nanga Jnr was to go to the airport, where a plane would fly him to France. From there, he would be driven to the prestigious Saint-Cyr, the military academy where de Gaulle had been trained. Nanga Jnr was to spend a year training to be a military officer. Houphouet-Boigny's approach worked, in that the pastor's son later became a brigadier in the Ivoirian army.

Another young man who was summoned to the president's office at the time was a history professor and trade unionist called Laurent Gbagbo. He had been raised near the cocoa fields of the southwest during the worst of French forced labour, and was fiercely opposed to his leader's Francophile tendencies. Gbagbo made Le Vieux feel uneasy. He had a rare talent for rallying crowds, and was unafraid of pointing out the failings of the authoritarian, single-party state. Gbagbo was invited into the leader's office and given a stern rebuke. Later Houphouet-Boigny had him arrested and thrown in jail for two years. Gbagbo would become the president's main political rival.

The clearing of settlements and scrubland around Yamoussoukro began in the early 1970s. Labourers moved in from across the country. Youngsters abandoned their family farms to learn scaffolding, bricklaying and concrete-mixing. Houphouet-Boigny wanted to build the city fast. Surveyors arrived equipped with maps and sketches that were eagerly transformed into whatever structure the president desired. Decisions were made on the ground, plans changed, buildings moved. There would be no industry, no factories or production lines, nothing to sustain any new workforce once the city was complete. He wanted prestige buildings, a scientific institute, tasteful government offices, and wide carriageways for the hordes of tourists. The purpose of Yamoussoukro wasn't to cater for the masses; it was an aristocratic retreat in the Roman tradition, a place to escape the busy markets and congested roads of Abidjan for the calm exclusivity of the president's birthplace.[9]

A lunch invitation arrived for Judith Chapman one day in 1976, delivered by a clerk of the presidential household. By now the family had moved to San Pedro, little more than a seaside village at the time, but soon to be the country's main cocoa and coffee port. Her presence was requested at the seaside home of Houphouet-Boigny's wife. By this time, the president had divorced his first wife, and taken a woman twenty-five years his junior. Marie-Thérèse was glamorous and beautiful, and shared her husband's tastes for the high life. She was photographed in Paris dressed as Marie Antoinette, all diamonds and long satin gloves. In Washington, she received roses from the Kennedys, and excitedly toured the capital with them, photographed wherever she went. The press referred to her as 'Africa's Jackie Kennedy'.

In San Pedro, Judith Chapman arrived at Marie-Thérèse's residence, and found it surprisingly modest, aside from a single architectural flourish: the swimming pool was half in and half out of the house. Beyond lay the beach and the lagoon, and beyond that the Atlantic Ocean. It was certainly in better taste than the president's palace in Abidjan. Judith's husband, Philip, had visited there. 'Gilding and false Empire' is how he described it: French antique furniture, marble statues and walls of ornate mirrors.

Marie-Thérèse was warm and unpretentious, and sat among the other young women laughing and gossiping as if it were a meeting of the Ladies' Circle rather than lunch with the president's wife. The talk was largely about children and schools: why there were too few of them, and how to reach out to more remote communities. Marie-Thérèse wanted to understand what improvements could be made, something in which she appeared to take genuine interest. Her husband would consult her about political decisions; she was the only person he felt he could truly trust.

The port of San Pedro was starting to take shape, soon cargo ships from America and Europe would be queuing out to sea. But for the moment, all it offered was an insight into how the culture of corruption was percolating down from Le Vieux through every stratum of society. Philip Chapman was approached by a worried member of his congregation, Germain, a smartly dressed, family man who thought deeply about issues. He had got a new job as a customs officer in the port, but his colleagues had quickly turned against him. He had seen them all taking kickbacks in return for allowing even the smallest consignment of cocoa through the port. When a company refused to pay, their beans were 'lost' somewhere in a warehouse at the far end of the docks, and next time they were more co-operative. Germain never complained, he let his colleagues get on with it. But that wasn't enough. His non-involvement in such a ready source of backhanders was seen as weird, even immoral. Why did he not want money for his children's education, or his parents' medicines? Didn't he care?

Côte d'Ivoire society had been turned on its head. Those who *refused* kickbacks were seen as deviants. Parents financed a good education precisely so their children could choose a career with good bribe-potential. If someone secured a job in the civil service, at whatever level, it was their *duty* to make it pay.

Rumours of presidential corruption were of little concern to most people, who reasoned they would do the same in his shoes. But occasionally a story would emerge of such spectacular misuse of public funds that the president was expected to make a statement. It usually entailed the creation of more toothless anti-corruption laws, or the vague promise of an inquiry. On several occasions, though, Houphouet-Boigny was so penitent, he promised to donate all his private land to the state. It sounded like a genuinely selfless act, and the papers often reported it as such. But since Houphouet-Boigny was 'the state', it was a meaningless gesture. He repeated the announcement on many occasions, without ever explaining how the plantations had fallen back into his hands since the last time.

The speed of building work at Yamoussoukro was following the same exhilarating curve as the price of cocoa. The wide roadways provided a curious spectacle for the locals, almost empty of cars, but with donkeys and traps eagerly testing the delights of the glass-smooth surface. There was a palace too, which was strangely brutalistic in its architecture, considering Houphouet-Boigny's taste for gilding and Second Empire kitsch. In the lagoon around its grounds, he began introducing crocodiles, creatures he believed to be sacred. There were half a dozen of them, which he treated as exotic pets, and fed personally in front of astonished foreign dignitaries. Still to come was its centrepiece, which he now envisaged as a cathedral rather than a mere church, perhaps something to rival what the pope had in Rome.

By 1978 the building programme at Yamoussoukro had become a serious drain on the public purse, absorbing one-third of the country's entire urban investment fund outside Abidjan. People had noticed how money was being diverted from their own towns and cities. But while cocoa prices remained high, and salaries were among the best in Africa, they were prepared to look away. In March 1983, Houphouet-Boigny declared that his previously obscure home village was sufficiently well-developed to become the political and administrative capital of Côte d'Ivoire, replacing Abidjan. The question was, how long before the cocoa bubble burst?

When Jean-Bédel Bokassa, self-styled 'emperor' of the Central African Republic, flew into Côte d'Ivoire in September 1979 he was homeless, stateless and fortunate to be alive. Events had moved swiftly during his final days in office. Bokassa had been president of the former French colony, which lay just north of Mobutu's Zaire, for thirteen years. In April that year he had issued an ill-considered presidential decree concerning school uniforms. From now on, all children were to wear clothing bearing Bokassa's image. It wasn't the narcissism of the man that rankled – they were used to that – but the fact that the contract for the compulsory, and expensive, new clothing had been awarded to a member of his own family. Demonstrators took to the streets, on a small scale at first, but their numbers quickly grew. Bokassa decided to send in troops. A large number of elementary schoolchildren were arrested, and crammed into small cells. There the beatings began. Some reports placed Bokassa himself at the scene, killing children with his own cane. In the end more than 100 schoolchildren were dead. After that, the demonstrators didn't just want a reversal of the uniform decree, they wanted Bokassa's head.

In Paris, the French government was watching with increasing alarm. This was one of their own – Bokassa had fought in de Gaulle's Free French army during the war and taken part in the capture of the Vichy government's African capital at Brazzaville in French Congo, as well as being part of the Allied landings that liberated southern France. He was a close friend of the French president, Valery Giscard d'Estaing, and the French had helped finance his bizarre 'coronation' with a diamond-encrusted crown. Bokassa had been eccentric from the start, but now he was out of control.

Shortly after the child murders, he had taken off to see his old friend Colonel Gaddafi on a state visit. Giscard d'Estaing's government took the opportunity to stage a coup. Code-named Operation

Barracuda, French Special Forces were airlifted into the capital, Bangui, on 20 September 1979, to overthrow Bokassa in what became known as 'France's last colonial expedition'. When they searched the president's villa they discovered chests full of diamonds. In his fridges were body parts. There were also human remains in the pond where he kept his crocodiles.

The French reinstated David Dacko as president, the man Bokassa had himself overthrown. Bokassa was outraged. He had always referred to President Giscard d'Estaing as his 'dear cousin'. And what about the diamonds he had given French politicians as gifts? His immediate concern, though, was finding somewhere to live.

Zaire seemed an obvious choice, but President Mobutu was too concerned about his international reputation. Bokassa tried Omar Bongo of Gabon, a man of few scruples who had embezzled millions in oil money from his own people, but even for him Bokassa was too toxic. Togo and Senegal also said no. Bokassa even had the cheek to ask the French for asylum. In the end, only one man was prepared to take him.

Houphouet-Boigny believed France should have shown more loyalty to one of its military veterans and, as France's trusted agent in West Africa, he was prepared to do a little housekeeping on their behalf.

Bokassa's plane landed at Abidjan airport on 24 September 1979 and the 'emperor' was whisked off to a villa owned by Felix Houphouet-Boigny, a grand three-storey property overlooking the lagoon in the exclusive residential district of Cocody. He soon settled into a routine, receiving daily meals from a local hotel, listening to military marching music, eating Camembert and drinking Beaujolais.[10] Soon he felt confident enough to venture to the local nightclubs and bars, although his popularity among the waitresses waned when they found out about the body parts and the child-killing.

By this time, Houphouet-Boigny was a rarity, one of the few among the first generation of post-independence African leaders still standing. If he glanced around his own immediate neighbours, there was only violence and instability. To the east, in Ghana, there had already been four coups d'état. North, in Mali, three coup attempts had failed. To the west, the president of neighbouring Guinea-Bissau had been overthrown by his own prime minister. In Liberia, a junior army officer, Samuel Doe, had just led a particularly bloody coup, killing the president and following it up with the public execution of thirteen members of his cabinet. Houphouet-Boigny held on, not only because of his wealth creation and moderate temperament, but also because he had reduced the size of his army, and placed it under French control.

Herman J. Cohen was not the kind of American you would expect to be doing business with dictators. He looked like a man who might keep bees or restore antiquarian books, but Ambassador Cohen was America's top man in Africa, and had become close to several autocrats: Mugabe, Gaddafi and Charles Taylor. Mobutu had grown so fond of him that he had invited Cohen to his sixtieth birthday party at Cape Martin in the South of France. 'Listen, don't lecture' was his motto, and Houphouet-Boigny was a man who liked to talk.

When Cohen arrived in Abidjan in the summer of 1987, Houphouet-Boigny had wanted to see him so urgently he had flown him in by private plane. The president was an octogenarian by then, shrunken by the years, 'a roly-poly little guy whose feet barely reached the floor'.[11] But he was still sharp, a master-manipulator. He told Cohen he had a problem on his hands.

It concerned his northern neighbour, Thomas Sankara, the president of Burkina Faso. Sankara was a dashing Marxist revolutionary rarely seen out of military fatigues. His politics couldn't have been more distant from those of Houphouet-Boigny. But the two countries were deeply interdependent. Around thirty per cent of Houphouet-Boigny's population originated in Burkina Faso, and had crossed the border to work in the cocoa fields. He needed Sankara on his side.

Originally the two men had been friends. Houphouet-Boigny had helped finance the coup that brought him to power in the first place, but Sankara turned out to be too wild. Seen from Abidjan, Burkina

Faso's president was a populist troublemaker in a scarlet beret, frightening the region's old guard and daring to suggest they were all corrupt. Everyone knew he was pointing the finger at Houphouet-Boigny. To make matters more interesting, Sankara's deputy, and almost certain successor, was one of Houphouet-Boigny's closest friends, Blaise Compaoré. Compaoré's wife was even closer. Houphouet-Boigny had made no secret of his fondness for her, and it was widely assumed she was one of his many dozen illegitimate children.

Whatever the truth, it would clearly suit Houphouet-Boigny if Burkina's Number 2, his old friend Compaoré, were to become Burkina's Number 1. It would also suit the United States of America, which preferred not to have a Marxist revolutionary whipping up trouble in West Africa.

Herman Cohen sat opposite Houphouet-Boigny in his presidential office, and threw in a remark he assumed would land on fertile ground. Sankara, he said, was destabilizing the whole region, and something needed to be done.

Cohen didn't expect the Ivoirian leader to explicitly announce a desire to see Sankara dead, but he did expect at least some vitriol. Instead, Houphouet-Boigny was uncharacteristically demure. 'Don't worry,' he said. 'Sankara is just a boy; he will mature quickly.' Cohen was confused as to why he had been flown in with such urgency. He could only assume the Ivoirian president was hiding his true intentions, and using the meeting to give himself deniability later.

In October 1987, President Sankara was sitting in a staff meeting in Burkina's capital when an armed group stormed into the room and riddled him with bursts of automatic gunfire. His body was then dismembered and buried in an unmarked grave. As expected, Blaise Compaoré became the country's new president. It was no mystery to Herman Cohen who was behind it. The plotters couldn't have executed such a high-risk plan without money and support. Afterwards they relocated to Côte d'Ivoire, and lived with Houphouet-Boigny's blessing in Abidjan.

★

When the economic crisis struck, it was as if Houphouet-Boigny was cruising along his smooth six-lane freeway in Yamoussoukro, revelling in his wealth and security, his enemies dead or in exile, and then the road suddenly collapsed beneath him. The bottom fell out of the world cocoa markets.

Prices had been on a downward trend throughout the 1980s. There was just too much cocoa on the market. Indonesia, Brazil, Ecuador, Nigeria: they were all pushing hard to increase their share by lowering prices and expanding output. Côte d'Ivoire was already the biggest cocoa producer in the world, and its capacity to produce more was unrivalled. During the 1980s it responded to the competition by doubling its output, until it controlled forty per cent of the market. But there was only so much chocolate the world could consume.

Faced with a seemingly endless queue of eager cocoa exporters, chocolate manufacturers chose the cheapest. Houphouet-Boigny was not going to be pushed around. He had promised to pay his farmers a good price, a mandatory minimum for each kilo sold at the farm gate, and he was determined not to let them down. But he couldn't control world markets. Forced to sell at a steadily reducing price, he continued paying his farmers what he had promised, leaving the Côte d'Ivoire government making a loss. Houphouet-Boigny's farm-gate prices were twice as high as any other cocoa-producing country. A wave of cocoa smuggling began, with Ghanaian farmers pouring across the border to sell at the artificially inflated price. Houphouet-Boigny was defiant. He continued shovelling more cocoa onto the docksides of San Pedro and Abidjan, predicting that an upturn was inevitable.

World prices slid further. Buyers accumulated mountains of spare cocoa in foreign warehouses. They had reserves that would last for months. The IMF and World Bank advised Houphouet-Boigny to slash his farm-gate prices in half, but he refused. He blamed the commodity brokers on the trading floors of London and New York. 'They amuse themselves by playing with our cocoa as if they were at the race track or cockfight,' said the president. Partly out of loyalty to his farmers, partly because the grand old man of cocoa could never be wrong, he continued on his obdurate course.

He was wildly over-leveraged. His village-capital at Yamoussoukro had required massive capital investment, for which he had borrowed extensively when times were good. Now his arrears were approaching $2 billion. The cathedral on its own had cost $500 million, and still wasn't finished. Creditors were queuing at his door. He tried to diversify, hurriedly encouraging his farmers to grow cotton, rubber and palm oil instead. But it was far too late. In May 1987, the cocoa markets buckled and then collapsed altogether.

Houphouet-Boigny was glued to his television set. He followed world prices obsessively, cursing the international speculators, and clinging onto the myth that he could single-handedly steer the markets back in his favour; in the past, even a rumour about the eighty-four-year-old's ill-health had been enough to affect prices in Ghana and Brazil. As the figures on the screen tumbled, and traders were shown in a frenzy of buying and selling, the president decided on a high-risk power play.

In January 1988, he boycotted the world cocoa markets, withholding forty per cent of the world's crop with a flourish. Côte d'Ivoire would sell no cocoa except at the price he decreed. It was a huge gamble. He tried to persuade other countries to join him, and create an OPEC-style cartel to fix their own prices. They declined. Houphouet-Boigny was on his own.

At the ports, cocoa wagons waited in the equatorial sun, engines churning out acrid smoke as their drivers slept nearby in hammocks. Pallets of cocoa rotted on the docksides. Piles of uncollected sacks waited by jungle roadsides.

Houphouet-Boigny stopped payments on what was now a $12 billion foreign debt. The IMF suspended a $200 million lending fund. Creditors gave up on Houphouet-Boigny ever reimbursing them, and raced around selling on the debts to third parties for half what they were originally worth. Côte d'Ivoire's banks became insolvent. When officials turned to the 'cocoa stabilization fund' for help, they discovered it had been looted.

Official government cocoa agents had no further capacity for buying the crop. With no one to sell to, Côte d'Ivoire's farmers resorted to the black market, trying to smuggle beans out of the country for half the previous price. Houphouet-Boigny came down hard. Anyone caught doing so would face a jail sentence of twenty years. The rest of the cocoa-producing world simply moved on without him.

Over in Yamoussoukro, his pet building project was reaching its conclusion. The vast marble cathedral that was to be a monument to God and to himself had taken four years to complete. Its giant columns were finished, the marble was laid seamlessly across its floors, the dome pieced together like a giant Fabergé egg. In the circumstances, 'The Basilica of Our Lady of Peace' seemed like a work of utter folly rather than a visionary's gift to the nation. Houphouet-Boigny insisted he had paid for it with his own personal fortune, but his people knew the truth.

His last stand against the world's cocoa buyers persisted for eighteen months. In the summer of 1989 Houphouet-Boigny surrendered. He staggered back into the world markets slashing his prices and releasing hundreds of thousand of tonnes of cocoa. The wise old man had been defeated. In ailing health, and half-blind, he returned to his palace in Yamoussoukro to lick his wounds.

With his country near bankrupt, he had little choice but to embark on an austerity programme, cutting public-service jobs and halving the income of cocoa workers. Facing a fall in their wages, the police and army began setting up extra road blocks to shake money from motorists. Cocoa drivers went on strike. Gradually people began taking to the streets, mainly students and teachers at first, but even former loyalists soon joined them. It wouldn't have escaped the president's notice that the favourite chant was 'Corrupt Houphouet'.

Resentment over falling living standards turned into demands to move away from a single-party state and introduce multi-party elections. Leading the protests was the young history professor he had chastized in his study all those years before. Laurent Gbagbo could smell blood; the president had never experienced such public dissent. In panic, Houphouet-Boigny hit back with tear gas and stun-grenades, dismissing the protestors as *loubards*, petty thieves and drug addicts. That only served to inflame the situation. Army and airforce recruits joined the protests, and occupied the international airport.

Houphouet-Boigny had little choice. On 3 May 1990, he capitulated, announcing the legalization of opposition parties and his intention to hold elections. After months of dragging his feet over every economic decision, suddenly he was in a hurry. The elections would be in October, short notice for a country that had no history of opposition politics. There were dozens of small pressure groups, often with contradictory aims, but no unifying movement. Now they needed to find candidates and organize a plausible opposition in the space of just five months. In the event, twenty-six political parties were created. Houphouet-Boigny couldn't have hoped for better news. His people, having been starved of choice for three decades, were now faced with too much. The candidate who came closest to unifying them was Laurent Gbagbo, leader of the Ivorian Popular Front, but he was running out of time. His presidential bid only got properly under way a matter of weeks before the polls opened.

On 28 October 1990 Felix Houphouet-Boigny put himself at the mercy of his electorate. He was filmed on the day, relaxed, enjoying the moment, as if, uncannily, he knew the result before it happened.

Large numbers stayed at home, suspecting their votes would have little effect on the eventual outcome. At several polling booths fights broke out when opposition members claimed the ballot boxes had been stuffed with Houphouet-Boigny votes. They tried to smash the boxes open.

The president's extensive network of bent party officials and bribable election staff carried out their job a little too well. Houphouet-Boigny won with an implausible 81.7 per cent of the vote, with Gbagbo receiving just 18.3 per cent. Unofficial estimates by Western observers gave Gbagbo between 30 and 40 per cent. In addition, Houphouet-Boigny's PDCI took 163 of the 185 seats in the legislature. Even without the ballot-tampering, his almost mythical status as the father of independence and his loyalty to his cocoa farmers would have been enough to win him the election. The five-year term as president would take him beyond his ninetieth birthday.

In the fall of that year, Felix Houphouet-Boigny sat in a front pew, waiting. He was small and crumpled now, an eighty-five-year-old schoolboy in his own basilica, smiling nervously and wondering how long it would be. Behind him were rows of hats: blue polka-dots and pink satin saucers. There were suited security officers in dark glasses, French diplomats and tribal chiefs in flowing golden gowns. The church was full, everyone straining for a view of the main door. For once, Houphouet-Boigny was not the person they had come to see.

He didn't know it, but his guest had not been keen on coming. Only months before, Ambassador Herman J. Cohen had been at the Vatican's Foreign Ministry in Rome when an official told him, 'We consider the basilica to be a tremendous extravagance for a poor African country.' It seems they had thought about boycotting, but had found themselves boxed in. 'To make matters worse, Houphouet wants to give it to the pope,' said the official. 'We are trying to dodge this one but we will not be able to do so.'[12]

When the procession entered the building it passed through a corridor of bowing bishops. Above them, in a stained-glass window, was that image of Houphouet-Boigny kneeling at the feet of Christ.

He raised himself from his pew, his wife Marie-Thérèse by his side. The whole congregation was on its feet. An official touched his sleeve and Houphouet turned around to see Pope John Paul II standing before him. The pope raised a hand in blessing, and Houphouet reached out, head bowed, face exultant. For a moment the dictator and the pope touched. Houphouet had given his basilica to the Church: the symbol of his hubris and corruption in return for his elevation to a place above the masses and their cocoa farms, above the protests and the fighting over who would be his successor, above his copy of St Peter's basilica, and into the cloudless African sky where Houphouet-Boigny could sit for eternity beside the most powerful leader of them all.

*

After his death from cancer at the age of eighty-eight on 7 December 1993, the country sank into the kind of political turbulence that had befallen so many of its neighbours. Two of Houphouet-Boigny's protégés tried to assume the presidency: his prime minister, Alassane Ouattara, and the president of the national assembly, Henri Konan Bédié. A bitter power struggle ensued, with the security forces divided on who they should back. In the end, they rallied behind Bédié, and it was he who became president. But instead of offering a consolation job to Ouattara, he banned him from public office. Watching from the sidelines, a weary Laurent Gbagbo commented, 'This is what happens when power is offered publicly for auction. When it is time to share the cake, they tear each other apart.'

Bédié's approach was dramatically different from that of Houphouet-Boigny. He championed a philosophy of *Ivoirité*, or Ivoirian-ness. At its heart was a belief that only the largely Christian southerners were true Ivoirians. The largely Muslim northerners, into which category he placed Ouattara, were immigrants who had more in common with ethnic groups in Burkina Faso and Mali than the tropical south of Côte d'Ivoire. It was racism disguised as patriotism. *Ivoirité* resurrected long-dormant tribal antagonisms, and introduced fresh ones.

Condemned to the political wilderness by his beloved PDCI, Ouattara formed a new party, the Rally of the Republicans (RDR), which drew its support from the marginalized north of the country. Côte d'Ivoire was dividing into two distinct regions. Two coups followed, and a lengthy civil war that drew in the French. There were several attempts at elections, but each time a candidate lost, he refused to accept the result and the violence continued. Among those jockeying for power was Laurent Gbagbo, transformed from a mild-mannered history professor during the years of Houphouet-Boigny to a hardened and corrupt politician. When he was defeated in the 2010 elections by his old adversary Ouattara, he refused to accept the result, and both men declared themselves president. Gbagbo unleashed a wave of sectarian violence.

His security officials began touring restaurants in Abidjan, hunting down leaders from Ouattara's newly formed coalition and bundling them into waiting vehicles. Their bodies were later found in local morgues, riddled with bullets. Women were gang-raped simply for the crime of wearing pro-Ouattara T-shirts. Suspected Ouattara supporters were stopped at road blocks and shot. Others were captured in their homes, and beaten with bricks or burned alive beneath piles of tyres and petrol-soaked-wood. It became known as an 'article 125': 100 francs for the petrol, plus 25 francs for the box of matches.

Gbagbo was eventually caught and arrested in a French-assisted raid, and is now standing trial for crimes against humanity at The Hague.

A quarter of a century after the death of Felix Houphouet-Boigny, his gift for keeping the country together appears near-miraculous. He achieved stability not through force but by a long period of economic growth and an almost reckless loyalty to his cocoa farmers.

But what had happened to all the money?

A bitter legal dispute continued for years after his death, with claims of forged paperwork, theft and corrupt lawyers. The former president had accumulated a spectacular fortune that placed him among the richest men in the world: an estimated $11 billion, some in cash deposits held in Zurich and Geneva, the rest in property. He had several mansions in Paris, a home in Chêne Bourg in Switzerland and another at Castel Gandolfo in Italy, near to the summer residence of the pope.

His second wife, Marie-Thérèse is still alive, an elegant eighty-eight-year-old who looks two decades younger. She spends most of her time in her grand house on the Swiss–French border, where liveried servants float around with trays of champagne. She receives few visitors now, but sometimes Catherine Bokassa flies in, the widow of the 'emperor' of the Central African Republic to whom Houphouet-Boigny gave sanctuary all those years ago.

Marie-Thérèse occupies herself by making embroideries seated among the Louis XV furniture that she managed to salvage from her husband's main address in Paris. The property at 11 Rue Masseran was seized, without compensation, by the Côte d'Ivoire government.

Its exquisite furnishings and paintings were auctioned at Sotheby's, but Marie-Thérèse says she didn't receive a penny. She claims to live off a pension of less than €2,000 a month, a sum supplied to her by the Ivoirian state. The benefactors of her husband's fortune, she says, were the four children from his first marriage to Kady Racine Sow. Only two of them are still alive today, and live discreetly in Paris. The rest of the money has fallen into the hands of lawyers, bankers, notaries and Côte d'Ivoire officials.[13]

PART FOUR

A Modern Slavery

CHAPTER NINE
Eritrea

ERITREA

I know him better than anyone. He is the army,
the security service, the legislature, the executive,
the judiciary and the economy. He is everything.

MESFIN HAGOS, PRESIDENT ISAIAS AFWERKI'S
FORMER NUMBER 2

SOMEWHERE ON THE vast ochre moonscape between Eritrea and Sudan where dust flats are creased by ancient winds, the road bends beneath an escarpment and a shack appears: a single room, sculpted from mud and sand, and baked brick-hard. And then another, perched higher on the hillside, a square window cut roughly through its side. A twist of smoke, more shacks, two, three, then boys chasing plastic bags through an empty plain, goats grazing on litter, thatched huts with beehive walls, a whole corrugated village of them, tea sellers beneath makeshift canopies, men sitting on top of firewood on top of donkeys, camels folded into Toyotas, and then the first concrete buildings – a gridwork of featureless boxes, walled gardens, creeping vines, occasional European-style villas, as humanity wrestles back control from the desert and we drive into a desert town.

Kassala is on the Sudanese side of the border, facing Eritrea, and huddled beneath the smooth pink domes of the Taka Mountains. 'My beautiful town has changed,' says the man sitting beside me in the Land Cruiser. He is from Sudan's much-feared National Intelligence and Security Service (NISS). NISS shuts down opposition newspapers, jails journalists, and uses lethal force with impunity to keep in power Sudan's President Omar al-Bashir, who is wanted by the International Criminal Court on charges of war crimes and genocide. This NISS operative is unexpectedly reserved and thoughtful. He spends the long car journey writing English love poems in a notebook, and asks politely if I will check them for grammatical errors. He is also preoccupied with the exodus from the country next door. 'Every week, hundreds arrive from there,' he says, putting down his pen and staring out of the window towards the Eritrean border. 'I feel for them, but Kassala can't take any more. We are the first place they come, the closest refuge.' We pause at a half-hearted roadblock where groggy young Eritreans stand in line, jumbled belongings strewn across the dirt: water bottles, chunks of dry bread, flip-flops. They are fleeing a homeland of which the world knows little, ruled by an enigmatic tent-dwelling dictator who won a glorious liberation war a quarter of a century ago, and then lost his way.

President Isaias Afwerki followed this same route from Eritrea into Sudan when he was their age, fleeing his homeland because it was occupied by a foreign power. He joined the liberation movement in exile, at a camp beneath the egg-shaped mountains of Kassala. Isaias (Eritreans don't have family names, and are formally addressed by their first names) was an impetuous, free-thinking, troublemaker who had studied Marx and was spoiling for a fight with the occupying Ethiopian army.

Arriving in Kassala in the early 1960s, he joined a ragtag brigade of feuding young men whose objective – to take back control of Eritrea – seemed far-fetched. It was a time when heroes of the liberation movement were being made, and there are still some who see Isaias that way: the Father of the Struggle, the guerrilla fighter who pulled off a near-miraculous victory, the beneficent leader whose citizens he treats as his own children. But there are many more who view him as a despot presiding over a slave state, imagining coups and assassins behind every door.

Back at the road block, the young Eritreans pick up their belongings and board buses bound for the Sudanese capital, Khartoum. Most will move on from there, northwards, attempting to cross the Sahara Desert. Many will die in the process. The rest might reach Libya, where they will pay people-smugglers for a place on an overcrowded boat, hoping to make it to the beaches of Europe. Eritrea is one of the largest contributors to the deadly migration route across the Mediterranean Sea. The others tend to be from war zones, such as Syria and Afghanistan. Few ask why tens of thousands are fleeing peaceful Eritrea.

The NISS operative stares through the window at the scene around the checkpoint. 'Young men, women, even children: what can we do?'

He shrugs and then thinks for a moment. 'We can't send them back; we know they would suffer.' An hour or so later we are cruising through vast powder fields on the wilderness frontier between the two countries, the driver hunched over his wheel, squinting through ink-black goggles to keep out the glare, headscarf writhing in the wind. I drape an arm out of the window. The sides of the car are as hot as a kettle. Bleached animal bones, rusting engine parts, shepherds' huts narrow as upended coffins, the rest is dust. This is the territory Eritreans stumble through trying to reach safety. Out here, miles from water or habitation, is considered the safest route out of their homeland. Closer to known patrol routes and checkpoints, Eritrean border guards often shoot on sight.

The man from NISS makes some hurried calls and says we can go only as far as the final police checkpoint on the Sudanese side. It's a concrete hut occupied by a plump officer drinking fizzy pop and sheltering beneath a single, stunted tree. He is puzzled that anyone would want to venture any closer, but agrees that I can walk the final few hundred metres to Eritrea.

The border is unspectacular. A line across a track marks the start of Eritrean territory. Not even a line, just a change in the colour of the asphalt. The plump officer watches from a distance, shrugging his shoulders at some colleagues who have just arrived. The NISS officer sits in a wooden shelter with some local tribesmen who are hoping for accreditation to pass through with their sheep. I can see some military-style buildings on the other side, but no movement, so I walk through, into the most secretive nation on earth. Eritrea is bottom of the world's press-freedom rankings, one place below North Korea.[1]

On the other side, hidden behind a bush, and sheltering from the sun, are four men sitting on brightly coloured plastic camping chairs. They raise themselves and wander over, wearily batting flies from their filthy shirts. They are curious. All appear to be in their twenties, shoeless, narrow-faced, torn trousers flapping around emaciated limbs.

These are Eritrean border guards, behind them acacia trees and desert for 300 miles, all the way to the capital Asmara. It's intriguing just to catch a glimpse. Few outsiders have been here in recent years. It exists far beyond the daily discourse of the global community, hidden away on the Red Sea coast, steadily pursuing its own course. Some countries have barred their diplomats from meeting Eritrean officials. Foreign capital is in no hurry to beat a path to Isaias's door. There are few diamonds here. Gold is limited to a handful of mines, operated in a joint-venture with the Chinese and the Canadians. There is copper, lead and zinc, but the infrastructure is too primitive to make it easily available. Oil is thought to exist in large quantities, but the country has been so secretive no one knows for sure, and Isaias seems uninterested in exploiting it. With a government so suspicious of outsiders, Eritrea remains one of the least-developed countries in the world.

Isaias's most plentiful and exploitable resource is his own people.

The men in rags, the border officials, want to look at some foreign coins, not for acquisitive reasons. Pitifully, they simply want to see and touch something from outside. They examine a pound coin, roll it in their hands, point to the image of Queen Elizabeth, and hold it to their chests like a medal. I give them one each, and they are thrilled. It had been my intention to walk to the military buildings in the trees, but a stony-faced official approaches, and the mood changes.

The man from NISS signals we should leave.

Nearby is Shagarab, a dusty refugee camp the size of a town. It lies on the Sudanese side of the border, a grass-fenced community way out in the desert. There are men herding donkeys, women selling flour, a modern office unit, concrete living quarters, even a church. There is a reason why Shagarab has a sense of permanence – some inhabitants have lived here more than thirty years. They arrived during the Eritrean War of Independence, and hoped Isaias's victory might herald the start of a new era. Now they expect to remain until he has gone, an island community adrift in the desert waiting for the storm to pass.

Dusty young men drift through the arrivals gate, skin tight on their skeletal faces. They are dressed in torn tracksuit bottoms and football shirts: 'Beckham', 'Ronaldo', 'Zidane'. Some have shoes. Five thousand more of them will cross the border before the end of the month. In the absence of independent journalists or NGOs reporting freely from Eritrea, the cause of such a sustained exodus can only be found in the testimonies of the men and women in Shagarab.

'So what was your job in Eritrea?' I ask one of them, in a crowded passageway between the residential blocks.

'Soldier! Soldier!' several shout at the same time.

'And how long were all of you soldiers?'

'Seven years…' says one.

'Army cadet!' shouts another. 'Military Conscription.'

'How long?'

'Ten years,' says one man. 'Conscription.' He is quieter than the rest, subdued. Some of the younger ones lean against him as he speaks. I ask him if he knows others who have served so long.

'More than ten years, twenty years, at least to thirty years,' he says calmly.

'They keep you until the end of your years,' another man chips in. 'Some of them they will die in service. They will die. It is limitless.'

'And what would happen if you try to leave?'

'They will come to your house and take another family member,' says an older man in his forties. 'They will put them in prison, and if you are hiding, they will find you and they will put you in prison also.'

This is the account given repeatedly wherever you talk to Eritrean refugees: London, Sudan, Libya, Italy, France – I have met them in all those places, and the stories are similar – endless military conscription, and prison or worse for those who try to evade it. They explain that at some point the military work turns into manual labour on building sites, farms and factories, but that they are still officially in the military. They live in vast prison-style camps, often far from home, and are paid barely enough to feed themselves, certainly not enough to live privately away from the state system. They are bonded labour, effectively slaves working for the Eritrean government – women, students, pensioners, prisoners, teachers, even judges, all are in the Eritrean military and none, unless they are close to Isaias's inner circle, can leave. In 2015, a United Nations report described Eritrean citizens as 'subject to systems of national service and forced labour that effectively abuse, exploit and enslave them for indefinite periods of time'.[2]

At Shagarab, the conversation stops at military conscription. If you push further, for information about daily life or about the political situation, the crowd quickly disperses. Men run away and hide. Even here, outside the country, they imagine Eritrean spies are eavesdropping, that a misplaced word might lead the secret police to their family home.

But the UN report is unequivocal. 'Since independence,' it says, 'extrajudicial executions and arbitrary killings have been widely perpetrated.' It goes on to list those responsible: the Eritrean Army, the National Security Office, the police, the Ministry of Justice, the Ministry of Defence, and ultimately, the man who makes every decision of any importance in the country: President Isaias Afwerki himself.

Isaias Afwerki was raised in a country torn between colonial powers; an ancient land of soaring mountain peaks, cloud-hooded rainforests and muddy coastal plains – a place the size of New York State, with a vast panhandle of land stretching more than 1,000 kilometres along the waters of the Red Sea. Not only was it ideally positioned as a crossroads for trade, with European ships anchoring there after passing through the Suez Canal, it was a coastal gateway into other promising lands, like Ethiopia and British-run Sudan. Everyone wanted a piece of the action.

The Italians were late-starters in the game of modern colonialism, but eager to catch up. They were ushered into the region by Britain, which was playing various underhand territorial games in the final decades of the nineteenth century, and preferred the Italians next door to their protectorate of Sudan rather than the French. Italy's territorial acquisitions began with the busy and strategically important Red Sea port of Massawa, agreed in a secret deal with Britain in 1886. Then came a narrow sliver of coastal land further south that was to become Italian Somaliland. Four years later they pushed inland from their coastal enclave of Massawa, conquering vast swathes of territory which, on 1 January 1890, they named Eritrea. Although parts of the territory had previously been under the control of the Abyssinian empire (the northern half of today's Ethiopia), most had not. It was a loose collection of diverse and often competing ethnic and religious interests, ruled over by local chieftains. The coastal lowlands were known for their ancient bustling ports where traders from India, the Persian Gulf and all over East Africa haggled over ivory and rhino skins. They were inhabited largely by Muslims. The cooler plateaus and hillsides of the highlands were predominantly Coptic Christian. But within each area was a stew of different tribes, languages and loyalties. There were Islamized pastoral nomads in the Barka region of the west who launched cattle raids against their Christian neighbours. Descendants of the Ottoman Turks worked the port of Massawa, but also inhabited the mountainous highlands of Sahel in the north. Various fragmented Sultanates had taken root on the parched volcanic wilderness of the southern coast along the Ethiopian border. In short, the people of this newly constituted land had little in common but for 'the accident of their residence in the territory Italy conquered and named Eritrea.'[3]

On acquiring its new possession, Italy signed treaties establishing territorial borders with Sudan to the north and west, and Ethiopia to the south. It then set to work expropriating vast tracts of Eritrean land as *terre domaniale*, crown property, for the production of cotton, tropical fruits and coffee, which was cultivated by cheap indigenous labour and exported back home to Italy. In the capital, Asmara, located on the northwestern edge of the highlands, an early form of apartheid was introduced. Superior whites occupied the capital's newly developed European quarter, with its clean water and smart new buildings, while Eritreans were confined to the sprawling slums and alleyways of the 'native' districts. The Italians wasted little time in exploiting their new supply of manpower, forcibly conscripting thousands into their colonial army to help seize further territory in Africa. The Eritrean *ascari* fought under Italian officers, seven thousand of them in the disastrously failed attempt to take over Ethiopia, which ended for the time being with the wiping out of an Italian army at Adwa in 1896. Four thousand Eritreans were killed or wounded in the conflict, and several hundred were taken as Ethiopian prisoners of war, during which time they were mutilated either by castration, or by having their right hands and left legs amputated. The next Italian territorial offensive came in 1911 when they conscripted 60,000 Eritrean *ascari* for the conquest of what is now Libya.

However, Italy's designs on Ethiopia were far from over. Ethiopia was one of only two nations that had remained independent during the scramble for Africa, the other being Liberia. Italy's fascist dictator, Benito Mussolini, in much need of a popular triumph, viewed the territory as the missing piece of a jigsaw – once joined to Eritrea and Italian Somaliland it would give him a sweep of territory in the Horn of Africa that would represent an unrivalled power base in the Red Sea area and much influence in the Middle East. The question was, how to acquire it?

In a blatantly provocative act, his troops built a fort in Ethiopian territory at the Walwal Oasis in 1930, which they staffed with Italian-conscripted Somali *ascari*. The wary Ethiopians stationed themselves nearby but chose to leave the fort alone. Then, in 1934, the inevitable happened. A clash erupted between the two sides, leaving 110 Ethiopians dead, and 50 Italians and Somalis. It looked very much like the start of a territorial offensive by Mussolini, but just when a unified voice of international condemnation was required, the world fell silent. Britain and France slunk away, hoping they might still retain Italy as an ally in the looming conflict with Germany. While the League of Nations prevaricated, Mussolini used the time to organize an attack.

Ethiopia's emperor, the self-styled 'King of Kings' Haile Selassie, could see what was coming. He raised 500,000 conscripts to fight alongside his army of 300,000 professional soldiers. Most new recruits were armed with spears and bows and arrows, while his soldiers carried pre-1900 rifles. Their communications and transport were woefully primitive and unreliable. In contrast, the Royal Italian Army possessed cutting-edge technology and the most advanced weapons money could buy.

In the early hours of 3 October 1935, Italian forces stormed across the Mareb River, which runs along the border between Eritrea and Ethiopia, and into Haile Selassie's land. They attacked using tonnes of poisonous chemicals dropped from planes and fired from artillery – the Ethiopians called it 'the terrible rain that burned and killed' – capturing city after city, until all that remained in Ethiopian hands was Addis Ababa. In early May 1936, when Italian tanks rolled into the capital, most Ethiopian troops had already fled, leaving just an underground resistance movement of 'Ethiopian Patriots' who continued guerrilla strikes against the Italians for the next five years. By this time, Haile Selassie was heading in the opposite direction, on a train of the Imperial Railway, with all the gold he could carry, fleeing for the coast and exile in Britain.

In Rome there was jubilation. Fascist youth movements marched and sang on the streets. A triumphant Mussolini announced he was merging Somaliland, Eritrea and Ethiopia into one vast colony that would be called Italian East Africa. 'At last, Italy has her empire,' he announced. 'The Italian people have created an empire with their blood. They will fertilize it with their work. They will defend it against anyone with their weapons. Will you be worthy of it?' The League of Nations felt powerless to intervene.

Mussolini considered the Eritrean capital, Asmara, the centrepiece of his new Roman empire, and set to work making it a sumptuous colonial playground. Along the city's boulevards he constructed eye-catching modernist buildings: a villa curved like the bow of an ocean liner, a petrol station with gravity-defying concrete wings. Smart European cars cruised the palm-lined streets. More Italians poured in. Eritrea was industrialized faster than any other African colony. Although Eritreans themselves were very much subjects of the Italian fascist state rather than citizens, the experience gave the diverse groups a sense of nationhood that they had hitherto not experienced. It was the birth of an Eritrean identity that would strengthen

with each successive occupation. But Mussolini's occupation was
almost over.

On 10 June 1940, the Italian leader entered the Second World
War on the side of Nazi Germany. He used his African colony as a
base from which to attack Allied forces in the region. First he took
British Somaliland and then began advancing into Sudan, occupying
Kassala, the strategic border town that is today the transit point for
migrants. But British forces soon drove the Italians back, through
Somaliland and Eritrea, and finally into Ethiopia. Assisted by
Ethiopian Patriots and de Gaulle's Free French Forces, they liberated
Addis Ababa in May 1941. Haile Selassie, 'God's chosen emperor',
returned from exile at a country house in Bath to reclaim his throne.

Britain was now the occupying power in Eritrea. British forces set
up a POW camp in Asmara, and went about capturing the remnants
of Mussolini's army, some of whom stayed on to fight a guerrilla campaign against the Allies, hiding out on the mountainsides of Eritrea and
Ethiopia from where they would launch ambushes and assassinations.

Just weeks earlier, the British had been fighting Eritrean *ascari*
conscripted by the Italians; now they needed to transform themselves
into a benevolent, inclusive administration.

There was a mini-revolution in education. The British administration established fifty-nine elementary schools, tripling the number
that the Eritreans had had before. The old syllabus, with its focus on
'Great Italians', was torn up and thrown away. People were exposed
to many diverse cultures as Allied soldiers from India, Free France
and Somalia passed through. Political parties were legalized, as
were labour unions and independent newspapers, none of which the
Ethiopians next door were fortunate enough to enjoy. Eritreans were
encouraged to take part in governance. Administrative councils were
established. Local chieftains were given back limited control. It all fed
into a heightened sense of nationhood, quickly politicizing a people
whose self-expression had been anaesthetized under the Italians.

However, while Britain was feeding Eritrean minds, it wasn't
feeding their stomachs. An economic depression gripped the country.
Thousands of unemployed *ascari* suddenly needed to be housed and

fed. The cost of living soared by 600 per cent, and social divisions began to appear that would have a profound effect on the nation's future. The mainly Muslim traders of the coastal region continued to live relatively well from business at the ports. But the Christians in the towns and rural areas of the highlands were hit by unemployment and hunger. They viewed the Muslims as 'exploiters'. The acrimony had begun.

The British administration then began stripping the country of its assets to assist other territories in the British Empire and aid the war effort on other fronts. An aerodrome was dismantled and shipped to India for use by the Royal Indian Air Force in bombing raids against the Japanese in Burma. Rail tracks were ripped up and exported to Kenya, where Britain had relocated its entire Eastern Fleet. A floating dock and two giant cranes were divided between Malta and Egypt to help boost key Allied supply lines.[4] Even today, some Eritreans speak of suing the British government for reparations.

As the war came to a close, one question above all others dominated Eritrean lives. Who would govern once the British had gone? On the face of it, there seemed little doubt. In the coffee shops of Asmara they reminded each other of the leaflets dropped by British aircraft during the war:

> Eritrean soldiers, listen! Desert the Italians and join us!... You people who wish to live under the flag of His Imperial Majesty and to have your own flag, we give you our word you shall be allowed to choose what government you desire.[5]

In the event, deciding Eritrea's future was going to be an extremely messy business. Haile Selassie saw the end of the war as an opportunity to expand his landlocked Ethiopian empire and give himself invaluable access to the Red Sea. Eritrea, he said, belonged historically to Ethiopia. He sent a flood of telegrams to the British, urging them to return the territory to its rightful owner. But the Allied powers had their own interests to serve. Each saw Eritrea's strategic position as a potential tool of empire.

The Eritreans themselves were only half-heartedly consulted about whose governance they would prefer. Most of the mainly Christian highlanders favoured a union with their Christian neighbours in Ethiopia. Most of the Muslim lowlanders wanted independence. But in the end, their views hardly mattered. Eritrea's fate would be decided by the fledgling United Nations. In December 1950, under pressure from Britain and the US, the UN announced that Eritrea would become part of an Ethiopian Federation ruled from Addis Ababa by Haile Selassie. The country was supposed to retain much of its autonomy and be treated as an equal partner to Ethiopia, not as a subordinate. But in his spectacular palace in Addis Ababa, surrounded by liveried servants, the quietly ruthless and expansionist King of Kings had other plans.

Isaias Afwerki was just seven years old when the British finally left Eritrea in 1952. Thousands gathered on the streets of Asmara that day to witness the truly surreal spectacle of the British administrator, top hat in hand, lowering the Union Flag as a British military band swung by, dressed in tiger-skin capes, twirling drumsticks as if it were a summer parade in a provincial English town. Afwerki's family were highlanders and Christians, and lived in a middle-class suburb of the capital. Their son showed early promise. He was athletic and articulate, but he also displayed flashes of temper. His academic abilities, though not dazzling, were enough to gain him access into the elite Prince Makonnen secondary school in Asmara, which was to become a hotbed of nationalist dissent.

Within months of British withdrawal, Haile Selassie began a systematic erosion of Eritrean freedoms. Writers and journalists were jailed. Trade unions were banned. The Eritrean flag was lowered, the Ethiopian flag raised. The two main Eritrean languages, Tigrigna and Arabic, were outlawed and replaced with Ethiopia's Amharic. The Eritrean assembly had its powers slowly stripped away. Britain and America, key allies of the Ethiopian emperor, did nothing to stop it. By the time Isaias Afwerki was coming of age, the country was being run as a police state, and things were about to get even worse.

In November 1962, Haile Selassie abandoned any pretence that Eritrea was part of a federation. He disbanded its assembly and annexed the country. Ethiopian troops flooded in to put down any opposition. At a time when the rest of Africa was being decolonized by Europeans, Eritrea was being frog-marched in the opposite direction. By the time the young Isaias Afwerki was sixteen years old, his country had become the fourteenth province of Ethiopia.

It set the nationalist cause alight.

At Prince Makonnen school, a small cell of young activists began to mobilize themselves in an anti-Ethiopian underground movement. Their operations were carried out largely at night. They daubed graffiti on buildings, and left piles of leaflets in public places to be discovered when the sun rose over Asmara. With Ethiopian soldiers regularly on the streets, it was an extremely risky business.

Isaias was making a name for himself more for his volcanic temper than his academic abilities. He was a tall, physically dominating teenager, but also something of a loner, tongue-tied and shy in the company of his contemporaries. He spoke so quietly the rest could hardly hear what he was saying. When they organized political meetings he would sit on the sidelines, intimidated by their precocious understanding of Eritrean history. His adoption by the inner circle came quite suddenly, and had little to do with his political beliefs.

In physics lessons, they had an American Peace Corps teacher, who would announce his pupils' marks in front of the whole class. Isaias rarely performed well in homework, but on this occasion he was awarded a particularly poor mark. When it was read out to the class, he rose from his desk, walked quietly to the front and slapped the teacher in the face. Such a defiant, anarchic recruit was just what the young activists required. He joined the others, and soon they began organizing student strikes and demonstrations in the capital. These were the future leaders of the Eritrean armed struggle taking their first, hesitant steps.

Away from the highlands, other groups of Eritrean nationalists were already coming together, and acquiring weapons. Muslim exiles in Cairo, galvanized by Haile Selassie's ban on political parties and trade unions, had left for Egypt and a taste of Colonel Nasser's popular Arab nationalism as early as 1958. A decision was taken in December 1959 to create a *Jabha*, or Front, that would become the famous ELF, the Eritrean Liberation Front. Organized from Cairo, it undertook its first guerrilla engagement in September 1961, when Hamid Idris Awate, a former Eritrean *ascari*, regarded as the father of the Eritrean armed struggle, led a unit of eleven peasant fighters in a fierce battle with Ethiopian soldiers on Mount Adal. The fight continued for seven hours and ended in stalemate, but the bravery of his small band of guerrillas inspired many more to join the struggle. The call to arms was spread by word of mouth through Muslim areas of Eritrea. Eritrean police officers were prized recruits, coming, as they did, ready-armed. More weapons were acquired from Syria and Sudan. But the Christian half of the country was not affected. The two communities were separate and distinct. The ELF was an almost exclusively Muslim group.

It was students from the Prince Makonnen secondary school who bridged the gap. Situated in the mainly Christian highlands, the school fell outside the ELF's traditional recruitment area. But the students were self-starters. Their nationalism grew out of personal experience. It spread quickly from school to school, opening up a home front right in the heart of the Eritrean capital. Inspired by news of ELF successes the students began organizing themselves into their own ELF cells. By the mid-1960s the ELF was attracting many Christian recruits too. Young men and women were signing up for a war of independence that would go on for the next thirty years.

Mesfin Hagos was a bright but surly youth, comfortable in his own company and confident enough to handle himself in a fight. He needed to be. Mesfin found himself at school in the capital city of the enemy, Addis Ababa, and the other pupils, all of them Ethiopian, wouldn't let him forget it. For them, being an Eritrean made him a misfit, 'a child of the Italian Empire' they called him, 'a product of Italian fascism'. Mocked and isolated, he began to study his ancestry and became passionate about Eritrea's right to a separate, autonomous state.

Mesfin had heard rumours about the Eritrean Liberation Front. The problem was, it was so secret he had no clue how to find it. On the streets of Addis Ababa, any loose talk about the ELF would be met with a visit from Haile Selassie's security services. The emperor knew that Eritrean nationalism was beginning to spread through his schools and universities, not only in Province 14, but in his capital city too. Anyone suspected of involvement would be neutralized swiftly.

One day Mesfin struck up a conversation with an elderly Eritrean man in a coffee shop. Nothing controversial, just reminiscences of home. He bumped into the same man again. They chatted, and nudged each other towards a few political matters. After several meetings, Mesfin plucked up the courage to ask the man if he had heard of the ELF. There was a pause. Mesfin has never forgotten the older man's response.

'You are speaking to a person who is one of them.'

Mesfin left the coffee shop in a hurry, carrying a handwritten letter of introduction addressed to the local ELF commander. He was soon in the hands of the ELF recruitment network, spirited off to Kassala at the foot of the mountains on the Sudanese border, with the ELF guerrillas who were gathering in exile.

Isaias Afwerki would take a different route. He had reluctantly made his way from the provincial capital to Addis Ababa to attend college in 1965. As the location of the country's only university, he had been left with little choice. Every Tuesday evening at 8 p.m., a small cell of nationalist students would hold clandestine ELF meetings at the back of a local teashop. Isaias would turn up late, if at all. They assumed he was disinterested. Then, in October 1966, after failing his first-year exams, he contacted an old friend, Wolde-Yesus Ammar, to ask if he would be good enough to accompany him to the bus station. Isaias told his friend he was going on a long journey and wanted someone to wave him off. In fact, he, too, was leaving for Kassala in Sudan to become a guerrilla fighter for the ELF.

Military camps were erected around the border town. Isaias and Mesfin joined other young recruits, cooking on open fires, singing songs about Eritrean folk heroes, and studying Marx, Engels and Lenin, books that quickly became the fighters' sacred texts. While their leaders grappled with organizing a few hundred untrained guerrillas to take on Haile Selassie's professional army, the new recruits debated philosophy, and awaited their first consignments of weapons.

They were old British army rifles. The recipients took them and cleaned them, and nursed them back to life. They didn't realize that a rifle only became available when it was retrieved from the hands of a former owner, lying dead on the battlefield.

Isaias and Mesfin were soon armed, placed in field units, and dispatched over the border into Eritrea. They ambushed small groups of Ethiopian soldiers in daring raids, and then melted away into the wilderness, sleeping rough in caves and mountain hideaways, trapping animals and collecting rainwater. This was bush war at its purest and most primitive. Ammunition was in such short supply that they salvaged old bullets, carefully removed the casing, and scraped inside the pink heads of matches so the phosphorous would act as a propellant.

I met Mesfin Hagos at a workman's café in a bleak north London suburb. Aged sixty-eight, with metallic curls and the remnants of a proud brush-moustache, he sat at a formica table among the tattooed builders and the pushchair mums: slow, purposeful, still an oak of a man with a voice used to being listened to. In the old photos he had a wayward, dusty Afro, and the same intimidating stare. Invariably, he was sitting alongside Comrade Isaias in field camps and political meetings, among filthy, wild-eyed men recently returned from action. Mesfin explained the turbulent years that defined Eritrea's future, and raised him and Isaias to the status of legends.

The ELF was, in the early days, still seen as representing the Muslim half of Eritrea. It was the Muslims who saw themselves as the natural opposition to Emperor Haile Selassie, the Christian, pro-Western occupier. They felt doubly wronged, persecuted both for being Eritrean and for worshipping a different god. The Muslims in camp would remind their Christian colleagues that the movement had been founded by Hamid Idris Awate in Cairo, under the protection of Colonel Nasser. It was, they said, a Muslim army. Christians like Mesfin and Isaias felt discriminated against. 'Before I went to [the camp in] Sudan,' said Isaias, 'the ELF was something like a magic organization to me – maybe some kind of fairy tale – but the first day I arrived I became frustrated. People began telling me about the ugly nature of the ELF, and Kassala became a nightmare for me. For some reason we were ostracized, even accused of being agents for Ethiopia.'

Broadly speaking, neither Muslims nor Christians were particularly devout. Isaias didn't attend church, and nor did any of his colleagues. Religion was just a convenient shorthand through which to define a person's tribe, schooling and social class. Distrust between the two was more about ancestral antagonisms, lifestyle and choice of regional allies than sincerely held religious beliefs. The Muslims tended to look to nearby Arab countries for support; the Christians, who had once looked to Ethiopia, were left isolated in the region. Religious and tribal labels were significant in those early years of the ELF because whoever seized power was expected to impose their own culture on the rest, and reward members of their own tribe.

Despite these tensions, the mainly Muslim ELF leaders identified both Isaias and Mesfin as future commanders. The pair were selected to undergo training in the People's Republic of China, and arrived at the Nanjing Military College at the height of the Cultural Revolution. It was a time when the Maoist Red Guard was purging the country of intellectuals, artists and writers, and targeting 'revisionists' in the Communist Party. Millions were transferred to work camps and tortured. 'Spies' and 'running dogs' were hunted down and forced to confess to imagined crimes in front of packed stadiums. Urban youths were relocated to the countryside as forced labour for state-run farms. Most of the killing took place between 1966 and 1969, with a death toll estimated between 400,000 and 1.5 million. Isaias and Mesfin were on separate trips, but both arrived in 1967, at the height of the tumultuous campaign. Both saw the trip to China as a great privilege, and were treated as honoured guests of the regime. There is a photograph of Isaias, dressed in an old anorak and surrounded by earnest-looking young Chinese men in high-collared Mao tunics on a misty mountainside. He and Mesfin were to spend six months studying Mao and Marx, along with the science of explosives, and the fundamentals of guerrilla warfare. Key to their future survival in the field back home in Eritrea would be learning how to operate behind enemy lines, and recruiting the masses to rise up against an occupying army. But shortly after their return to camp in Kassala, Christian recruits began disappearing.

In the workman's café in London, Mesfin Hagos sips his sugar-free lemonade. He speaks in voluminous detail, eyes focused on a dirty wall behind me. It has become the wall of a room in Kassala, a stale, empty room beside the headquarters of ELF Command.

One morning, sometime in the mid-1960s, he was invited to lunch with a group of ELF leaders. All were Muslim, but it hardly mattered to him at the time. Mesfin was scheduled to return to the field, and was busy organizing food supplies and trying to link up with other members of his unit. He politely turned down the lunch invitation, but two of his Christian comrades agreed to attend.

Later that afternoon, Mesfin was passing by the building and decided to see if anyone was still around. The place was a room of rough furniture and dirty walls. It was empty. But he noticed a layer of sawdust on the floor.

'I wiped it away,' he says, brushing the formica table gently with his giant hands, 'and underneath the sand...' he rolls his thumb against his fingers to recall the stickiness and struggles to finish the sentence. 'The ELF had its own assassination squads.'

In Eritrea, Haile Selassie's forces unleashed terror against his increasingly independent-minded province, targeting the Muslim low-lands from where most ELF members were recruited. Villagers were rounded up and executed. Entire villages were obliterated by aerial bombing. Livestock and people were machine-gunned from passing helicopters. But in the Kassala camp, instead of focusing on defending their countrymen from the Ethiopian enemy, the ELF was imploding.

Highland and lowland recruits, Christians and Muslims, all feared each other. For their protection, groups of like-minded comrades forged secret alliances. The dispute is more accurately described as one between young urbanite students from Asmara, and old Muslim leaders educated in Arab capitals rather than religious conflict. It was a power struggle for control of the liberation movement, and Isaias and Mesfin, as potential leaders, would have been inviting targets. In 1969 several splinter groups abandoned Kassala under cover of night. One unit set up camp on a remote mountainside south of Asmara. It consisted of just twelve men, all Christians from the highlands. Their leader was Isaias Afwerki.

When the ELF leadership heard about the defection of one of their most promising recruits, they were incensed, believing that any sectarian differences could still be overcome. They accused Isaias of narcissism, of being obsessed with power, of wanting to form a movement in his own image. When word reached Isaias's old friend, Wolde Ammar, back in Addis Ababa, he was not surprised. After he had dropped Isaias at the bus stop that day, he had returned to friends in the ELF cell and predicted, 'Isaias won't last long. Either he will desert, or create his own splinter group and divide the struggle in two.'[6]

Isaias's departure from Kassala, however, had been precipitated by genuine fear. His primary aim, of defeating the Ethiopians, was shared with the ELF and there was no credible prospect, at that moment, of him usurping their position as the paramount liberation movement; they had 4,000 fighters, compared with Isaias's bare dozen.

In the remote Dankalia region of the Great Rift Valley, orange lakes of lava bubbled through the earth's thin crust. Hot winds raced across fields of cinders picking up clouds of stinging dust and depositing them around the foothills of long-extinct volcanoes. Few could survive outdoors here for more than a few hours without water and shelter. The temperature regularly reached 50°C, and the only surface liquids were sulfurous yellow pools which vaporized into spectacular spires of salt. It was located on a narrow strip of Haile Selassie's Province 14, between the Red Sea and the rest of Ethiopia. As such it was symbolic, and would block the emperor's access to the sea should the Eritreans manage to regain independence.

This was the landscape that Isaias Afwerki chose for an historic meeting of ELF defectors in 1971. Three different groups attended, having walked for days through one of the most hostile regions on earth. They gathered in a remote village, eating camel meat roasted over an open fire, and discussed the future of the movement late into the night. They agreed to form a new guerrilla group to rival the ELF. Its name was to be the Eritrean People's Liberation Front, the EPLF, and although, at twenty-five years old, Isaias was deemed too young and inexperienced to be its leader, he would be its driving force. As the guerrillas toasted the creation of their new movement that night, among them sat a young fighter who would become Isaias's second-in-command: Mesfin Hagos. But what to do about their former comrades in the ELF?

The Dankalia unit of ELF guerrillas led a nomadic lifestyle interspersed with gunfights around the volcanic wilderness, weeks of boredom followed by intense moments of sensory overload. Among their number was Goitom Mebrahtu: a hard man with a ready sense of humour, who had learned to live on bread made from flour and saltwater which he baked on rocks heated by the sun. For Goitom the breakaway of the EPLF wasn't to be taken seriously. He had heard of Isaias and thought the whole thing a vanity project. The discord between Muslims and Christians was largely contrived, in his opinion, by a disruptive young man bent on forming his own army. After all, Goitom himself was Christian, and by this time, with the rush of highland recruits joining the ELF, he believed Christians were in the majority. But it wouldn't be long before he encountered men from the new, rival splinter group while out patrolling the region.

The first encounter was brief. The ELF invited their rivals from the EPLF for a meeting to co-ordinate activities.

'Welcome,' they said, when Isaias's men arrived.

'You didn't invite us here,' responded Isaias's men. 'Our Kalashnikovs invited us here.'

The tone was set.

The two groups would run into each other in oasis towns, never quite sure whose side the other group was on. Neither had uniforms; they wore shorts and T-shirts with belts of ammunition hanging around their necks. It was, perhaps, symbolic that two armies with a common aim and a common enemy couldn't tell each other apart.

'Who are they?' shouted one of Goitom's men as they cruised through a marketplace in a pickup one day.

The men they were pointing at seemed to be having a similarly hectic conversation across the other side of the road. One of them fired a shot. Goitom's men responded with a storm of bullets, and raced off into the desert.

The Dankalia region became a dangerous battleground. Isaias's men wanted control of its Red Sea port, a valuable source of revenue from tolls on ships passing through. They also sought to control, or at least tax, the trade in salt. ELF leaders tried to negotiate a power-sharing pact, dividing income and preventing unnecessary deaths, but Isaias's men kept breaking the agreement.

One day in 1980, Goitom and his men stumbled upon an EPLF base hidden away in a small oasis. It consisted of just four wooden huts, encircled by a trench. They decided to attack.

That night, fifty ELF fighters stretched out in a line across the desert, silently taking their positions, guns at the ready. Goitom found he could see in the dark, as if some dormant, animal instinct had been lit by the prospect of death. He was armed with a pistol in one hand and a Chinese hand-grenade in the other. The only sound was that of their own bare feet, treading carefully in the ash. The ground still felt warm from the searing heat of the previous day. The moon was out, and there was a little light wind. On the horizon was a clump of black trees and bushes around a shallow pool. The air smelled of sulphur. Goitom glanced down his line of men. They were keeping their positions, trying not to hurry. He felt for the metal clip on top of his grenade, and instinctively slipped his thumb through the ring. Still 100 metres to go. He could make out the shape of the huts now, made of grass-bound branches. They were larger than expected. Room for perhaps twenty men. Crack. The first shot sounded like the bough of a tree snapping under tremendous pressure. The oasis erupted with the sound of automatic gunfire. The EPLF had been waiting for them.

Goitom ran forward, hurling his grenade as he went. In the chaos he didn't even see where it landed. A man went down beside him. Goitom picked up his dead colleague's Kalashnikov and used that instead of the handgun. He leaped into a trench. As he pulled himself out, he felt something cold on the inside of his leg. No pain, just the sense that something was running down his thigh.

Three guerrillas ran over to him. He assumed they were from the other side, and drew his pistol ready to shoot himself.

Goitom tells me his story in a London pub. He's in his mid-sixties now, with a hole the size of an inkwell in the side of his leg. Even while recuperating in a Yemeni hospital, he considered the ELF and EPLF brothers, and was optimistic they would eventually reunite. It would have made sense, he says, each would have acted as a counterbalance to the other, preventing either from taking absolute power or giving birth to a dictator. But the quarrel between the two groups had moved away from supposed religious differences. By the end of the 1970s, the ELF had become largely Christian, and Isaias's group, although secular, attracted many Muslims – any earlier religious distinction had gone. Although issues of personality and tribal loyalty persisted, the difference was now in ideology. The ELF was a loosely organized coalition that included political views from across the spectrum. Isaias's EPLF was avowedly Marxist, with a tightly disciplined centralized structure committed to Maoist-style guerrilla warfare.

In Addis Ababa the enemy was changing shape. In September 1974, God's chosen emperor had been evicted from his Imperial Palace and jailed in a military coup. An even more brutal regime – a committee of apparently Marxist Ethiopian military officers, 'the Derg' – had replaced him. They set about systematically killing anyone connected with Haile Selassie, and then began executing each other in a barbaric scramble for power. The strongman who eventually emerged was Mengistu Haile Mariam. Mengistu oversaw the jailing and execution of tens of thousands of opponents in the 'Red Terror' purge. Then he turned his attention to the guerrilla groups fighting for independence in Province 14.

Out in the field, Isaias Afwerki's EPLF desperately needed to gather more recruits. Isaias still wasn't leader, but considered himself the group's visionary and theorist. As such, he decided to compose an EPLF manifesto to help increase numbers and formalize its political agenda.

We can imagine him hunched over his typewriter, a pile of Maoist and Marxist literature by his side. He is dressed in military fatigues, sitting at a makeshift table beneath a canvas shelter on a remote mountainside. Music drifts in from the nearby clearing, where his comrades are seated on ammunition cases, singing along to handmade instruments as they clean their weapons. Isaias punches the keys of his typewriter. *Our Struggle and its Goals*, he writes. He wants this to be received as a grand theory that might one day bear his name:

> The impoverished and the workers rise against the rich, as do the slaves against the masters. The village militates against the chief, the weak unite against the powerful and the new erupts over the old. It is an historic truth.

He grandly addresses his manifesto to 'the people of the world'. But it is his portrayal of his former colleagues in the leadership of the ELF that makes for the most interesting reading. 'They cultivated differences and discord and aggravated them increasingly,' he writes.

> They became increasingly preoccupied with the devising of schemes aimed at gratifying their lust for power. In an effort to capitalize on [ethnic differences], they magnified these minor contradictions and then

used them to manipulate the liberation forces. This corrupt pursuit of
personal aggrandizement eventually led to dissensions within the front.

They are, of course, the very same allegations that the ELF levelled
against Isaias himself.

There is archive footage of Isaias from the time. He seems more
like a mumbling academic than a volatile, visionary leader: narrow-
shouldered, neat-haired, hesitant under the gaze of the lens. It was
1975. He had just been appointed chairman of the EPLF's Military
Committee, and was delivering a stone-dry tour of standard-issue
1970s Maoist Marxism, in the form of an educational film: 'We must
build a society that is free from exploitation of man by man,' he
recites over pictures of a tractor. 'Self-reliance is the order of the day.'
No Gaddafi flourish, none of Mugabe's intellectual arrogance, just
quiet, unblinking austerity. But to his largely uneducated followers it
was hugely inspirational.

There was no warning, nothing in Dawit Isaak's behaviour to explain
why he had suddenly disappeared. He was an A-grade student from
a middle-class suburb of Asmara, a boy so smart the other kids
found him too intimidating to play with. Dawit spent his spare time
sitting beneath a bougainvillea writing poetry. After school he helped
at his parent's Italian delicatessen, selling thin-sliced ham, goat's
cheese and fat green olives. But just recently he had begun asking
uncomfortable questions.

'Where is everyone?' he had said to his mother, after returning
from the empty streets where boys normally played football. Then
to neighbours, 'Where's your brother?' 'Your father, we haven't seen
him for months; is he coming back?' Shutdown shops, abandoned
cars, litter blowing through the streets. Asmara's inhabitants were
retracting into their homes like turtles into their shells.

Asmara still had its own Eritrean police, but they were employees
of the Ethiopian state. They could do nothing about the extrajudicial
killings committed by bands of Ethiopian security officials. Instead

they were reduced to traffic duties and investigating scuffles that took place over the dwindling supplies of food. Far away in Addis Ababa, Mengistu viewed Asmara as an infected wound that needed to be gouged and cleaned.

The exodus from Asmara could not be defined by age or gender. Men slipped away at night through the backstreets into the grassy plains beyond, and then hiked up into the mountains where the camps were based. Young girls were as likely to run off and join the ELF and EPLF as were young boys. Between 1974 and 1977, the population of Asmara dropped by almost two-thirds. The majority of those were leaving to become guerrilla fighters. Among them was a teenage Dawit Isaak. As a result, his mother went into steady decline. 'If you find him, bring him home,' she would say, to other young men heading for the hills, 'even if he is dead; at least then we can bury his body.' Dawit had chosen to join Isaias's EPLF. He couldn't have done so at a more dangerous moment.

The swelling numbers of recruits were causing a headache for Isaias, Mesfin Hagos and the other EPLF leaders. They didn't have enough guns to go round, and the whole organizational structure was better-suited to a small band of trained and motivated guerrillas. Of particular concern to Isaias was the influx of students and intellectuals.

Ideologically, they came from the same place, but they had preconceived ideas about how the EPLF should be run. They wanted debates on every aspect of the group's organization, committees to formalize its rules, votes and collective decision-making. None of that suited Isaias at all. His approach was for the core leadership to make decisions and impose them on the rest, Soviet-style democratic centralism, without consultation or appeal. There wasn't time to listen to opposing views. They were at war. Fierce discipline was required.

The students had expected to live like Che Guevara, in a world of Marxist literature and open debate. They were progressives, with an internationalist outlook. The men who greeted them at camp were tough, scowling soldiers, in need of a readily compliant workforce.

Some students dared stand their ground. They were given the disparaging label *Menkae*, which meant bats: blood-sucking demons, spiriting themselves through the night and holding secret meetings while the good men of the EPLF were fast asleep. The name caught on. *Menkae* were mocked and bullied. The leaders accused them of being spies, trying to undermine the liberation movement on behalf of Ethiopia. Some even said they were Cold War agents, working for the CIA. A security unit was set up, and suspects put under surveillance. Based on little evidence, and often unreliable testimonies, *Menkae* were detained in specially built EPLF prisons attached to guerrilla camps. They were beaten, whipped and starved to death.

An American journalist who spent three and half months with the EPLF at that time wrote, 'When I left the EPLF zone and got back to Port Sudan I felt as though I had just gotten out of prison.'[7]

In 1977, the men alleged to be key leaders of the *Menkae* were rounded up and detained. The EPLF needed to decide their fate. It was left to a committee chosen by Isaias, who by then had been elevated to vice-secretary general of the movement. The decision was taken that the *Menkae* should be sentenced to death.

During a seven-year period of purges, the EPLF killed an estimated 3,000 of its own fighters. Mesfin Hagos remembers these events clearly, and insists that they need to be understood in their context. His fighters were sandwiched between the ELF and the Ethiopians, being attacked on two fronts. It was 'a time of survival and death', he says. In the circumstances, the *Menkae* were jeopardizing the possibility of achieving an independent Eritrea.

Later that same year, 1977, the EPLF were on the cusp of doing just that. Using Mao-style tactics – small bands of guerrillas in constantly shifting mobile warfare, escalating to large-scale assaults on Ethiopian positions – the EPLF had liberated every important town and city in Eritrea. Men and women had taken to the streets, celebrating imminent victory. All they needed was Asmara. Their fighters were already massing at its gates.

Then, suddenly, the entire conflict was turned on its head.

Under Haile Selassie, the Ethiopian military had been funded by the Americans in return for strategic Cold War support. Now, with Mengistu at the helm, the Soviet Union was their friend. Moscow was eager to help its newly acquired ally. It didn't matter that it was supplying arms to fight Marxist guerrillas. This was an important foothold in east Africa, and all the more satisfying for having been poached from the Americans. Throughout the closing months of 1977, Soviet assistance arrived on a spectacular scale. They donated dozens of supersonic fighter aircraft, $2 billion-worth of arms and ammunition, and sent hundreds of military advisors. More support arrived from Cuba and East Germany. Almost overnight, the Ethiopians became the largest and most well-equipped army in sub-Saharan Africa.

Isaias had little choice. He ordered his fighters into tactical retreat. On foot, pushing heavy artillery, and carrying crates of ammunition on their backs, they walked 600 kilometers, returning to positions they had held five years before. The decision wasn't greeted with scorn by Isaias's comrades. Quite the reverse; it had saved his men from near-certain annihilation. Isaias had made a strategic sacrifice of territory that enabled the EPLF to conserve its assets, regroup and plan its next step. It is still remembered by his supporters today as a defining moment in his ascent to greatness.

On a torpid day in 1978, stray dogs were all that wandered through the decaying Italian quarter of Asmara. It felt like the province was gradually being strangled into submission. Few even dared leave their homes to find food. Then, strolling nonchalantly through the front door of his family home, came Dawit Isaak; thinner, with yellow bruising around his face and dressed in rags that seemed to have been baked in mud. Before he could tell them about the liberation movement, and his spell in an Ethiopian jail, his mother gave him the sternest telling off of his life. During the next few years, Dawit was to see profound changes in his home city.

With much of the rest of Ethiopia terrorized into submission, Mengistu now turned his full attention to taming the recalcitrant folk of his Eritrean province. Ethiopian soldiers roamed the streets of Asmara, hunting down suspected nationalists and hanging them by piano wire. Gangs of secret police smashed down doors and hauled people away, taking them to police stations from which they would never reappear.

The whole of Asmara was being punished for the activities of the EPLF. In 1982, Mengistu decided to relocate his entire regime to the city and arrived by helicopter, announcing that 'the secessionist bandits will be smashed within ten days'. Flush with Soviet money, he deployed 120,000 troops into the province. They attacked EPLF positions with poisonous gasses. The guerrillas fought back, wearing homemade charcoal masks. Dawit Isaak's family took a last look around their home, packed a few belongings and fled. Soon after they were on a boat bound for Europe.

Above the clouds in Eritrea's north, the mountain ribs stretch, row after lifeless row, skinned and bleached clean by the sun. Rocks clatter down vast scree basins. Entire hillsides slide into valleys. But follow the scars from the seasonal streams and brief rivers, into the green valleys below, and you might find a hole in a rock face, an opening framed by stones. Look closer and the stones are hand cut, and the dried streams are actually pathways, and the hole is not a hole but a door. And if you pass through that door you will find a long, narrow corridor on the other side. This is an entrance to the hidden town of Nakfa, where the EPLF's subterranean headquarters were once based.

They constructed this place after Isaias Afwerki's legendary retreat. The fighters climbed out of reach of Mengistu's patrols and dug miles of tunnels, creating underground offices, hospitals, schools and factories. Workshops were insulated with the scavenged remains of Ethiopian parachutes and powered by colonial-era generators manufactured in Birmingham. EPLF craftsmen made guns and ploughs from the wreckage of crashed fighter planes. Disabled veterans stitched military uniforms for new recruits and clothes for children. Nakfa withstood countless offensives. Mengistu's troops were defeated by the steep mountain terraces, and the invisible army that could break cover at will from any of the town's hidden caves. From Nakfa, the EPLF slowly worked its way back into Ethiopian-held territory. By this time, they had driven the remnants of the ELF out of the country. Isaias's fighters could concentrate on a single enemy.

Death often came from the skies. A metallic wind screaming through a still day... a plane arcing skywards... a thump in the soft earth, followed by an explosion and a shower of gravel. Soviet helicopters dropped napalm, flaming petroleum jelly that adhered to the skin and charred the human bodies it touched.

The EPLF stuck to its Maoist guerrilla tactics. They would dress as shepherds, in flowing nomadic robes, and ride donkeys behind enemy lines. They might buy livestock, which they would herd towards an Ethiopian position. When they were close enough, the shepherds would pull out their rifles and launch a surprise attack.

Once in control of a town, they would introduce systems of healthcare, education and food distribution. In true Maoist tradition, some of them would stay on, settle down and raise families, giving lessons in leftist politics, and converting the masses.

On the front line, men and women fighters married in the trenches. War babies born in the field became known as 'Red Flowers'. The war continued so long, right through the 1970s and '80s, that when the Red Flowers came of age, they, too, were tutored in the ways of guerrilla warfare. Several lost their lives, having known nothing but the struggle.

The watershed moment occurred in March 1988. There was a town called Afabet, a grid-work of whitewashed cottages and live-stock farms situated in a remote desert basin ringed by desolate wind-whipped mountains. Its surroundings gave it some natural protection in a region of otherwise flat, barren plains. Afabet had caught the eye of the Ethiopian military. They had decided to station the rump of their war effort there: tanks, artillery and 20,000 men. They still had several Soviet military advisors, though this was the twilight of the communist regime and their commitment to foreign adventures was weakening. From anywhere in town, the Ethiopians had visibility over the steep mountainsides, and could quickly detect any attempts to overrun them. They laid landmines around the entrance roads and fields, and placed lookouts on the mountaintops. Afabet was as close as they could get to a natural military fortress.

Commander Mesfin Hagos was viewed as the best tactical mind in the EPLF. Always outnumbered by the Ethiopians, he had pulled off some legendary military victories. By constantly stinging the enemy with small but deadly attacks, he would provoke them into lashing out with large-scale but often ill-conceived retaliation, during which the guerrillas would wait in ambush. It had the effect of turning the civilian population against the Ethiopians, and towards the under-resourced, heroic underdogs. The EPLF seemed to have more spirit, more dedication. They were fighting for an ideal, not a pay packet. Even when they captured Ethiopian soldiers, they used clever psychological tactics to further the cause. Instead of beating and killing them, they would look after them, giving them food and clean leaving quarters. As word spread, the Ethiopians realized there was no need to fight to the death and would surrender more readily.

Mesfin got word from EPLF headquarters in Nakfa that he was to attack and overrun the town of Afabet. He counted his troops, and estimated he could muster, perhaps, 5,000. It was a tiny number in comparison with the 20,000 Ethiopians inside the town. The rule of thumb was that an attacking force should have three times the number of its enemy. Mesfin had around a quarter.

He didn't need to rush. He sent a small unit of his most able men through the minefields by cover of night. They knew the patterns the Ethiopians used, and took their chances. Another team moved in behind, isolating the mines and carefully defusing them to open a route. Once the units were in town, some mingled on the streets and gathered intelligence, others camouflaged themselves in the foothills and studied troop movements. In this way, they were able to build an extensive catalogue of intelligence: positions of ammunition dumps, movements of key officers, the rotation of lookouts.

When the EPLF attacked, the Ethiopians were taken by surprise. They began to retreat, backing the tanks out of town through a narrow mountain pass. Mesfin gave orders to shell the lead tank as it tried to squeeze through. They hit it, and the vehicle burst into flames. With the pass now blocked, the rest of the convoy was trapped behind it. A hellish scene unfolded. The Ethiopians, realizing the whole of Afabet was surrounded, began to shell their own tanks and artillery to prevent them falling into the hands of the EPLF. Men leapt from blazing tanks, hair and clothes on fire, screaming for help, but meeting further friendly fire. As the panicking Ethiopian troops tried to escape, they ran straight into the EPLF line. EPLF forces swept through Afabet, tightening the noose, fighting house to house while the civilian population hid in their homes. When they arrived at the narrow mountain pass with the burning tanks they found smoldering skeletons by the side of the road.

Three days later Mesfin radioed Isaias at Nakfa headquarters to report a remarkable victory. His fighters had captured or killed 20,000 Ethiopian troops. But it would be another three years before they snuffed out the final remnants of Mengistu's army.

In May 1991, EPLF fighters marched jubilantly into Asmara to liberate its people and declare that the war was won. There was dancing and singing. Women ran from their homes to give food and water to the weary troops. The thirty-year war had cost the lives of 60,000 fighters, and 90,000 civilians.

In Gothenburg Cathedral in Sweden, Dawit Isaak spent the day sliding a brush beneath the pews, picking up sweet wrappers and polishing the marble floors. He heard news of the EPLF victory from friends, immediately excused himself from work, and raced around the city trying to raise money from other Eritrean refugees to help with the rebuilding effort back home. Isaias was the leader now, not just of a guerrilla movement, but of a newly independent country, ravaged by three decades of war. Dawit needed to get back there as soon as possible. He put on a black leather jacket and a tie patterned with silver and black barley-twist stripes and went to a photographer's studio in town. The picture came out well. He looked thoughtful, a little vulnerable, perhaps, but at least he looked like *something* to show the people back home, more than just a church cleaner. He had been writing in his spare time – poetry, journalism, a few experimental plays – now he could return to Eritrea and chronicle its first steps towards freedom.

Asmara had changed. Houses had been reduced to rubble, long grass sprouted from the boulevards, beggars and prostitutes hung around dingy bars, twisted metal and burnt-out tanks blocked the narrow streets. Dawit joined the rebuilding effort. There was an outpouring of collective industry: men and women in fatigues mixed cement and laid bricks; oil drums were recycled into plates; rusting military equipment was 'rewound' into gutters, hairpins and combs; tanks were melted down into iron girders. Salvaged cardboard and tubing from medical drips was used to make flip-flops. The war had left tens of thousands of veterans severely disabled. Blindness, mental illness and missing limbs were the most common disabilities. But even these survivors set to work on projects, continuing the self-help philosophy that had helped them to win the war.

Dawit's life raced along at a similar breathless pace to the reconstruction. He married, had a family, bought a house, and wrote optimistic articles about Eritrea's future. All his hope lay with President Isaias, and he was encouraged by what he saw.

The president was married by now, with two children, and had moved into a modest four-bedroom house located in a neighbourhood near to the government buildings. He lived among other families, his children attending the same schools, his wife shopping at the same markets. He showed no interest in exploiting his new position to become wealthy. In fact, he continued living the frugal life of a guerrilla fighter, even down to the plastic sandals he wore. He set aside his Marxist ideology, replacing it with moderate pragmatism but continuing the philosophy of self-reliance that had evolved during the war. He promised to be more pluralistic, introducing elections and open government. But trying to adapt a militarized state into a successful civilian society was going to be a challenge.

There were early signs of trouble, with suspicions that Isaias himself was struggling to adapt to civilian life. Skills that had enabled him to rally and organize a victorious guerrilla army were different from those required to run a country of 3 million peace-starved inhabitants. There was no one in his team with professional qualifications, no one who could balance a budget, no one who knew how to negotiate with the IMF or World Bank.

The most worrying aspect of Isaias's leadership was that he transplanted his military system of decision-making directly into government. For all his talk of openness, he rejected the advice and opinions of his own ministers. There was no consultation. Isaias made a decision, and instructed them to execute it. Two years after independence there was still no hint of an opposition, no judiciary, and no free press. A national assembly had been created that was supposed to be organizing elections and formally selecting the president, but it couldn't meet without Isaias's permission. He was in no hurry to give it.

Early after independence, Mesfin Hagos, by now an EPLF celebrity, became minister of defence and the president's closest political confidant. Even he wasn't allowed to make decisions in his area of responsibility. In 1995 he wrote to Isaias, warning, 'Either I am allowed to be a real minister, or I will go.' The response was silence, and he stepped down, putting all his energies instead into the national assembly, an executive made up of the leading figures of the EPLF.

To the war veterans on the streets of Asmara, Isaias was beyond criticism. Teething problems were to be expected. They still viewed him as the embodiment of the struggle. To criticize him was to criticize the dead: the EPLF martyrs. But a small group of progressive writers were becoming troubled. They had been denied a free press on security grounds, but believed enough time had elapsed to allow them to question and debate political issues openly. They began publishing articles that directly criticized Isaias. It was a risky thing to do. They were poets, playwrights and journalists, the very types he had rounded up during the war and executed.

One day in 1996 Dawit Isaak received a call. It was the president's office. Would he report straightaway? Others were summoned too, four of them. One was Dawit's best friend, the poet Joshua Fessehaye.

They were shown into Isaias's shabby office, with its bare walls and utilitarian furniture, and told to wait. Dawit had made an effort, dressing in his best jeans and blazer, and he sat among the others, chatting quietly. They had no idea what to expect.

When Isaias appeared, he was in a mood of quiet reflection. He had been thinking about their demands, he said, and although unhappy about the way they had gone about it, he had decided to agree. Not only would he grant a free press, he would help pay for an independent newspaper. At that point, a photographer entered the room, and the men posed awkwardly for a picture. Dawit is taller than the rest, arms behind his back, staring warily into the lens; beside him Joshua, bearded, with an awkward smile. In the middle stands Isaias. The writers have left a wide gap on either side, no one comfortable about standing close to him.

When news filtered through to the national assembly that an independent newspaper was being launched, its members were encouraged. They were in the process of drawing up a constitution that would bring about elections, ban torture and introduce criminal trials. Six years on from independence, it was already long overdue. And then the president surprised them again. He told them the constitution would be ratified. Not yet, of course, but when he was ready. His pretext for never doing so was just about to present itself on Eritrea's southwest border.

It began in a tiny border town located on a barren plain, a farming community grazing its cattle among the landmines. The place was called Badme.

Badme was close to the border with Ethiopia. Maybe in some strict geographical sense it was *in* Ethiopia. The residents considered themselves Ethiopian, but few outside Badme really cared. It was a remote backwater, a line of shacks clinging to a single tarmac track.

In 1998 a group of Eritrean officials were killed in mysterious circumstances nearby. Isaias viewed it as a hostile act by Ethiopian spies, who he believed were hiding among Badme's tiny population.

He ordered the town to be overrun, and sent in tanks, artillery and two brigades of soldiers. It came as a shock to his ministers, none of whom had been consulted. It was even more of a shock to the authorities in Addis Ababa, who considered Badme an Ethiopian town. They interpreted the arrival of Isaias's forces as an invasion.

The response was immediate. Ethiopia bombed Asmara airport. If Isaias had consulted his ministers, they would have cautioned against further escalation. The country was still healing after the liberation war, they were not prepared for a new conflict. But Isaias kept his own council. He launched a retaliatory air strike against an Ethiopian airport.

Days later, across the shared 620-mile border, poured thousands of Ethiopian troops. This was a full-scale invasion. The Ethiopian army swept into its former province, and began to retake towns and villages, digging in for a long war. Eritrea was losing territory because of an impetuous, belligerent decision by the very man who had built his presidency on securing his nation against the threat from the dangerous country next door. It was a catastrophic misjudgement by Isaias, and there was no one else to blame. He was president, minister of defence, commander-in-chief and military strategist.

The border war did more damage to Eritrea in two years than the war of independence had in thirty. Seventy thousand Eritreans died. A quarter of the population was displaced. The country's infra-structure, painstakingly patched together by the collective work of a war-weary population, was almost completely wiped out. Roads, buildings, train lines and hospitals were left in ruins. The country had been pushed back to Year Zero.

Isaias's response was to shut down government, cancel all demo-cratic processes, suspend the constitution and place his country on a war footing. Under the pretext of preventing further Ethiopian invasions, he decreed that all men and women between the ages of eighteen and fifty would be conscripted into the military. Gangs of security officials took to the streets to enforce the order. People were rounded up and carted off to military camps. Those who resisted were beaten and taken to jails, as were their terrified families. The entire country was transformed into a militarized state. This was conscription of a sort never seen in Africa before. The length of service would be indefinite.

It was with some trepidation that Mesfin Hagos arrived at the home of the president in March 2001. He was greeted, as usual, by the security detail positioned outside Isaias's gate. Inside he found the familiar domestic scene. Isaias welcomed him into the family room which was decorated with portraits of his three children and his wife, and motioned for him to sit down. He was offered tea or whisky, and chose the former. From the kitchen he could hear the sound of cooking. Isaias's wife would often bring them something if the meeting dragged on.

Mesfin had guessed what it was about; Isaias thought a coup was brewing.

Senior figures in the party – the EPLF had been rebranded as the People's Front for Democracy and Justice, PFDJ, shortly after independence – had finally had enough of Isaias's despotic behaviour. They were all veterans, fellow fighters who had been prepared to give him time, but since the border war, he seemed even more intent on monopolizing power. They had met discreetly, fifteen of them, and composed a letter. It accused him of 'betraying trust... abandoning collective action...' and trying to 'control preparation for elections at any cost'.

Given Isaias's erratic nature, and his tendency towards paranoia, they had been careful to keep the letter private. No one outside their circle knew of it. They had also used measured, though strong language. 'If we do not get a positive reply,' they told him, 'we shall be forced to express our views openly. We shall not be responsible for the consequences.'

The president had responded with disdain. 'In general,' he wrote, 'I only want to say that you are all making a mistake.' But it had rattled him. He summoned Mesfin because he trusted him as a go-between.

'These people are CIA and Ethiopian agents,' Isaias told him. 'That is why they are doing this.'

'No,' replied Mesfin. 'They were with me in the field. They fought with me. They are not spies.'

'Well, you need to stop them.'

Mesfin was puzzled. The president referred to the fifteen as 'them'. Surely he had looked down the list of signatures and seen Mesfin's name there. Either he could not accept his old friend was part of the group, or he was giving him a final chance to disown them.

'I am one of them,' said Mesfin. 'How can I drop the idea if it is my idea?'

The meeting ended soon after. The next letter, and Isaias's reaction to it, would change the course of Eritrean history.

In fifteen closely argued pages, it took apart every aspect of Isaias's presidency: the derailed constitution, the secrecy, the catastrophic border war, the refusal to create a judiciary, the absence of elections. The president was, they said, 'conducting himself in an illegal and unconstitutional manner'. But the authors still exercised some restraint. There was no direct threat to his position, and no suggestion they would take their grievances to the street. 'We shall continue in our struggle to establish the rule of law,' they wrote, but only through the 'legal and democratic means available'. It was signed by the same group of fifteen men, calling themselves the G-15.

Shortly after the letter was finished, Mesfin Hagos took it to the newspapers. It was the only way, he thought, that Isaias would start to listen. One of the journalists who dared to publish the letter was Dawit Isaak.

Mesfin Hagos was at Dulles Airport in Washington in 2001, waiting for a flight, when he heard the news. It was four months after the publication of the G-15 letter, and he was about to return home, having undergone medical treatment for a bad back. He had been scheduled to fly the previous week, but Al-Qaeda had attacked New York, and he had been stranded in the United States.

'They have arrested them all,' the voice said. It was his wife, desperate, tearful, phoning from Asmara. 'The G-15: they have all been taken to prison.'

Mesfin was supposed to be travelling home via Frankfurt. He decided to board the plane, and stop in Germany to reappraise the situation. He phoned his wife again as soon as he landed. 'Don't come to Eritrea,' she said. 'They will take you.'

Dawit Isaak was driving home through Asmara, with two of his children in the back, when a red car pulled in behind. His young daughter Betlehem noticed the change in her father's driving. He made a sudden U-turn. The car in pursuit did the same. Her father said nothing. He glanced at the rearview mirror, and then turned down a side street. The red car followed.

At home, Dawit parked outside his gates. The red car slowed as if to do the same, then sped off. The next morning there was a knock on the door. It was 9 a.m. and Betlehem went to answer. She saw the red car parked outside, and two men standing in the doorway.

'Does Dawit Isaak live here?' one asked. Her mother, Sofia, appeared behind her. The man repeated the question. Polite, but firm. Sofia turned and looked back into the house, towards the front room. 'My husband?' she hesitated. 'Yes,' and then added 'maybe.' The two men followed her inside.

When Dawit appeared he was wearing shorts and a T-shirt. He shook hands with the men and sat down with them. Sofia brought breakfast of mozzarella, bread and ham, and the men ate, and chatted about mundane things. At some point, while the talking continued, one of the men eased Dawit's arms behind his back, and put chains around his wrists. Dawit didn't resist. The conversation barely missed a beat. Then they rose, and escorted Dawit to the front door. 'Just a simple interview,' he called over his shoulder, 'nothing to worry about.' A week later, when he had failed to return, Sofia toured Asmara's police stations looking for him. 'You must be mistaken,' said on officer. 'You have never been married to a man with this name.'

There were more open letters to newspapers. Security officials surrounded the University of Asmara and detained 2,000 students.

Journalists were abducted. An Eritrean ambassador fled for his life. Isaias was moving against his old foes once again – intellectuals, writers, progressives – this time to stop an imagined coup. He had been preparing for this eventuality ever since the mid-1990s. Isaias had educated himself in authoritarian methods of control, studying examples from the Stasi in East Germany. Under the pretext of streamlining the army, he had demobilized his most capable and most educated officers, those he judged to be a threat, and replaced them with generals unable to read and write. No one remained in their role, or in a single geographical location for long. He rotated them, preventing friendships and alternative loyalties from developing. It meant he had an illiterate army command, but one that was in thrall to Isaias, and dependent on his patronage for their lives and careers.

He had insured himself well. During whispered conversations among members of the national assembly, they tried to ascertain the strength of Isaias's support among the military. If the opportunity were to be seized, they must be certain that senior officers would move smoothly in behind them and have Isaias arrested. Word came back from a commander they had known in the field that, although large parts of the army would support a coup, the majority would not. They concluded it would turn into a bloodbath. The moment was lost.

A month after his arrest, Dawit Isaak reappeared at home, accompanied by his jailers. He played with his children, told them they should always do their homework, picked up some towels and spare clothes, and was led outside again to the waiting car. A few weeks later the family were told he was in hospital, and were given permission to visit. His face was gaunt, even his mannerisms had changed. He had a different walk, like an animal trying to protect an injury. After that, Dawit Isaak drifted away from them, deeper into Eritrea's network of secret prisons, as did members of the G-15 – apart from Mesfin Hagos.

Eyob Bahta was a boyish, softly spoken thirty-year-old, and one of the few people who knew the fate of the G-15. He was a guard at one of Eritrea's secret prisons, a role he disliked so intensely that he fled the country – in Eritrea it's not only the inmates who try to escape but their jailers too. Eyob made it across the border to Ethiopia in 2010, where he claimed asylum and described to human rights groups what he had seen.[8]

At the start of their incarceration in 2001, he says, the G-15, along with the journalists who had published the letter, were kept in rooms at a 'training centre', from where they could see a road and vehicles and had the right to use the toilet twice a day. They assumed that they would be released soon, and so obeyed the rules. Even so, they were handcuffed twenty-four hours a day, each of them alone in a bare cell. The isolation was intensified by walls so thick that, even when they shouted to see if other prisoners were nearby, nothing could be heard. While this was happening, Isaias's security officials were on the rampage, rounding up thousands of suspected opponents and jailing them in a network of detention facilities he was constructing across the country.

Quickly, the regime built thirty of them,[9] along with military jails for each army unit and their sub-divisions, amounting to an estimated 300 or so prisons. There was a cluster around Asmara, including 'Track B', a former US storage facility near the airport, which was reported to hold draft-dodgers who had refused to serve in Isaias's conscripted army. Track B also held migrants captured attempting to cross the border to Sudan, and former EPLF fighters who were said to have voiced criticism of Isaias and his regime.

In Asmara itself was Karchele prison, six military-style blocks surrounded by high walls in a residential area. It was said to be run by Isaias's 'Special Security Unit', and housed dozens of journalists and religious prisoners. Most of the prison-building programme took place in remote and inaccessible locations, to prevent escape or attempts at rescue. Three were constructed in the vast cinder-fields of the Dankalia region, where Isaias had held the inaugural meeting of the EPLF. They transported metal shipping containers from ports on the Red Sea Coast, which were used as punishment blocks. Heated all day by the ferocious sun, prisoners would be placed inside without water, and left to themselves. Many died. Some days the metal became so hot, the prisoners' skin stuck to the floor.

In the 'training centre' where the G-15 and Dawit Isaak were being held, any hope of imminent release quickly faded. After two years of solitary confinement, said former prison guard Eyob Bahta, three of the group had died. One of them was Dawit's best friend, the bearded poet Joshua Fessehaye. He is said to have hanged himself.

The next phase of their incarceration was to be spent at a prison built especially for them. Eiraeiro, north of Asmara, is hidden in a remote cinder valley far from the nearest road. It consists of two blocks of windowless concrete cells, arranged in lines beside a dry riverbed. Each cell measures five paces by four with an airhole in the ceiling. There is a hole in the floor which serves as the toilet, and a metal sink. The prisoners are chained twenty-four hours a day. This is where Eyob was a prison guard. 'They don't even know whether it is day or night,' he told human rights workers.

The surviving members of the G-15, and the journalists, were transferred to Eiraeiro in the summer of 2003. The guards would take them food but were not allowed to talk with them. Doing so would be breaking the rules, and lead to punishment. Inmates who are ill, no matter how seriously, are given painkillers and nothing more. They sit alone, every day, with chains long enough to reach the toilet but no further.

All the G-15 were senior members of Isaias's government. Eyob says most of them have died. Some, he says, succumbed to the heat, others to unspecified medical conditions. Two committed suicide. Dawit Isaak, he says, is one of the few still alive.

It was a blowy autumn day in Gothenburg in 2015, and inside the cathedral a woman handed me a small yellow badge that carried the silhouette of a young man with an Afro haircut wearing a silver and black barley-twist patterned tie. The words 'Free Dawit' were written beneath. 'He used to work here,' she says, and shows me a book of poetry and remembrance that carries his story in the opening page. When Dawit Isaak's daughter, Betlehem, enters the building, she walks around quietly, breathing in the smell of wood polish and white lilies, and then turns to me and says, 'One day I will get married here.'

Betlehem is twenty-three now: articulate, outwardly tough, and a campaigner for her father's release. Her mother, brother, and little sister all live in Sweden. We sit in a coffee shop and discuss what she thinks has happened to her father in the years since he was taken from her in chains. 'He's still alive,' she says calmly. 'If he were dead, it would be easy for them to say, "He was ill and he died in prison", but they haven't said that.'

She has a point. Isaias Afwerki was asked directly about the whereabouts of Dawit by a Swedish journalist in 2011 and replied, 'I don't know. I don't even care where he is or what he is doing. He made a big mistake.' The use of the present tense has given Betlehem some hope.

Four years into his incarceration, when he was in the purpose-built Eiraeiro prison, the family received a phone call. It was Dawit. The conversation was brief and confusing. It seemed that he had been allowed out for a visit to hospital. He knew it would be temporary. His jailers were with him. He asked about the children, and said he was going to visit his mother and elderly grandmother. He also planned to visit his father's grave. Forty-eight hours later he was back inside, and has not been heard from since.

Isaias's paranoia has led him to jail between 5,000 and 10,000 political prisoners. There is no opposition party, and no independent journalist in the country to hold him to account. When a visiting US national was invited to an official dinner with Isaias and staff from the US embassy, she asked about the detention of two members of its staff, both of them Eritrean nationals. She reported later that the president 'glared stonily' at her and replied, 'Would you like me to hold a trial and then hang them?'

As he purges his country of imagined opposition, Isaias himself has increasingly become a recluse. He spends his days at home, painting and tinkering with gadgets and carpentry work. Sometimes he sleeps elsewhere, in safe houses around the capital. When he is away on official business, he is said to swap his food with subordinates in case it has been poisoned.

The veterans, particularly out in the countryside, still eulogize him as the leader of the glorious struggle, the man who defeated the Ethiopians in the thirty-year war, and Isaias regularly travels out to meet them, posing for photographs and listening to their everyday problems to do with farming and raising livestock. He is driven in a cavalcade of security vehicles from one destination to the next, dropping in unexpectedly, and delighting the locals. When he stays overnight, he chooses a bar, and his security detail clears the building of other drinkers. Residents in nearby homes are told to remain indoors, and Isaias sits alone, drinking whisky or beer. There is no one he trusts enough to be a friend. The closest was Mesfin Hagos, who has not returned to the country since the arrest of the G-15, and would certainly be detained if he did. He now lives in Frankfurt.

Isaias still lives a relatively frugal life, although some of his senior army officers and loyal ministers live in large, ostentatious homes. They have taken advantage of the occasional foreign construction or mining contract and Isaias allows them to do so. The patronage is small beer in comparison with other African dictatorships, but in a country of such extreme poverty, it has created and maintained a small elite, loyal to the president.

So what is driving Isaias? There are oil companies queuing up to explore a country where relatively few surveys have been done because of the endless wars. But Isaias isn't interested in personal financial gain. He sometimes lives alone in a tent, on the edge of a dam-building project which he hopes will be a testimony to his greatness. Even there, he needs to be in control, instructing the engineers and labourers, hurrying them along, trying to imbue them with the spirit of self-sacrifice.

He was the underdog guerrilla leader who, against all odds, vanquished the Soviet-backed oppressor. Now it suits him to be the embattled president, constantly on a war footing against the same aggressor. By convincing his supporters that Eritrea is still under siege, he can continue to play the heroic guerrilla leader, building his revolution while being shunned by the rest of the world. Isaias will not stand down, nor is he grooming a successor.

Mesfin Hagos was mulling over why he was spared, when the rest of the G-15 are either dead or in prison. 'I think about it a lot,' he says, spreading his fingers across the formica table in the workman's café. 'Isaias knew I was in America; he could have waited for me to return home and then made the arrests. Why did he spare me?' He repositions himself on his plastic chair and takes a sip of bottled water. 'Maybe out of fear. Because he knew I had the support of the army, and if he jailed me he knew they might respond.'

'Perhaps because you were good friends, and he wanted you to escape?' I suggest.

'We weren't friends,' says Mesfin, emphatically.

He didn't have friends. Isaias was a good person. I know him better than anyone else, but we wouldn't talk about personal things – just about the party, about work.

Isaias wanted to create society in his own image, without consultation. Since 2001, his actions have all been defensive, he can't trust anyone. He has even cut off members of his own family. Now he is emptying Eritrea of its children. He wants to be the first and only leader of Eritrea and he is creating the conditions so that, after him, the country will descend into war. He is doing the job of Ethiopia for them, destroying the state of Eritrea.

As we walk towards the Tube together along a busy north London road, Mesfin pauses at a building site. 'What do you call those?' he asks, pointing to a pile of metal shipping containers stacked high against the autumn sky. 'You know what they use those for in Eritrea?' I nod and we carry on walking.

'So hot...' he whispers, 'so hot they melt the skin.'

Acknowledgements

I vanished for long periods of time while writing this book, hiding away at the British Library or embarking on whirlwind research trips, or barricading myself into my cave-study among a sea of books with little regard for personal hygiene, surfacing only occasionally to rant about my latest Africa-related discoveries to weary friends and family, and for that I would like to apologize. My wife, Flavia, got the brunt of it and reacted with patience and encouragement, enduring many spontaneous and needy readings and always offering valuable suggestions. She countered all my frailties with a beaming smile and gusts of energy which pulled me through.

My editor, Neil Belton, allowed me the freedom to experiment at the beginning, and gradually took a firmer grip when I was drifting off course. His quietly encyclopaedic knowledge of African history – and indeed all history – was startling, and something I hope I have exploited to the full. He never tired of reading and re-reading the manuscript and offering clever suggestions.

I must also thank my agent, Georgina Capel, for encouraging me to write the book in the first place. She called me when I was under siege in Crimea, reporting on the Russian occupation for the BBC, and suggested I might want to write a book about Africa and the men who had stolen its resources. It couldn't have been further from my mind, but her enthusiasm and clear-minded persistence had me hooked on the project that very night.

Congo. On the ground I was assisted by Emery Makumeno, who tirelessly sought interviewees, as well as translating, researching and introducing me to his own family members with fascinating stories to tell. I am also indebted to Glenn Kendrick, a rare breed of diamond explorer who is also a humanitarian, and who shared with me many details of his early work during Mobutu's rule in Congo. Thanks also to Simon Taylor of IDC Holdings in London, who briefed me on his company's early diamond-mining experiences in several post-colonial African countries.

Colonial Oil. When I began research for my chapter on colonial oil I imagined I would be extremely lucky to find any of the early explorers or industry operatives still alive; after all we are talking about the immediate post-war era, and anyone sent to Africa would have been expected to possess considerable experience in the field already. I was thrilled to find the only surviving member of the Rover Boys, the geological commando unit set up by Esso, Dr Dave Kingston. He was generous with his time and his anecdotes, and in explaining the basics of oil geology. Sadly he passed away before the book was finished. I must also extend my thanks to BP, whose Linda Fernley kindly circulated an appeal to all their pensioners who had worked in Africa. That yielded many sources, and several extraordinary anecdotes. It led me to BP's Rex Brown, who invited me into his home and shared sandwiches and beer with me as he relived his days in his beloved Nigeria. It also introduced me to BP's Edgar Lloyd, an old Libya and Nigeria hand who had written several beautifully poetic stories from the time, which he was kind enough to share with me, and which provided much inspiration. David Thomas, an independent oil explorer, is a generation younger than the rest, but he furnished me with books, contacts and industry literature that were invaluable.

Libya. For much inside information on the early years of the Libyan revolution, I am indebted to David Orser, formerly of Mobil and then Occidental, who had a ringside seat on some of the biggest deals of the early Gaddafi era. I am also grateful to my fixer, Mohammed Miloud, who carried out a series of interviews on my behalf with his Uncle Atti in Tripoli, a rare survivor of the Abu Salim prison massacre who went through much psychological discomfort to relive those terrible experiences.

Nigeria. Barnaby Pace at Global Witness gave me indispensible assistance on the story of Dan Etete and his corrupt attempts to seize ownership of Nigeria's largest oil concession. The distinguished silk Mark Howard QC of Brick Court Chambers gave me an entertaining account of questioning Dan Etete at London's High Court.

Equatorial Guinea. I am grateful to Raimundo Ela Nsang, secretary general of the Equatorial Guinea opposition group, CORED, living in exile in Paris, whose father was a minister under the Macías regime. He patiently explained his family's experiences and his father's narrow escape from death. I met several other survivors who wish to remain anonymous for fear of recriminations against their families in Equatorial Guinea. The courageous former US ambassador John E. Bennett, who dared openly criticize Obiang's regime and was threatened with assassination, gave me valuable insights into the president's character, having met him on numerous occasions. Another exile, Joaquin Makuba Mavindi, spent time finding victims of Obiang in the UK, and supplying valuable background material.

For description of the landscape and geography of a country I have never been able to visit, I relied on Oscar Scaffadi's beautifully written guidebook published by Bradt Travel Guides.

Côte d'Ivoire. I am indebted to the US ambassador Herman J. Cohen, US assistant secretary of state for African affairs 1989–93, and now CEO of lobbying firm Cohen and Woods International, who generously gave me his precious time to talk about his personal experiences of Felix Houphouet-Boigny.

I must also thank the inspirational Dr Phil Clark at SOAS, whose briefing on Houphouet-Boigny convinced me that this story had to be included in the book. Also, Dr Jean Pierre Bat, who enthused in equal measure from Paris, and Dr Vincent Hiribarren, lecturer in modern African history at King's College London, who pointed me to some crucial texts.

Special thanks go to Judith and Philip Chapman, who were young church missionaries during Houphouet-Boigny's early years, and invited me into their home to share their experiences of how it was to be a European living under his regime.

Eritrea. Mesfin Hagos, Afwerki's closest confidant for many years and his commander on the battlefield, flew to London to see me and patiently led me through his role in events that have become landmarks in Eritrea's recent history. For personal experiences of the War of Independence I met with several former fighters from both the ELF and EPLF. Chief among them were Haile Woldan, who fought for the ELF alongside his wife, and Goitom Mebrahtu, whose colourful stories of fighting on the scorching-hot plains of Eritrea were worthy of a book in their own right. Wolde-Yesus Ammar, author and head of foreign relations for the Eritrea Peoples Democratic Party (EPDP), gave his time to brief me when I knew next to nothing, and patiently pointed me in the right direction. As a former friend and classmate of Isaias Afwerki, he was able to paint a detailed picture of the dictator's early years. His colleague, Mengisteab Asmerom, also from the EPDP, was also eager to assist from the start. The author and principal director of Justice Africa, Dawit Mesfin, helped me make sense of some of the more arcane disagreements between the ELF and EPLF, and was good enough to do so when he was writing his own book on Eritrea.

Special thanks go to Betlehem Isaak, the courageous and determined daughter of the jailed journalist Dawit Isaak, who has been detained in solitary confinement by Isaias Afwerki since 2001. Betlehem welcomed me to Gothenburg, where she lives, and spent two days describing in detail the story of her father's life and her campaign to have him freed.

Finally, thank you to the two institutions where I hid away to continue my writing when I could no longer face the clutter and tumbling paperwork of my cave-study. The proprietor of Sufi restaurant in London W12 gave me a table on which to write quietly at the back of his establishment whenever I needed – and often a glass of wine too – and many days were spent tucked in a quiet corner of Proud Mary's coffee shop off Uxbridge Road, tapping away until well beyond closing time.

Notes

Africa cannot be tamed into words on a page. There are times you imagine you might have mastered a single episode in history, hacked through a sweltering, tangled jungle of literature until the trees are finally thinning onto some airy mountain peak from where you can see the contours of everything below, only to find that this was merely a knoll in the gentle lowlands and that the jungle proper still lies ahead.

Most writers on Africa are faced with a choice. Either they survey the entire continent from the highest point they can climb, tracing the course of every arterial river to see how events and people have fed through Africa's immense and complex history, or they plunge beneath the jungle canopy and focus on a single rare and colourful bloom, dissecting every filament beneath a microscope, so that a solitary event or person might make sense of the whole. I have attempted a combination of the two, and am thus indebted to a wide range of authors and source material.

I have listed below the sources for direct quotations, statistics and points of disputed information. Where information is not in dispute and can easily be found in one or several books I have not identified a source. The full details of the key source publications, and those that have significantly helped inform the narrative, are listed in the bibliography. Those from which I have just taken a quote or two are listed in the notes, but not in the bibliography.

Because most events described in this book happened within living memory, I have tried to gather first-hand testimonies whenever possible. Many of those sources preferred not to be mentioned, but those who agreed are referenced in the acknowledgements.

Among those who climbed high for a sweeping panorama of the continent, I must make special mention of historian and journalist Martin Meredith. His faultlessly researched, broad-canvas digests of African history have been of great assistance. Special mention must also go to David van Reybrouck's modern masterpiece *Congo: The Epic History of a People*. For the history of the chocolate scandal involving Cadbury, Lowell J. Sartre's *Chocolate on Trial* and Carol Off's *Bitter Chocolate* are the stand out reads.

Chapter One: Congo

1. ...the prisoner had become a statesman. Remilleux 1989, p. 39.
2. ...systematically ripped off by city slickers. *Ibid.*, p. 40.
3. ...taking their tax revenue with them. Reybrouk 2014, p. 262.
4. ...rendering the discussions pointless. Remilleux 1989, p. 41.
5. thousand million Belgian Francs. O'Brien 1962, ebook location 1784.
6. ... the state now just a minority shareholder. Remilleux 1989, p. 263.
7. ...Mobutu had already been approached by the CIA. Wrong 2001, p. 66.
8. ...personal currency transfers out of Katanga and back home to Brussels. O'Brien 1962, ebook location 1709.
9. ...not for pillaging or to serve the ambitions of some little princeling. Remilleux 1989, p. 263.
10. ...replacing Lumumba with a pro-Western group. Wrong 2001, p. 68.
11. ...at the invitation of Lumumba. *Ibid.*, p. 68.
12. ...I order you to go and arrest ex-President of the Republic Kasavubu. Remilleux 1989, p. 49.
13. ...had put Mobutu on his payroll the week before. Weissman, Stephen R., *Studies in Intelligence*, Vol 59, No. 4, December 2015. p. 54.
14. ...and the subsequent tribal fighting which had left so many dead. O'Brien 1962, ebook location 1903.
15. ...they exhumed the bodies, sawed them into pieces, and dissolved the remains. Reybrouk 2014, p. 308.
16. Full text of Lumumba's last letter to his wife can be found on Friends of the Congo website, accessed 5 August 2016.
17. a country that does not want to fight. Guevara 1997, p. 127.
18. ....suddenly lost faith in their magic. Remilleux, p. 57.
19. ...a major was despatched to cut the telephone lines of President Kasavubu. Reybrouk 2014, p. 330.
20. ...the other three condemned politicians had been watching, awaiting their turn. *Ibid.*, p. 339.

21. ...he was estimated to be the world's eighth-richest man. *Ibid.*, p. 357.

22. ...which controlled the notorious underground cells known as OAU2. 'Prison conditions in Zaire', Human Rights Watch/Africa Watch Human Rights Watch/Prison Project, January 1994, p. 13.

23. ...and shot him again, in his hospital bed. Amnesty International appeal announcement. UA 351/93. 5 October 1993.

24. ...in a cell and shaved with a broken bottle. Amnesty International. 'ZAIRE: Violence against democracy', 16 September 1993. AI Index: AFR 62/11/93.

25. ...he must think we are out of our damn minds. Bechtolsheimer, Götz. Phd thesis *Breakfast with Mobutu: Congo, the United States and the Cold War, 1964–1981*, Department of International History, LSE March 2012. p. 143.

26. ...guardian of one of Mobutu's sons. Blumenthal 1983.

27. ...which they wanted for their General. *Ibid.*

28. ...Who is going to shout THIEF! *Ibid.*

29. ...gave him an another $3 billion. United Nations. Report of the Independent Expert on the effects of foreign debt. Cephas Lumina. UN, 11 June 2012, p. 6.

30. ...UN transportation trucks were stolen, apparently by Mobutu's own troops. Bechtolsheimer, Götz. Phd thesis *Breakfast with Mobutu: Congo, the United States and the Cold War, 1964–1981*, Department of International History, LSE March 2012, p. 214.

31. ...and properties in Italy, Spain, and Portugal. 'Biens mal acquis... profitent trop souvent: La fortune des dictateurs et les complaisances occidentales' Mars 2007, CCFD (Comité Catholique contre la Faim et pour le Développement) 4, rue Jean Lantier – 75001 Paris, pp. 34–38.

32. ...begun calling him Mobutu Sesescu. Reybrouck 2014, p. 393.

33. ...fights were breaking out over a piece of burnt crust and banana skin. 'Prison Conditions in Zaire', Human Rights Watch/Africa Watch Human Rights Watch/Prison Project, January 1994, p. 37.

34. ...Rumour had it he regularly procured a new fourteen-year-old virgin for himself. Cohen 2015, p. 92.

Chapter Two: Zimbabwe

1. ...it must have come from God. Holland 2008, p. 6.

2. ...the first time he had ever 'seen red'. Pimlott 1992, p. 370.

3. ....because of the red flashes before my eyes. Pimlott 1992, p. 370.

4. ...the calm of a madman. *Ibid.*, p. 372.

5. ...Should we live in trees today? Where can we go? Meredith 2009, p. 116.

6. ...dustbin we are now throwing him. Holland 2008, p. 42.

7. ...for what was to come later. Smith 1997, p. 343.

8. ...there could be hope instead of despair. Smith 1997, p. 342.

9. ...that's what the war was about. Meredith 2009, p. 42.

10. ...needed to be 'crushed'. Meredith 2009, p. 60.

11. ...still moving in their stomachs. Report on the 1980s disturbances in Matabeleland and The Midlands. Compiled by the Catholic Commission for Justice and Peace in Zimbabwe, March 1997. p. 57.
12. ...sing songs in praise of ZANU-PF. *Ibid.*, p. 58.
13. ...tangible action is required. Zvobgo 2009, p. 278.
14. ...more farms than are considered necessary. Meredith 2005, p. 631.
15. ...'a scar on his left knee' and 'ulcers'. Meredith 2009, p.135.
16. ...during a three year period. United Nations. Final report of the Panel of Experts on the Illegal Exploitation of Natural Resources and Other Forms of Wealth of the Democratic Republic of the Congo. S/2002/1146. p. 8.
17. ...same period topped US$10,000. *Ibid.*, p. 8.
18. ...justified for her to have more land. Chikuhwa 2013, p. 92.
19. ...discovered 75,273 were 'ghosts'. *Ibid.*, p. 62.
20. ...Zimbabwean by pain of death. Barclay 2010, p. 109.
21. ...as the King of Matabeleland. Report entitled 'Reap What You Sow: Greed and Corruption in Zimbabwe's Marange Diamond Fields'. Partnership Africa Canada, 2012, p. 19.
22. ...diamonds were plundered from Marange. *Ibid.*, p. 1.

Chapter Three: Before the Dictators
1. ...shut the furious Americans out. Yergin 1991, p. 743.
2. ...them falling into enemy hands. *Ibid.*, p. 1308.
3. ...land area of the same extent. BP, Our Industry, 3rd edition (1958), p. 349.
4. ...the witches' brew in Macbeth. Huxley 1955, p. 181.
5. ...spending another cent on the concession. Steyn, P. *Oil Exploration in Colonial Nigeria, 1903–1958.* University of Stirling, p. 21.
6. ...they were searching for palm oil. Andrew Walker, 'The day oil was discovered in Nigeria', BBC News Website, 17 March 2009.
7. ...as if we were trained monkeys. *Ibid.*
8. ...£1, per acre, per year. Peel 2009, p. 25.
9. ...spree of urgent drilling began. Hallett 2002.
10. ...accounts of a man called Omar Shelhi. Epstein 1996, pp. 216–36.

Chapter Four: Libya
1. ...he secured an extra $1 billion of income. St John 2012, p. 255.
2. ...on (America's) cold insolent face. Bamberg 2000, p. 474.
3. ...the language of our enemies? Anderson 2002, p. 120.
4. ...interception should be a matter for the Irish government. Andrew 2012, p. 1437.
5. ...officer say 'don't move'. *Ibid.*, p. 1438.
6. ...piling them into lorries for despatch. Heikal 1976, p. 197.
7. ...his conduct as 'hair-raising'. Foreign Office document, National Records Office – 'Gaddafi's Personality', January 1977.

8. ...one of the demonstrators should have been killed. Security Service archives, quoted from Andrew 2012, p. 1590.
9. ...demonstration through diplomatic pressure. *Ibid.*, p. 1617.
10. ...the triviality of the twentieth century. Jana (Tripoli) 3 Feb 1981, FBIS, 4 Feb 1982.
11. ...twenty-five per cent of the world's problems. Elwarfally 1988, p. 153.
12. ...not going to join them in their lack of morality. *The New York Times*, 23 October 1997.
13. ...on liberal democratic principles. Amelia Hill, 'Gaddafi's son will be in turmoil says LSE professor who acted as advisor', *The Guardian*, 21 February 2011.
14. ...would call a team player. Richard Spencer, 'Saadi Gaddafi involved in shootings, rich rewards and wooden legs during bizarre football career', *The Daily Telegraph*, 29 October 2011.
15. ...recruit Saadi for the sake of government relations. *The New York Times*, 25 February 2011.
16. ...that the journalist would love it. Mark Allen to Musa Kusa, 18 March 2004, (Letter from my own collection, seized from Intelligence Office in Tripoli).

Chapter Five: Nigeria
1. ...with the fuse almost burnt out. Omoigui, N. 'Operation "Aure": Northern Nigerian Military Counter-Rebellion, July 1966. (http://www.omoigui.com, accessed 01 August 2017).
2. ...warm afternoon air, and shot dead. Omoigui, N. 'Operation "Aure": Northern Nigerian Military Counter-Rebellion, July 1966', Urhobo Historical Society 2002 (accessed on internet).
3. ...anything that comes in its way. Saro-Wiwa 1992, p. 58.
4. ...cursed neglect and cursed Shell. *Ibid.*, p. 71.
5. ...2.5 million barrels of oil. Human Rights Watch. 'The Price of Oil', January 1999.
6. ...greatly outweighs any disadvantages. Saro-Wiwa 1992, p. 51.
7. ...and overpower coup plotters. Omoigui, N. 'Nigeria: The Palace Coup of November 17th 1993' (dawodu.com, accessed 14 December 2016).
8. ...$12.2 billion over a six-year period. Okonta and Douglas 2003, p. 36.
9. ...raging down his study phone. Saro-Wiwa 2012, p. 272.
10. ...raising pressure on the federal government of Nigeria. Saro-Wiwa 1995, p. 165.
11. ...would be 'an insurance against coups'. Omoigui, N. 'Nigeria: The Palace Coup of November 17th 1993' (dawadu.com, accessed 14 December 2016).
12. ...Most Urgent and IMMEDIATE PRIORITY. Anyanwu 2001, p. 24.
13. ...a fairly brutal person. Okonta and Douglas 2003, p. 138.
14. ...I will take care of the situation. *Ibid.*, p. 130.
15. ...Their permits cost them $10 million. London's High Court (sitting in Paris), Energy Venture Partner v Malabu Oil & Gas, 10 December 2012.

16. ...again made someone else's dreams come true. Olusegun 2005, p. 80.

17. ...sorry, there is nothing we can do. BBC world Service, 'Witness', 7 July 2015.

Chapter Six: Equatorial Guinea

1. ...they are either dead or in exile. Fegley 1989, p. 52.

2. ...a hundred million dollars in foreign currency. *Ibid.*, p. 165.

3. ...to command all the peoples of Europe. Aetas de la Conferencia Constitucional sobre Guinea Ecuatorial, Madrid, 3 November 1967. Quoted in Fegley 1989, p. 51.

4. ...if you vote for me, I will give it to you. Klinterberg 1978, p. 45.

5. ...fifty or sixty people a day were being executed. Fegley1989, p. 153.

6. ...team asked for the death penalty. Liniger-Goumaz 1988, p. 57.

7. ...Of you for a long time. (song). Fegley 1989, p. 82.

8. ...the profits from his coffee plantations. Dr Alejandro Artucio, ICJ observer. 'The trail of Macías in Equatorial Guinea: The story of a dictatorship', International Commission of Jurists and the International University Exchange Fund, 1979, p. 36.

9. ...military officers and even a police commissioner. Ambassador John E. Bennett, farewell speech in Malabo, Equatorial Guinea, 28 July 1994.

10. ...and even by President Obiang himself. 'Money Laundering and Foreign Corruption: Enforcement and Effectiveness of the Patriot Act', UN Senate report, 15 July 2004, p. 38.

11. ...walked through the door with a suitcase. Peter Maass, 'A Touch of Crude', *Mother Jones*, issue Jan/Feb 2005.

12. ...that I met there because of you. 'Keeping Foreign Corruption out of the US', US Senate report, 4 February 2004, p. 46.

13. ...his fellow citizens lived in extreme poverty. 'Second Vice-President of Equatorial Guinea Agrees to Relinquish More Than $30 Million of Assets Purchased with Corruption Proceeds', US Department of Justice statement, 10 October 2014.

Chapter Seven: Before the Dictators

1. ...steamed like a gigantic hothouse. Nevinson 1906, p. 182.

2. ...well treated and cared for. Professor Glyn Stone, 'The Foreign office and Forced Labour in Portuguese West Africa, 1894–1914'. Accessed at http://eprints.uwe.ac.uk/11757/1/ForeignOfficeandSlaveryB.doc

3. ...ill is of slight importance. Satre 2005, p. 18.

4. ...purchased a fleet of coastal steamers. Clarence-Smith 1985, p. 104.

5. ...Which he bravely admits. Satre 2005, p. 32.

6. ...as a result of his own eloquence. *Ibid.*, p. 155.

7. ...slavery of an atrocious character? All quotes from the Cadbury trial are from Satre 2005, p. 171 onwards.

Chapter Eight: Ivory Coast

1. ...and to give it an educational role. Zolberg 1969, p. 56.
2. ...remains faithful to this principle. El Hadj Moussa Kome, a member of the legislative assembly, 1959. Quoted in Zolberg 1969.

3. ...ten years' time we shall compare the results. Meredith, M. 2005, p. 66.
4. ...had needed to silence their bourgeoisie. 'Discours pronounce par M Houphouet Boigny', 7 Sept 1958. From the US Library of Congress (available online), p. 18.
5. ...as the first peasant of Côte d'Ivoire. From the documentary 20 ans, Félix Houphouet-Boigny, RTI in Cote d'Ivoire and FRAMES, Motion Graphics & VFX Film Production.
6. ...containing Houphouet-Boigny's corpse in effigy. Zolberg 1969, p. 353.
7. ...he smiled during one interview. Madelin, 1993, p. 307
8. ...in his personal bank accounts. Meredith 2005, p. 288.
9. ...exclusivity of the president's birthplace. Elleh 2002, p. 134.
10. ...eating Camembert and drinking Beaujolais. Titley 1977, p. 138.
11. ...whose feet barely reached the floor. Cohen 2015, p. 18.
12. ...but we will not be able to do so. *Ibid.*, p. 29.
13. ...supplied to her by the Ivoirian state. Tilouine, J., Article in *Le Monde*, 2 April 2015.

Chapter Nine: Eritrea

1. ...one place below North Korea. *Reporters Without Borders 2015*, World Press Freedom Index. Eritrea has been ranked last in the world for the last eight years.
2. ...for indefinite periods of time. UN Human Rights Council, 'Report of the Commission of Inquiry on Human Rights in Eritrea', 4 June 2015.
3. ...in the territory Italy conquered and named Eritrea. Ammar 1992, p. 15.
4. ...help boost key Allied supply lines. Pankhurst 1952, p. 15.
5. ...choose what government you desire. Ammar 1992, p. 22.
6. ...divide the struggle in two. *Ibid.*, p. 46.
7. ...I had just gotten out of prison. Duggan, J. *The Eritrean Newsletter*, January 1982 (published by the ELF Foreign Information Centre, Beirut).
8. ...human rights groups what he had seen. Eyob Bahta was interviewed by Elsa Chyrum of Human Rights Concern Eritrea, 4 January 2011. The full transcript can be read on the organization's website.
9. ...the regime built thirty of them. Amnesty International, 'Eritrea: Rampant repression 20 years after independence', 9 May 2013.

Bibliography

Ammar, Wolde-Yesus. 1992. *Eritrea: Root Causes of Wars and Refugees*. Sinbad Publishing Company.

Anderson, B. 2002. *Joe Cahill: A Life in the IRA*. O'Brien Press.

Andrew, C. 2012. *The Defence of the Realm, The Authorised History of MI5*. Penguin Books, digital version.

Anyanwu, C. 2001. *The Days of Terror*. Spectrum Books Ltd.

Bamberg, J. 2000. *British Petroleum and Global Oil 1950–1975: The Challenge of Nationalism*. Cambridge University Press.

Barclay, P. 2010. *Zimbabwe: Tears of Hope and Despair*. Bloomsbury.

Blumenthal, E. 1983. 'Zaire, A report on the credibility of its international finance'. (From the appendix of Emmanuel Dungia, *Mobutu et l'argent de Zaire*, Harmattan, 1992.)

Chikuhwa, Jacob W. 2013. *Zimbabwe: The End of the First Republic*. AuthorHouseUK.

Clarence-Smith, W. G. 1985. *The Third Portuguese Empire, 1825–1975: A Study in Economic Imperialism*. Manchester University Press.

Cliffe, L and Davidson, B. 1988. *The Long Struggle of Eritrea*. The Red Sea Press.

Cohen, Herman J. 2015. *The Mind of the African Strongmen*. Vellum, an imprint of New Academia Publishing.

Dowden, R. 2008. *Africa: Altered States, Ordinary Miracles*. Portobello Books.

Elleh, N. 2002. *Architecture and Power in Africa*. Praeger.

Elwarfally, M. G. 1988. *Imagery and Ideology in US Policy Toward Libya, 1969–1982*. University of Pittsburgh Press.

Epstein, Edward, J. 1996. *Dossier*. Carroll and Graf Publishers, Inc.

Fegley, R. 1989. 'Equatorial Guinea, An African Tragedy'. American University Studies: Series 11, *Anthropology and Sociology*, vol. 39.

Guevara, C. 1997. *The African Dream: The Diaries of the Revolutionary War in the Congo*. The Harvill Press.

Hallett, D. 2002. *Petroleum Geology of Libya*. Elsevier.

Hochschild, A. 2012. *King Leopold's Ghost*. Macmillan.

Heikal, M. 1976. *The Road to Ramadan*. Ballantine Books.

Holland, H. 2008. *Dinner with Mugabe*. Penguin Books.

Huxley, E. 1955. *Four Guineas*. The Reprint Society Ltd, by arrangement with Chatto and Windus Ltd.

Klinterberg, R. 1978. *Equatorial Guinea, Macías Country, The Forgotten Refugees*. The International Student Exchange Fund.

Liniger-Goumaz, M. 1988. *Small is Not Always Beautiful: The Story of Equatorial Guinea*. C Hurst and Co.

Madelin, P. 1993. *L'or des dictatures*. Fayard.

Meredith, M. 1988. *Diamonds, Gold and War*. Simon and Schuster.

Meredith, M. 2009. *Mugabe: Power, Plunder and the Struggle for Zimbabwe's Future*. PublicAffairs.

Meredith M. 2005. *The State of Africa*. The Free Press.

Meredith, M. 2014. *The Fortunes of Africa*. Simon and Schuster.

Nevinson, H. 1906. *A Modern Slavery*. Harper and Brothers Publishers.

Nugent, P. 2012. *Africa Since Independence*. Palgrave Macmillan.

O'Brien, C. C. 1962. *To Katanga and Back*. Faber and Faber, ebook edition.

Off, C. 2006. *Bitter Chocolate: Investigating the Dark Side of the World's Most Seductive Sweet*. Random House.

Okonta, I and Douglas, O. 2003. *Where Vultures Feast: Shell, Human Rights and Oil*. Verso.

Olusegun, A. 2005. *The Last 100 Days of Abacha*. The Bookhouse Company.

Pankhurst, S. 1952. *Eritrea on the Eve: The Past and Future of Italy's "First-born" Colony, Ethiopia's Ancient Sea Province.* New Times and Ethiopia News Books.

Peel, M. 2009. *A Swamp Full of Dollars: Pipelines and Paramilitaries at Nigeria's Oil Frontier.* I. B. Tauris & Co Ltd.

Pimlott, B. 1992. *Harold Wilson.* Harper Collins.

Remilleux, Jean-Louis. 1989. *Mobutu: Dignity for Africa.* Editions Albin Michel SA.

Reybrouck, David Van. 2014. *Congo: The Epic History of a People.* Fourth Estate.

St John, Ronald Bruce. 2012. *Libya: From Colony to Revolution.* Oneworld Publications.

Saro-Wiwa, K. 1992. *Genocide in Nigeria: The Ogoni Tragedy.* Saros International Publishers.

Saro-Wiwa, K. 1995. *A Month and a Day.* Penguin.

Saro-Wiwa, Noo. 2012. *Looking For Transwonderland: Travels in Nigeria.* Granta.

Satre, Lowell. J. 2005. *Chocolate on Trial.* Ohio University Press.

Smith, Ian. 1997. *Bitter Harvest: Zimbabwe and the Aftermath of its Indpendence.* John Blake.

Titley, B. 1977. *Dark Age: The Political Odyssey of Emperor Bokassa.* Queen's University Press.

Wrong, Michela. 2001. *In the Footsteps of Mr. Kurtz: Living on the Brink of Disaster in Mobuto's Congo.* Fourth Estate, ebook edition.

Yergin, D. 1991. *The Prize: The Epic Quest for Oil, Money and Power.* Free Press, ebook edition.

Zolberg, A. R. 1969. *One Party Government in the Ivory Coast.* Princeton University Press.

Zvobgo, Chengetai J. M. 2009. *A History of Zimbabwe, 1890–2000* and *Postscript, Zimbabwe, 2001–2008.* Cambridge Scholars Publishing.

Image credits

1. Colonel Joseph Mobutu, 1960. © Marilyn Silverstone/Magnum Photos
2. Capture of Patrice Lumumba, 1961. Universal History Archive/Getty Images
3. President Joseph Mobutu and Muhammad Ali, 1974. Moviestore collection Ltd/Alamy Stock Photo
4. Robert and Grace Mugabe, 2017. Tafadzwa Ufumeli/Anadolu Agency/Getty Images
5. The Rover Boys
6. Colonel Muammar Gaddafi, 1969. Genevieve Chauvel/Sygma/Getty Images
7. Colonel Muammar Gaddafi and his bodyguard, 2011. Sergei Supinsky/AFP/Getty Images
8. Paul Kenyon and Saadi Gaddafi, 2011. © BBC
9. General Sani Abacha, 1997. Issouf Sanogo/AFP/Getty Images
10. Dan Etete, 1998. Heinz-Peter Bader/Reuters
11. Ken Saro-Wiwa, 1993. © Tim Lambon/Greenpeace
12. President Macias and Obiang. Sigfrid Casals/Cover/Getty Images
13. President Teodoro Obiang and President Robert Mugabe. Jekesai Nijikizana/AFP/Getty Images
14. Teodoro Obiang. © Instagram
15. President Houphouet-Boigny at Our Lady of Peace Basilica. Patrick Robert/Sygma/Getty Images
16. Isaias Afwerki, 2015. Eritrea-Mining/Nevsun Reuters/Mohamed Nureldin Abdallah

Index